The Beginning of WISDOM

A Devotional Study of Job,
Psalms, Proverbs, Ecclesiastics
and Song of Solomon

Warren Henderson

All Scripture quotations are from the New King James Version of the Bible, unless otherwise noted. Copyright © 1982 by Thomas Nelson, Inc. Nashville, TN

The Beginning of Wisdom – A Devotional Study of Job, Psalms, Proverbs, Ecclesiastes, and Song of Solomon

By Warren Henderson
Copyright © 2016

Cover Design: Benjamin Bredeweg

Editing/Proofreading: Kathleen Henderson, Daniel Macy, and David Lindstrom

Published by Warren A. Henderson
3769 Indiana Road
Pomona, KS 66076

Perfect Bound ISBN: 978-1-939770-30-1
eBook ISBN: 978-1-939770-31-8

ORDERING INFORMATION:
Gospel Folio Press
Phone 1-905-835-9166
E-mail: order@gospelfolio.com

Also available in many online retail stores

Table of Contents

PREFACE 1
INTRODUCTION TO HEBREW POETRY 3
JOB 11
    DEVOTIONS IN JOB 17
PSALMS 185
    DEVOTIONS IN PSALMS 201
PROVERBS 351
    DEVOTIONS IN PROVERBS 357
ECCLESIASTES 415
    DEVOTIONS IN ECCLESIASTES 421
SONG OF SOLOMON 445
    DEVOTIONS IN SONG OF SOLOMON 455
ENDNOTES 479

Other Books by the Author

Afterlife – What Will It Be Like?
Answer the Call – Finding Life's Purpose
Be Holy and Come Near – A Devotional Study of Leviticus
Behold the Saviour
Be Angry and Sin Not
Conquest and the Life of Rest – A Devotional Study of Joshua
Exploring the Pauline Epistles
Forsaken, Forgotten, and Forgiven – A Devotional Study of Jeremiah
Glories Seen & Unseen
Hallowed Be Thy Name – Revering Christ in a Casual World
Hiding God – The Ambition of World Religion
In Search of God – A Quest for Truth
Knowing the All-Knowing
Managing Anger God's Way
Mind Frames – Where Life's Battle Is Won or Lost
Out of Egypt – A Devotional Study of Exodus
Overcoming Your Bully
Passing the Torch – Mentoring the Next Generation
Revive Us Again – A Devotional Study of Ezra and Nehemiah
Seeds of Destiny – A Devotional Study of Genesis
The Bible: Myth or Divine Truth?
The Evil Nexus – Are You Aiding the Enemy?
The Fruitful Bough – Affirming Biblical Manhood
The Fruitful Vine – Celebrating Biblical Womanhood
The Hope of Glory – A Preview of Things to Come
The Olive Plants – Raising Spiritual Children
Your Home the Birthing Place of Heaven

Preface

The overall theme of Job, Psalms, Proverbs, Ecclesiastes, and Song of Solomon is succinctly stated in Proverbs 9:10: *"The fear of the Lord is the beginning of wisdom, and the knowledge of the Holy One is understanding."* Concisely put, to know God is what knowledge means and, as Psalms, Proverbs, and Ecclesiastes repeatedly declare, such understanding should prompt fearful awe of Him. In his early years, Solomon's son learned that *"The fear of the Lord is the beginning of knowledge, but fools despise wisdom and instruction"* (Prov. 1:7). As Solomon's son advanced into the school of life, wisdom instructed him that it was foolish to live without God in the world. True wisdom is inseparable from the fear of the Lord; it is man's starting point in understanding the mind of God, which enables him to resolve questions otherwise inscrutable. Those who choose to walk in the path of godly obedience find life and blessing, and demonstrate their understanding of who God is and of His ways.

The Lord has displayed His holy character in all His gracious actions; thus, He should be feared and His name revered – *"Holy and awesome is His name"* (Ps. 112:9). Indeed, the psalmist follows this statement by saying, *"The fear of the Lord is the beginning of wisdom"* (Ps. 112:10). This implies that those who have the proper disposition towards the Lord will do His commandments and praise His name! The "fool" of Psalms and Proverbs is not a mentally challenged person, but someone who rejects divine knowledge and wisdom: *"The fool has said in his heart, 'There is no God'"* (Ps. 14:1). A person who has no time or respect for God is a fool because he is morally and spiritually bankrupt and doesn't know it. Accordingly, foolishness is closely linked with death; while this can refer to a single event that ends physical life, more often in these books it speaks of the entire realm that is in conflict with life. May God's people learn true wisdom and avoid deadly foolishness.

The Beginning of Wisdom

    These Poetry Books provide divine counsel and wisdom in how to properly respond to life's various, often arduous, seasons in a God-honoring way. Job teaches us that human suffering is inevitable, and that even the innocent and God-fearing cannot escape it, yet God's way is not sorrowful. Psalms, the Jewish Hymnbook, teaches us the art of prayer and praise to God. Proverbs informs us how to live wisely in fear of God during our earthly sojourn. Ecclesiastes explores the true meaning of life. The Song of Solomon conveys the genuine intimacy and commitment that a man and woman are to enjoy in God's design for marriage.

    The Beginning of Wisdom is a "commentary style" devotional which upholds the glories of Christ while exploring Job, Psalms, Proverbs, Ecclesiastes, and Song of Solomon within the context of the whole of Scripture. I have endeavored to include in this book some of the principal gleanings from other writers. *The Beginning of Wisdom* contains dozens of brief devotions. This format allows the reader to use the book either as a daily devotional or as a reference source for deeper study.

— Warren Henderson

Introduction to Hebrew Poetry

God understands our limitations to comprehend spiritual and eternal matters. As a declaration of grace, He exercised various literary forms in the Old Testament to declare His word to us. These include but are not limited to word-pictures, prophecies, shadows, types, allegories, symbols, metonymies, paradoxes, personifications, plain language, and poetry. The latter form of expression is not limited to the five Old Testament books normally categorized as poetry: Job, Psalms, Proverbs, Ecclesiastes, and Song of Solomon. In fact, about one third of the Old Testament is poetic in nature. For example, nearly ninety percent of the book of Isaiah is comprised of poetic arrangement; other prophetic books such as Jeremiah and Hosea are also largely poetic in nature. As God's written word was not widely available to the common people, inspirational poetry permitted easier memorization and oral transmission among the Jewish nation.

Canon Placement

The Hebrew Bible, the Old Testament in the complete canon of Scripture, is composed of twenty-five books. Since the Old Testament in our Bibles contains thirty-nine books, one might ask, "What is different?" The answer is that the content is the same, but the order, names, and collection of the books vary somewhat. In the Hebrew Bible, 1 and 2 Samuel are "Samuel," 1 and 2 Kings are "Kings," and 1 and 2 Chronicles also are joined under the single title, "Chronicles." The last twelve books of the Old Testament are all contained within one book in the Hebrew Bible entitled "The Minor Prophets." This explains how we derive an Old Testament with thirty-nine books from the Hebrew Bible's twenty-five book arrangement ($39 - 3 - 11 = 25$).

The Old Testament is canonized as follows: five books of *Law*, twelve books of *History*, five books of *Poetry*, and seventeen books of *Prophecy*. Job, the first of the Poetry Books and perhaps the oldest book in the Old Testament, will not be considered at this time. The remaining four Poetry Books (Psalms, Proverbs, Ecclesiastes, and Song of Solomon), which are primarily the writings of David and Solomon, will be explored in this work. All four of these books were written during the same era (approximately tenth century B.C.). The historical narrative within 2 Samuel, 1 Kings, and 1 and 2 Chronicles relate to the same timeframe.

Themes

These five Poetry Books provide divine counsel and wisdom in how to properly respond to life's challenging seasons in a God-honoring way. Psalms, the Jewish Hymnbook, teaches us the art of prayer and praise to God (see Ps. 5 and 33, respectively). Proverbs informs us how to live wisely in fear of God during our earthly sojourn (Prov. 1:7, 9:10). Ecclesiastes teaches us what the true meaning of life is all about (Eccl. 1:2-4, 2:24-26, 12:13-14). The Song of Solomon, or the Song of Songs (Song 1:1), conveys the genuine intimacy and commitment that a man and woman are to enjoy in God's design for marriage (Song 8:6-7).

Overview of Poetry Construction

Most of us are familiar with poetry that rhymes similar sounding words to express a central meaning; in contrast, Hebrew poetry rhymes thoughts and ideas with each other to convey its message. By design, this format would promote memorization and enhance retention of God's Word. Although Hebrew poetry uses a variety of different types of patterns, the most common format is called *parallelism*. In parallelism, a grammatical pattern or idea is introduced in the first line and then repeated on subsequent lines to balance, reinforce, expand, and/or crescendo the obvious conclusion.

In regards to composition, there are two main types of parallelism, *Grammatical* and *Semantic*. As Grammatical Parallelism uses Hebrew word forms in its rhyming scheme, much of its style is lost in translation. In contrast, Semantic Parallelism correlates Hebrew ideas and thoughts, which do transfer into other languages. There are six forms of Semantic Parallelism used throughout the Old Testament, especially in the Poetry Books: synonymous, antithetic, synthetic, emblematic, composition, and climactic. A brief overview of these parallelism forms will enable the reader to more easily identify and appreciate each poetic style.

Synonymous Parallelism:
This style of parallelism is commonly employed in the prophetic books. In short, the central idea of the first line is repeated and reinforced with slightly different words in the second line without any intention to enlarging the idea; thus, both lines are synonymous in meaning.

Example: *"A false witness shall not be unpunished. He that speaks lies shall perish"* (Prov. 19:19).

Antithetic Parallelism:
In antithetic parallelism, the idea of the first line is contrasted with that of the last line, thus clarifying both extremes. By confirming the opposite aspect of the first line, the value of the theme is confirmed or completed.

Example: *"A wise man's heart is at his right hand, but a fool's heart at his left"* (Eccl. 10:2).

Synthetic Parallelism:
Synthetic parallelism uses subsequent lines to complete or compliment the idea or question conveyed in the first line. The following statements explain or add information to the original thought to draw together a complete idea or logical conclusion. There are several types of synthetic parallelism which are widely used throughout the Old Testament: completion, comparative, rationale, situational, etc. Rather than explain each type, it suffices here to merely note the nature of the synthetic form: if you sense an incomplete thought or are prompted to ask a question after reading the first line, but then the thought is completed or the question is answered in the following line, that is synthetic construction. Phrases such as *"better is ... than..."* such as in Ecclesiastes 7:5 identify synthetic parallelism.

Example: *"Give unto the Lord, O you mighty ones* [incomplete thought], *give unto the Lord glory and strength* [thought completed: glory and strength are to be given]" (Ps. 29:1).

Example: *"Yea, though I walk through the valley of the shadow of death, I will fear no evil* [why?]; *for You are with me; Your rod and Your staff, they comfort me* [the answer]" (Ps. 23:4).

Emblematic Parallelism:

Emblematic parallelism compares two lines of poetry by a simile or metaphor, that is, a symbol or a metaphor is placed side by side with its meaning. This form is often identified by the use of "is like" or "like" in the first line, and "is," "so is," or "as" in the following line. The original line serves as an illustration or emblem of the second line. This prompts the reader to consider and to compare experiences in life to understand the message, much in the same way a parable does.

Example: *"A word fitly spoken* **is like** *apples of gold in settings of silver"* (Prov. 25:11).

Example: *"**Like** an earring of gold and an ornament of fine gold,* **is** *a wise rebuker to an obedient ear"* (Prov. 25:11-12).

Composite Parallelism:

This form of parallelism uses three or more phrases to develop a theme. Through multiple expressions the meaning of a term or concept can be clarified. The main idea may be expressed in the first line and then refined by following lines or the reader may have to deduce the central point by reasoning all the thoughts together.

Example: *"Blessed is the man* [main point – but what does the blessed man do?] *who **walks** not in the counsel of the ungodly, nor **stands** in the path of sinners, nor **sits** in the seat of the scornful"* (Ps. 1:1).

Climactic Parallelism:
Climactic parallelism employs a highly repetitious, progressive set of lines until a theme is developed in a main idea or statement. In this form of poetry, part of one line, either a word or phrase is repeated in the following lines to advance to the conclusion. The main difference between composite and climactic parallelism is the use of repetitious words or phrases in each of the lines.

Example: *"Give unto the Lord, O you mighty ones; give unto the Lord glory and strength. Give unto the Lord the glory due to His name; worship the Lord in the beauty of holiness"* (Ps. 29:1-2).

Summary
Knowing something about the construction of Hebrew poetry, especially how various parallelistic forms are developed should assist the reader to better appreciate and properly interpret poetic Scripture. These passages are packed with practical wisdom for daily living, encouragement during challenging times, comfort for the brokenhearted, and the praise and worship of real people who found the Lord trustworthy and honorable in all His doings. May the reader be blessed by studying Job, Psalms, Proverbs, Ecclesiastes, and Song of Solomon and sing along with David:

Good and upright is the Lord;
Therefore He teaches sinners in the way.
The humble He guides in justice,
And the humble He teaches His way.
All the paths of the Lord are mercy and truth,
To such as keep His covenant and His testimonies (Ps. 25:8-10).

Job

Job

Introduction

The book of Job possesses a character quite different than any other portion of Scripture. Although it is usually categorized with the other four Old Testament books of poetry, it might well stand alone as a unique genre. This literary classic explores the subject of human suffering, an ageless impasse with which both philosophers and theologians have often wrestled. Why does God sanction human misery, especially of the innocent? Why does God permit His faithful servants to suffer adversity and premature death? These are just some of the questions that righteous Job agonized over while experiencing the greatest trial of his life.

Job was a God-fearing man with vast wealth, a large, happy family, and many loyal friends. Yet, for reasons never fully revealed, God allowed Satan to strip Job of all his earthly possessions, take the lives of his ten children, and inflict Job with a grievous boil-causing disease. In fact, it was God who drew Satan's attention to Job's honorable conduct, resulting in Satan's accusations and subsequent attacks against him.

Satan asserted that Job was only upright because God had protected him and ensured his prosperity. The king of slanderers then suggested Job was self-centered and only worshipped God because he had received God's favor. To prove this assertion false, God permitted Satan to take away nearly everything that Job had divinely received. Although Job does later question God's wisdom in the matter, he continues to honor and worship the Lord despite his personal losses and what he perceives to be injustice. What is the outcome of all Job's suffering? In the end, God is glorified, Satan is dejected, and Job is refined, blessed, and honored.

Purpose

Job shows us man possesses an inherent desire for preservation but resides in a world plagued with evil. This means that human suffering is inevitable, and that even the innocent and God-fearing cannot escape it. Although God does not originate evil, the narrative demonstrates He is in complete control of it. God is sovereign over all His creation, and even though it has been ruined by sin and rebellion, He is able to affect His own glory and our betterment in it, no matter the circumstances.

Without God, suffering would be a most miserable experience! It is only through Him that our human misery can have a foreknown and profitable purpose. He ensures the outcome of our suffering can accomplish a greater good; hence, we can be thankful despite the hardship (Rom. 8:28; Eph. 5:20).

Our affliction may be the consequence of sin (Heb. 12:6), or for personal refinement (Jas. 1:2-3), or to prepare us for further blessing (42:12), but it is always for the glory of God (John 11:4). Thus, Paul could confidently write: *"For I consider that the sufferings of this present time are not worthy to be compared with the glory which shall be revealed in us"* (Rom. 8:18). In this sense, suffering for righteousness better prepares believers for heaven! Righteous Job would learn through adversity what it means to be delivered from himself for God's glory.

> No pain, no palm; no thorns, no throne; no gall, no glory; no cross, no crown.
> — William Penn

Date

It is quite possible Job is the oldest book in our Bibles. Most conservative scholars place the events of the book during the days of the patriarchs, though the actual book may have been written much later. Within the text, we witness Job acting as a priest for his family by offering burnt sacrifices to the Lord (1:5). Abraham, Isaac, and Jacob did likewise, and this points to a time period prior to the Exodus and the giving of the Law and establishment of the Levitical priesthood.

Another clue that suggests Job was a contemporary of the patriarchs is Job's age. He lived 140 years after his troubles ended and hence was permitted to know his great-great-grandchildren (42:16-17). Jewish tradition suggests that he lived twice as long after the events of this story as he had before them, dying at the age of 210 (i.e., 70 years plus 140 years). The human lifespan dropped from several hundred years to 140–180 years in only five generations after the flood. Abraham lived to be 175; Isaac, 180; and Jacob, 147; a few centuries later Moses and Joshua lived to be 120 and 110, respectively. A few more centuries later, David, having lived out his days, died at the age of 70. Job's longevity, then, fits well with the timeframe of Genesis chapters 12-50. This would be true even if the reference to 140 years in chapter 42 is a poetic expression pertaining to the summation of Job's lifespan, as some believe.

Additionally, Job refers to Adam and the fall of man (31:33), and various facets of the creation account (9:8, 12:10), but he does not mention any of the Jewish patriarchs, who were probably unknown to Job. The information he had was most likely passed along to Job by oral tradition rather than any written form of Genesis, which did not exist until the fifteenth century BC. The most likely timeframe for the book would be between 2100 and 1700 BC.

Historical Setting

The entire book takes place outside of Israel, though Job had apparently profited from the oral transmission of the creation account. As just mentioned, Job may have been a contemporary of Abraham, though not living in the same area. The young man Elihu, introduced later in the book, was a Buzite; Buz was the second son of Nahor, the brother of Abraham (Gen. 22:20-21). Perhaps the knowledge of Abraham's God came to Job through Nahor's descendants, or later by Esau or his clan who dwelt in the region in which Job lived.

Job, a Gentile, lived in the land of Uz (1:1), which is connected with eastern Edom, the land of Esau's descendants (Lam. 4:21). Eliphaz resided in Teman, which lies south of Petra (also in Edom's territory). Teman was named after Esau's grandson (Gen. 36:11). C. I. Scofield also notes that "Uz was the object of raids from Chaldea and Sabea (1:15, 17). It is probable therefore, that Uz included eastern Edom and northern Arabia."[1] The fact that Job lived near a desert (1:19) further substantiates this conclusion. Much of this region will later be referred to as Idumea.

The Beginning of Wisdom

Authorship

The writer of the book of Job is unknown. Many believe Moses wrote the book, perhaps during his forty-year stay in Midian, just prior to the Exodus (Ex. 2-3; mid-fifteenth century BC). It is conjectured that the story of Job, who faithfully suffered in the purposes of God and was rewarded for doing so, would have been a great comfort and encouragement to God's covenant people after their deliverance from Egypt. It is also possible that Job was penned during the days of Solomon (971-931 BC), when most of the other poetry books, works of wisdom, were written. Some prefer an even later date and correlate the book with the return of the Jewish captives from Babylon in the sixth century BC. Not knowing the author of Job or when the book was written in no way undermines the validity or value of this inspired literary classic.

Outline

A prologue in chapters 1-2 contains discussions between God and Satan concerning Job and Satan's ensuing attacks on the man. The prologue also confirms Job's integrity before and after Satan's destructive onslaught. In the next section, Job laments his condition and has several dialogues with his three friends, (Eliphaz, Bildad, and Zophar), pertaining to the reasons people suffer and to Job's stated innocence (Job 3-31). There are three rounds of discussions with these men in which Eliphaz and Bildad each speak three times, and Zophar speaks twice. Job answers each interchange with an eloquent and spirited rebuttal.

After Job and his miserable counselors are talked out, a younger man named Elihu launches into a six-chapter monologue. He is angry with Job for justifying himself rather than God, and also with Job's three counselors for condemning Job without resolving his problem (Job 32-37). From a whirlwind, the Lord then rebukes His servant Job for questioning His wisdom and for asserting God misused His authority in dealing with him (Job 38-41). Job humbles himself and is fully restored (42:1-6). In the end, Job is refined and significantly blessed by God, and God is honored by the entire outcome (42:7-17).

A concise outline for the book would be:

I. Prologue – Job 1-2

II. Job's Dialogue With His Counselors – Job 3-31
III. Elihu's Monologue – Job 32-37
IV. The Lord Speaks – Job 38-41
V. Job's Confession – Job 42:1-6
VI. Epilogue – Job 42:7-17

A Fictional or Real Character?

Did God's servant Job really exist and suffer as indicated in the book entitled after his name? Some have suggested the entire book is metaphorical and, though it contains charming poetry, the narrative of artificial characters should not be considered seriously. Before explaining why the story of Job should be considered as non-fiction, A. R. Faussett explains why some favor an allegorical understanding of the book:

> The sacred numbers, *three* and *seven,* often occur. He [Job] had *seven* thousand sheep, *seven* sons, both before and after his trials; his *three* friends sit down with him *seven* days and *seven* nights; both before and after his trials he had *three* daughters. So also the number and form of the speeches of the several speakers seem to be artificial.[2]

Is Job a fictitious character in a contrived story? Certainly not, but as William Kelly explains, the Jews of old had two major difficulties with accepting Job as an actual, real person:

> That there was not a man upon earth that God had such pleasure in looking upon as Job, and yet such a man passing through deepest trial from God. It is a great difficulty with the Jews; they cannot understand it. They want to make out that Job was an imaginary being, because it seems so strange to them that after Abraham, Isaac, and Jacob, there should be a man outside Israel altogether that God had such a high opinion of — and he not a Jew! Yes. So there it was a great blow to their pride and their narrowness.[3]

How could a man outside of Israel be so appreciated by God? Why would God sanction such intense misery for a God-fearing and righteous man? The answer to both questions is the same one that God gave Habakkuk, when he inquired of the Lord as to why He would use

The Beginning of Wisdom

evil Babylon to punish His own rebellious people. He told the prophet, *"The just shall live by faith"* (Hab. 2:4). The meaning is a simple truth repeated throughout Scripture: trusting in God and His Word results in life, but pride and rebellion lead to death. The lesson for Habakkuk and also for Job was not to trust in their feelings or emotions, but rather to have faith in God's character and choices. As demonstrated in Genesis 22, when God asked Abraham to sacrifice Isaac (his only son of promise), the greatest test of our faith often occurs when it seems as if God is contradicting Himself. The greatest outcome of such bewildering circumstances is accomplished when man lives by faith and trusts God with his fate. To this end, Job's existence in Scripture as a suffering, upright man challenges our minds to contemplate the mysterious purposes of God.

    The wider context of Scripture supports a literal interpretation of this book. The prophet Ezekiel referred to Job alongside Noah and Daniel, validating his non-fictional status (Ezek. 14:14, 20). James wrote of Job's trial and how he benefitted from it to encourage us to exercise patience and faith in the Lord during grim and threatening times (Jas. 5:11). Job was a real man and the narrative conveys his story for our gain.

Devotions in Job

A Righteous Man Attacked
Job 1

The opening five verses furnish a panoramic view of the man Job: his location, his character, his family life, his prosperity, and his piety. In short, he is surrounded by everything that could make the world agreeable to him, and he is esteemed in it. Job likely lived during the time of the patriarchs. He dwelled in the arid land of Uz, which included eastern Edom and northern Arabia (v. 1). It is interesting that his name is derived from the Hebrew word *'ayab*, which means "persecuted" or "hated." As we will soon see, Job's friends thought he was being persecuted by God for his sins, which was not the case; in fact, they were ignorantly the oppressors of an innocent man.

Addressing his character, the text indicates Job was a rare specimen of a man. He was perfect, that is, he had a well-rounded moral character. He was upright; honesty and integrity marked his relationship with others. He was a God-fearing man, which is the foundation of true wisdom. Job shunned evil; his outward walk was one of rich integrity – he genuinely hated what God detested and lived accordingly. Roy Zuck summarizes other biographical information pertaining to Job found elsewhere in the book:

> Job was highly respected (29:7-11), a fair and honest judge (29:7, 12-17), a wise counselor (29:21-24), an honest employer (31:13-15, 38-39), hospitable and generous (31:16-21, 32), and a farmer of crops (31:38-40).[4]

Whether God directly rewarded Job for his righteous character, or merely established him to acclaim His glory, we are not told. Regardless, God chose to immensely bless Job and to protect him, his house, and his affairs (v. 10). As a result, Job's prosperity and posterity were the envy of everyone.

Unlike many other patriarchs, Job was monogamous, and his wife bore him seven sons and three daughters (v. 2; 2:9). His substance was incredible: seven thousand sheep, three thousand camels, five hundred yoke of oxen (i.e., one thousand oxen), five hundred female donkeys, and a very great household (servants, buildings, supplies, etc.). In short, Job *"was the greatest of all the people of the East"* (v. 3). Job had all that any man could want: a wife, many children, high status, immense wealth, and a pleasant and peaceful existence. Accordingly, Job's children had not a care in the world; they frequently feasted and enjoyed a merry existence (v. 4).

After their days of feasting were finished, Job would call his family together early in the morning and offer burnt offerings on their behalf. There was no Levitical priesthood at this time, so the patriarchal duty of offering burnt sacrifices for one's family was a common practice, and one Job engaged in routinely (v. 5).

Job's cup of temporal bliss was overflowing, but though the outward display of the man seemed flawless, God knew that the inner man still required testing, inspection, and refinement. There were still elements of carnality in Job's heart, which Job himself was not yet aware of; these must be exposed and self-judged. God's Spirit works on our heart and mind to affect changes in how we think and in what we do. Any external effort to reform the inner man cannot succeed, for that would be of the flesh, which can never prompt true spiritual vitality.

Self-righteousness is often the handmaiden of religious show and outward piety. Some commentators believe Job revealed such a motive when presenting his burnt offerings to the Lord for his children, but not for himself: *"It may be that my sons have sinned and cursed God in their hearts"* (1:5). While Job's concern for the spiritual condition of his children is honorable, his contemplation of their sins and not his own *may* be reflective of something in his heart that was not right. This is C. H. Mackintosh's understanding of the narrative:

> A soul really self-judged, thoroughly broken before God, truly sensible of its own state, tendencies, and capabilities would think of his own sins, and his own need of a burnt offering.[5]

Regardless of what may or may not have been an indication of a self-focused attitude, Job was a godly man with an honorable and blameless testimony; that is without question. Yet, as we all know, on this side of glory, none of us are perfect and none are sinless; rather, all believers are a divine work in progress – and we thank the Lord for His faithful diligence (Rom. 8:29; Phil. 1:6).

Moreover, Job never considered that personal sin may have been the cause of his suffering, in fact, he vehemently denies the matter (9:17). While it is true that sinful behavior was not the issue, it seems presumptuous of Job not to consider the possibility. Job's pitiful lament in Job 29 over the faded glory of bygone days seemingly indicates that a root of self-complacency existed in his heart. From his perspective, the basis of his self-worth was, to some extent, established by the tokens of divine favor he had received, not in the deeper spiritual aspects of life. All this is to say that God determined it was necessary for Job to be tested through the removal of blessings; this would permit Job to see more clearly what God valued within him. Self-righteousness, self-confidence, and self-importance are always an impediment to enjoying deeper communion with God. He reserves His fellowship for those who are of a humble and contrite spirit:

For thus says the High and Lofty One who inhabits eternity, whose name is Holy: "I dwell in the high and holy place, with him who has a contrite and humble spirit, to revive the spirit of the humble, and to revive the heart of the contrite ones (Isa. 57:15).

Job was an upright man who in all his outward behavior demonstrated immense reverence for the Lord. Yet, his heart was not perfect; there were secret attitudes that needed to be dealt with, which no one was aware of but the Lord. No matter how much we try to hide from God's penetrating scrutiny, He clearly sees into the deepest recesses of our hearts, into the undergirding of our souls. The writer of Hebrews puts the matter this way: *"there is no creature hidden from His sight, but all things are naked and open to the eyes of Him to whom we must give account"* (Heb. 4:13). Because God sees and knows what is best for us, He must act against that which is not pleasing to Him. As we will soon see, the process can be quite painful, but the end result is closer fellowship with God and Christ-likeness.

Abraham was a man of immense faith and *"the friend of God"* (Jas. 2:23); however, it was still necessary for God to test him, to prove the validity of his faith by challenging the longings of his own heart (Gen. 22). To be drawn nearer to the heart of God, every man and woman of faith must tread this needful heavenward path. Paul confirms two important truths concerning the flesh: *"No flesh should glory in His [God's] presence"* (1 Cor. 1:29) and *"in my flesh* [and ours too] *nothing good dwells* (Rom. 7:18). This means that all the unlovely things within us (our carnal motives, selfish thoughts, and proud impulses) hinder our communion with a God who has no such thoughts. For this reason the Spirit of God diligently seeks to expose and eradicate what hinders us from experiencing all the joy and power of divine fellowship. Thankfully, God does this refining work in His best timing and through the most appropriate means to uphold His glory and to gain the optimum outcome for us. This is evident in the story of Job. If Job had not needed further moral sifting, would not the Lord have exalted His name in a different way? Hence, we must have confidence in a sovereign God to see, to know, to do good, and to honor Himself in all that He does.

In verse 6 we transition from the delightful earthly scene of a righteous, God-fearing man worshipping His Creator to the throne room of heaven. On a particular day, or rather at an expected time, *"the sons of God came to present themselves before the Lord, and Satan also came among them."* The expression, *"the sons of God"* is from the Hebrew phrase *bene elohim* used to describe angels in Job 1:6, 2:1, and 38:7. Excluding the latter reference, Satan is among these angels as they submit reports and render homage to God in heaven. A similar Hebrew phrase *bene elim* is also employed in Psalm 29:1 and 89:6 to refer to angels.

The Lord created and established the earth and reigns supreme over creation from His holy hill above (Ps. 24:1-2). Although Satan wanted to *"ascend to the hill of the Lord"* and rule as God, his pride was judged and he lost his privileged status as a covering cherub and was cast off God's holy mountain (Isa. 14:12-15; Ezek. 28:12-17). David then reminds us that only those with clean hands and a pure heart may be with the Lord in His hallowed dwelling place (Ps. 24:3-4). Yet, all God's creation is subject to Him, and all moral beings, fallen or not, must give a personal account to Him; such is the scene before us. Later, during the midpoint of the Tribulation Period, Satan and his demonic host will be constrained to the earth and no longer have access into God's presence to accuse the brethren (Rev. 12:7-12).

But how can an evil being like Lucifer approach the sacred throne of God and not be consumed by His awesome presence? Perhaps the events recorded in Exodus 14 pose a possible explanation. Pharaoh and his army had Moses and the Israelites boxed in at the Red Sea with no possible means of escape. A terrible slaughter seemed imminent, but the pillar of cloud that had been to the east of the Israelite camp moved to the far western side of the camp and blocked Pharaoh's approach.

The Angel of the Lord (a theophany) was within the cloud and His glory illuminated the camp of the Israelites during the following nighttime hours, but the cloud provided no light to the Egyptians. This supernatural phenomenon may explain how Satan can venture into God's presence in heaven (e.g., Job 1) and survive the encounter. When permitted, Satan is allowed to come into God's veiled presence for communication purposes, but to him God appears as darkness, while to various holy creatures His glory is visible: *"Clouds and darkness surround Him; righteousness and justice are the foundation of His throne"* (Ps. 97:2). It is the same God, but to the one He seems veiled by darkness and to the other, He reveals His glorious light.

In the scene recorded in the first chapter of Job, God interrogates Satan about his doings. Having no responsibilities, Satan restlessly and relentlessly roves about the world causing havoc. Satan answers God truthfully, for he knows he cannot deceive the Lord on any matter (v. 7). However, when speaking to humans, Satan always distorts the truth to some degree in an attempt to solicit sin through deception. We see this even in his interactions with the Lord Jesus when he was on earth. Obviously, Satan knows it is impossible to cause God to err, and thus, by failing to entice Christ to sin, Satan served God's purpose of proving the Lord Jesus' divinity.

While it is obvious that Satan does communicate and has influence throughout the Bible, his actual voice is recorded only three times. In Genesis 3, he spoke to undermine and cast doubt on the Word of God and was successful in enticing our first parents to sin against God. In Job 1 and 2, Satan spoke to undermine Job's character, which later caused Job to doubt God's goodness. Lastly, in Matthew 4 the devil spoke to cast uncertainty on the integrity of the Son of God. To summarize Satan's recorded communication in the Bible, we see three verbal attempts to cast doubt on what is righteous. Let us be wise to his deceit.

It is noteworthy that God is the One who initiated the conversation with Satan concerning Job: *"Have you considered My servant Job, that there is none like him on the earth, a blameless and upright man, one who fears God and shuns evil?"* (v. 8). One can only image how a Jewish reader would shudder at such a declaration. Jehovah's servant – a Gentile! None like Job in all the earth! Was he more righteous than the patriarchs? If the patriarchs were Job's contemporaries, God thought so. Another possibility is that Job lived after the death of Joseph, a time when Scripture does not mention any notable men of faith. If this were the case, Job's long life span (eighty to ninety years longer than those of the time period) would have been quite a testimony of God's blessing to all in the region.

God's emphatic statement to the devil showed He was not only aware of Job's heart and conduct, but also knew everyone else on the entire planet to the same degree. Satan could not contradict God's assessment of Job's godly behavior, but he could allege the man had wrong motives for worshipping God. Such was Satan's bold indictment against Job:

> *Does Job fear God for nothing? Have You not made a hedge around him, around his household, and around all that he has on every side? You have blessed the work of his hands, and his possessions have increased in the land. But now, stretch out Your hand and touch all that he has, and he will surely curse You to Your face!* (vv. 9-11).

The accuser of the brethren suggested that Job was not serving God because he loved Him, but rather because of the prosperity he received from God. The enemy proposed that no one would want to serve God, unless he or she benefitted for doing so. In other words, Lucifer is putting forth the same proud philosophy which resulted in his own downfall: God is not worthy of honor on the mere basis of who He is. Satan's response proves he is not in control of the future, nor does he know what the future holds; otherwise, he would not have asserted what soon would be proven to be a self-abasing lie. The Lord's response was concise: *"Behold, all that he has is in your power; only do not lay a hand on his person"* (v. 12). Quite eager to commence mayhem in a Jehovah-worshipper's life, and now having divine permission to do so, *"Satan went out from the presence of the Lord."* As we will see, he wastes no time in bereaving Job of his children and despoiling him of all his wealth.

Demonic blow after blow fell in quick succession upon the devout head of Job. First the Sabeans stole his oxen and donkeys, and slew his servants (vv. 14-15). Second, fire from heaven (possibly lightning strikes) consumed all his sheep and his servants watching over them (v. 16). Third, a raid by the Chaldeans stripped him of all his camels, and they also slew his servants (v. 17). Lastly, a messenger informed Job that all ten of his children had been killed when a great wind storm (possibly a tornado) collapsed the house of his eldest son, where they had all gathered to feast (vv. 18-19). Can Satan control the armies of men, orchestrate devastation through nature's fury, and cause fire to fall from heaven? Yes, when permitted to do so.

For example, no satanic fire fell from heaven on Mount Carmel when the prophets of Baal were crying out to their false deity. Why? Because at the same time Jehovah's prophet Elijah was set to honor Him before the people; fire did sweep down from heaven to consume his water-soaked sacrifice and, in fact, the entire altar. The dramatic demonstration proved to idolatrous Israel that Jehovah and not Baal was the God of Israel. God only permits Satan to do the spectacular when it is in keeping with His sovereign purposes.

Hardly had one messenger arrived to tell Job of his agonizing loss, when yet another lone survivor arrived to deliver even heavier tidings. In a few moments of time, Job had been stripped of his commerce (oxen and donkeys), his comfort (his wool-producing sheep), his transportation (his camels), most of his labor force, and his posterity (all his dear children). All that remained to Job was his health, his wife, a few servants, and perhaps a roof over his head – the prosperity and posterity of the richest man in the East had been swept away in an instant of time!

It is further observed that the destroyer of God's creation, the first murderer, did not hesitate to kill as many people as possible in the dastardly attack. If Satan cannot receive the worship of men, he would ensure that no voices lift up praise to the only One who should be worshipped. This reality will never be more apparent than during the Tribulation Period, when most the world's population will perish. Many will die for not worshipping Satan's public representative, the

Antichrist, but most will be slaughtered in vengeful rage against God (Matt. 24:21-22; Rev. 12:12).

On hearing of the final catastrophe, the afflicted servant of God arose and responded in a way few would. He tore his robe, shaved his head, and fell to the ground to worship: *"Naked I came from my mother's womb, and naked shall I return there. The Lord gave, and the Lord has taken away; blessed be the name of the Lord"* (vv. 20-21). By this amazing statement Job was affirming God's sovereign authority over himself and all that he had, thus transforming a most miserable situation into an occasion of adoration and praise. Job did not cling to his wealth or maintain confidence in it, but rather he viewed it as a God-given resource which was to flow through him to bless others. He was not an owner, but merely a steward of what was God's, who had now removed this responsibility from him. Job could say blessed be the name of the Lord, because he had been righteously wealthy and not filthy rich. Mike Mason observes that Job's religious friends could have never uttered such a statement as it would have been too arbitrary and illogical for their liking:

> Good religious people do not believe in luck; they believe in finding reasons for everything. They are always trying to figure out why they are having a bad day, or why they are sick, or why they are not more happy or prosperous. This type of thinking, which forever tries to appease and manipulate the god behind every bush and rock, is a kind of paganism. In this tight theology there is not room for the sheer arbitrary unreasonableness of the Lord. By contrast, the mind that is able to live with unanswerable questions, letting the roulette ball spin at will and yet still seeing the Lord's hand at work – this is the mind of true faith.[6]

Though emotionally devastated by the entire ordeal, his faith was intact, *"Job did not sin nor charge God with wrong"* (v. 22). In other words, Job did not believe God was acting out of character in all that he had suffered. It is an astounding affirmation by a cherished servant of the Lord, one who honored God and outraged Satan. All the false accusations of the devil were now flung back in his face. Job had shown he was devoted to the Lord apart from receiving any material gain for serving Him.

God was in full control; the enemy could do no more than permitted and only what God deemed necessary to expose to Job the depths of his own heart. What will be revealed to Job about himself will lead to self-judgment and a deep mistrust of himself; only then can the servant of God rest in and fully delight in the eternal mercies of God.

Meditation

> Gaining spiritual life is conditional on suffering loss. We cannot measure our lives in terms of "gain"; they must be measured in terms of "loss." Our real capacity lies not in how much we retain but in how much has been poured out. The power of love is attested by love's sacrifice. If our hearts are not separated from the love of the world, our soul life has yet to go through the cross.
>
> — Watchman Nee

Satan's Second Assault
Job 2

We return again to the heavenly scene in Job 2. Satan returns to present himself before God as in the last chapter (vv. 1-2). After the Lord questions Satan as to where he has been and receives his answer, the Lord again raises the subject of His loyal servant Job: *"Have you considered My servant Job, that there is none like him on the earth, a blameless and upright man, one who fears God and shuns evil? And still he holds fast to his integrity, although you incited Me against him, to destroy him without cause"* (v. 3). In the throne room of heaven before all powers and principalities, the devil is reminded of his past failure. Given his previous proud disposition, this must have been an infuriating discourse. Not only had he failed to entice Job to sin, but Job's faithful allegiance despite immense hardship disproved his previous assertion against Job's motivation for honoring God. Indeed, Job had chosen to worship the Lord, even without receiving His good favor.

Yet, Satan is unabashed by his failure to rob God of glory and halt the worship of one of His servants. Satan levies a new accusation against Job: *"Skin for skin! Yes, all that a man has he will give for his life. But stretch out Your hand now, and touch his bone and his flesh, and he will surely curse You to Your face!"* (vv. 4-5). Satan suggests that Job would surrender everything, including his piety for God, in order to save his life. In response to this evil claim, the Lord gave Satan authority to physically afflict Job, but he could not take his life (v. 6).

The enemy of God wasted no time; he promptly departed and *"struck Job with painful boils from the sole of his foot to the crown of his head"* (v. 7). So grievous was the affliction that Job took up residence on an ash heap and passed the days and hours by scraping himself with a potsherd (v. 8). While it is not necessary that we should know the exact nature of the disease which fell on Job, Samuel Ridout proposes a couple possibilities:

Some have thought it to be leprosy, the most hopeless, loathsome and deadly of all human afflictions. Others have named it elephantiasis, a repulsive and fearful disease in which every part of the body is affected. It is accompanied not only by the distortion and swelling of the limbs which give it its name, but by putrid inflammation extending throughout the entire frame. It begins with the rising of tubercular boils, and at length resembles a cancer spreading itself over the whole body, by which the body is so affected that some of the limbs fall completely away.[7]

Despite Job's agonizing and debilitating condition, he held fast to his integrity, which was an affront to his grief-stricken wife. For a marriage to have survived the sorrowful events of chapter 1 is a testimony to the mutual strength and comfort a husband and wife can afford one another when unified. She had jointly suffered with her husband during Satan's first assault and had said nothing. However, in his second attack, Satan had struck her lifetime mate, provider, and protector. Her husband was beyond helping and she was now helpless also. When Job needed her most, she abandoned her husband (19:17) and, worse, turned her back on the Lord – the only One able to console her.

It would be hard for any of us to genuinely empathize with Job's wife, who, having just lost all her children and perhaps grandchildren in one day, now saw her husband stricken with a horrific, incurable disease. In utter anguish of soul, she counseled her husband: *"Curse God, and die"* (v. 9). Job responded by telling his wife that such talk is foolish and then inquired of her, *"Shall we indeed accept good from God, and shall we not accept adversity?"* (v. 10). In other words, if our God is good and does good, shall we not be willing to accept all that He has for us? The implied answer is "yes." Hence, Job rejected the foolish counsel of his wife, and with an unnatural calmness accepts all his troubles as a mysterious allowance from the hand of his God; at least, this is his initial reaction. This monumental declaration of faith is the last clear-minded expression of Job for some time; in the next chapter he becomes fully engulfed by despair.

None of us can identify with Job, for we have not suffered as he did. Our human minds struggle with the fairness of such a harsh recourse by the Lord. Frankly, we do not like any of it. Job's story makes us feel vulnerable, as we realize that just living a moral life is not enough to please God. William Kelly attempts to put Job's affliction and response in proper perspective for us in reference to God's desired outcome.

> Many of you know what it is to have a raging toothache; that is a very small thing comparatively – the tooth only. ... Well, think of this. It is not as if all the teeth were raging; that would be nothing, comparatively; ... but the whole body from head to foot in every part of it; not an exception; the most tremendous disease known, among the diseases of a terrible character in the Eastern world. This most pious of men was allowed of God to come into it for the purpose of doing him far greater good than if he had never had any of these trials. That is what comes out in the Book. And, accordingly, even then Job did not sin. He had been even now not only marked by the greatest grace in his prosperity, but by the most exemplary patience in his adversity. If God had stopped there, there would have been no lesson at all, comparatively. It would only have turned to Job's glory.[8]

Thankfully, God is more interested in bettering Job than just seeing him honored. He knows of something in Job which must be exposed and removed. Satan knows nothing of it; in fact, Job's response to his attacks has humiliated him and proven him once again to be a liar. Undoubtedly, Job was struggling with his thoughts, and wrestling with inner feelings and various questions. Yet, Scripture affords him a high accolade: *"In all this Job did not sin with his lips"* (v. 10).

Sadly, this remarkable testimony would be somewhat marred during Job's later discussions with his three friends: Eliphaz the Temanite, Bildad the Shuhite, and Zophar the Naamathite (v. 11). We should not question the good intentions of these men who jointly came to mourn with Job and comfort him in his distress; however, their influence on Job was not a positive one. What Satan could not accomplish through direct attack, he was able to somewhat achieve through Job's friends. As we will later learn, they did not speak for God and would be rebuked for that reason. This is a good reminder that we should be careful as to how we counsel and comfort those reeling in pain or grieving over the loss of a loved one. We certainly do not want to find ourselves aiding the enemy in a cause that is contrary to the will of God.

Eliphaz, Bildad, and Zophar were stunned when they saw Job. His condition was so abhorrent that they did not even recognize him. To see their friend in such agony caused them to weep and wail, to rend their clothes, and to put dust on their heads (v. 12). For seven days they sat with Job on the ground and in complete silence (v. 13). In the Far East, it was customary to mourn the dead for seven days and nights (e.g., 1 Sam. 31:13) and in their estimation Job was a living-dead man. Job's grief became their grief and if they had only remained quiet, their efforts to comfort Job may have succeeded.

Indeed, these men showed much kindness to their bereaved and afflicted friend by leaving their homes, setting aside all business and family affairs to console him. However, their presence had the effect of stirring up thoughts and feelings in Job's heart which until their visit had not been outwardly expressed. In the next chapter, Job finally does speak to them, but it is to curse the day of his birth. Job cannot bear his adversity any longer; he wants an end to it – he wants to die (3:1).

Meditation

> Our vision is so limited we can hardly imagine a love that does not show itself in protection from suffering.... The love of God did not protect His own Son.... He will not necessarily protect us – not from anything it takes to make us like His Son. A lot of hammering and chiseling and purifying by fire will have to go into the process.
>
> — Elisabeth Elliot

Job: Death Is Welcome
Job 3

Chapters 3 through 31, the largest section of the book, contain a series of discourses between Job and his three companions. These speeches are full of poetic language, ancient metaphors, and complex expressions, much of which is either accusatory or defensive in nature, or flat-out rude and sarcastic. It is tempting for the reader to skip over this argumentative portion of text to get to the "and they lived happily ever after" ending. But as Samuel Ridout points out, in doing so we would not learn several valuable lessons for life that God has for us:

> We have in this division the largest and, in many respects, the most complicated part of the book. It has been well named *The Entanglement*, for it is a mass of argument, denunciation, accusation, suspicion, partly correct theories, and withal flashes of faith and hope – all in the language of loftiest poetry, with magnificent luxuriance of Oriental metaphor. To the casual reader there may seem to be no progress, and but little clarity in the controversy. And it must be confessed that God's people at large seem to have gained little from these chapters beyond a few familiar, beautiful and oft-quoted verses. But can we think that God would have permitted a useless book to be included in that "all scripture," which is profitable? Let us then come with confidence to these controversies and patiently seek their meaning.[9]

This section begins with a drawn-out visit by Job's three friends, Eliphaz, Bildad, and Zophar. So astounding was Job's deplorable condition and so profound his grief that they gazed on their friend in utter bewilderment. They rent their garments, covered their heads with dirt, and sat with their friend in complete silence for an entire week. Their presence invoked Job to break this long silence with a bitter lamentation lasting an entire chapter.

It is painful for us to listen to a fellow believer who desires to be covered with darkness, to die, or even cease to exist altogether in order to escape the emotional trauma he or she is enduring. From this perspective, Job 3 is one of the bleakest passages in our Bibles. Some readers will join ranks with Job's friends and condemn Job for such irreverent whining; others will just assume Job is delirious with grief and does not know what he is saying. Yet, he does. He is articulating his thoughts and feelings with painful honesty that we might in a limited way perceive his mental agony. Should we fault him for being transparent? Would it have been better for him to say something deeply spiritual that he did not mean? Better to honestly express our doubts and pain to the Lord than to camouflage our true feelings with a false spirituality – God is not fooled by hypocrisy. What Job says is not wise, but at least it reflects how he really feels and is not a lie. All sin is foolish, but not all foolishness is sin.

It would be natural for anyone suffering as Job was to curse the day he or she was born, but C. H. Mackintosh reminds us that this should not be the response of an heir of glory:

> Ah! if Job had been in the presence of God, he never could have uttered such words. He would have known full well why he had not died. He would have had a soul-satisfying sense of what God had in store for him. He would have justified God in all things. But Job was not in the presence of God, but in the presence of his friends, who proved, very distinctly, that they understood little or nothing of the character of God or the real object of His dealings with His dear servant Job.[10]

Job wanted to die, but God determines the length of our earthly sojourn, as well as its difficulties and resulting glory.

The most striking aspect of this chapter is not Job's lament – being human we can understand his depression and his desire to escape life; rather, it is the contrast of this chapter with the preceding two that is shocking. Can this be the same man who humbly bowed his head and worshipped God after successive billows of adversity crashed upon him? Is this the one who patiently suffered a dreadful disease and even rebuked his wife for suggesting that he curse God and kill himself? Indeed, this is Job, but the shock of the previous calamities has passed and now the cold reality of ongoing pain and daily misery has gripped his mind and is in control of his tongue.

The satanic battlefront has shifted from outward calamities to the inner man. Solomon tells us, *"The spirit of a man will sustain him in sickness, but who can bear a broken spirit?"* (Prov. 18:14). During the initial attacks, Job's response had been sustained by a joyful and refreshed spirit, but now his mind is riveted in depression and doubt. He cannot reconcile his blameless life with his present suffering. He therefore rejects what God has permitted in his life and he wants to die to escape it. Mike Mason suggests that Job has shown us that there are times when spiritual hope can take the form of despair:

> As someone has said, "Only the desperate are truly hopeful." To be sure, there are varieties of despair and depression that are without hope at all, that are full of godless self-pity and destructiveness. But there is also a kind of despair that is realistic, courageous, and preserving in the highest degree. This is the despair that a person will have when he knows that things are wrong – that they are all wrong – and that they absolutely must get better or else he will die. The reason he despairs, then, is that he knows in his heart that there is a better way, and he has made up his mind that he will not rest until he finds it. He will not settle for anything less. ... This is not despair; this is hope. ... A lazy and self-satisfied person will never despair in this manner. Only a person who believes ardently in God will have the courage to endure such despair.[11]

This is the type of confidence that the Lord Jesus demonstrated while contemplating His imminent crucifixion in the Garden of Gethsemane. He was in utter anguish of soul; yet, He did not pray to escape His circumstances, but that God's will be done in them: *"Now is My soul troubled; and what shall I say? Father, save Me from this hour: but for this cause came I unto this hour. Father, glorify Thy name"* (John 12:27-28). Despite His distress over the horrific cost to Him personally, the Lord Jesus fully accepted His Father's will for Him. Only in the Lord's life do we find such a perfect example to follow; Job's responses to his difficulties, as well as our own reactions, merely reveal areas of needed growth and refinement.

None of us is able to point the pharisaical finger at Job and criticize his spirituality, for none of us has passed through his decimating hardship – we have not been tested in the same way. Frankly, few saints would have surpassed the first satanic assault in the way Job did. Throughout the entire ordeal, which lasted months, Job retained his faith and his sanity, though he often wrestled with haunting doubts.

Job was a true and devoted child of God, but he still needed to learn more about himself through brokenness, as, indeed, we all do. Roy Hession reminds us that we are prone to live in an illusionary world rather than honestly recognizing the un-Christ-like motives and attitudes residing in our own hearts:

> Beloved, if we feel we are innocent and have nothing to be broken about, it is not that these things are not there but that we have not seen them. We have been living in a realm of illusion about ourselves. God must be true in all that He says about us. In one form or another, He sees these things expressing themselves in us (unless we have recognized them and allowed God to deal with them) – unconscious selfishness, pride, and self-congratulation; jealousy, resentment, and impatience; reserve, fears, and shyness; dishonesty and deception; impurity and lust; if not one thing, then another. But we are blind to it. We are perhaps so occupied with the wrong the other man has done us that we do not see that we are sinning against Christ in not being willing to take it with His meekness and lowliness. Seeing so clearly how the other man wants his own way and rights, we are blind to the fact that we want ours just as much; and yet we know there is something missing in our lives. Somehow we are not in vital fellowship with God. ... Unconscious sin is, nonetheless, sin with God and separates us from Him. The sin in question may be quite a small thing, which God will so readily show us if we are only willing to ask Him.[12]

God would lay Job's heart bare; he would then discover what God wanted to remove from it and he would genuinely agree with God that this was needful. Through brokenness and this rooting out process, Job would gain a deeper understanding of his God, and learn to loathe what God did not appreciate within himself. It would be a painful learning experience, but an invaluable one.

During an arduous time in David's life, he wrote: *"I would hasten my escape from the windy storm and tempest"* (Ps. 55:8). It is not natural for us to cherish threatening circumstances or to desire ongoing pain; David wanted to flee from the storm that was pursuing him. Later, however, David could write, *"God is my strength and power, and He makes my way perfect"* (2 Sam. 22:33). God could make David's way perfect because God's way is perfect; this is a reality that Job would also discover for himself to be true (2 Sam. 22:31).

Presently, however, Job yearned to escape his calamity through the doorway of death. He wished he had never been conceived (vv. 6-7), or that he would have died in the womb (v. 3), or at least expired shortly after his birth (v. 11). He even desired that his existence would have been shrouded in the darkness of oblivion, that is, that God would never have contemplated him at all (vv. 4-5). In this poetic sense, Job personified himself with the night and with darkness – in the absence of light he would have no association with reality.

If he had died at birth, there would have been mourning; there would not have been any joyful celebration or annual birthdays to regard. But because he was born and nursed by his mother, he was forced to suffer this manifold trial, rather than to experience what he considered the quiet tranquility of death, a rest that kings and notable rulers had already received (vv. 9-15). In verses 16-19, Job again voices his desire to join the dead, who have been freed from life's struggles; death would release him from his debilitating disease and overwhelming grief. Job never contemplated suicide, but he did long to die (vv. 20-23). In his bitterness of soul, he thought death was the only means of escaping his harsh reality, but God had a different plan.

Depressed saints often do not think properly (e.g., 1 Kgs. 19:4) and in his grief and sorrow, Job wrongly asserts that death brings rest and peace to the dead. While the doctrine of eternal judgment of the wicked and the resurrection of the just unto eternal life is more clearly expounded in the New Testament (Mark 9:42-48; Rev. 20:10-15), several Old Testament passages do mention this future reality (Prov. 14:32; Isa. 66:22-24; Dan. 12:2). Abraham clearly looked forward to dwelling in a heavenly city with God (Heb. 11:10). Scripture does not state that death puts the human soul into a state of unconscious sleep (rest), as Job suggests: *"I would have been asleep"* (v. 13), *"as infants which never saw the light"* (v. 16). Rather, the Lord Jesus affirmed that *"God is not the God of the dead, but of the living"* (Matt. 22:32) and that both the wicked and the just are fully conscious after death (Luke 16:19-31).

Job did not have the benefit of Scripture to know there is a distinction between the condition of the wicked and of the righteous after death. He did believe in bodily resurrection (14:14), but in his present despondency favored annihilation or nonexistence. We therefore conclude that not all of what Job says while in his depressed state is infallible or divinely inspired. Scripture records his proclamation of hopelessness for us to learn from, but not to build doctrines on. In the New Testament, we not only have more information about suffering, death, and the afterlife, but also more hope concerning the outcome of these:

We also glory in tribulations, knowing that tribulation produces perseverance; and perseverance, character; and character, hope (Rom. 5:3-5).

For I consider that the sufferings of this present time are not worthy to be compared with the glory which shall be revealed in us (Rom. 8:18).

For the fifth time in his lament, Job asks, "Why?" (v. 23). But heaven is silent; in fact, the Lord never explains His reasons to Job at any time in the entire book. Elisabeth Elliot reminds us that there is nothing wrong with sincerely asking God "why," as it demonstrates genuine faith which cannot make sense of His ways:

There are those who insist that it is a very bad thing to question God. To them, "why?" is a rude question. That depends, I believe, on whether it is an honest search, in faith, for His meaning, or whether it is the challenge of unbelief and rebellion. The psalmist often questioned God and so did Job. God did not answer the questions, but He answered the man – with the mystery of Himself.[13]

The child of God must learn that the "whys" of God's prerogatives rest with Him; man is only responsible to honor the revealed "whats" of life. "May God's will be done" is the right response for all the activities of life, the good and the bad; it is not necessary for us to know why God chooses what He does, but rather to rest in Him. But Job was in distress; he had neither rest nor appetite; he was sighing rather than eating (v. 24).

In the closing verses of chapter 3, Job recounts the day in which he lost everything. He shares his inner feelings about the matter in what has now become a famous verse of Scripture: *"For the thing I greatly feared has come upon me, and what I dreaded has happened to me"* (v. 25). It is possible there was a nagging concern in the back of Job's mind which pertained to losing what he had, an anxiety that often afflicts rich people. However, given the popular worldview of that day, there really would be no cause for such a calamity if he were living a God-fearing life. Logically speaking, the expression probably relates to the quick repetitive losses that Job experienced in one day. After hearing of the first loss, Job feared more harm would occur. Then, when he learned that another disaster had befallen him, he continued to fear further calamity. He confessed to being oppressed by terror throughout the entire ordeal, and though he longed for peace and quietness, he had only experienced repetitive turmoil since then (v. 26).

Job ends his first lament by again welcoming death's arrival to release him from all his woes. It is noteworthy that throughout this entire discourse, Job does not speak of injustice or speak ill of God, but rather describes his intense plight, which could have been avoided if he had died at birth or had never been born. Hence, he curses his existence, but he does not curse God. As he previously told his wife, such behavior would be utter foolishness.

Job believed to never have existed would be better than his present existence. When severely depressed, we often permit the *here and now* to overshadow *forever* and *never*. Contemplations of suicide or even statements welcoming death are affronts to God's sovereignty. In effect, what one is really saying is: "God cannot work this situation for my good! There will never be a positive outcome of this trial! God is not with me. God cannot use my suffering to further His glory." Thankfully, Job would learn the same lesson David did when he experienced a frightening tempest in his life:

> *The righteous cry out, and the Lord hears, and delivers them out of all their troubles. The Lord is near to those who have a broken heart, and saves such as have a contrite spirit. Many are the afflictions of the righteous, but the Lord delivers him out of them all* (Ps. 34:17-19).

Indeed, it is better to journey through the threatening unknown with the Lord than to venture anywhere else, especially death, without Him. Solomon rightly exhorts, *"Do not be a fool – why die before your time?"* (Eccl. 7:17; NASV). Job begins this journey by lamenting his situation; he will end it as a new man, refined, restored, vindicated, and blessed. Let us remember that *"a righteous God tests the hearts and minds"* of His people (Ps. 7:9).

Meditation

> Character cannot be developed in ease and quiet. Only through experience of trial and suffering can the soul be strengthened, ambition inspired, and success achieved.
>
> — Helen Keller

> This is God's universal purpose for all Christian suffering: more contentment in God and less satisfaction in the world.
>
> — John Piper

Eliphaz: The Innocent Do Not Suffer
Job 4-5

Before evaluating the dialogue between Job and his three companions, the reader is reminded that neither the words of Satan, nor much of what the main characters utter is inspired by God, though we have an inspired account of their statements and interaction. Most of what is said is incorrect, or correct but misapplied, or at least open to question. This demonstrates the fallacy of humanism to resolve the question of human suffering, even when promoted by a child of God. As F. B. Hole surmises:

> We must never overlook the difference between **revelation** and **inspiration**. All Scripture is inspired of God, but not every word found therein is a revelation from God. When Solomon wrote, for instance, *"There is nothing better for a man, than that he should eat and drink..."* (Eccl. 2:24), he was not uttering a **revelation** from God but rather his own foolishness – **inspired** to put it on record for our warning.[14]

Instead of acknowledging that their world was in a fallen state resulting from original sin, Job's well-to-do friends insisted that the world was not inherently bad, but rather sorrowful events occurred as an expression as to how God felt about those in it. Samuel Ridout summarizes the philosophical tenet exhibited in the unified message of Job's three comrades:

> That principle is that all suffering is of a punitive rather than of an instructive nature; that it is based on God's justice rather than on His love – though these are ever combined in all His ways. Such a principle necessarily fails to distinguish between the sufferings of the righteous and those of the wicked.[15]

In short, it was believed that well-doers do not suffer calamity, but only the wicked do. As well-established inhabitants, Job's friends undoubtedly considered themselves in the first category of earthly citizens and Job, regrettably, in the latter group.

The concept that all human suffering is directly punitive is, of course, not a principle supported by Scripture. James informs us that God permits His people to experience trials to build stronger patience into their faith (Jas. 1:2-3). Likewise, Peter informs a group of persecuted Christians that their trials were precious to the Lord because of what they accomplished for them personally and for His glory:

In this you greatly rejoice, though now for a little while, if need be, you have been grieved by various trials, that the genuineness of your faith, being much more precious than gold that perishes, though it is tested by fire, may be found to praise, honor, and glory at the revelation of Jesus Christ, whom having not seen you love. Though now you do not see Him, yet believing, you rejoice with joy inexpressible and full of glory, receiving the end of your faith – the salvation of your souls (1 Pet. 1:6-9).

Because of Job's grim emotional outburst of the previous chapter, Eliphaz, likely the oldest, and closest of Job's friends, is hesitant to answer Job (4:1). He is concerned that he might provoke further angst from Job, but at the same time feels that it is necessary to confront Job, because he has insulted God by his lamentation. So refined and diplomatic Eliphaz initiates his first discourse by asking Job if he will patiently listen to what they have to say (4:2). In a kind and considerate fashion, Eliphaz reminds Job that in times past he had been wonderfully used as a source of instruction, counsel, and strength for many (4:3-4). But the intent of this compliment becomes plain in the next verse; it is merely an impetus for rebuke: You advised others to patiently endure trials, but yet you do not heed your own counsel when calamity challenges your faith (4:5). This statement, as pertaining to Job, could be true, as well as the following one: *"Is not your reverence your confidence? And the integrity of your ways your hope?"* (4:6). F. B. Hole suggests that indeed Eliphaz put his finger on the weak spot in Job by this statement:

> That Job's character and ways were excellent has been guaranteed by God Himself, but that being the case, how subtle the snare to make them the basis of one's confidence and hope, and to build everything upon them, before God as well as before men. It is what many a very godly saint has done since the days of Job.[16]

In short, it was not Job's perseverance in well-doing that could secure his livelihood and enjoyment in life; rather, such things were controlled by the counsels of a supreme God whom Job worshipped. Let us be care not to adore what we have, what we are doing, or what we have done; God could blow it all away with one puff of air (Hag. 1:9). Our security and prosperity are in Him alone, not in the relationships we establish, nor in our accomplishments, nor in our stockpiled resources, and definitely not in the organizations to which we belong.

Job apparently could not encourage himself, and needed encouragement, but what Eliphaz says next was not helpful. He suggested that true God-fearing piety rests in God's sovereignty, and should therefore not be so easily abandoned (4:6). Later, Eliphaz questions Job's reverence for the Lord (15:4), so this statement was probably meant as a follow-on reprimand of Job's present conduct.

Eliphaz then presents his thinking about human misery by imposing a sowing and reaping illustration from nature. Verse 7 forms the basis for his argument: *"Remember now, whoever perished being innocent? Or where were the upright ever cut off?"* It has been Eliphaz's observation that the innocent and upright do not reap suffering unless they have plowed iniquity and sown trouble, for God ensures that those who do wicked deeds are judged. His analogy poses a vague, but stinging indictment against Job: *"Those who plow iniquity and sow trouble reap the same"* (v. 8). In other words, Job, you are getting what you deserve!

While it is true that *"by the blast of God they* [the wicked] *perish,"* it cannot be logically concluded that everyone that perishes is wicked (v. 9). Job would agree that God sturdily judges the evildoers, but does every calamity on earth translate to His retribution for personal sin?

The elder orator likens Job to a mighty lion who doubtlessly caused others trouble, and therefore through divine measures had his teeth broken and cubs scattered (4:10-11). Eliphaz was implying that because of Job's sin, he had lost his social status, economic power, and all his children. Without teeth, the lion cannot eat and starvation prevails in time; likewise Eliphaz was suggesting that Job, having received divine reprisal for sin, was now being slowly devoured by his guilt.

Eliphaz's reasoning was solely based on his personal observations; however, he seeks to further substantiate his conclusion by relating a frightful vision he had experienced in a dream (4:12-14). William Kelly associates the fear that beset Eliphaz during his nighttime vision to the erroneous and ungracious way he conveyed its message to Job:

> It was evidently not enough of grace that he had; grace does not make people fear in this kind of way. It is judgment that does so, and this is what these good men are full of; they were full of the spirit of judgment. And yet that is the very thing we are called not to do. *"Judge not, that ye be not judged."* When there is evil found on the part of one who bears the name of the Lord, we are bound to judge him; but there was no evil found on the part of Job at all. And when evil is not found, we are bound not to judge; we are not to yield to our own thoughts; we are to wait upon God to make it all plain.[17]

In his vision, a formless spirit was passing by him, it stopped, remained quiet for a moment and then spoke to Eliphaz (4:15-16). There is nothing in the text to suggest that this vision came from the Lord, and there are several reasons to reject the idea. Perhaps the two most outstanding reasons are, first, Eliphaz received "a word," but not a "word from the Lord," and second, Eliphaz assumed that God was removed from and unconcerned about the affairs of men, which is not true (4:18-21).

This formless spirit then asked Eliphaz two questions: *"Can a mortal be more righteous than God? Can a man be more pure than his Maker?"* (4:17). The answer to both questions is "no." The apparent meaning is that man has no right to question God or reply against God; if man suffers, it is his own fault. The implied conclusion is that Job should not think he was innocent of sin. If God charges His angels (fallen angels) with error, He certainly cannot trust man, who was created lower than the angels (4:18). Eliphaz concludes by addressing the fragility and the mortality of man, especially of those who live sinfully; they are likened to a clay house that soon falls, a toppled tent, a shattered vessel, or an effortlessly smashed moth (4:19-20). This was a terrible way to die, unnoticed and without understanding (4:21).

Eliphaz's questions and his implication take the form of an exaggerated truth which is then used as a putdown – this is a frequent tactic of the devil.

According to Eliphaz, Job lacked wisdom; otherwise he would realize that he was suffering because he was a sinner. While it is true that all men are impure before God (i.e., are sinners), Eliphaz fails to understand that by his own logic, all would then suffer because of sin, including himself. Therefore in Eliphaz's world there should be no difference between the righteous and the wicked; all would be suffering. The idea that individuals can be positionally justified through faith by grace is not a concept that had been revealed yet. Thankfully, in Christ, believers today have the confidence that though sin and suffering occur, God's plan of salvation cannot be thwarted. He is concerned and He notices every detail of our lives – He is connected with us and will make us better, even if the worst, from our perspective, happens.

However, Job's companions did not understand this operation of God and unfortunately, Eliphaz, in his holy zeal, further pushes his conclusion that Job is being chastened by the Lord:

> *Call out now; is there anyone who will answer you? And to which of the holy ones will you turn? For wrath kills a foolish man, and envy slays a simple one. I have seen the foolish taking root, but suddenly I cursed his dwelling place* (5:1-3).

And there is the root of the problem. Eliphaz is not prompted to have pity on those who suffer or to pray for them, but rather he curses them. He surmises that no holy one (i.e., a saints or perhaps angels) can help to ease their plight because they are getting the divine retribution they deserve! While the conclusion is the same, Matthew Henry perceives that Eliphaz is referring to the "holy ones" for a different reason: "When were any of the saints or servants of God visited with such divine judgments as Job, or did they ever behave like him under their sufferings?"[18] The implied answer is that no righteous person had ever suffered like Job; therefore, Job must be guilty of serious offenses.

As an older man, Eliphaz was prone to judge the issues of life from his past observations and experiences without having the specific facts available to discern Job's situation (5:4-5). The phrase *"I have seen"* repeatedly occurs in Job 5 and characterizes Eliphaz's self-proclaimed expertise. Sadly and inappropriately, he interprets Job's crisis based on what he has previously witnessed, not on its own merits.

This is deductive reasoning at its worst: All I see are black ducks, therefore all ducks are black, yet without evaluating every duck in existence, such a conclusion is presumptuous. Did Eliphaz know for sure that all suffering results from personal sin? Had he reviewed every example of travail in human history to formulate his conclusion? Did Eliphaz know that every wicked person had not prospered on the earth because of divine judgment? The answer to all these questions is "no." Therefore, it was audacious to lump poor Job in with the wicked because of his dismal situation. Eliphaz's conclusion was unmerited, especially in view of Job's well-acclaimed upright and blameless testimony. Such behavior is a stern warning to us not to judge things by their apparent form or to assume one situation is just like another. A wise person will fully consider each set of circumstances before answering a particular matter, as the first appearance of things is usually not the correct assessment (Prov. 18:13-17). It is foolish for anyone to grip a one-sided story, especially since God will judge those who condemn the just (Prov. 17:15)!

To add insult to injury, Eliphaz adds:

For affliction does not come from the dust, nor does trouble spring from the ground; yet man is born to trouble, as the sparks fly upward. But as for me, I would seek God, and to God I would commit my cause (5:6-8).

Eliphaz did not think that Job was seeking God in the situation, but rather complaining bitterly against Him. However, Eliphaz, being of a calm and serene disposition, could say with confidence, "If I were in your shoes, I would seek the Lord and commit my cause to Him, instead of whining about it." There is no way of proving the validity of Eliphaz's statement, as he was not the one being refined by fire. With this said, it is likely that he would attempt to suppress outward expressions of his anger, rather than speak his true feelings. His version of God would surely reimburse wrath for venting anger – not a good trade. On the contrary, Job is completely honest with God and willingly expresses his feelings because he has a higher perception of God's character than Eliphaz does. Job shows us that it is better to be honest with the Lord when we are hurting and do not know how to best articulate it than to be a hypocrite and try to hide our true thoughts, which He knows anyway.

Eliphaz continues by explaining what he has witnessed throughout his life: that the Lord blesses the upright and relieves the poor, but frustrates and destroys the works of the crafty and deceitful (5:9-16). While his limited observations may have been correct, Eliphaz had inadequate understanding of God's grand prerogative in dealing with humanity. To broad-brush all God's activities in such a speculative manner is foolish and, in effect, limits His sovereign rule in creation.

Eliphaz offers several sound (though misapplied) statements in this chapter: *"Man is born to trouble"* and *"He [God] catches the wise in their own craftiness"* are good examples, as is his statement in verse 17: *"Behold, happy is the man whom God corrects; therefore do not despise the chastening of the Almighty."* The inspired writer of Hebrews affirms the same idea (Heb. 12:6-7). Yet, when combined with subsequent verses, Eliphaz uses the latter statement as a club over poor Job's head. Why was Job miserable and bitter? Why was he not experiencing God's love through correction? The implied answer to these questions was because Job was being divinely rebuked for sinfulness; otherwise he would be happy in his circumstances (5:18-27).

Because Job did not have the right attitude, he was not obtaining God's comfort, deliverance, and blessing, but rather His displeasure. Job's counselors had a narrow field of vision; they believed that Job could fix all his problems if he would just get right with God. But they were nowhere near the truth – Job could not resolve his situation; rather, he must experience brokenness and yield the pieces of his heart to God, who would then gladly and promptly end his trial.

If Job were repentant, Eliphaz promised that God would deliver him from *"six troubles, yes, in seven no evil shall touch you"* (5:19). To follow a number with the next highest was to symbolize completeness (e.g., Prov. 30:15). God's deliverance would be perfect and complete, if Job would just acknowledge his sin. Eliphaz even mentions the type of calamities that Job could be delivered from: famine, war, slander, destruction, and wild beasts (5:20-22). He further ascribes the types of blessings that a righteous man enjoys: agricultural prosperity (not even hindered by stones in the fields), security, good health, many descendants, and a long life (5:23-25). Such a man goes to the grave having lived a full and fruitful life (5:26). Eliphaz smugly concludes his *matter of fact* speech, with, *"It is true."* Based on a lifetime of observations, he urged Job to heed his instruction and rebuke – he should admit his sin and get right with God (5:27)!

Meditation

> Humility alone unites patience with love; without which it is impossible to draw profit from suffering; or indeed, to avoid complaint, especially when we think we have given no occasion for what men make us suffer.
> — John Wesley

> Why should the righteous suffer? Why not? They're the only ones who can handle it.
> — C. S. Lewis

Job: A Plea for Pity in the Day of Vanity
Job 6-7

Job replies to Eliphaz's speech: *"Oh, that my grief were fully weighed, and my calamity laid with it on the scales! For then it would be heavier than the sand of the sea"* (6:2-3). Eliphaz had been arguing from a balanced-scale theology, that is, that God always renders tit for tat. Job contended that his confused friends did not have proper balances to weigh out and understand his misery, which was heavier than wet sand. They had a limited and nebulous perspective, so Job challenges them in this chapter to get specific on what he has done wrong.

Job's unrelenting pain and grief had caused his mind to swirl with emotions, and admittedly to utter impetuous words (6:3). He further affirms that the arrows of the Almighty had smitten him (i.e., God had inflicted him). Job is being consumed by his misery; it is controlling him: *"My spirit drinks in their poison; the terrors of God are arrayed against me"* (6:4). Because his companions were full, they could neither empathize with him, nor assist him in his agony. They were like well-fed animals who do not bray because they are content; he, on the other hand, had ample cause to bemoan his distress; he was eating loathsome food, not the good things in life (6:5-7). Though Eliphaz thought he had fed Job good things, he had actually denied him real spiritual food. Why did Eliphaz think that Job was as strong as stone and unresponsive as bronze (6:12)? In reality, Job's strength was depleted and he could not go on; hence, once again he asks the Lord to end his days and to cut him off (6:8-13).

Job then reprimands his colleagues: If they were God-fearing, they would not act deceitfully, but would be willing to show him pity (6:14-23). *"To him who is afflicted, kindness should be shown by his friend"* (6:14). They were like desert streams that dried up in the heat, just when the traveling caravans from Tema or Sheba most needed water. Likewise, when Job needed his colleagues the most, they proved to be utterly useless. Because Job could not admit that he justly deserved such a crushing trial, H. L. Rossier suggests that the words of his associates were harder to bear than the sufferings of his tortured body:

> The death of his children and the loss of his goods were terrible blows; the sickness with which Satan had visited him was of the most trying and horrible kind, but both the silence and the speeches of his friends were as the innumerable poisonous arrows which pierced his soul. In these three men Satan had found unconscious but all the more efficient tools. Instead of really comforting Job, they brought him to despair. Instead of reminding him that the goodness of God endures forever, and that the reason of his ways although hidden for a time, would in the end be revealed as glorious, they accused the poor man, first in their hearts, then openly, of the grossest crimes, simply because they could not account for his sufferings in any other way. Who then can still be surprised that Job became vexed and wished that God might destroy him (6:9)?[19]

Accordingly, Job levies a direct challenge to his companions to abandon vague suggestions and insinuations and supply detailed allegations (6:24-25). He promised to hold his tongue if they could specifically prove to him where he had legitimately erred (6:26-30). Right words have force, but inappropriate words dig a pit for the innocent. In verse 30, Job alludes to his guiltlessness – he knew what iniquity was and had not indulged in perverseness. Accordingly, he knew the faultiness of Eliphaz's argument just as his tongue could discern the taste of food.

Job's challenge to his friends is a good one for us all to heed, suggests William Kelly: "How often among brethren in Christ have vague insinuations, or even accusations, brought havoc, where 'right words,' based on specific facts, would have proved forcible and brought good."[20] It is our nature to jump to conclusions without all the facts and then deliberately and ungraciously share these presumptuous verdicts with others. This is what Job's companions did. Such behavior distorts the truth concerning the guilty and even worse, defames and defrauds the innocent. God is not honored in either case.

In the multitude of words sin is not lacking. But he who restrains his lips is wise (Prov. 10:19).

The Beginning of Wisdom

> *There is one who speaks like the piercings of a sword, but the tongue of the wise promotes health* (Prov. 12:18).

> *A prudent man conceals knowledge, but the heart of fools proclaims foolishness* (Prov. 12:23).

Words can heal or hurt; let us be wise in how we use them, especially when conversing with those who have locked themselves into a cell of despair.

Job continues his response into chapter 7 by addressing the Lord. Verses 1-10 contain a moving discourse, which enables the reader to better understand Job's mental and physical condition and the sense of hopelessness that had gripped his heart. Job began by using the brevity of man's existence on the earth as an example: despite the vanity of man's brief days, he still had something to hope for. A slave, for example, longed for shade and rest after laboring all day in the hot sun, and a hired servant expected to be paid after completing his contracted service (7:1-2). But Job considered his situation much more desperate. First, he had nothing to hope for and, second, there was no reprieve in his suffering.

Indeed, his situation was acutely miserable: *"months of vanity"* and *"wearisome nights"* (7:3), and the *"tossing to and fro until the dawning of day"* (7:4; KJV). Job was suffering from severe sleep deprivation. Most of us can tolerate a night or two without sleep and still carry on, but what type of disposition might we have after months of sleeplessness? He also was in gnawing pain: *"My flesh is caked with worms and dust, my skin is cracked and breaks out afresh"* (7:5). Job was covered head to toe with oozing sores that were encrusted with dirt and infested with squirmy worms.

Furthermore, nothing changed day after day, month after month; thus, he understandably concludes: *"My days ... are spent without hope"* (7:6). Like the swift weaver's shuttle, or a short breath of air, or a vanishing cloud, his hopeless days flew by in endless procession. The Hebrew word translated "hope" is *tiqvah*, which is rendered "thread" in Joshua 2:21. Rahab's hope of salvation rested in a scarlet thread that she secured at her window. The thread was a reminder of what she longed for. Since Job is speaking of life's brevity, the weaver's shuttle running out of thread may be Job's intended meaning, but the concept of *hopeless* is the same in either case. Job believed that he would never

Devotions in Job

see *good* again in his remaining lifetime, which was quickly wasting away (7:6-10). His friends should have been moved with compassion by his pathetic state, rather than adding to his misery with condescending speech.

Job turns his thoughts heavenward in the remainder of the chapter. While it is true that Job's prayers throughout the book are often self-focused and he bemoans God's apparent absence, rather than appreciating His nearness, his prayers are decisive proof of his genuine faith. Although David had not yet penned Psalm 62, Job practically understood its meaning: *"Trust in Him at all times, you people; pour out your heart before Him; God is a refuge for us"* (Ps. 62:8). Accordingly, Job often breaks into prayer while confronting his friends; in contrast, they never utter one prayer in the entire book. Indeed, they uttered lofty dialogue about God, but were not prone to talk with Him personally. It is a trap that religious people often fall into – it is easier to talk about God, rather than to pray to Him. Leonard Ravenhill reminds us that, "No man is greater than his prayer life." What is accomplished in secret is powerful, but what is done for the esteem of others is nothing but pride and God hates it (Matt. 6:4-6)!

At this juncture, Job is disillusioned with God's ways and lifts up a bitter complaint to Him (7:11). He begins by acknowledging his own smallness, for even the sea and the sea monster are greater than he is (7:12). Why then did God consider man to be so significant that He would cause him to suffer continually? This did not make sense to Job. He sought comfort on his bed during his remaining days, but could find no reprieve because God continued (at least he thought) to torment him with dreams and terrible night visions (7:14). So he pleads to God, *"Let me alone"* (7:16). He loathes his present life and desires that the days of his vanity would come to an end – Job just wants to die (7:15).

Though a grief-stricken discourse overall, F. B. Hole notes a change in Job's tone when complaining to the Lord instead of his friends (7:16-19):

> He at once is made to realize the insignificance and even the sinfulness of mankind. His cry is, *"What is man . . . ?"* and though he could not answer the question with the clearer light vouchsafed to David in Psalm 8, or the full light of the New Testament, he knew enough to admit that man is not what he ought to be, and that it is a wonder that God should set His heart upon him.[21]

In verse 20, Job further applies his previous statements about God's mysterious interest in humanity in the form of personalized "what" and "why" questions:

> *Have I sinned? What have I done to You, O watcher of men? Why have You set me as Your target, so that I am a burden to myself? Why then do You not pardon my transgression, and take away my iniquity?* (7:20-21).

Job knew that he was under God's scrutiny and that his God could perceive sin and error in a way that he could not. Hence, he asks God what his sin was and why, given his brokenness, God had not granted him a full pardon – surely he had suffered enough for any possible offense he had committed! He knew God was a forgiving God, but he did not feel forgiven because he was still suffering. What good was all his faith, if it did not remove the weight of his sin from him? Job had to learn that it is not his faith that affects forgiveness; only God can forgive individuals of their sins and cleanse the sinner's guilty conscience.

At this juncture of the narrative, we are starting to understand better why God is testing His honorable servant Job; J. N. Darby explains:

> In Job we have man put to the test ... an upright man and righteous in his ways, in order to show whether he can stand before God in presence of the power of evil, whether he can be righteous in his own person before God. On the other hand, we find the dealings of God, by which He searches the heart and gives it the consciousness of its true state before Him.[22]

Though Job had lived a blameless and God-fearing life, he never said that he was sinless; on the contrary, he was vaguely aware of the guilt residing in his conscience. It is not likely that he understood what was causing those feelings, as God had yet to reveal it to him. We also know, all too well, how encumbered our minds are with wrong thinking, tainted motives, and lusting. Sometimes we cannot quite put our finger on specifically what is tapping our moral compass, but we know that something is. The symptoms of guiltiness relate to far more than what we do; they also include who we are, a matter that Paul rightly summarizes: *"I know that in me (that is, in my flesh) dwells no good thing"* (Rom. 7:18). At this juncture, Job was only nebulously aware of the sin that was within him. In the unfolding chapters God will plow furrows on Job's heart to expose the hidden pride that presently resided there. Job must see what is not pleasing to the Lord for himself and repudiate it. Presently, he did not know specifically what it was, though he sensed its presence.

Like Job, we too need our hearts tilled up, spiritually speaking. How can this be accomplished? Thankfully, being in the Church Age we have more resources available than Job did. First, each believer must examine his or her own heart as exposed by the Word of God to determine his or her own spiritual state. Next, we must ask the Holy Spirit to search our hearts and expose sin, whether it is hidden or blatant, sins of commission and sins of omission. Hidden sins might include pride, hypocrisy, unloving attitudes, and disrespect for God's order and authority. Sins of omission may include a lethargic prayer-life, an absence of faith, a lack of concern for the lost, or a deficiency of love for the Church. We must realize that all sin grieves the Lord, and therefore must be dealt with. Job did not have the Word of God to ponder or the indwelling Spirit of God to immediately convict, as we do. Therefore, let us cooperate with God on this grand prerogative by asking Him to show us our sin, and to see it and loathe it as He does. Only then can we enjoy a walk of holiness with the Lord.

As we will soon witness in the life of Job, the Lord knows best how to refine each of us to be more like Christ (Rom. 8:29). The Lord loved Job too much to leave him the way he was or to leave him alone, so death, though Job longed for it, would never be an option. Job could not escape the providential care of His great God and neither can we!

Meditation

The readiest way to escape from our sufferings is to be willing they should endure as long as God pleases.

— John Wesley

Bildad: You Are Not Upright
Job 8

While Bildad and Eliphaz sat in the same religious pew, Bildad's vantage point for addressing Job is quite different than that of Eliphaz. Where Eliphaz relied solely on past personal experiences and observations to censure Job, Bildad never refers to his own experiences. Bildad's authority pertains to ancient traditions of *"the former age"* and *"of the fathers"* (v. 8). He is the staunch voice of antiquity, and in his view he had greater credibility than Eliphaz. As one might expect, his discourses abound with well-known proverbial sayings and virtuous clichés.

Bildad believed that by examining the past (which was a much wider basis of information and consensus than Eliphaz applied) we gain accurate guidance for the future: *"Will they not teach you and tell you, and utter words from their heart?"* (v. 10). While it is true that we should learn from the past, C. H. Mackintosh explains why both past experience and developed traditions are inadequate to assist Job:

> Now, it must be admitted that Bildad conducts us into a much wider field than that of Eliphaz. The authority of a number of "fathers" has much more weight and respectability than the experience of a single individual. Moreover, it would argue much more modesty to be guided by the voice of a number of wise and learned men than by the light of one's own experience. But the fact is that neither experience nor tradition will do. The former may be true, so far as it goes, but you can hardly get two men whose experience will exactly correspond; and as to the latter, it is a mass of confusion, for one father differs from another; and nothing can be more slippery or uncertain than the voice of tradition – the authority of the fathers.[23]

Consequently, Bildad's traditionalist viewpoint has no more worth to Job than Eliphaz's lifetime of experiences; both are bantering about the same prosperity gospel message that many are erroneously embracing today: Tangible faith ensures an individual a health and wealth outcome. It is conjectured that because God is righteous, He must reward positive faith, and, of course, it must be in the prescribed way that we want Him to. While it is true that the resurrection life of Christ, which all true believers enjoy, ensures power and joy, the unfolding of God's blessings are not always pleasant or appreciated at a particular moment. The life and arduous ministry of Paul as shown to us in Acts demonstrates this statement to be true. Because we are self-focused, we do not often perceive God's doings as positive, especially when they result in suffering and disappointment. Those who only expect God to do them good if they do good will ultimately become disillusioned with the Christian faith and fall away. This is why Peter instructed suffering believers to *"gird up the loins of your mind, be sober, and rest your hope fully upon the grace that is to be brought to you at the revelation of Jesus Christ"* (1 Pet. 1:13). Expect hardship for living for Christ and expect His grace alone to sustain you – not your biased expectations or your perceived good works!

Job's friends needed divine revelation to truly understand Job's situation, but that was not made available to them until later. When we do not know what God thinks on a particular matter, it is best to stay quiet, but Eliphaz, Bildad, and Zophar did not follow that course of action. The experiences of one man (Eliphaz) or the combined history of many men cannot be the grand standard to measure another man's doings. There is only one paradigm that matters and that is God's revealed will. The words of men may have merit in directing the affairs of life, but the voice of God is absolutely perfect in governing all that we do. In a future day, God will not judge us according to how well we followed the experiences of others or held to human tradition, but how we adhered to His Word (John 12:48).

Eliphaz had reprimanded Job for resenting the chastening of God, but Bildad goes further to accuse Job of subverting God's justice through endless windy words (vv. 2-3). This implied that Job was indeed guilty of sin, deserved his present misery, and should cease rejecting God's righteous judgment. If this were not enough, Bildad ruthlessly drags Job's dead children into the argument: *"If your sons have sinned against Him, He has cast them away for their transgression"* (v. 4). How does bringing up such a sensitive matter enhance Job's recovery? We learned from Job 1 that Job meticulously offered atoning sacrifices on behalf of his children, just in case they had sinned against the Lord; all this to say that Job held a clear conscience on the matter of sin. Bildad's attempt to plant doubt in Job's mind concerning his children is a brutal and counterproductive rabbit trail.

In a taunting fashion, Bildad then counsels Job to seek God out to plead for restoration, if he felt he was innocent. Bildad felt that it was presumptuous for Job to expect God to search him out or to agree with him (7:21, vv. 5-7).

Bildad's name means "son of contention," and he clearly lived out the meaning of his name when speaking with Job. After asserting the basis for his arguments, Bildad devotes the remainder of the chapter to summarizing what we learn from tradition: God always rewards or punishes individuals according to their deeds. He uses three illustrations from nature to substantiate his conclusion (two from plant life and one from the insect world). Job might as well lean on a spider web for support than to depend on his self-proclaimed guiltlessness to thwart God's judgment. If man is wicked, God cuts him off. If good, God prospers him. Several statements infer Job's guilt in this chapter:

Does God subvert judgment? Or does the Almighty pervert justice? (v. 3).

If you were pure and upright, surely now He would awake for you, and prosper your rightful dwelling place (v. 6).

So are the paths [of judgment] *of all who forget God; and the hope of the hypocrite shall perish* (v. 13).

Behold, God will not cast away the blameless, nor will He uphold the evildoers (v. 20).

Bildad likened Job to a well-watered plant that God had pulled up out of the ground, roots and all, and now was withering away (v. 12). In summary, Bildad's message to Job was: The fathers agree with me, Job: You are not upright, or you would have God's blessing, not His rebuke. To emphasize this conclusion, Bildad concludes his harsh discourse by throwing Job's words *"I will no longer be"* (7:21) back in his face by affirming his statement, *"the wicked will come to nothing"* (8:22).

Although Bildad's rebuke was different than Eliphaz's, the reasoning of both men is founded in the same worldview, that is, God's moral government alone dictated His interaction with humanity. This meant that it was impossible for God to disfavor a righteous individual and that certain judgment would fall on every wicked person (v. 20). Thankfully, God the Father did not hold to this protocol when He judged His perfect and upright Son for our sin! Thus, to suffer with Christ means that a believer must suffer undeservingly in righteousness; this has nothing to do with suffering justly for wrongdoing, for Christ was sinless (1 Pet. 2:18-20). Hence, God's great prerogatives transcend the limits of human reasoning and we should be thankful that they do.

William Kelly explains that the distorted worldview of Job's friends was not founded on faith in God's revealed Word, but rather was the fallout of man's moral awareness (i.e., his guilty conscience):

> There was conscience, conscience toward God; but conscience, however useful and highly important, as it is, for the soul, never does, nor can it ever, reveal God. It detects our bad state, and the more it is purged by divine grace through redemption, the clearer is its judgment. But that was not the case then. Everything was more or less confused, and God was merely regarded as a righteous God. But God is the God of all grace. And many people confound God's grace with His goodness; but the goodness of God is quite a different thing from the grace of God. The goodness of God is that which flows out in every sort of kindness, and in patience with us and consideration of our weakness. But the grace of God means not merely His love, but His love rising above sin; His love triumphing over all our evil.[24]

In short, the responses of Eliphaz and Bildad were derived from the moral awareness that God had placed within them (Rom. 2:15). They did not have the benefit of direct revelation to know truth or experienced redemption to know God's grace – their understanding of God and His ways was limited. In ignorance, they sought to uphold the righteousness of God, but failed to do so. Their viewpoint limited God's sovereign rule over man and, additionally, wrongly indicted and injured God's righteous servant Job.

God is much more than just a righteous God who must judge sin; He is also a gracious God who knows how to overcome sin and make us triumph for His glory! *"Now thanks be to God who always leads us in triumph in Christ, and through us diffuses the fragrance of His knowledge in every place"* (2 Cor. 2:14). In Christ, we do not receive what we did deserve and we get much more than we do deserve.

Meditation

> We must learn to regard people less in light of what they do or omit to do, and more in the light of what they suffer.
>
> — Dietrich Bonhoeffer

Job: No One Is Righteous and All Suffer
Job 9-10

Job's response to Bildad's accusatory insinuations is quite remarkable; he begins by stating his concurrence, *"truly I know it is so"* before fully developing his thematic question (v. 2). He agreed with Bildad's statements: the wicked do perish (8:22) and the hypocrite who forgets God does suffer a vanishing hope (8:13). But then Job infers that he is not that hypocrite. He had not forgotten God, so why was he suffering? This was a baffling contradiction to his ontological reckoning and the cause-and-effect relationships that he understood to govern life under God's rule.

After further considering God's dealings with the wicked and the hypocrite, Job wonders by what basis God could accept any man as righteous. In forming his question, he uses words similar to those uttered in irony by the spirit voice in Eliphaz's vision (4:17): *"But how can a man be righteous before God?"* Eliphaz and his friends did not believe that there was an answer to this question, but Job earnestly believed that there was a divine resolution and that every individual's eternal destiny depended on it. No one could ever pacify Bildad's exacting God of righteousness; therefore, Bildad's understanding of God's ways clearly did not go far enough to resolve man's need of righteousness in order to be accepted by God.

Job knew God to be faithful, without really knowing why He could be faithful to a sinner. God's steadfast faithfulness to Job was his assurance of security, though he had no theological foundation for explaining why a perfect God could accept an imperfect man. The reason for this would not be revealed for a couple more millennia: Christ would become the righteousness of the believer, the means of acceptance before God throughout all dispensations. A sinner is justified when he or she exercises faith in the salvation message that God has revealed in different ways throughout human history (e.g., Gen. 15:6; Rom. 3:28).

Job agreed with Eliphaz that man could have no dispute with an all-wise and powerful God (9:3), though later he will attempt to subpoena God to somehow cause Him to explain His actions (10:2, 13:22, 14:15, 31:35-37). However, when God did speak to Job from a whirlwind, he found out that he could not challenge God at all; in fact, he could not even answer His questions. But putting aside his distraught emotional condition, Job was a God-fearing man, and he knew that no man could confront God and benefit from doing so (v. 4). He reasoned: who would be so foolish to stand against a God who overturns mountains in His anger, causes earthquakes, solar eclipses, spreads out the heavens, controls the stars and constellations and *"does great things past finding out, yes, wonders without number"* (9:5-10)?

Not only is God all-powerful, but He is unperceivable unless He chooses otherwise; He could pass near to Job without him being aware of His presence (v. 11). As the presence of an imperceptible God could not be affirmed by Job, this statement is likely an attempt to upstage Eliphaz's viewable, chattering spirit in Job 4. No one can control God or question His actions, and those proud enough to do so will reap His anger (9:12-13). So Job is utterly perplexed as to what to do: *"How then can I answer Him, and choose my words to reason with Him? For though I were righteous, I could not answer Him; I would beg mercy of my Judge"* (9:14-15). Job's response in this section strikes a sour note of self-righteousness, suggests Matthew Henry:

> His answer, though it sets forth the power and majesty of God, implies that the question between the afflicted and the Lord of providence is a question of might, and not of right; and we begin to discover the evil fruits of pride and of a self-righteous spirit. Job begins to manifest a disposition to condemn God, that he may justify himself, for which he is afterwards reproved. Still Job knew so much of himself, that he durst not stand a trial. If we say, "We have no sin," we not only deceive ourselves, but we affront God; for we sin in saying so, and give the lie to the Scripture. But Job reflected on God's goodness and justice in saying his affliction was without cause.[25]

If granted a personal meeting with God, Job wondered how he could even speak; he reasoned that it would be best for him to be silent and hope in God's mercy. Job was under such a crushing load that he did not think he would live long enough to bring his case before God anyway, and even if he did, he was concerned that he would just condemn himself by his own words, even though he was blameless (9:17-20).

In verse 20, he logically concludes the futility of a mortal man questioning an eternal God, even if he were blameless; but then utters a profound paradox in verse 21 by declaring his innocence: *"I am blameless."* Probably without realizing it, Job had acknowledged the great moral chasm that naturally exists between a holy God and every sinner, even those who try their best to be righteous.

Job repeatedly announces or implies his innocence throughout the narrative (e.g., 6:10, 9:21, 10:7-8, 16:14-17, 23:7, 27:2-6), but here he reasons that it did not really matter, as God was set to indiscriminately destroy him, despite his blamelessness (9:22-24). The outcome of this reasoning caused him to completely despise his life. God's perceived injustice angered Job; this is the first of several occasions in which Job accuses God of being unfair, and as J. N. Darby asserts, Job was actually declaring himself more righteous than God by doing so:

> We see in Job a heart which, although rebellious, depends upon God, and would rejoice to find Him. ... We see one who has tasted that God is gracious, whose heart, wounded indeed and unsubdued, yet claims those qualities for God – because it knows Him. ... But these spiritual affections of Job did not prevent his turning this consciousness of integrity into a robe of self-righteousness which hid God from him, and even hid him from himself. He declares himself to be more righteous than God. Elihu reproves him for this.[26]

We are now afforded a further glimpse of what was with Job that God wanted Job to discover, to loathe, and to purge out. In the remainder of the chapter, Job expresses his despair because he felt his case before God was hopeless, whether he was guilty or not: life was brief and his days on the earth were quickly vanishing (9:25-26). We might wonder: is such spiritual despondency a valid response for a man or woman of faith? Mike Mason suggests that despair is often permitted in the Christian experience to enable us to better experience and appreciate the miracle of divine deliverance:

> Our creed may be ever so orthodox, but how shall we fare when God Himself begins doing the unorthodox? "I will strike the shepherd,"

quotes Jesus in Mark 14:27, "and the sheep will be scattered." Oddly enough, if our faith makes no practical allowance for confusion, alienation, and oppression, then Christianity becomes a Pollyanna religion in which the very possibility of the Lord's direct and supernatural intervention has been leached away. As believers we need to remember that profound disillusionment is one of the essential stages in the training of the disciple. Without three days of despair, there could not have been the wide-eyed, astonished disbelief of resurrection morning (Matt. 28:17). ... Yet without this skepticism, there could never have been the greater comfort and the sealed conviction that came only with the gift of the indwelling Holy Spirit at Pentecost. Unless our faith has a healthy component of skepticism, there will be no surprises for us in Heaven.[27]

In his present state of mind, Job was skeptical; he felt that God had deemed him guilty, regardless of what he had actually done (9:27-31). Furthermore, no man, including himself, could adequately mediate his case before a divine tribunal, nor would anyone have the authority to revoke God's rod of affliction, even if it could be proven that He had acted unjustly (9:32-35). To Job's companions, the whimsical notion of a human mediator pleading and arguing on behalf of another human in God's courtroom must have seemed heretical. How dare a man deem himself equal with God! Yet, this would be, as indeed was, God's very solution to resolve humanity's condemnation; His incarnate Son, the Lord Jesus Christ, as a righteous Mediator took the place of sinners in judgment and then was raised from the dead to be our continual High Priest and Advocate before God the Father in heaven (1 Tim. 2:5-6; Heb. 4:13-16; 1 Jn. 2:2). What Job's friends considered fanciful and unorthodox was God's plan for redeeming repentant sinners. Rejoice, dear Christian: there is a man in the glory who even at this very moment is advocating our best interests before the throne of the universe. He proved His love for us at Calvary and continues to do so each and every day. Will it not be wonderful to spend eternity with such a genuine lover of our souls? What a wonderful Savior indeed!

In overviewing the chapter, F. B. Hole observes that Job devises four possible answers to his initial question as to how a man might be found righteous before God. Each of these logical assessments initiates with a distinct "if" statement:

1. The first "if" is in verse 3. Man can adopt a defiant attitude and contend with God about the matter and, of course, receive no justification.
2. The second "if" is in verse 20. Man can justify himself before God, but Job surmised that to do so would be self-condemning, as God knows everything about us and His standards of perfection are above human standards.
3. The third "if" is in verse 27. Since Job could not defy God or justify himself before God, perhaps he "should then give up hope, abandon his quest for the answer, and give himself up to the careless pursuit of enjoyment. Human nature has not changed, for many of us have pursued just the line of thought which Job disclosed here; only he immediately discarded the idea, realizing how vain it was. If we carelessly forget, God does not forget."
4. The fourth "if" is in verse 30. What about a course of self-improvement? "He knew that melted snow would give distilled water of the purest kind, having the greatest power of absorbing and removing defilement. The figure he used is most graphic. If he achieved something like this in his own character and life, what then? Why, God would plunge him in a dirty ditch as the only fit place for him. And even then, he himself, beneath his clothes, would be dirtier than they! The defilement was in himself and not in his surroundings. His rejection of the idea of achieving justification by a process of self-improvement could not be more decisive." [28]

Job has investigated four potential means of being justified before God, but through sound reasoning has rejected each one. Defiance, self-justification, careless forgetfulness, and self-improvement will not achieve a good standing before God or improve his situation. In the latter option, Job realized that he could not just pull himself up by his bootstraps and smile and say today is a happy day and everything is going to be great. True faith is not displayed with fake smiles or by acting happy when all is disturbing, but rather in knowing God and trusting Him to not act contrary to His character or His promises. In mourning and grief, Job first displayed that kind of resolve (Job 1 and 2), but now doubts are swarming about or in his mind.

Being in bitterness of soul and sensing that he has nothing to lose, Job decides to directly challenge God to list His charges against him and to disclose His evidence (10:2). Knowing that there is no one else to plead his case, he decides to be his own defense attorney, even though this decision is contrary to his conclusion in the previous chapter (10:1). Job then imagines the types of questions he would ask God if granted entry into His courtroom. Roy Zuck summarizes Job's postulated queries (10:3-6):

1. Does God get some kind of sadistic pleasure out of abusing Job, whom He had made with His very hands?
2. Does God have eyes like a man and have to investigate Job?
3. Are God's days short so that He has to probe after Job's sins?[29]

Obviously, the answer to each question is "no." God was not like that at all; so why was God punishing an innocent man (v. 7)? Of course, Job is judging the matter by his own belief system, so the premise was wrong – Job was not being punished by God; rather He was being purified as gold in the refiner's furnace (23:10; Mal. 3:3).

Besides being fickle in judging an innocent man, Job surmised that God was also being inconsistent as an all-wise Creator (10:8-12). Verse 12 reads: *"You have granted me life and favor, and Your care has preserved my spirit."* The Hebrew word translated "favor" is *checed*. In an attempt to convey its virtually unfathomable meaning, *checed* is often translated into compound words, such as "loving-kindness" or "tender mercies." So what sense did it make for God to fashion Job in his mother's womb, bring him into the world, and show him incredible kindness, and then to suddenly want to destroy him? It was not that Job was denying that he was a sinner, or that sinners suffer for their offenses, but rather in comparison to the wicked, God's extreme judgment upon him was hugely unfair and, in his view, inconsistent (vv. 14-15).

Thoroughly confused, Job then wondered if God had determined to afflict him long ago for his sins and had just been watching and stalking him like a lion, waiting for the right moment to pounce on him all at once. But, if that were true, then God would have misled Job as to what his actual relationship with God was previously (10:15-17). What we are witnessing is a man of faith wrestling with his own doubts. Job desperately wants to make sense of his miserable situation, but cannot. He does not want to give up on God, nor reject Him, but yet cannot reconcile his understanding of God and His ways with his terrible circumstances. Have you ever been in a situation where, like Job, you doubted the Lord's goodness or methods? If so, did you feel guilty for not simply trusting the Lord? Mike Mason suggests that there is a relationship between faith and doubt that is often misconstrued by Christians:

> We tend to think of doubt as an intellectual problem, when really it has more to do with the emotions and the will. Many people who have no intellectual doubts about their creed are nevertheless wracked by a different kind of doubt, by something that is closer to shame. This sort of doubt does not question the basic truth of such doctrines as the virgin birth, the authority of Scripture, the deity of Christ, or the physical resurrection. Where such questions are persistently present, they usually have less to do with doubt than with plain unbelief. To stand apart from these great and glorious realities and to try to evaluate them with the human mind is not doubt but a kind of trust: trust in oneself. With real doubt it is different. Real doubt begins with such a profound distrust of self that one is driven into the arms of God because there is literally nowhere else to go. To be cast upon God in such a way that it is like being adrift on the wide open ocean in a tiny raft without rudder or sail or oars – this is doubt.[30]

This is how we should understand Job's feeble attempts to make sense of his feelings. Intellectually speaking, Job knew what the truth about God was; there is no issue of unbelief, but rather of a doubting heart being strangled by the emotional inability to understand what God is doing. The issue was not whether a good God actually existed, but rather because there is a good God, why is He allowing me, a good person, to meaninglessly suffer so terribly? This is doubt, not disbelief, and it is natural for doubt to bridge the transition between chaos and the unfolding purposes of God in a believer's life. We know such things are irrefutable, but sometimes our impatient emotions get the best of us.

Not being able to make sense of his situation, Job again pleaded for the rest of death (10:18-22). As in his first speech (Job 3), he wishes that he would have died in his mother's womb or shortly after birth. Since he felt he was near death, which offered a one-way door permitting no return, Job pleaded with God to provide him a brief reprieve to experience a moment of joy before dying.

The Beginning of Wisdom

Meditation

When we long for life without difficulties, remind us that oaks grow strong in contrary winds and diamonds are made under pressure.

— Peter Marshall

Zophar: You Are Not Innocent
Job 11

Though Zophar has patiently waited until now to voice his opinions, he wastes no time blasting Job by calling him a self-righteous scoffer and an egotistical windbag: *"Should not the multitude of words be answered? And should a man full of talk be vindicated? Should your empty talk make men hold their peace? And when you mock, should no one rebuke you?"* (vv. 2-3). Zophar is incensed by Job's idle words, proclaimed innocence, and for insinuating that God was mismanaging His affairs.

His quick assault gives the impression that he shoots from the hip rather than taking care to aim at what he wants to hit. C. I. Scofield suggests that Zophar "presumes to know what God will do in any given case, why He will do it, and what His thoughts about it are."[31] He is the voice of trigger-happy legalism and religious hypocrisy. He believed that all Job's problems would go away if he simply repented of his sins and got right with God, as if this was all God cared about. To think that repentance is the only human strategy to resolve any of life's difficulties is a limited perspective of God's interaction with mankind. Zophar's view actually limits divine omniscience and transforms God into a wrathful, tyrannical brute, who is always posed to pounce on you when you do wrong.

Although God's ways are hard to understand, Zophar hoped that God would expound wisdom to self-righteous Job: *"For you have said, 'My doctrine is pure, and I am clean in your eyes.' But oh, that God would speak, and open His lips against you"* (vv. 4-5). Zophar then assumes an authority that he did not have by rebuking Job. And, as one might expect, a pompous pharisaical tone permeates his entire speech.

Because God's ways are so far above human understanding, Zophar renders God virtually unknowable. Zophar is correct that God is far above human comprehension, but He is not a vague entity; rather He is a God of communication and revelation. Again, it is important to remember that Zophar's speech is not inspired by God, though he believes he is speaking for God. Scripture has afforded us a historical record of Zophar's reproof to Job that we might be brought along in our own learning. In fact, many of Zophar's statements are astoundingly true, yet misapplied:

1. *"Know therefore that God exacts from you less than your iniquity deserves"* (v. 6). The scribe Ezra says something similar while on his knees and making intercession for his rebellious countrymen (Ezra 9:13). And to this statement we would say, "Amen and praise the Lord," but Zophar used it to tell Job that God was letting him off easy and he deserved worse punishment for his sins than he was getting.

2. *"Can you search out the deep things of God? Can you find out the limits of the Almighty? They are higher than heaven – what can you do? Deeper than Sheol – what can you know?"* (vv. 7-8). The answer to the first two questions is "no" and the last two is "nothing." God must reveal Himself for us to know Him. So through the revelation He supplies and the understanding He confers through the Holy Spirit we are able to understand in a measure who God is.

3. *"If He passes by, imprisons, and gathers to judgment, then who can hinder Him? For He knows deceitful men; He sees wickedness also"* (vv. 10-11). The implied answer to the question is, of course, "no one." Because of His omniscience, God is infallible in His judgments and is all-powerful in executing them.

4. *"If you would prepare your heart, and stretch out your hands toward Him"* (v. 13). Now this was the best counsel that Job could have received. This is what Job needed to do. David puts it this way: *"Wait on the Lord; be of good courage, and He shall strengthen your heart; wait, I say, on the Lord!"* (Ps. 27:14). But Job sought answers from within himself; he did not look to the Lord and wait on Him.

5. *"The eyes of the wicked will fail, and they shall not escape"* (v. 20). This is a truth repeated throughout Scripture: the wicked cannot escape judgment. A day is coming in which God will set right all wrongs and those rebelling against His authority and rule will be recompensed accordingly.

Job did not deserve this hurtful verbal flogging; he was suffering in the will of God without knowing the reason why. Zophar added to Job's misery by suggesting simple answers for a painful and complex situation, which could not be easily explained. In fact, only God knew the true reality of the entire ordeal. We do not find doctrinal error with Zophar's statements per se, but fault in their application; they were used to insinuate and indict Job of wrongdoing.

For example, Zophar rightly surmises: *"For an empty-headed man will be wise, when a wild donkey's colt is born a man"* (v. 12). Since man's fall in Eden, his uncontrolled and unrestrained behavior often resembles the nature of a wild donkey or even a savage beast. Zophar encourages Job not to be a witless man (like the wild donkey in his own reasoning), but rather seek the Lord and His wisdom: *"If iniquity were in your hand, and you put it far away, and would not let wickedness dwell in your tents; then surely you could lift up your face without spot; yes, you could be steadfast, and not fear"* (vv. 14-15). Like Eliphaz and Bildad, Zophar assumed that Job had committed sin and was suffering for it, and that if he would just humble himself and repent, he would be restored to God and experience joy again. He then reminds Job that the wicked are doomed (v. 20). However, this was the wrong counsel for Job; he was not suffering because of his iniquities. Job's friends just could not imagine a righteous God putting an upright man through such cruel adversity.

Zophar's words resemble the high talk of the Pharisees, who often condemned the behavior of others by the Law and their traditions, yet they could not help others overcome what displeased God (Rom. 7:7-14). At best they can only identify the problem, not fix it. For this reason, Samuel Ridout suggests that Zophar lived up to the meaning of his name:

Zophar, "a sparrow," from the root verb "to twitter," is the masculine form of Zipporah, Moses' wife, and like her he was an unconscious opponent of God's judgment on the flesh, though he was very zealous in condemning the fancied works of the flesh in Job. His vehement denunciations were utterly out of place and were as harmless as the "twitterings" of the bird for which he was named.[32]

Zophar's speech to Job is a good reminder of the damage that misapplied truth, the main tool of the heretic, can cause in the Body of Christ. While truth is the basis for genuine Christian fellowship, it can also result in much division in the Church if abused. Christ desires that there be no divisions in the Church, but rather that all believers enjoy fellowship to the fullest degree possible in reference to their common foundation of scriptural truth. Only in truth can unity be secured and only by ongoing love can it be maintained; and both realities of fellowship are only possible through the Holy Spirit.

The teaching and understanding of truth is vital to the building up of the Church: *"He who prophesies* (i.e., declares divine truth) *speaks edification and exhortation and comfort to men"* (1 Cor. 14:3). We also recognize that Scripture is the tool God uses to remove from us what is not sound in our lives to establish that which pleases Him (2 Tim. 2:15). Yet, doctrine alone is insufficient to guide believers in proper conduct; we need a work of grace in our hearts also: *"Knowledge puffs up, but love edifies"* (1 Cor. 8:1). Love and grace must temper our actions to ensure the edification of others (1 Cor. 8:1; Eph. 4:15-16). Separation to holy living occurs when divine truth is embraced and false doctrine is shunned (2 Thess. 3:6). Yet, not all division among brethren is profitable. If love does not guide one's activities, isolation of the members within the body of Christ will occur over minute points of disagreement, the result of which will hinder the Church's working and growth.

On this point, Paul commands, *"But, speaking the truth in love, may grow up in all things into Him who is the head – Christ"* (Eph. 4:15). The challenge, then, is to have fellowship with all believers to the degree that doctrine allows. I can walk farther in harmony with some Christians than with others, but I can go some distance with all Christians (e.g., we at least have agreement in the gospel message). Those within our own local churches and our homes will likely share a high degree of commonality.

Unfortunately, Zophar's misapplication of the truth caused division between him and Job, prompted others to further embrace an erroneous conclusion, did not resolve Job's problem, and angered the Lord. Let us not repeat Zophar's offense. If we are speaking for God, let us use His Word accurately and wisely apply it with a spirit of humility and grace – as only the Lord Jesus Christ would.

Meditation

Tis better to suffer wrong than do it.

— Thomas Fuller

Job: The Wicked Are Punished Eventually
Job 12-13

Although Job agrees with Zophar's last statement (11:20), that the wicked will perish, there is no common ground after that. Job commences his retort by mocking his companions' supposed wisdom with what has now become a well-known saying: *"No doubt you are the people, and wisdom will die with you!"* (12:2). A. R. Fausset expresses Job's sarcasm this way: "Ironical, as if all the wisdom in the world was concentrated in them and would expire when they expired."[33] They certainly deserved that rebuke; being older men (15:10), they should have been more sensitive in their interaction with pitiable Job (8:8-10, 12:12). Zophar had compared Job's understanding of man's moral existence to that of a stupid donkey, but Job reminded them that when they died, they would have no wisdom at all.

Job follows with a more amiable statement: *"I am not inferior to you. Indeed, who does not know such things as these?"* (12:3). They had not really said anything beyond what was common knowledge – God is wise and powerful. Job had already considered obvious information and was frustrated with his companions for continually restating what he already knew. Simply put, he was just far ahead of them in his contemplations of God and His ways. Job's companions had not provided an explanation as to how a God-fearing man might be made to suffer in God's grand prerogative. In reality, they had no more wisdom on such things than Job possessed and even less discernment in exercising compassion. How easy it is to judge things by their initial appearance, or our past experiences or developed traditions – these things often cloud clear perception and hence we do not properly discern things as God does.

In former days, God had responded to Job's prayers, but now He was silent and though Job was blameless, he had become the laughingstock of those who were at ease (like his three accusers; 12:4-5). This seemed wholly unfair to Job, because the wicked (e.g., those who carried their idols in their hands) dwelt safely in their tents: He reasoned that they should be the ones punished, not him (12:6). Job 12:5 reminds us of the maddening dichotomy we often experience on earth: When life is trouble-free, we do not ask God questions, and when things go bad, we do not perceive His answers.

Zophar had implied that Job's understanding of spiritual things was like that of a donkey. Job turns that statement around on his friends and exhorts them to learn from the animals, birds, fish, and the earth, because they all knew about the ups and downs of life, that is, arbitrary hardships which God permits. William Kelly expounds further this idea:

> That is, the whole creation – the lower creation of God upon the earth – is a proof that things are not yet according to God. Do they not prey upon one another; do not the great swallow up the small; and is not man the great executor of death upon beasts and birds and fishes, and everything, for his own gratification? I do not mean merely for food, but to please himself at all costs. In short, it is not merely what the Lord allows, but man makes it for his lusts, for his luxury, for everything except God.[34]

Creatures living on the earth know all about suffering (e.g., the food chain, natural disasters, drought, lightning strikes, blizzards, etc.). In this sense, they were wiser than Job's friends, who were affirming that the righteous do not suffer during their earthly sojourn (12:7-11). Job then rightly emphasizes the fact that it is God's determination alone when a human life will end (12:10). This truth should help those in despair not to consider suicide as a means of escaping God's will, but rather permit Him to work His will in their difficulties.

While God's name, "Jehovah," is referred to several times in the opening narrative (Job 1 and 2) and once directly by Job (1:21), *Jehovah* is only found once in the dialogue section of the book and again it is Job who utters His name (12:9). Some have questioned whether or not the reference was later inserted into the text, but its mysterious usage here seems to further substantiate Job's point that he is not deficient in wisdom, as compared to his tormentors. Job's focus on the wisdom shown in nature is a preview to God's answer to Job later in the book, which brings him to repentance. Perhaps this is another reason Jehovah's name is mentioned here – creation was a

The Beginning of Wisdom

direct and accurate reflection of Himself. Job's theology is objective; he does not rely on the subjective experience (like his friends do), but on the external revelation of God and His just and gracious character. Accordingly, Job's friends never refer to Jehovah by name, but use less-personal and vague terms for God.

In the remainder of the chapter, Job launches into a discourse about the wisdom and power of God, which often produces paradoxical results: In His sovereignty, God can break down, overturn, shut up, withhold, dry up, overturn, despoil, remove, increase, destroy, build up, etc. (12:13-25). In application, God discriminately and inexplicably spoils the wisdom of counselors, makes judges fools, overthrows the mighty, removes the wisdom of years, and increases weak nations, while destroying strong ones. Therefore, what one may expect to happen in life is not always the case.

Job then implies two conclusions: First, though his friends were older and therefore should be wiser, that was not the case. Second, because Job had experienced God's "breaking down," he felt that he knew more about the mysterious ways of God than they did. Whether or not either point is true is arguable; yet, we would agree with Job that often the Lord does uncover the darkness as we experience difficulties under His care (12:22). That is, He illuminates the hard-to-understand aspects of life with His wisdom.

In chapter 13, Job summarizes what he has said: I am sound in mind, I know and *"I am not inferior to you"* (13:1-2). But Job quickly moves on; he does not want to waste time bantering about with *"forgers of lies"* and *"worthless physicians"* who would show more wisdom if they remained silent, instead of speaking erroneously for God (13:4-5, 7). Rather, Job wanted to take his complaint straight to God and debate Him on this matter. For this reason, he preferred that his agitators listened to his plea in silence (13:3, 6). To his friends the notion was heretical, but it is appropriate for people of genuine faith to desire personal interaction with God, especially when they feel that only God can understand and can exonerate them. Job desired vindication by God even more than escaping his desperate circumstances.

Job asserts that his colleagues could not speak for God, because they had their own fallacies to be divinely reckoned with and they were also partial; God was completely impartial in His judgments (13:8-11).

Consequently, their counsel was worthless to Job, literally a proverbial *ash heap* (13:12). Hence, he demands of his friends: *"Hold your peace with me, and let me speak, then let come on me what may!"* (13:13). It would have been easier just to agree with their arguments, but Job chooses the arduous and more tiring path of standing his ground and rebuffing their false insinuations.

But now he again comes to a point of desperation and realization. He felt that he had nothing to lose by arguing his case directly with God, not with those who thought they were God's prosecutors (13:14): *"Though He slay me, yet will I trust Him. Even so, I will defend my own ways before Him. He also shall be my salvation, for a hypocrite could not come before Him"* (13:15-16). The Hebrew meaning of Job's statement does not pose a questionable outcome, but rather an anticipated one, *"He will surely slay me."* Job knew the risks of defending himself, but he felt that if there was even a remote chance that God would exonerate him, it would be better than lingering despondently in his present agony (13:17-19). No matter the outcome, Job would trust in the Lord, his salvation. So much for Satan's initial denunciation of Job's character: *"Does Job fear God for nothing?"* (1:9). Job's reverence for God was not to be rich as Satan taunted; Job loved and trusted in the Lord unconditionally.

Of course, his day in Jehovah's courtroom was a bit whimsical; Job did not know anything about approaching God in terms of mediation. The Lord Jesus Christ would later be revealed as the sole mediator between God and man, but this had not been revealed to Job at this time (1 Tim. 2:5). Previously, Job said that God would not acquit him if he were given a chance to defend himself against injustice (9:28), but now he seems to think that there was at least a possibility of an acquittal.

Having stated his determination to defend himself, even though God might strike him dead, Job then turns his attention from his colleagues and addresses the Lord directly (13:20-14:22). Roy Zuck summarizes what Job asks of the Lord (13:20-25):

First, he requested that God not intimidate him (9:34), the defendant, in court. It was only right that he be given a fair trial (9:16-19). Then Job offered to meet God as either defendant or plaintiff. But when he asked God to enumerate his sins, God did not appear in court (6:24). Job asked God why He remained silent and considered Job His enemy

(19:11). To torment a ... leaf or chase after ... chaff was to molest the worthless, to hit a frail, helpless person who was down.[35]

Job desperately wanted to discover the reason for his suffering; if he had sinned, he was unaware of it; if he had offended God, he wanted to know. True repentance is a willingness to know the worst about ourselves, being willing to agree with God about it, and then repudiating whatever displeases Him. This Job is willing to do, but he has no idea what kind of sin he might have committed to deserve such divine oppression.

Perhaps God was remembering and punishing Job for juvenile sins, but then he surmised that would not be appropriate since he had lived a blameless life since his youth (13:26-27). Job never claimed to be sinless, but rather that he was undeserving of the immense cruelty he was enduring. Yet, we well know, that no one senses or feels his or her sin with the same clarity and weight that God does (Isa. 43:24; Ezek. 6:9; Amos 2:13).

Job was on an emotional roller coaster ride, as evidenced by some of his statements in this chapter which contradict his previous conclusions. Therefore, it is no surprise that Job quickly vacillates from his bold dare to overwhelming despair; this mood swing sets the tenor for the next chapter. Job felt like a rotting corpse or a moth-eaten garment that no longer had any value to anyone (13:28).

Meditation

> If there were no tribulation, there would be no rest; if there were no winter, there would be no summer.
>
> — John Chrysostom

Job: Longing for Resurrection
Job 14

In the last chapter, Job expressed hopeful confidence that he would be exonerated by God, if he were permitted to have his day in heaven's Supreme Court. But Job's emotions vacillate again to one of pessimistic dismay as he laments the frailty of life and the futility of death. Verse 1 summarizes the brevity of one's earthly existence: *"Man who is born of woman, is of few days and full of trouble."* In the ancient Near-East culture, women were looked down upon, and since man came from a feeble woman, how robust or pure could he really be? Hence, Job concludes man is born unclean, lives but a few days under God's continuous scrutiny, and then vanishes like a withering flower or fading shadow (vv. 2-4).

Since God alone determines the lifespan of each person, Job felt like a hireling counting down his remaining time of compulsory service. Job did not want to live out his final days wasting away; so he wondered why God did not focus His attention elsewhere and cease troubling him (vv. 5-6). This is poetic venting; Job deeply yearned for a brief period of peace before his rapidly approaching death.

Having acknowledged the brevity of life and his desire to have a restful reprieve before dying, Job turns his attention to the futility of death. In considering the decisiveness of death, Job ponders a tree that has been chopped down, but still has an active root system. The roots sense water, draw it up, and the once-dead-looking stump begins shooting up new branches – it is alive again. But man does not have such an opportunity; at death, one's body is put in a grave where it lies disabled and slowly decays (vv. 7-11).

Job then says something that might be interpreted in various ways, if it were not for the established context of the passage: *"So man lies down and does not rise. Till the heavens are no more, they will not awake nor be roused from their sleep"* (v. 12). A. R. Fausset suggests that Job was simply implying that he …

had no hope of living again in the *present* order of the world, not that he had no hope of life again in a new order of things. Ps. 102:26 proves that early under the Old Testament, the dissolution of the present earth and heavens was expected (compare Ge 8:22). Enoch *before Job* had implied that the *"saints shall live again"* (Jud. 1:14; Heb. 11:13-16). Even if, by this phrase, *Job* meant "never" (Ps. 89:29) in his gloomier state of feelings, yet the *Holy Ghost* has made him unconsciously (1 Pet. 1:11-12) use language expressing the truth, that the resurrection is to be preceded by the dissolution of the heavens. In Job 14:13-15 he plainly passes to brighter hopes of a world to come.[36]

Job is not promoting annihilationism, soul sleep, the destruction of the earth as the end of humanity, nor is he denying that there is a resurrection of the dead. Rather, he is merely saying that death is final, and that we cannot relive our lives on earth in the bodies we once had (v. 12). The writer of Hebrews confirms this truth: *"It is appointed for men to die once, but after this the judgment"* (Heb. 9:27). Death seals the eternal fate of the quality of faith one lived in life!

Although Job recognized that reviving a dead body was impossible, he still preferred the dark, gloomy rest of a grave instead of his present suffering under God's anger, or so he perceived (v. 13). This was a viable solution because eventually he believed that he would experience resurrection: *"All the days of my hard service I will wait, till my change comes"* (v. 14). Not having divine revelation on the topic of heaven, Old Testament saints hoped to enjoy God's presence on the earth after escaping the cold confines of Sheol through resurrection (Isa. 26:19; Dan. 12:2). Old Testament saints understood that death was unavoidable, and that beyond the grave their souls would be sequestered in a spiritual abode called Sheol. The Lord spoke of this place during His earthly sojourn: redeemed souls were consciously residing in Abraham's bosom, while the wicked were suffering in Hades (Luke 16:19-31). It is the author's opinion that the realm of Abraham's bosom was emptied after Christ's resurrection (Matt. 27:52).

Though not afraid of death itself, David was not too enthusiastic about the finality of death or his future stay in Sheol: *"The sorrows of Sheol surrounded me; the snares of death confronted me"* (2 Sam.

22:6; Ps. 18:5). Yet, he rejoiced and hoped in his future resurrection from Sheol in a new body:

Therefore my heart is glad, and my glory rejoices; my flesh also will rest in hope. For You will not leave my soul in Sheol, nor will You allow Your Holy One to see corruption (Ps. 16:9-10; also Ps. 86:13).

David is still waiting for his new resurrected body. His earlier body did see corruption in the grave, but the body of Jesus Christ, of whom he prophetically spoke, did not; He was raised up from the grave after three days. This event not only fulfilled David's words, but also reaffirmed his hope and Job's too. This is why Job never speaks about dying and going to heaven – that is a mystery not revealed until the New Testament (2 Cor. 5:8; Phil. 1:23; 1 Thess. 4:13-18).

Earlier, Job wondered how he might find and speak with an invisible God and also how a sinful man could ever be justified before a righteous God. Now, he considers another quandary: *"If a man dies, shall he live again?"* (14:14). Indeed, these are important questions for all of humanity to consider. Job does not sugarcoat the harsh reality of death, but he does boldly approach its inevitable reality with confidence that there was blissful life after the grave. Thankfully, Job's seemingly incredible quandaries are actualities in Christ: Through the incarnation of Christ, God communicated His Word to mankind. Through Christ's death repentant man can be justified (declared right). Through Christ's resurrection, man can possess and experience eternal life. The Lord Jesus explained how the believer's resurrection, speaking of glorification, was made possible through His life:

I am the resurrection and the life. He who believes in Me, though he may die, he shall live. And whoever lives and believes in Me shall never die. Do you believe this? (John 11:25-26).

All the abundant blessings of eternal life are found in Christ alone (John 5:24, 10:10).

Though Job despaired over the temporary nature of human life and the finality of death, he did believe that he would experience a bodily resurrection in the afterlife, though he had no idea how that was possible. Centuries later, Elijah, Elisha, the Lord Jesus, Peter, and Paul would all demonstrate God's power in reanimating a dead body, but no such miracle had occurred in Job's day. What is remarkable is that without scriptural revelation, ancient men like Job and Abraham believed in resurrection.

Abraham demonstrated his belief that God had the power to raise the dead by his willingness to offer Isaac, as commanded (Gen. 22:1-5). He instructed His two young men assisting him to wait at the foot of Mt. Moriah while he and Isaac offered a sacrifice on the mount. He also told them that he and Isaac would return again. How did Abraham know that Isaac would return with him? Hebrews 11:17-19 provides the answer to this question: By faith, Abraham knew that Isaac was the promised seed and that God could not breach His word – if he struck Isaac down, God would have to raise him back to life. This took an extraordinary amount of faith, considering this was his only son and that there had never been a resurrection from the dead before.

The Lord Jesus later taught that He, as the Son of God, created all life and that all life was in Him (John 1:3-4). He also stated that at His command all the deceased would be resurrected to stand in judgment before Him. That is, every disembodied soul would be joined to an immortal body that would never die just before giving an account of their life before Christ:

> *Most assuredly, I say to you, he who hears My word and believes in Him who sent Me has everlasting life, and shall not come into judgment, but has passed from death into life. Most assuredly, I say to you, the hour is coming, and now is, when the dead will hear the voice of the Son of God; and those who hear will live. For as the Father has life in Himself, so He has granted the Son to have life in Himself, and has given Him authority to execute judgment also, because He is the Son of Man. Do not marvel at this; for the hour is coming in which all who are in the graves will hear His voice and come forth – those who have done good, to the resurrection of life, and those who have done evil, to the resurrection of condemnation* (John 5:24-29).

From this passage we learn that there will be two types of resurrection: a resurrection of the just to enable eternal residence in heaven and a resurrection of the condemned to be punished for eternity in the Lake of Fire (Rev. 20:10, 15). The Lord Jesus has received authority from His Father to initiate both of these resurrections, but

Scripture informs us that the first resurrection (i.e., of the just) occurs in several stages, while the resurrection of the condemned occurs all at once at the Great White Throne judgment (Rev. 20:11-15). The *resurrection of life*, also called the *first resurrection* (Rev. 20:5-6), occurs for the righteous at several distinct points (e.g., Christ's own resurrection, 1 Cor. 15:23; the rapture of the Church, 1 Thess. 4:13-18; and the resurrection of tribulation saints, Rev. 20:4) in time prior to the Great White Throne judgment.

While Scripture affords us a more complete overview, William Kelly explains that Job had a limited concept of what resurrection entailed (vv. 12-13):

> Now you have in this world the righteous and the wicked all confused together. But that is only till the judgment come; that is only till the Lord come. And when the Lord comes, there will be the separation of the righteous called not only from the dead (other dead being left in their graves), but to heaven where He is now. They are going to be like Himself – "the resurrection of the just." But there remains the great mass of mankind; and that is what Job describes in this chapter ... the resurrection of the unjust. And therefore you observe how beautifully the language suits. "Man that is born of a woman" – not a word about anyone that is born of God. Those that are born of God will be the righteous. But "man that is born of a woman" (and all are) "is of few days" – it looks at man since the fall – "and full of trouble."[37]

Job was speaking about a future day when the heaven and earth would pass away; at that time, those remaining in their graves would rise in resurrected bodies to stand judgment. How Job perceived all this is unknown, but the actual event is verified by John as being true (Rev. 20:11-15). In verse 13, Job connects resurrection with the manifestation of God's wrath on the wicked, something he did not desire to experience and did not think he would because of God's mercy.

Job viewed death as a temporary discharge from active duty on earth, to be followed sometime later by a final transfer of a righteous soul into a new body fit for God's presence. For this reason, Job looked forward to the day that God would summon him into His courtroom to be questioned; he would then gladly give an account of his deeds (vv. 15-16). Job's delight in this future day when God would

The Beginning of Wisdom

count his steps (good deeds) and not remember his sins anymore is the high watermark of this chapter (v. 17). How did Job know that God could righteously forgive his sins? In the same way that David knew, by accurately recognizing the character and attributes of God and trusting in His mercy.

Under the Law, adulterers and murderers were to be executed, meaning there was no provision to spare David's life, yet he knew the character of God, and thus chose to trust in Him. God is a covenant-keeping God and had made unconditional promises to David; therefore, by faith, David knew there must be an unrevealed means beyond the Law by which the Lord could righteously forgive his capital offenses (see Ps. 32 and Ps. 51).

Job's delightful contemplation of divine forgiveness was a fleeting moment, for he swiftly plunges into fathomless despondency. The fact that death would eventually come and release Job from his present woes, and that there was a faint hope of afterlife through resurrection, did not alleviate his present suffering. Job again protests his present plight. He likened himself to a mountain that was slowly crumbling under nature's fury, and to a rock being worn away by rushing water, and to soil that was carried away by steady erosion (vv. 18-19). His ongoing agony had completely exhausted him. Job then lamented that when his countenance was no longer flushed with life, God would send him away from all that he knew and possessed (v. 20). Although death would bring rest from his sufferings, Job viewed death as a loathsome state that had to be endured prior to resurrection.

Job firmly believed in the consciousness of the human soul after death, even though the body of the deceased decayed. He also thought, however, that experiencing bodily decay in the grave must be a painful process; certainly it would be an emotionally challenging experience (v. 22). For example, after experiencing death, parents would no longer be a part of their children's lives, neither partaking in their honor, nor their problems (v. 21).

Job concludes his third rebuttal and his first round of discussions with his associates in this morbid, hopeless tone. He is a dear servant of God who is suffering terribly, but does not know why. W. H. Westcott provides this summary of Job's overall response since suffering the calamities of chapters 1 and 2.

At his wife's suggestion he might have cursed God and died, and so ended his misery, which *she* felt to be insupportable. But *he* felt it was a poor thing to give God a bad name; for although he knew Him but dimly, he knew Him too well to do that. All the past when recalled could be considered with a good conscience in the fear of God; in the present, although he was so crossed, burdened, and suffering, he was sure God would explain everything satisfactorily *if only he knew where to find Him;* as to the future, far from being diverted from piety by any calamities undergone, or by any lust of sin or gain – he was determined that even if God slew him, yet he would trust in Him.[38]

While Job does question the fairness of God's actions, he does not blaspheme God's name, nor does he speak disgracefully of the Lord. This chapter indicates that by faith Job anticipated an afterlife with God, in which the matter of his present suffering would be set straight. In the face of unending despair, Job still had a glimpse of hope. Dear believer, we have so much more to delight in than Job ever could, because God has revealed so much more truth to us. Job had experimental notions of God and his conscience to guide him, but we have the immutable, everlasting promises of God recorded for us in Scripture – in these we can greatly rejoice!

The Church's hope is the imminent coming of the Lord Jesus Christ in the air to gather His Church from the earth to be with Him forever. This is part of the "First Resurrection." The anticipation of bodily resurrection and glorification is indeed a living hope! It is a purifying hope that should consecrate and sanctify each day of a believer's life (1 Jn. 3:3). Believers then should not hope for the grave to escape hardship, but rather live for the Lord in whatever calling He puts them. Paul puts it this way: *"For none of us lives to himself, and no one dies to himself. For if we live, we live to the Lord; and if we die, we die to the Lord. Therefore, whether we live or die, we are the Lord's"* (Rom. 14:7-8). For this reason, the apostle endured much suffering to fulfill his ministry for the Lord (2 Cor. 11:23-28; 2 Tim. 2:10).

Job was correct; man's days are few (and ours are about two-thirds fewer than Job's), but our lives are only vain, if we choose to live for ourselves, instead of the One who died for us and was raised for our justification! The Lord Jesus said, *"For whoever desires to save his life will lose it, but whoever loses his life for My sake will save it. For what profit is it to a man if he gains the whole world, and is himself destroyed or lost?"* (Luke 9:24-25). It is truly a joy and privilege to live for Christ now!

Meditation

> Our sorrows are all, like ourselves, mortal. There are no immortal sorrows for immortal souls. They come, but blessed be God, they also go. Like birds of the air, they fly over our heads. But they cannot make their abode in our souls. We suffer today, but we shall rejoice tomorrow.
>
> Let this one great, gracious, glorious fact lie in your spirit until it permeates all your thoughts and makes you rejoice even though you are without strength. Rejoice that the Lord Jesus has become your strength and your song – He has become your salvation.
>
> — Charles Spurgeon

Eliphaz: The Wicked Do Not Prosper
Job 15

In his first speech, Eliphaz exercised some courteous restraint, but he assumes a more dogmatic and forthright stance against Job in his second discourse. He begins with a volley of nearly a dozen questions, to preamble his specific indictments against Job later in the chapter. When all boiled down, Eliphaz suggested that Job was irreverent in his speech, disrespectful to his elders, deceived by his own vanity, and obviously a hardened sinner, as the righteous prosper in God's economy and the wicked do not.

Eliphaz likened Job's vain words to a hot desert wind, which blew hard but had no moisture (vv. 1-3). It is difficult to ascertain Eliphaz's exact meaning from the Hebrew text in verse 2, but he is likely implying that wise men do not belch hot air and that Job was. He then throws Job's earlier words back in his face: *"You are right, Job your own mouth condemns you"* (9:20). From his vantage point, the fact that Job had been willing to defend himself, even if it meant dishonoring God, was proof enough that Job was harboring sin in his heart (vv. 4-6). Eliphaz's reaction to Job's speeches serves as a warning to those who genuinely want to assist those imprisoned by despair: Do not sour in goodness when their badness challenges you. You cannot help others unless you are unconditionally willing to suffer with them in their recovery. This is the example that Christ left us to follow (1 Pet. 2:19-21).

Exasperated by Job's claim that he had as much wisdom about rudimentary affairs as they did (12:3, 13:2), Eliphaz scolds Job. How dare Job claim that he had more wisdom than they did, especially since they were older than Job; he even suggests that Job knew nothing that they didn't know (vv. 7-10). Eliphaz had spoken first, which suggests that he was the oldest of Job's visiting friends. It would also seem that he was the most offended by Job's comments; as a younger man, he should show more respect to his elders. Additionally, he argued that

Job should appreciate the kind consolation that God was providing to him through them (5:17-27), rather than venting anger towards them and God (vv. 11-12). Did Job think that such uncontrolled outbursts would go unpunished (v. 13)? Eliphaz did not think so.

Eliphaz then repeats his previous argument, that no man born of a woman could possibly be righteous before God, for he surmised that even the holy angels were tainted in comparison to God's holiness (vv. 14-16). Later, Bildad will further suggest that the stars are impure in God's sight, perhaps acknowledging that sin has had a devastating effect throughout creation (25:5), his point being that all of humanity, by nature, is corrupt before a holy God. But would not this conclusion mean that Eliphaz was in the same situation as Job? Absolutely. Yet, because of Job's vicarious situation, he assumed that Job was much more sinful than himself and thus he could condemn Job in pharisaical pride (Rom. 2:1-4). Samuel Ridout wonders why Eliphaz ever confronted Job with such high-minded religiosity in order to cause him to repent:

> If the very heavens are unclean in His sight, how much less is mortal, sinful man! But is not *Eliphaz* one of these, as well as the poor sufferer? Why then apply it to Job as though it proved *him* a sinner above all others? This, surely, is more like crafty speech than all the hot utterances of Job. Let Eliphaz take his place beside Job and confess that he too is "abominable and filthy." The poor sufferer might have responded to that.[39]

Referring to his own observations and also to what was known from the annals of human history, Eliphaz argued that sometimes a wise man (referring to Job) becomes corrupted by the strange philosophies of wicked men and loses his way (vv. 17-19). Of course, as an Arab, he was touting that his ancestors had ever been in the land untainted by outside influences (i.e., foreigners). This ideology led Eliphaz to an outlandish conclusion: *"The wicked man writhes in pain all his days, and numbered are the years stored up for the ruthless"* (v. 20, NASV). Not only was Job's unrelenting agony the result of stubborn pride and personal corruption, but he had also become a terror-invoking tyrant in Eliphaz's view. This was not true, but the heartless suggestion that people were now afraid of Job certainly had to compound his overall grief.

In the remainder of the chapter, Eliphaz lists several calamities to show what would befall a sinner according to history. Consequently, Job should expect to hear terrifying reports, to be despoiled by marauders (v. 21), to be haunted by the darkness of death, to be a victim of violence (v. 22), to wander aimlessly without provisions (v. 23), and to be hounded by imminent distress (v. 24). These ills were well-chosen by Eliphaz, who could then argue that Job had already experienced all of these outcomes, thus proving his point: Job had been rightly recompensed for shaking his fist at almighty God (vv. 25-26).

Before continuing his lists of troubles that beset the reprobate, Eliphaz paused to explain why they were judged by God. He inferred that the wicked were fat, implying that they were self-indulgent, undisciplined rebels (v. 27). Therefore, God was obliged to destroy their homes and cities, to strip them of their possessions, to blow away their wealth, and to destroy their crops (vv. 28-30). Such would suffer darkness, anguish, and insecurity and would learn the futility of their riches, which could not safeguard their future affluence (v. 31).

Like a vine without grapes, the wicked will suffer premature death (vv. 32-33) and have no posterity to rejoice in (v. 34). A specific example is afforded: a person who takes a bribe and causes the mistreatment of others will have their tents burned with fire (v. 34). Remembering how Job's sheep had been destroyed by fire from heaven may have invoked this imagery in an attempt to prove to Job that he had already been judged by God. Unlike Job, Eliphaz cannot envision God judging the wicked post-mortem, as the hope of resurrection is beyond him. In summary, those with deceitful hearts effortlessly conceive sin and in time give birth to vanity, which then distresses them. Well, Eliphaz did not convince Job of anything. In fact, as we will see in the next chapter, Job is quite appalled by his logic and insinuations.

While much of what Eliphaz said was true, it was not categorically so. His information and reasoning ability were limited; it was therefore foolish for him to broad-brush all human experiences into narrow corollaries of cause-and-effect logic. To do so philosophically limits God's omnipotence and leads to wrong conclusions about God's dealings with humanity.

What did Eliphaz need to realize? First, God knows that the heart that beats for Him will do what is right (Deut. 11:13). Second, the human heart is naturally depraved: *"The heart is deceitful above all things, and desperately wicked"* (Jer. 17:9). Third, only God searches and knows what really dwells in the human heart: *"Who can know it? I, the Lord, search the heart, I test the mind"* (Jer. 17:9b-10a). Fourth, God often requires extreme measures to expose hidden roots of sin and ungodly dispositions within our own hearts: *"even to give every man according to his ways, according to the fruit of his doings"* (Jer. 17:10b). Eliphaz was judging Job's situation with an impure heart, from an outward perspective, and with limited information. This is not so with God. In holy purity God perceives and judges with all the facts at hand (both seen and unseen) to ensure the best approach ensues for our good and His glory! This wonderful reality becomes evident in the final five chapters of this book.

Meditation

> Jesus has no tenderness toward anything that is ultimately going to ruin a man in service to Him. If God brings to your mind a vise which hurts you, you may be sure that there is something He wants to hurt.
>
> —Andrew Murray

Job: You Miserable Counselors
Job 16-17

Condemning an innocent, acutely diseased, grief-stricken person is a terrible offense and reflects the tenets of a deficient theology. Any view of God which affixes guilt without evidence, justifies the oppression of the poor, and inflicts cruelty on the downcast and brokenhearted is plain wrong. Jehovah is a perfectly holy and righteous God who will judge sin, but He also desires to demonstrate His long-suffering, merciful, and gracious nature to those who desire His love and help. He is slow to anger and quick to forgive and believers are to reflect His character in all that we do, especially while ministering to those in need.

Job's companions had begun well; they put aside their household affairs to silently identify with him and to console him. No doubt, seeing their loyalty after a week's time is what prompted Job to converse with them. However, in the course of time, Job's friends went from a ministry of comfort to one of accusations and rebuke; they suggested that Job was suffering for his own sin and that he needed to repent to receive God's forgiveness. Having repeatedly rejected their long-winded indictments, Job now provides an audit of their assistance: *"Miserable comforters are you all"* (16:2). From his perspective, his colleagues had only scorned and mocked him; they were not a solace to him (16:20, 17:2). He found no wisdom, nor anything to benefit from in their endless babblings (17:10).

A suffering person does not need a lecture – he needs a listener.

— Billy Graham

To be effective comforters and counselors, we must follow the Lord's example; otherwise, we will likely be "miserable comforters" to others also. John writes of the Lord: *"We beheld His glory, the glory as of the only begotten of the Father, full of grace and truth"* (John 1:14). The Lord Jesus was not just balanced, but all that He did and said was full of grace and truth. Just as grace and truth are inseparable aspects of the Lord's character, the believer should not invoke one quality without the other. The apostle Paul puts it this way: *"Let your speech be always with grace, seasoned with salt"* (Col. 4:6). If it is not necessary to say, or cannot be said in love, or is not true, then the Lord would not have us say it.

Paul further reminds us that as we rely on the Lord to overcome various trials we become better equipped to help others face the same challenges with confidence:

> *Blessed be the God and Father of our Lord Jesus Christ, the Father of mercies and God of all comfort, who comforts us in all our tribulation, that we may be able to comfort those who are in any trouble, with the comfort with which we ourselves are comforted by God* (2 Cor. 1:3-4).

So, why were Job's companions such miserable comforters? They failed to help Job because they opened their mouths without knowing the truth, with a lack of grace, and said what was not necessary. Because they had not experienced specifically what Job was going through, they could not rightly empathize with him or know how to encourage him through the trial. Even Job was surprised that Eliphaz was emboldened to return a second time to attack him with more *"vain words"* (v. 3). Job then states that if their roles were reversed, he would not do so, but instead would provide encouragement and comfort (16:4-5). May we learn from Job's friends' mistake and not repeat their sin, lest we also suffer God's rebuke for adding to the misery of one He loves. It is better not to speak than to do so wrongly and needlessly hurt another.

Turning from his miserable comforters, Job again laments, before the Lord, his loathsome situation. God had emotionally worn him down by the deaths of his family and servants, and physically, through the fatigue and pain of a cruel, ongoing illness; he was now quite frail, just a shadow of the man he once was (16:6-8). He likened God's hostility towards him as to a growling, vicious beast that had brutally torn him in an unprovoked attack (16:9). Then, to make matters worse, God had permitted the people to mock and persecute Job; he was oppressed by the wicked, perhaps speaking of his friends' speeches (16:10-11). F. B. Hole suggests that there are both positive and negative aspects to what Job is saying:

> It looks as if verses 9, 10 and 11 are a reference to what he had suffered by the speeches of his friends, and if so, even this he took as chastisement from the hands of God as well as all the losses and disaster that had come upon him. That he did take it all from the hands of God was indeed good, but we still perceive that note of self-righteousness and self-vindication marring his prayer, especially in verse 17. This being so, his prayer did pass into a complaint that he was being hardly dealt with by God, and this especially because he felt he could speak of God as being on high the Witness to his integrity, even though his friends scorned him.[40]

While Job had legitimate reasons to seek answers from the Lord, it is never a good idea to do so in a self-righteous manner or to blame God for our problems. To illustrate his complaint, Job said that God had grabbed him by the neck and had shaken him to pieces (16:12). Additionally, Job was a mere target for God's skillful archers, and God, being an elite warrior, had mortally wounded Job (16:13-14).

Of course, none of this was correct; God was not a hostile oppressor, but in his emotional condition Job could not determine another explanation. He had humbled himself before the Lord by wearing sackcloth and being covered with dirt, but though he had prayed with many sincere tears, God had not answered him (16:15-17). Desperate for vindication, Job pleaded with the earth to not cover up the injustice that had been done to him (16:18). Since Job's scornful friends (literally, "my mockers – my friends") had not pleaded in prayer for him, he hoped that some heavenly mediator, someone who had clout with God, would appear and show himself friendly by interceding on his behalf (16:19-21). Job fundamentally knew that God was high and holy and therefore could not interact directly with sinful man, unless someone of equal virtue would willingly represent man to resolve his plight.

Ironically, this was God's ultimate plan to restore humanity, but not His immediate solution for Job. Ultimately, the Lord Jesus Christ, whom God the Father loves and respects most of all, would stand in the gap between fallen humanity and Himself and be a successful Mediator

(1 Tim. 2:5). He not only experienced the judicial penalty of sin, death, for every man (Heb. 2:9; 1 Jn. 2:2), but also ever lives to make intercession for those who trust in Him for salvation:

> *He, because He continues forever, has an unchangeable priesthood. Therefore He is also able to save to the uttermost those who come to God through Him, since He always lives to make intercession for them* (Heb. 7:24-25).

Although Job would have been dead for many centuries when Christ suffered at Calvary, the Lord did so to pay the righteous debt of Job's sins (Rom. 3:25). This is why the Lord Jesus could confidently say: *"I am the way, the truth, and the life. No one comes to the Father except through Me"* (John 14:6). Christ was Job's intercessor, but not exactly in the way Job wanted; he, being near death, needed immediate legal advocacy, not the continued provocation of his present mockers (16:22-17:2). Indeed, God's assistance would come in its proper timing, as He was in full control of all the events that were occurring in Job's life, thus no other intercessor was required.

Though Job thought that God was against him, he also knew that only He could post security for him (i.e., a pledge to protect a defendant until he could be legally tried in court; 17:3). This was necessary because Job had no supporters, just those who hoped to gain some divine reward for denouncing him, as they believed God had. Rather than reward, Job surmised that his disloyal friends would reap God's vengeance for misrepresenting Him; he supposed that God might strike their children with blindness (17:4-5).

Besides wishing for a court mediator and that God would post his bail to obtain some relief before his trial, Job further hoped that there was still some righteous person who would exercise pity on his behalf. This earnest expectation showed Job's disgust for his miserable comforters, who were unrighteous men in his estimation. Job had been sneered at, spit on, and insulted, but surely his frail frame and dim eyesight (perhaps because of continuous crying) would invoke the pity of some honorable person (17:6-9). Job then extends a sarcastic invitation to his accusers to try again to prove his guiltiness – implying that they would fail and prove their own folly (17:10).

His friends had high hopes that Job would repent of his sin and be divinely restored before death overtook him, but Job had no such hope. Job had many unfulfilled dreams, but his light on the earth (i.e., his life) was nearly extinguished. Death was near; the grave and corruption were waiting for him. This really meant that all his plans were quickly fading into the darkness (17:11-14). The Hebrew word translated "grave" in verse 13 is rendered "Sheol" in verse 16, which is the equivalent of the Greek *Hades*, used in the New Testament. In Luke 16, as noted earlier, we learn that this spiritual domain secures disembodied spirits into one of two compartments: Abraham's bosom where faithful souls await resurrection unto life through Christ, and a place of torment where the wicked continue to reside for their resurrection unto final judgment in the Lake of Fire. Job knew that after experiencing death he would be conscious, but be constrained in Sheol.

Job's dreary address concludes with the realization that he had no expectation of rescue and that his only hope of ending his saga was the grave (17:15-16). God had other plans for Job. May we take to heart the words of David who often faced seemingly hopeless situations: *"Why are you cast down, O my soul? And why are you disquieted within me? Hope in God; for I shall yet praise Him, the help of my countenance and my God"* (Ps. 42:11). David forced himself to proclaim the goodness of God to his own soul and was refreshed for doing so. When darkness abounds, may we hope afresh in the bright promises of God.

Meditation

> The best we can hope for in this life is a knothole peek at the shining realities ahead. Yet a glimpse is enough. It's enough to convince our hearts that whatever sufferings and sorrows currently assail us aren't worthy of comparison to that which waits over the horizon.
>
> — Joni Eareckson Tada
> (left a quadriplegic after
> a diving accident)

Bildad: Proverbial Condemnation
Job 18

We read in Proverbs 15:1, *"A soft answer turns away wrath, but a harsh word stirs up anger."* No doubt we have before us four God-fearing men (though of different understandings), who genuinely cared for each other, but who have now lost perspective and are allowing their pride and emotions to guide their speech. The effect was not comfort or peace, but rather increased strife and more futile rhetoric. We are reminded by Solomon that ...

> *In the multitude of words sin is not lacking, but he who restrains his lips is wise. The tongue of the righteous is choice silver; the heart of the wicked is worth little. The lips of the righteous feed many, but fools die for lack of wisdom* (Prov. 10:19-20).

The more we talk, the more likely we are to slip with our lips – sin! On the contrary, wise speech blesses and edifies others. While Bildad's speeches tend to be brief, he says much more than he should. When interacting with people, fit words, spoken softly, can deescalate hostility, but contentious speech merely fuels strife. The latter choice would well characterize the communication between Job and his friends, and, as to be expected, the result was harmful, not helpful.

Bildad commences his second speech on a cruel note: *"How long till you put an end to words? Gain understanding, and afterward we will speak"* (v. 2). From Job's viewpoint, his companions had offered no sound counsel or reasonable arguments that would cause him to quit countering their insinuations or defending his reputation. They had accused him of wrongdoing; Job believed that they were in error and so he was not going to back down as long as they continued their verbal offensive. Yet, it was Job's condescending self-assurance that continually drew his associates back into the ideological fray. No one wanted to cease from promoting his position (i.e., from arguing). Job had expressed surprise that Eliphaz had returned to confront him a second time; now Bildad accuses Job of endless words. It is most unfortunate that many of us engage in the same proud and shameful practice. In so doing, we exalt ourselves, dishonor the Lord, and cause further injury to His people.

Clearly, Bildad was offended by Job's dismissal of their prudent assertions. Job had made them out to be wild beasts attacking their prey (or were stupid as cattle; NIV); so he counters with an insulting tirade (v. 3). It would have been far better for everyone to cease speaking and be still before the Lord. Yet, with that said, then we would not be able to learn from their interchange which so eloquently reveals the sinful impulses of the human heart when offended and injured.

Bildad's speech is a regurgitation of what Job's friends had already said: God judges and destroys the wicked, but sustains the righteous, thus inferring that Job was a hypocrite – a wicked man receiving divine retribution. Job had said that they were unwise (17:10), but Bildad implied that Job was the one being insensible. In reference to Job's earlier statement about God tearing him to pieces, Bildad suggested that Job was hurting himself by his own angry words and that all his vain babblings could not change the reality of God's judgment against him (v. 4). William Kelly further explains this point:

> Let Job be as violently agitated as he may, he will find out in the end that, as they are not to be counted cattle for stupidity, so the moral government of God is as immovable as the course of the earth, or the stubborn rock. What a man sows he reaps: if evil, ruin; if good, blessing. But of the latter Bildad has not a word to say. Did he know that grace works through faith? Faith can not only remove the rock, but cast a mountain into the sea.[41]

Bildad was correct; the earth, and all God's operations in nature, did not revolve around Job, but God was not limited by Bildad's deficient worldview – there was much more in this situation than any man could possibly understand. In application, let us remember that many words spoken do not change what we do not have control over. However, if carefully chosen, words spoken to others and prayers uttered to God can enable us to endure with the hopeful expectation that God is overseeing the trial and guiding its outcome.

The Beginning of Wisdom

No matter what extremes they employ, Bildad argues that the wicked eventually ensnare themselves in their own evil scheming (vv. 5-12). Roy Zuck observes Bildad's zealous use of metaphors in this section to depict this entangling outcome:

> In fact dangers await him like a net (for catching birds) and its mesh (the covering over a pit), a trap, a snare, a noose on the ground, and a trap in his path. Here Bildad used six Hebrew words for traps, more synonyms for these objects than in any other Old Testament passage. Whatever Job would do, Bildad affirmed, would ultimately ensnare him.[42]

This implied that until Job repented, he would continue to live in terror because calamity and disaster were poised to pounce on him at any time. Bildad then provides some examples of how God deals with the wicked. (Notice that each one is carefully chosen to relate to Job's situation.) The wicked suffer: The worst kinds of skin diseases (v. 13). The terror of their households being torn away (v. 14). The burning of their homes so that they have no security (v. 15). The wicked are like a tree pulled up by its roots, with its branches broken; it is discarded and left to wither away (v. 16). In the end, no one remembers someone who walks in darkness, as they are banished from the earth and have no posterity to perpetuate their name (vv. 17-19).

Finally, Bildad counters Job's statement that any true righteous person would see his condition and have pity on him (16:9). Rather, Bildad suggests that the upright would be astounded that Job would suffer such a horrible end because he would not get right with God (v. 20). This point is punctuated by the worst charge against Job thus far: *"Surely such are the dwellings of the wicked, and this is the place of him who does not know God"* (v. 21). Not only did Bildad suggest that Job was suffering as a wicked man, but he further implied that Job did not even know God. If Job possessed a true comprehension of God, he would realize that what Bildad was saying about God's interaction with evildoers was true and Job would repent. This parting jab sank Job further into depression; in the next chapter we witness Job's lowest point of despair. He was truly alone, all alone, or so he thought.

Meditation

You may never know that Jesus is all you need, until Jesus is all you have.

— Corrie Ten Boom
(a WWII concentration camp survivor)

Job: My Redeemer Lives!
Job 19

During his dispute with God (Job 1 and 2), Satan had attempted to discredit Job's faith, but then disappears from the story altogether. Afterwards, Job's friends appear to continue the evil effort by clashing with Job for thirty chapters. Clearly, the battle that was won in heaven continued on earth by those representing the heavenly participants. The "accuser of the brethren" was still involved, yet discretely behind the scene. Almighty God was completely engaged in the confrontation and would soon appear to ensure the earthly conflict ended well to accomplish the most good. Mike Mason summarizes how Satan used Job's friends to continue his assault on a man of faith:

> Herein lies the great, terrible, beautiful secret of the book's unity, as we see Satan attacking Job not only through disaster and disease and depression, but through the faithlessness of his friends. We need not go so far as to class these men as deliberate accomplices of Satan, but they are certainly his pawns, and for us the sobering lesson is that Christians are not above being used as instruments of the Devil. If the Devil himself were to appear on Job's doorstep and attack him verbally, would his accusations be any more subtle and stinging than those of the friends? With friends like these, one is tempted to ask, who needs enemies?[43]

Satan's efforts against Job were continuing through his friends. Why the Lord permitted this man to endure such hardship for so long is a mystery, but obviously it was needful.

Bildad's spiteful retort in the previous chapter is followed by Job's counter argument (v. 1). Rather than referring to the actual number of their verbal assaults, Job used the Hebrew idiom of "ten" (e.g., Gen. 31:7) to signify that his accusers had already reproached him "many" times (v. 3). He threw Bildad's own question of *"how long?"* back at him to inquire how much longer his friends would vex his soul by their many words (v. 2). Job then asserted that if he had sinned against God, it was his own problem, not theirs, so they should not presume to be superior to him in their judgments (vv. 4-5). He then contended that he had not sinned, but that God had caught him in His net; he was the helpless victim of divine injustice (v. 6). Job believed that God had needlessly mistreated him.

What further exasperated Job is that God did not respond to his desperate cries to correct the grievance (v. 7). Was God indifferent to justice? It seemed so to Job, who then employs eight specific illustrations to accuse God of wrongdoing: God had unfairly obstructed his path in life, covered him with darkness, and removed his status in the community (vv. 8-9). Furthermore, the Lord had demolished Job (i.e., like an old building), had uprooted all of Job's hope, and had poured out His wrath on Job, as if he was an enemy (vv. 10-11). In the latter sense, Job likened God to an army that had surrounded him and was building up a siege ramp in order to conquer and destroy him (v. 12).

Not only was God aloof, but Job felt abandoned by everyone else also. Distant relatives, near kinsman, friends, and acquaintances had deserted him at the time of his greatest need (vv. 13-14). Even his household servants, his own personal servant, and his wife refused to respond to Job; they would not risk coming near him because of his disease (vv. 15-17). Although his three companions were nearby, Job felt estranged from them socially and emotionally – it would have been better if they were not with him. The younger generation did not show Job the respect his age deserved, and his most intimate companions (probably referring to Eliphaz, Bildad, and Zophar) and loved ones disavowed him (vv. 18-19). Seeing his agonizing situation, as one smitten and forlorn of God, why did his allies not pity him (vv. 20-21)? Why did they persecute him so ruthlessly, like a pack of wild beasts devouring their prey – Job's flesh (v. 22)?

Job desired that all his words be engraved on a rock with the letters filled with lead to preserve his testimony – he wanted future generations to learn of his guiltlessness and his protest of injustice (vv. 23-24). This woeful treatise expresses Job's lowest point in the narrative; being disdained by God and man, he was all alone. He is an emotionally traumatized man who was in immense pain and had lost

The Beginning of Wisdom

everything. It is from this deep despondency that a sudden burst of faith springs up within him to declare his confidence of future vindication in the presence of God (vv. 25-29).

As previously mentioned, Job may be the oldest book in our Bibles, and, ironically, it is the first to speak of resurrection. Even after the loss of all his wealth, his children, and his health, Job would not blaspheme God, but instead told his three friends that he anticipated being bodily with God in the afterlife:

For I know that my Redeemer lives, and He shall stand at last on the earth; and after my skin is destroyed, this I know, that in my flesh I shall see God, whom I shall see for myself, and my eyes shall behold, and not another. How my heart yearns within me! (Job 19:25-27).

Even if God took Job's life, and his body rotted in the grave, he understood that he would be resurrected in a future day and that he would dwell with his resurrected Redeemer – *I know that my Redeemer lives!*

> I know that my Redeemer lives!
> What joy this blest assurance gives!
> He lives, He lives, who once was dead;
> He lives, my ever-living Head!
>
> He lives triumphant from the grave;
> He lives eternally to save;
> He lives exalted, throned above;
> He lives to rule His Church in love.
>
> — Samuel Medley

After everything pertaining to his natural body was destroyed, Job could declare by faith, *"In my flesh I shall see God."* Job's hope was to be raised up with an incorruptible body and to live again with his Redeemer. The Hebrew word *gaal* is rendered "my Redeemer" and speaks of someone who can fully restore something lost. Job knew that only God could fully restore all that man had lost by sin. His declaration expresses his deep desire to be one with his God and to be restored into perfect fellowship with Him. Charles Spurgeon explains why Job had such confident assurance:

> The longing desire of an afflicted child of God is once more to see his Father's face. His first prayer is not "O that I might be healed of the disease which now festers in every part of my body!" nor even "O that I might see my children restored from the jaws of the grave, and my property once more brought from the hand of the spoiler!" but the first and uppermost cry is, "O that I knew where I might find Him, who is my God! That I might come even to His seat!" God's children run home when the storm comes on. It is the heaven-born instinct of a gracious soul to seek shelter from all ills beneath the wings of Jehovah. ... Job's desire to commune with God was intensified by the failure of all other sources of consolation. The patriarch turned away from his sorry friends, and looked up to the celestial throne. ... Nothing teaches us so much the preciousness of the Creator, as when we learn the emptiness of all besides.[44]

Job was not afraid to be with the Lord, but rather was looking forward to that wonderful opportunity, *"whom I shall see for myself."* But how did Job know that death was not the end of man? How could he declare by faith that his Redeemer was the living One, and that at *"the last,"* He would stand on the earth? How did Job know that he would one day experience resurrection and have a glorious body? F. B. Hole supplies a likely answer to these questions:

> Though truth has been progressively revealed, certain great facts of a prophetic sort came to light in very early days. There was, for instance, the prophecy of Enoch, uttered before the flood, though not put on record in Scripture until the last epistle of the New Testament. Without a doubt Job would have known this prediction of Enoch, and it is remarkable that nothing he says here is out of harmony with what is revealed in later ages. When the glorious Christ raises the saints, Job amongst them, he will indeed "see God," and see Him, as he said, "in my flesh," though he did not know he would be raised with a spiritual body like unto the resurrection body of our Lord.[45]

There was no doubt in Job's mind that he had been accepted by God (though he did not know why) and that he would be received by God after death. This is why Job did not fear death, and even welcomed it. However, Job's death would have failed to yield the valuable lessons that God wants us to learn from this book.

Job knew that in the day of resurrection, God would stand with him on the earth, no longer as a stranger, but an advocate to declare him innocent. Then his accusers would learn too late that there was no pretext of a case against Job (v. 28). Rather than trying to convince Job that he was in sin and reaping God's judgment, they should consider their own accountability before Him in wrongly accusing him – God would judge them with the wicked (v. 29). Job's warning was forthright: If his friends continued to persecute him, they would be severely punished by God for doing so. They would be wise to cease their attack and stand with Job and defend his innocence.

Though Job suffered greatly, God did restore and bless him later in his life (Job 42). What was his hope during those long, difficult days beforehand? He knew that his resurrected body would not be covered with sores, but would fully enable him to be with and honor his God. What Job did not know was that his Redeemer would also experience resurrection and bring him into all the eternal blessings of His life.

Christ was raised from the dead three days after He gave His life as a ransom for humanity. Though there had been six bodily resurrections recorded in the Bible previously, Christ was the first individual to experience glorification (to receive a glorified body which would be suitable for the dynamics of heaven). The number seven is used in the Bible to symbolize completeness and perfection and Christ, the seventh human raised from the dead, was the first to experience perfect resurrection; as Paul puts it, the Lord Jesus was *"the firstfruits of the dead"* to appear before God in heaven (1 Cor. 15:20-23). In a coming day all believers will receive that same kind of body (Phil. 3:21).

Natural law governs us while we sojourn on earth, but that is not true in the spiritual realm of the afterlife. Whether one spends eternity in heaven or in hell, everyone will undergo a spiritual resurrection. This ensures that all individuals will have a body suited for their final destination. The wicked will experience resurrection just prior to the Great White Throne judgment at the end of the millennial reign of Christ (Rev. 20:10-15). The Eternal State, the everlasting reality of a new heaven and new earth without sin, follows this final judgment. Time ceases to have meaning after this, but believers, including Job, will never tire of praising God, learning of His infinite grace, or basking in His awesome glory!

Meditation

> We want to avoid suffering, death, sin, ashes. But we live in a world crushed and broken and torn, a world God Himself visited to redeem. We receive His poured-out life, and being allowed the high privilege of suffering with Him, may then pour ourselves out for others.
>
> — Elisabeth Elliot

Zophar: The Wicked May Prosper Briefly
Job 20

Exasperated by Job's insolence, Zophar cannot keep still any longer; his understanding of the situation has forced him to respond (vv. 1-2). He commences his second and final speech with this pungent retort: *"I have heard the rebuke that reproaches me"* (v. 3). Solomon would later write: *"Do you see a man hasty in his words? There is more hope for a fool than for him"* (Prov. 29:20). Especially when offended, we should not permit emotions to govern our speech; the damage caused by the eruption of harsh words can require years to heal. Zophar, affronted by his grief-stricken friend, moves to defend himself against the one he originally sought to console. It is a good reminder that hurting people often say things that they do not mean, or speak more sharply than they intend. Solomon reminds that *"a friend loves at all times"* (Prov. 17:17). A true friend must have thick skin and demonstrate genuine love by avoiding hasty and unnecessary responses:

> *Love suffers long and is kind; love does not envy; love does not parade itself, is not puffed up; does not behave rudely, does not seek its own, is not provoked, thinks no evil; does not rejoice in iniquity, but rejoices in the truth; bears all things, believes all things, hopes all things, endures all things* (1 Cor. 13:4-7).

Zophar did not exercise biblical love, but rudely confronts Job with a warning from the past (vv. 4-11), which can be summarized by verse 5: *"That the triumphing of the wicked is short, and the joy of the hypocrite is but for a moment."* Zophar contended that human history shows certain consistencies in reference to the wicked: their joy was brief because God brought them low, they vanished like a dream, their children suffer also to repay those they oppress, and they ultimately lost all the wealth they gained through fraudulent means. Zophar was philosophically squeezing Job into his ethical and spiritual vortex, but Job, a guilt-free man, just would not yield to the effort. Through several eloquent metaphors, he implied that Job had acquired his wealth dishonestly and was now being reimbursed for his wickedness.

None of Job's friends were rightly expressing the mind of God or His character accurately, though at times they were uttering truthful statements. Misapplied truth is more treacherous than rightly applied deception, for the latter may have a respectable outcome, but the former misrepresents God. If the three had been able to correctly characterize God to Job, they would have been able to lead Job into God's presence and self-judgment. However, because their ministry centered in self-vindication, that is all that they received back from Job – they never got past Job's pride to reach his conscience.

Regrettably, Job's companions led him into the vast arena of carnal debate, not into the Creator's presence. They shifted Job's focus from the root of his faith in God to its apparent lack of fruitfulness. Rather than dealing with the heart issue, they proudly judged what they perceived to be true – the externals (2 Cor. 5:12). They unknowingly were limiting the work of God's grace in Job's life by causing him to reflect on outward virtues, rather than inward attitudes. As a result, says C. H. Mackintosh, all of Job's defensive utterances prove how far Job was from true brokenness and humility, a feature of those who enjoy God's presence:

> No doubt the friends were wrong, quite wrong – wrong in their notions about God, wrong in their method of dealing with Job. But their being wrong did not make him right. Had Job's conscience been in the presence of God, he would have made no reply to his friends, even though they had been a thousand times more mistaken and severe in their treatment. He would have meekly bowed his head, and allowed the tide of reproof and accusation to roll over him. He would have turned the very severity of his friends to profitable account, by viewing it as a wholesome moral discipline for his heart. But no; Job had not yet reached the end of himself. He was full of self-vindication, full of invective against his fellows, full of mistaken thoughts about God. It needed another ministry to bring him into a right attitude of soul.[46]

The Beginning of Wisdom

Prejudice against the truth caused Job's companions to escort their friend into the vast hopeless realm of rhetoric. Eliphaz relied on personal experience, Bildad trusted in tradition, and Zophar was full of his own pharisaical confidence and insights. Human wisdom, historical accounts, personal experiences, social traditions, emotional appeals do not reach into a man's conscience as God's Word and Spirit do. These are God's tools for directing our feet onto the path of righteousness (Ps. 119:105). Let us be careful not to replace what God deems necessary for spiritual life with intellectual, religious, and emotional substitutes; otherwise we will also be miserable counselors. Moreover, let us not be easily offended or self-vindicating while assisting others, but rather in a spirit of humility may we lead them into God's presence (Gal. 6:1). Only there can the most worthy One teach us of our own unworthiness.

Zophar suggested that riches gained through deceitful means are like a sweet delicacy that is savored in the mouth, but when swallowed sours in the stomach and is soon vomited up. Meaning, what was initially enjoyed was lost and the end of the matter was far worse (vv. 12-15). In this sense, riches obtained through corruption have a quick end, like the deadly venom of a snake which suddenly and unexpectedly strikes (v. 16). Fresh streams of water, honey, and cream are used to symbolize prosperity, but Zophar asserts that God will not permit the wicked to enjoy what was wrongly seized from others, especially the poor, for He will return to them what was taken (vv. 17-19).

Although the wicked are full, they still crave more riches. Yet, their wealth will not save them when God rains down wrath upon them and strips away their possessions (vv. 20-23). Zophar maliciously implied that Job had lusted for wealth, obtained it through underhanded means, such as dispossessing the poor, and was now reaping divine justice for his crimes. All of which was not true. Zophar's conclusion was a possible answer for Job's situation, but not the right one. We can only imagine the further misery that this callous and misdirected counsel caused Job.

In conclusion, Zophar affirmed that God would not permit a wicked person to escape justice, so no matter how hard Job tried to avoid divine retribution, God would get him sooner or later (vv. 24-27). If Job was struck by one of God's arrows and was able to pull it out, then God would smite him with terror and darkness, or send down fire to devour all that he had. No matter what Job did to elude justice, heaven would reveal his iniquity and the earth would rise up to vindicate God's righteousness (v. 27). Zophar uses the illustration of a raging flood carrying away all one's household goods as an example of the type of earthly fury that Job could expect; God had appointed the wicked to suffer such calamities (vv. 28-29). This was Zophar's narrow-sighted worldview, which he used as a philosophical club over poor Job's boil-ridden head. Sadly, Job's friends are becoming crueler and are stuck in the rut of shallow redundancy, unlike Job, whose arguments are steadily advancing with spiritual insight.

God will certainly judge all the wicked in the resurrection, and often He invokes payback on them now, but that is not always the case, nor is personal hardship a sure sign of divine punishment for sin. On the contrary, the Lord Jesus told His disciples that they should expect adversity in the world that was hostile to Him:

If the world hates you, you know that it hated Me before it hated you. If you were of the world, the world would love its own. Yet because you are not of the world, but I chose you out of the world, therefore the world hates you. Remember the word that I said to you, "A servant is not greater than his master." If they persecuted Me, they will also persecute you (John 15:18-20).

These things I have spoken to you, that in Me you may have peace. In the world you will have tribulation; but be of good cheer, I have overcome the world (John 16:33).

Similarly, Paul informs believers that if they lived for Christ, they should expect to suffer and be persecuted in a world plagued by sin: *"Yes, and all who desire to live godly in Christ Jesus will suffer persecution"* (2 Tim. 3:12). To suffer faithfully for righteousness is an evident sign of being a true believer, as an unsaved person would not be willing to do so:

We are bound to thank God always for you, brethren, as it is fitting, because your faith grows exceedingly, and the love of every one of you all abounds toward each other, so that we ourselves boast of you among the churches of God for your patience and faith in all your persecutions and tribulations that you endure, which is manifest evidence of the righteous judgment of God, that you may be counted worthy of the kingdom of God, for which you also suffer; since it is a righteous thing with God to repay with tribulation those who trouble you (2 Thess. 1:3-6).

Unlike Job, we have a scriptural mandate which instructs us to expect suffering, if we live to please the Lord. Furthermore, God promises to amply repay those who do trouble us. It is often through the Church's trials and persecutions that the Lord declares His presence to the unregenerate. This was the case when Paul and Silas were beaten for their godly testimony and thrown into jail at Philippi without a civil trial (Acts 16). Their singing and praises to God after being so ill-treated spoke volumes to the jail-keeper who trusted Christ as Savior. Afterwards, his entire household received Christ also and a local church was founded in that city.

Years later, Paul wrote the saints at Philippi and told them how he was praying for them to triumph in their affliction: *"That you stand fast in one spirit, with one mind striving together for the faith of the gospel, and not in any way terrified by your adversaries, which is to them a proof of perdition, but to you of salvation, and that from God"* (Phil. 1:27-28). They knew that this was possible, because they had already witnessed the fruitful outcome of Paul's patience in adversity. Suffering patiently for the cause of Christ is evidence of true salvation, and is also a convicting testimony of the reality of Christ to one's persecutors!

Meditation

But pain insists upon being attended to. God whispers to us in our pleasures, speaks in our conscience, but shouts in our pains: it is His megaphone to rouse a deaf world.

— C. S. Lewis

Job: God Will Judge the Wicked
Job 21

In comparison to Job's previous counter responses, Job's reply to Zophar's pithy indictment of the last chapter is unique in that he does not directly speak to God at any time. Furthermore, Roy Zuck observes Job's unusual usage of plural nouns and verbs in this chapter: "In this speech Job responded to the view of the three arguers ('you' in vv. 2, 27-29, 34 is plural, and the verbs in vv. 2-3a, 5, 29, and 34 are plural) about the destruction of the wicked."[47] Though Job does refute many of Zophar's remarks in verses 7-33, it is evident that his overall response confronts the collective view of all three orators.

Job felt that his obstinate and calloused counselors were not listening to him. He requested them to be quiet and carefully consider what he had to say; afterwards, *Zophar* was free to continue mocking him (i.e., the singular verb implies the action of one person; vv. 1-3). From Job's point of view, there was no cause for them to be impatient with him because he was complaining to God, not them (v. 4). He also requested that they take a good look at him; his repulsive and abysmal appearance should invoke their pity and tolerance (vv. 5-6). According to Bildad's earlier statement, pity should be the appropriate response even if Job was a wicked person (18:20).

It is often hard for a hurting person to make sense of how they feel until they are able to talk things out. Job's reply is a good reminder for us not to interrupt a hurting person who is disclosing their feelings. This is not the proper time for questions, ideas for resolution, and especially correction or condemnation. Hear the entire matter out and carefully ponder and pray about what should be said. If you do not know what to say, it is better to be still and commit the matter to the Lord in prayer. Attentive listening and the human touch convey much love at such times. It is therapeutic for a suffering person to hear themselves talk things through. The verbalization of feelings causes us to organize our thoughts and try to reason things out. A distraught person will appreciate a listening ear, and a prayer afterwards rather than instant problem-solving. A husband, who wants to remain in happy standing with his wife, will soon learn the wisdom of this verbal protocol.

Job then counters Zophar's argument that the prosperity of the wicked is brief before they receive divine vengeance, a view held by all three counselors. This could not be true because Job had witnessed evildoers die of old age, having enjoyed their children and financial security all their lives (vv. 7-9). Even those who flippantly prayed to God were often permitted to appreciate the finer things of life, such as music, cattle, and even a peaceful death after a long life (vv. 10-15). Did not all man's affluence come from the hand of God (v. 16)? Absolutely. Hence, Job's observations not only implied that the wicked prosper more than a brief season, but in many cases God did not judge them at all during their earthly sojourn.

To punctuate his claim, Job repeatedly asks his friends, *"how often"* do we really observe the life of the wicked being snuffed out prematurely by sudden calamities, as Bildad had claimed (18:5, 12; v. 17). Job answers his own question: Seldom had they witnessed God blowing away the wicked like unwanted chaff or straw; thus, Zophar's assertion could hardly be supported by the facts (v. 18). Job anticipates that his colleagues might counter his conclusion by arguing that God would punish a wicked man's children, if he went unpunished in life; however, Job insisted that God did not punish innocent people for another's crimes (vv. 19-21).

Having supplied evidence and reasoned out a solid conclusion, Job turns the table on his friends (who have been endlessly harping on the inevitable misery of the wicked) by asking, "Why does God bless those who reject Him?" What is Job's line of thinking? If his friends would concede that God does bless the wicked at times, would it not also be reasonable that a sovereign God executing His eternal purposes might also cause the righteous to suffer hardship?

How dare men try to teach an all-knowing God how to rightly judge evildoers or to refine the righteous! We may observe another commit what we think is a sinful act, but only God knows all the details about it, and only God can discern what is in that person's heart and whether hypocrisy resides there. For instance, David says, *"The fool has said in his heart, 'There is no God'"* (Ps. 14:1). Such a person may have never uttered those words, but God understands the language of the heart. An evil or righteous person will live out what resides in their heart.

Consequently, it is possible for a believer to preach the imminent return of Christ for His Church (1 Thess. 4:13-18) and even say aloud, *"Come, Lord Jesus"* (Rev. 22:20), but not live devoutly or expectantly of Christ's coming. It is possible to share the gospel message with someone when it is convenient, but then ignore the multitudes of hell-bound sinners we rub shoulders with on a daily basis. Dear reader, do you really believe the gospel message is the only means of saving sinners from an agonizing eternal existence in the Lake of Fire? Do you really believe that the Lord might return before you finish perusing this page? William Kelly reminds us that it is important for us to examine our own hearts now, so that God will not need to act against us later:

> So that it is a very solemn thing — the way in which the Lord takes the crafty and reads the heart; and therefore, it is of all importance that we should judge ourselves, and look to the Lord, that we may have Christ Himself before our souls so habitually that we are filled by His mind and directed by His love, and led by the Holy Spirit who gives the needed power and grace to those that look to Christ.[48]

At this very moment, God not only knows what is in the hearts of the wicked, but in ours also. Job's associates were preoccupied with God's judgment of the wicked, but let us not forget that we must stand before Him and give an account of our lives also (Rom. 14:10-12; 2 Cor. 5:10).

In death, Job agreed that there was no disparity between the righteous and the wicked, but in life, prosperity, posterity, health, mental vitality, etc., were not necessarily indications of well doing (vv. 22-26). Anticipating the objection of his friends (i.e., that he provide an example of a wealthy wicked person to support his conclusion), he supplies them evidence: Had they not talked with travelers, such as merchants, who were prosperous, yet unscrupulous in their business practices (vv. 27-29)? Was that not the very reason that the wicked were prospering now? The implication was that they knew Job was correct on this matter.

Furthermore, though the wicked shall ultimately be judged by God, who would be so bold to confront a prominent and prosperous person about their evil deeds now (vv. 30-31)? It would not be socially acceptable to do so, but Job's companions were quite willing to attack him after he had lost everything. Job's point being that often when wealthy wicked people die, they have well-attended funerals, receive an honorable burial, and are often fondly remembered (vv. 32-33). Job concludes his speech by evaluating the benefit of all their consoling. In his view, their counsel was futile because their insinuations were founded on a false premise, namely, that the righteous do not suffer calamity (v. 34). In short, they were pathetic friends indeed! Job knew that any theological framework which cannot afford the believer the faith to live out each and every day and in all circumstances is worthless.

Asaph observed the same social incongruity that Job mentions and even wondered why he should continue pursuing godliness and suffer for doing so, since the wicked seem to prosper and avoid God's judgment:

Behold, these are the ungodly, who are always at ease; they increase in riches. Surely I have cleansed my heart in vain, and washed my hands in innocence. For all day long I have been plagued, and chastened every morning (Ps. 73:12-14).

However, Asaph had advantages that Job did not, Holy Scripture to consult and a Holy Sanctuary to inquire of the Lord. As a nation, the Law promised God's blessing for Israel's obedience and His cursing for rebellion, but God dealt with individuals in a personal way which could not be foretold by Scripture (Deut. 28). After spending time in God's presence, Asaph realized his attitude was wrong and could even be harmful to God's people if shared – the destruction of the wicked is sealed – do not envy them (Ps. 73:15-17).

We, too, may agree with both men: At times it does seem that the wicked flourish. While Scripture does confirm their ultimate doom, it may not occur during their earthly sojourn as Job's companions asserted. What is the lesson for us? We will not understand all that God is doing in our lives, but the Lord invites us to draw near at all times to receive comfort and direction. When doubts and quandaries arise, may we in faith choose to pray along with Asaph:

You will guide me with Your counsel, and afterward receive me to glory. Whom have I in heaven but You? And there is none upon earth that I desire besides You. My flesh and my heart fail; but God is the strength of my heart and my portion forever. For indeed, those who are far from You shall perish; You have destroyed all those who desert You for harlotry. But it is good for me to draw near to God; I have put my trust in the Lord God, that I may declare all Your works (Ps. 73:24-28).

Meditation

The shepherd imagery that Job employs in verse 11 is worthy of our appreciation. Spiritual leaders throughout the course of Biblical history are likened to shepherds, and those in their care are likened to sheep. In verse 21, Job applies the shepherd analogy to family leadership; a man's children are his flock of sheep. Biblical duties and affections of a father towards his family closely align with the instructions given to shepherds. Whether it be Christ shepherding the Church (John 10), church leaders pastoring local churches (1 Pet. 5:1-5; Acts 20:28-31), men caring for their families, or women caring for other women and their own children (Tit. 2:3-5), the functional responsibilities are basically identical. Shepherds are to lead, protect, feed, attend, and watch over the sheep, while being good examples and humble servants. Shepherding, like teaching, prophecy, and evangelism, is a genderless equipping gift to the Church (Eph. 4:11-12). When men and women are engaged in shepherding others, they must follow the Lord's example of sacrificial care: The Good Shepherd gave His life for the sheep. Job especially highlights that husbands and fathers are to be good shepherds of their families, for no authority and responsibility conferred by God is without direct accountability to Him also.

— Warren Henderson

The Beginning of Wisdom

Eliphaz: Job, Your Wickedness Is Great!
Job 22

This chapter commences with the third and final round of speeches by Job's companions Eliphaz and Bildad. Much of what is said is repetitive, but is conveyed with greater condescending zeal. Roy Zuck summarizes the three counselors' arguments thus far, previews their final discourses, and also Job's general response to them:

> In cycle one Job's visitors implied that he was a sinner and appealed to him to repent. In the second foray they insinuated that he was guilty and stressed the terrible fate of the wicked, but voiced no challenge for repentance. In the third verbal battle they attacked him by accusing him of specific sins, and only Eliphaz again gave a call for Job to turn back to God. Job stood his ground in response during all three rounds of attack. He denied (a) the premise of their implications, (b) their assertion that the wicked always suffer, and (c) that he himself was a deliberate transgressor.[49]

An incensed Eliphaz introduces the main point of his final rebuttal with a volley of five questions, the last being a bold indictment against Job:

> *Can a man be profitable to God, though he who is wise may be profitable to himself? Is it any pleasure to the Almighty that you are righteous? Or is it gain to Him that you make your ways blameless? Is it because of your fear of Him that He corrects you, and enters into judgment with you?* ***Is not your wickedness great, and your iniquity without end?*** (Job 22:2-5).

The first question suggests a major flaw in Eliphaz's understanding of why humanity should submit to God. Eliphaz believed that a man's good deeds did not add to, nor does a man's sinfulness subtract from God's pleasure. He suggested that it was not to God's advantage to send prosperity to some and to others calamity; therefore, when God did send blessing or disaster, it was man alone who was responsible. Eliphaz surmised that God was disinterested in the righteous and did not benefit from them. God did, however, notice and act against the wicked because He must uphold justice in the earth (vv. 1-2).

Eliphaz's entire argument hinges on a single question: What is the right motive for obedience? Possible answers included: To gain God's blessing, to avoid His judgment, or to demonstrate love to God. The Lord Jesus answers this question while instructing His disciples: *"If you love Me, keep My commandments"* (John 14:15). Therefore, it is not for personal profit that we should choose to fear and obey God, but rather to please Him (Rev. 4:11). Clearly, then, the answer to Eliphaz's second question was "yes," God did notice the righteous, as shown by His fine accolades of Job in the opening verses of the book. Eliphaz was quite wrong about God's attitude towards the virtuous and, hence, Job.

However, this does not mean that Job was a perfect man. He did not have the benefit of Romans 7 and 8 to understand the flesh nature that resided in him. In practice, God had already said that there was not a man on the entire earth that was as blameless and God-fearing as Job. However, as William Kelly points out, God also knew what was in Job's heart and that some selective purging was necessary:

> There was not a man on earth that was all round like His servant Job, and yet there was something there that God meant to bring out, of which Job had no idea, i.e., that he never recognized that it was wrong.[50]

Eliphaz's remaining three questions in the initial volley were to ensure Job felt the guilt of his supposed sin. In his view, God does not correct the innocent; therefore, given Job's circumstances, his wickedness had to be great (vv. 4-5). Eliphaz then imagines the types of offenses that Job (once a wealthy man that had abused his status) had committed to earn God's sore retribution. Sins hypothesized are: not returning the personal pledge of a garment during nighttime hours (this was to safeguard a debtor from getting cold; Deut. 24:10-13), neglecting the weary, and abusing the poor, orphans, and widows (Deut. 27:19; vv. 6-9). As a result of his mistreatment of others,

The Beginning of Wisdom

Eliphaz predicted that wicked Job would experience hindering snares, devastating perils, confusing darkness, and a flood of catastrophes (vv. 10-11). But his reasoning and conclusion were erroneous. Job was innocent of wrongdoing and will later defend himself against each of these charges (31:16-22).

Settled in his self-righteous status, Eliphaz then had the audacity to suggest that Job had never known God intimately, but he still could through repentance: *"Now acquaint yourself with Him"* (v. 21). Such a pompous demand had to further frustrate and sadden Job.

Job had previously suggested that God cannot be forced to behave according to man's perception of His justice: *"Can anyone teach God knowledge, since He judges those on high?"* (21:22). One technique of enhancing a weak argument is to twist the meaning of the opposing viewpoint and confront that altered version; this is what Eliphaz does (vv. 12-14). To paraphrase his conjecture:

> How dare you, Job, question the One who dwells above the clouds in heaven, our majestic God's awareness of man and wisdom to govern man's doings? Although He dwells high above, He is quite aware of what you have done.

That was not what Job had said; in fact, it was quite the opposite. In retrospect, we have a narrow-minded elderly man resorting to dishonorable tactics to convince Job that he was right and that Job was wrong. This is another practical lesson for us to contemplate: the truth never needs defending by what it despises, that is, hypocrisy, lying, and deceit.

Rather than stopping there, the senior confronter then likens Job to the evil generation destroyed by the flood in Noah's day. Similarly, those who perished had been blessed by God, but yet would not repent; they just wanted to be left alone and perished (vv. 15-18). Job had told his accusers that they were free to mock him, if they would only be still and carefully listen to him (21:2-3); now Eliphaz says that is just what he is going to do, because the righteous should rejoice when God renders justice to sinners (vv. 19-20).

So far, Eliphaz has imagined the type of sins that Job must have committed for God to judge him so harshly. Then, he misrepresented what Job had said to insinuate that he was mocking God. He now concludes by again calling on Job to repent:

> *Now acquaint yourself with Him, and be at peace; thereby good will come to you. Receive, please, instruction from His mouth, and lay up His words in your heart. If you return to the Almighty, you will be built up; you will remove iniquity far from your tents* (Job 22:21-22).

Adopting a less accusatory tone in verse 23, Eliphaz offers Job more tender words concerning his needed restoration (vv. 23-30). If Job would only repent, and trust God as his gold and silver, He would shine His light on Job again, that is, God would reinstate Job's prosperity, answer his prayers, and have fellowship with Job (vv. 23-28). He then would have pure hands and effective prayers to help others who had been brought low and were discouraged, as he was now (vv. 29-30). Much of what Eliphaz says in this section is wonderfully true for a repentant sinner; the problem was his application was misapplied – Job was not in sin. Little did Eliphaz know that the Almighty would cause Job's return, just as he had suggested, but it would be to his shame and for Job's honor.

Eliphaz's words in this section would prove to be prophetic: *"Then you will lay your gold in the dust ... Yes, the Almighty will be your gold ... So light will shine on your way"* (vv. 24, 25, 28), and so it would be and much sooner than he could have ever imagined. *"When they cast you down, and you say, 'Exaltation will come!' Then He will save the humble person"* (v. 29). Indeed, that is exactly what the Lord did, but it was Job's three accusers that were cast down and Job, who Eliphaz did not think was contrite, was exalted.

Meditation

> The will of God is never exactly what you expect it to be. It may seem to be much worse, but in the end it's going to be a lot better and a lot bigger.
>
> — Elisabeth Elliot

Job: Longings for God
Job 23-24

Having already declared his innocence repeatedly, Job does not bother to defend himself against Eliphaz's grave charges in this reply (though he will fully vindicate himself in chapter 31). For the moment, he is more concerned with God and His obscurity. The sudden burst of joyful expectancy witnessed in chapter 19 is now fully eclipsed by the thick, looming clouds of doubt. Having sunk back down into the mire of despair, Job will speak challenging, almost malevolent, things about the Lord. The Lord has yet to converse with Job and probe the recesses of his heart to reveal wrong attitudes. Until He does, we should expect Job's emotions to vacillate and expressions of doubt and aggravation to fill the narrative.

Samuel Ridout provides this helpful outline for Job's discourse of the next two chapters:

The reply may be divided into seven parts:
(1) His longing to lay his case before God (23:1-9).
(2) Protestations of righteousness (23:10-12).
(3) Afraid of God as his enemy (23:13-17).
(4) God's apparent failure in government (24:1-12).
(5) The wicked described (24:13-17).
(6) Their escape into Sheol (24:18-21).
(7) God seemingly their protector (24:22-25).[51]

Though grief-stricken and miserable, Job's bitterness related to his friends' false charges against him and God's unfair treatment, which he was being forced to endure (23:1-2). Contemplating the big picture for a moment, it must be remembered that, in Adam, we are all born condemned (John 3:18), and, therefore, God is not obliged to show us any kindness at all (Rom. 5:12, 15). Accordingly, man cannot justly accuse God of being unfair when trouble strikes. The reality of the matter is that God treats us better than we deserve; in Adam, we deserved hell and we prove it every day. Even when we try our best, we fall short of God's minimum standard of perfection required to enter into heaven (Rom. 3:23). No amount of righteous doings can compensate for even one past moral failure. God's solution to our problem was to judge a willing and perfect Substitute (Jesus Christ) in our place, that we might receive a righteous standing in Him (1 Tim. 2:5-6). Paul describes the exchange:

> *For when we were still without strength, in due time Christ died for the ungodly. For scarcely for a righteous man will one die; yet perhaps for a good man someone would even dare to die. But God demonstrates His own love toward us, in that while we were still sinners, Christ died for us* (Rom. 5:6-8).

God saw our pitiful condition and was motivated by love and mercy to pursue a righteous means of forgiving repentant sinners by judging His own Son in our place (Rom. 3:21-24). Salvation, then, is all of God. Scripture tells us, *"For by grace you have been saved through faith, and that not of yourselves; it is the gift of God"* (Eph. 2:8) and *"according to His mercy He saved us"* (Tit. 3:5). For this reason, every believer can agree with Paul, *"Thanks be to God for His indescribable gift!"* (2 Cor. 9:15). Consequently, any sinner thinking that they can argue their case with an all-knowing, holy God and gain an acquittal on personal merit is mistaken (Rom. 3:19). Unfortunately, Job settles into this type of self-righteous thinking in this chapter.

Job reasoned that if he could only find God, he could then argue his case before Him (vv. 3-4). He was confident that God would not stand against him, but rather God would agree with him and vindicate him before his accusers (23:5). However, no sooner is this uncanny defiance voiced, when Job reverses course to affirm his confidence that God would strengthen him, so that he could adequately defend himself (23:6). Mike Mason explains why, like Job, all believers should desire to be judged by the Lord:

> Unlike most people, Job sees the judgment–seat of God as a place of refuge, not of condemnation. In fact, what he longs for more than anything else is to be judged by God. Naturally there is also a part of Job that stands in fear of divine judgment; yet for him it would be a

far more fearful prospect if God's judgment never fell, and such is the case with all true believers.[52]

Only believers who walk with the Lord in accordance with His truth will yearn to be with Him and have confidence in His judgment (1 Jn. 3:3). Job was such a believer. If Job ever got such an opportunity, he knew his divine Judge would deliver him forever (23:7). These are not the words of a pagan, or a rebel, but a bewildered, God-fearing servant overcome by doubt who longs to be exonerated.

A self-righteous man can speak this boldly when the Lord is absent, but later when God personally visits Job, there would be no arguing with God; rather, Job is speechless. The Lord's response to Job then and after His restoration seems to indicate that it is far better for His suffering people to approach Him with their honest doubts than to not seek Him at all. The Lord is merciful and He seeks us out wherever we are, though at times we may be so emotionally numb we cannot sense His presence. Job even supposed that God was hiding from him so he could not present his case before Him, the Judge of all (23:8-9).

Turning from his obsession of not being able to find God, Job again protests the injustice done to him. Job believed that his heavenly trial would successfully establish his innocence: *"But He knows the way that I take; when He has tested me, I shall come forth as gold"* (v. 10). William MacDonald warns against misapplying the meaning of this verse from its direct context: "Verse 10 is often quoted to prove the sanctifying effects of trials, but in the context it is really Job's confidence in a 'not-guilty' verdict."[53] Job maintains his personal uprightness (he believes he has done the will of God; 23:11-12), but does not have the sense of grace that is necessary to actually survive a divine examination – this he will learn.

The lesson for us is that when we commend ourselves, as Job does here, we undermine the holy character of God: *"There is none righteous, no, not one; there is none who understands; there is none who seeks after God"* (Rom. 3:10-11). This is our natural standing before God; nothing but His mercy and grace through Christ can ever change that fact!

With that said, Job does, in the latter portion of this chapter, acknowledge God's sovereignty in all his affairs, that is, God certainly has the right and wherewithal to use adversity to refine His servants.

Peter goes further to inform us that such hardships are precious to God: *"The genuineness of your faith, being much more precious than gold that perishes, though it is tested by fire, may be found to praise, honor, and glory at the revelation of Jesus Christ"* (1 Pet. 1:7). Speaking of Job, Warren Wiersbe provides a panoramic understanding of what this verse means to a child of God:

> In Job's case, what was "the end [purpose] of the Lord"? *To reveal Himself as full of pity and tender mercy.* Certainly, there were other results from Job's experience, for God never wastes the sufferings of His saints. Job met God in a new and deeper way (42:1-6), and, after that, Job received greater blessings from the Lord. "But if God is so merciful," someone may argue, "why didn't He protect Job from all that suffering to begin with?" To be sure, there are mysteries to God's working that our finite minds cannot fathom; but this we know: God was glorified and Job was purified through this difficult experience. If there is nothing to endure, you cannot learn endurance. ... God permits Satan to try His children, but He always limits the extent of the enemy's power (1:12, 2:6). When you find yourself in the fire, remember that God keeps His gracious hand on the thermostat! (23:10). ... Satan wants us to get impatient with God, for an impatient Christian is a powerful weapon in the devil's hands.[54]

Of course, Job knew nothing about the devices and activities of Satan, or the spiritual warfare of Spirit-filled believers in the Church Age, but he could boast that he had walked in the way of godliness (i.e., gold-like purity). Consequently, he believed that God would have to acquit him of wrongdoing (23:11-12). Job suddenly becomes overwhelmed by the thought of standing before and confronting the One who is alone in majesty and does as He pleases (23:13-14). Because God is sovereign over all things and yet elusive, Job was terrified at the prospect of suddenly appearing before Him, but he was resolved to do so no matter what – his case must be heard (23:15-17). Job does not dread coming before God on the matter of his sin, as Eliphaz had suggested (22:10), for he believes he is innocent, but rather because of God's awesome disposition.

The balance of Job's speech (Job 24) shows a dichotomy in his thinking concerning God's judgment of the wicked: by observation he knew God was indifferent to the judgment of the wicked living on the

The Beginning of Wisdom

earth (24:1-17), but by faith he believed all evildoers would reap God's wrath, at least in the afterlife (24:18-25). Job asserted that God has a lackadaisical attitude in judging those committing sin; then he lists various crimes that seem to go unpunished: moving boundary stones to steal land, robbing from orphans and widows, and neglecting and even victimizing the poor and needy (24:1-8).

This is a rare moment in the ongoing dialogue; Job loses sight of his own misery to grieve with the mistreated and oppressed. It was baffling to Job that God did not execute immediate justice, when nursing babies were snatched from widowed mothers and sold, and the unclothed and hungry people were forced into slavery, and the innocent were wounded or killed by violent crimes (24:9-12). He then proceeds to list the secret sins that wicked people do under the cover of darkness that God seemingly ignored and did not punish: murder, burglaries, adulteries, etc. (24:13-17). All these observations were disturbing to Job because he, as a righteous man, had received the punishment that these evildoers, *"those that rebel against the light,"* deserved, but did not receive. Why had God chosen Job to be His enemy?

Job then affirmed his confidence that God would judge the wicked, but he did not believe that this had to occur immediately or even in this life, as his accusers did. He also did not agree with them that suffering was a sign of God's disapproval of personal sin. In Job's view, both the wicked and the righteous are blessed by God, the righteous are permitted to suffer, but the wicked, who are unstable as foam on the surface of water, will eventually experience His wrath (24:18). Some commentators believe that verse 20 actually begins Bildad's response, because the text seems to better agree with the arguments of Job's friends concerning God's immediate punishment of the wicked. However, Job is merely providing examples of how God does punish the wicked to ensure his point is understood – the wicked will be rendered justice by the means and timing God deems best.

Job argued that this often happens during their lifetime despite their high social position and the security of their wealth because God knows their ways (24:23-24). He might curse their land and vineyards to make them unproductive or He might snuff out their life prematurely, such that not even their own mothers would bereave them long after their burial (24:19-20). Those who oppress the needy for gain might be snapped like a tree at any moment, for none can withstand God's mighty power (24:21-22). Job believed that he had correctly considered all the facts, and ends his speech by challenging his companions to prove his viewpoint wrong (24:25).

Of course, the believer's joy will never be obtained through attacking our accusers or proving them wrong – such things gratify the flesh. Whether we are confronted by intense opposition, daily suffering, or the disappointing regression of the Church, we must learn to trust and rejoice in the Lord. In such times of distress, may we too recall to mind Nehemiah's charge to his distressed fellow countrymen: *"The joy of the Lord is your strength"* (Neh. 8:10). Rejoicing is a choice (Phil. 1:18), and it is a command (1 Thess. 5:16). Rejoicing in truth revives the heart of the redeemed and opens the way for God to perform the spectacular!

Meditation

> Though poor in this world's goods, though grieving the loss of loved ones, though suffering pain of body, though harassed by sin and Satan, though hated and persecuted by worldlings, whatever be the case and lot of the Christian, it is both his privilege and duty to rejoice in the Lord.
>
> — A.W. Pink

Bildad: How Can Man Be Justified?
Job 25

Each of Eliphaz's and Bildad's speeches were progressively shorter in duration, which demonstrated two things. First, any measure of compassion they initially had for Job was waning. Second, they had exhausted themselves and lacked any new arguments to convince Job of his folly. In his final discourse, Bildad addresses the highness of God (vv. 1-3) and the lowness of man (vv. 4-6). Besides Bildad's brevity, F. B. Hole observes a major flaw in his treatise:

> There appears to be little of reference to Job's statements in what he said. His description of the greatness and glory of God is fine and almost poetical, and what he says of the sin and uncleanness and insignificance of man, who is like a worm before his Creator, is equally true. But he could only reiterate the question Job asked in Job 9, "How then can man be just with God," without making any attempt to answer it, or express a desire for a mediator, as Job had done. To Bildad it was an unanswerable question, and perhaps he thought it gave some kind of excuse for the sin, with which he and his friends had been accusing unhappy Job.[55]

So rather than attacking Job personally or responding to his windy words, Bildad settles for a diminutive survey of God's majesty and man's depravity. Man is insignificant in comparison to God.

As Creator, God established order in all that He created and rules over it. He is sovereign not only over the material world, but also over all powers and principalities (including angelic beings). His glory and omniscience saturates all of His creation. Bildad concluded that such an all-knowing and all-powerful God should be respected; this inferred that Job was not doing so (vv. 1-3).

Bildad chooses to reiterate Eliphaz's previous rebuttal concerning God's greatness and man's insignificance by asking two questions

(4:17-18, 15:14-16): *"How then can man be righteous before God? Or how can he be pure who is born of a woman?"* (v. 4). These are good questions that every individual should ponder, but ultimately can only be answered by the Lord. If the moon (which reflects the light of the sun, a star) and all the stars are tainted in comparison to God's brilliance, how can man, who is more comparable to a lowly maggot than the heavenly stars, be accepted before God (vv. 5-6)?

While it is true that physical man is much less than a star in the material world, it is not so in the spiritual realm. Stars are not eternal and though they do reflect the glory of God, they were not fashioned in His image or likeness, as man was (Gen. 1:26). Adam was created as a unique moral being with an eternal essence. For this reason, man was God's crowning act to His creative work (Heb. 2:7-8) – he was to rule over creation and represent God in it; unfortunately, man disobeyed God in Eden and fell from God's favor. Thus, in our natural state, that is, "born of a woman," we are apart from God – the only way to be reconciled with God now is to be born again through spiritual regeneration (John 3:3; Tit. 3:5).

The flesh nature that we were all born with opposes the things of God (Gal. 5:17); therefore, there is nothing within our flesh that can perfectly please God. Jeremiah states: *"The heart [seat of emotion] is deceitful above all things, and desperately wicked"* (Jer. 17:9). Our good works do absolutely nothing to earn God's favor because of our depraved nature and our spiritual separation from God, which Scripture refers to as spiritual death (Eph. 2:1). The grand conclusion is that we all are sinners and that we can do nothing to persuade God to love us more than He already does. Good works are evidence of true salvation in Christ, not the basis for salvation (Jas. 2:17, 20).

We now know the answer to Bildad's question: How can man obtain a pure standing with God? The answer is that each individual must be justified (declared right by God). This is how Abraham received salvation: *"Abraham believed God, and it was accounted to him for righteousness"* (Rom. 4:3). If anyone could have merited salvation through personal effort, it would have been Abraham, but Scripture condemns him apart from receiving the righteousness of God. Justification is an accounting term which means "to impute or accredit to another's account." When an individual trusts Christ, God imputes a righteous standing to that individual's account (he or she is declared righteous before God, though in practice he or she will still sin). This reality is a positional truth which the Christian is to practically live out daily (Rom. 6:11-12, 13:14). If one dies without being justified (i.e. receiving forgiveness of sins and obtaining a righteous standing in Christ), there is no hope for that individual – they will suffer a horrible eternity away from God's presence (Heb. 9:27; Rev. 20:11-15).

Bildad desired to humiliate Job before his Creator, in an attempt to awaken Job to his own unworthiness and guiltiness before God. However, the attempt fails because Job has upheld the glory and sovereignty of God and has never denied that he was a sinner, or that God will judge sin. Rather, his position all along has been that he has done nothing to warrant the cruel treatment that he has been enduring. He believes that God has been unjust towards him and that his unwanted suffering is unwarranted. Later, after his restoration, Job will realize that his agonizing ordeal was a valuable experience in developing his character and faith.

Meditation

> I've never heard anyone say the really deep lessons of life have come in times of ease and comfort. But, I have heard many saints say every significant advance I've ever made in grasping the depth of God's love and growing deep with Him have come through suffering.
>
> — John Piper

Job: His Innocence and God's Greatness
Job 26-27

Before considering Job's response to Bildad's final speech (Job 26), and to his associates in general (Job 27 and 28), let us ponder how they failed to represent God and resolve Job's dilemma. Roy Zuck suggests ten reasons that Job's friends were worthless physicians (13:4) and miserable comforters (16:2):

1. They did not express any sympathy for Job in their speeches.
2. They did not pray for him.
3. They seemingly ignored Job's expression of emotional and physical agony.
4. They talked too much and did not seem to listen adequately to their advisee.
5. They became defensive and argumentative.
6. They belittled rather than encouraged Job.
7. They assumed they knew the cause of Job's problems.
8. They stubbornly persisted in their views of Job's problem, even when their ideas contradicted the facts.
9. They suggested an inappropriate solution to his problem.
10. They blamed Job and condemned him for expressing grief and frustration.[56]

Biblical counselors today would do well to learn from these mistakes and not repeat them in their own ministries. We read in Proverbs 20:5, *"Counsel in the heart of man is like deep water, but a man of understanding will draw it out."* To "draw it out" requires attentive listening, repeating back what has been heard, asking questions, rightly applying Scripture to lead the unsettled person into the peace of God. Unlike Job's companions, we have the full advantage of God's Word to illuminate the dark recesses of the human heart. A good counselor will skillfully and graciously apply Scripture to draw out into the light what others need to recognize for themselves as inappropriate thinking and abhorrent to God. May we remember that an offended and defensive counselor will fail miserably in helping the one who is not thinking straight and bound by despair.

In contrast to Bildad's brief speech, the shortest in the narrative, Job's retort goes on for six chapters and is the longest discourse of the book. Bildad had supposed that he had greater knowledge of the majesty and workings of God than Job (18:2-7, 25:2-3). But when we examined his counsel to Job, Bildad does nothing more than proclaim man's depravity, God's greatness, and God's prerogative to punish the wicked. He surmised that Job had offended God and that he must repent in order to escape God's punitive retribution, the source of his present suffering.

To confront Bildad's pompous assertions that Job had no power, strength, or wisdom in matters pertaining to God, a sarcastic Job highlights the irony to Bildad's insinuations (26:2-3): Bildad had said nothing that had encouraged or strengthened Job in his distress; in fact, the sum total of his counsel and insights were of no value to Job because no one, including God, had helped Bildad with his words (26:4). Rather, if Bildad wanted to learn something about Almighty God, then he should consider what Job knew about Him. In fact, Bildad's last words were virtually the same as Eliphaz's first words (4:17): *"How then can man be righteous before God?"* (25:4). Job's friends were stuck in an endless loop of meaningless rhetoric which merely offered variations of the same message. Rewording the same message and repeating it again and again did not make it more viable.

Where Bildad had generalized the greatness of God in the heavens, Job dwells on His specific power on earth, in the depths of the sea, in Sheol, and in destruction. For example, God was over the dead who were in anguish because they could not escape God's observation or control (26:5-6). The Hebrew word *rapha* is translated as "dead" (26:5), but is also translated "the giant(s)" or "Rephaim(s)" twenty-five times throughout the Old Testament to speak of a towering people of immense strength (Gen. 15:20; Deut. 2:20). Despite their once elite status on earth, these and other disembodied spirits now feared God in Sheol.

We must pause here to acknowledge some of the pagan deities that are often referred to throughout the book of Job. Awkwardly, many of these references have been lost in translation; for example, the word

Devotions in Job

"Destruction" (26:6) is derived from the Hebrew *abaddown* (or *Abaddon*). We read in Revelation 9:11 that the *"king over them the angel of the bottomless pit, whose name in Hebrew is Abaddon, but in Greek he has the name Apollyon."* In Job's day, Abaddon likely referred to the pagan god of the underworld. In Job 26:7, the Hebrew word translated "the north," *tsaphown,* comes from the root *tsaphan*. Saphon (also *Zaphon* in Isaiah 14:13) is the mysterious mountain associated with the Canaanite creation story. Consider Job 26:12: *"He stirs up the sea with His power, and by His understanding He breaks up the storm."* The Hebrew word for "sea" is *Yam*, the Canaanite god of the sea, and the Hebrew word rendered "storm" is *Rahab*, which according to medieval Jewish folklore represented the water-dragon of darkness and chaos. Job 5:7 reads, *"Yet man is born to trouble, as the sparks fly upward."* The phrase "as the sparks" is derived from the Hebrew *ben resheph*, literally interpreted "the sons of Resheph" spring up. Resheph was a Canaanite deity which protected from plagues and war. In Job 7:12 we are introduced to Tannin (Tanniyn), translated "a whale" but was considered to be the monster of the deep in Canaanite and Phoenician mythology. Tannin is usually translated "dragon" in the King James Version of the Bible. In fact, there are many other pagan references in the Hebrew text of Job, but most of these are lost in translation.

Why does the original text contain so many cultural and poetic references to pagan entities? It shows how Satan had thoroughly weaved his deception into the fabric of the society in which Job lived. Given Job's limited revelation of the truth, his strong faith in the one true God is that much more exhilarating to us. Even in the darkest domains of our sin-cursed world, God has provided sufficient revelation of Himself that we might know Him through faith. Given the limited revelation available to Job, F. B. Hole notes that his understanding of creation was astonishing:

> His description of God's creatorial power is striking. Verse 7 in particular shows how these early saints, living in the fear of God, as far as He was then revealed, had a true and simple knowledge of created things, far removed from the fantastic ideas entertained, even by the learned, when their minds had been darkened by lapsing into idolatry.[57]

The Beginning of Wisdom

Job shows us that we do not need to be inundated with information to be useful to the Lord, but rather God blesses those who simply obey what He has revealed to them (Deut. 29:29).

Returning to the narrative, Job seems to anticipate what God would eventually say to him; he mentally blocks out his pain and misery for a moment to utter a song of praise concerning Almighty God's creative power. Job informs Bildad that God hangs the earth on nothing: *"He stretches out the north* [or northern skies] *over empty space; He hangs the earth on nothing"* (26:7). Throughout the centuries philosophers, theologians and scientists have theorized as to how the earth was supported. The ancient Greeks asserted that either Atlas or Hercules shouldered the planet. The Hindu *Vedas* teach that the earth is flat, triangular in shape, and held up on the back of four elephants (perhaps turtles). However, the concept of a free-floating planet hanging in nothingness was a foreign consideration to ancient man, for all objects were witnessed to rapidly fall to the ground if not supported. Job rightly states that God sustains the skies over empty space, hangs the earth on nothing, and that He also gathers up moisture from the earth into the clouds according to His boundaries. This, of course, speaks of the evaporation and condensation of water (26:8-10).

Not only does God control space and the earth hovering in space, but He completely governs all that pertains to the earth also, such as great sea creatures, typhoons, and earthquakes (26:11-13). The *"pillars of heaven"* poetically speak of mountains which seem to hold up the heavens from man's perspective, yet these tremble at God's presence. Job suggested that these incredible evidences of God's power were only meager indications of His overall control of things on, above, and within the earth. God's mysterious rule over all creation could not possibly be comprehended by anyone (26:14). In summary, Job was implying that Bildad had no real understanding of God's mysterious influence in nature or His activities among men.

In chapter 27, Job will contrast his integrity with the judgment of the wicked. Before addressing Zophar's favorite topic, *"the portion of the wicked"* (20:29), Job will again affirm his innocence and that God had unjustly vexed his soul. As long as God lends him breath, he will not utter perverse words or deny his integrity (27:1-4). He seals this pledge with the most common oath in the Old Testament, *"as God lives."* Previously, Job's wife had desired him to curse God and die, but he ignored that request (2:9). He rejected his friends' assessment of his situation (27:5); rather, he had a clear conscience and was ready to stand before God in judgment (27:6). In reality, Job had been denied *due process.* But that is the point of the entire book; God chose to deny Job immediate justice in his circumstances in order to test and refine his faith. The end goal was to gain victory over Satan; this would honor the Lord and bestow blessing to Job. In faith, innocent Job could stand fast and wait for God's deliverance.

In contrast, the wicked (perhaps Job was thinking of his companions), have no hope before God when He ends their existence on earth (27:7-8). Then, it will not matter how powerful and wealthy the wicked have become or how much they cry out to the Lord for mercy; it will be too late (27:9-10). While the wicked did not understand the ways of God, Job knew enough to teach his associates that their empty accusations were wrong; God was not punishing him for evil (27:11-12). The brazen confidence of Job in the Lord, given his dire situation, is amazing. Here is a terribly diseased man, who is approaching death, who sits all alone on an ash pile, and he chooses to talk up his Creator. He has a clear conscience and he knows his God; therefore, he is not budging against the steady undercurrent of false accusations. As shown in the power of the cross, God knows how to righteously deliver those who will trust in Him alone for salvation!

In the remainder of the chapter, Job agrees with Zophar's assessment that God will ultimately punish the wicked, but not necessarily immediately. While it is true that a vile person may die in warfare, by starvation, by a plague, or in a calamity (such as a powerful storm), that was also true for the righteous individual (27:13-21). In either case, whether wicked or righteous, their possessions and wealth pass on to others and are of no assistance in altering divine judgment in the afterlife. God may choose to recompense a wicked person straightaway, but often does not, and the righteous also suffer loss by the sword, famine, pestilence and natural disasters. What is unmistakable is that the wicked cannot escape God's judgment no matter how hard they try, and in this matter the righteous can cheer and rejoice in God's just ways and powerful vindication (27:22-23).

Job was not perfectly correct in all that he said to his friends. Yet, he does teach us that during times of seemingly senseless misery it is profitable to uphold the greatness of God and maintain hope in Him.

The Lord will resolve our difficulties in His timing and for His glory, and in that we can always rejoice!

Meditation

> God delights to increase the faith of His children...I say, and say it deliberately – trials, difficulties and sometimes defeat are the very food of faith...We should take them out of His hands as evidences of His love and care for us in developing more and more that faith which He is seeking to strengthen in us.
>
> — George Muller

Job: Wisdom Is God's Alone
Job 28

In this chapter, Job will extol the priceless value of wisdom. He will continue to build on his assertion that man cannot fully understand God's mysterious and powerful ways. How then could his antagonists claim they comprehended what God was doing in his life? Job then uses a sophisticated illustration of mining to show how man is able to search for ore, precious metals, and gems deep underground, yet cannot discover true wisdom despite all his technological cleverness. The irony of the example is that man will expend all his time and resources to search for what he thinks is precious, but will not venture across the street to obtain the wisdom that God amply and freely provides.

The first eleven verses pose a logical premise for the entire chapter. In this section Job mentions three times that men venture into the earth to discover desirable metals and gems (vv. 1-2, 5-6, 10-11). The remaining part of the chapter then develops two ideas: First, that man searches randomly and blindly for what he deems as precious; however, God knows right were such things are buried thus; God is much wiser than man. Second, understanding this should cause man to seek from God what he cannot purchase or find on his own, despite all his laboring (vv. 13-19); God alone possesses true wisdom (vv. 21-28).

Human ingenuity may find ways of digging shafts into the earth, diverting the subterranean streams, and venture places that no strong beast or keen-sighted bird has ever been (vv. 7-8), yet wisdom cannot be found there. What is Job's point? Man really knows very little about God's doings in creation and how to sequester wisdom. He arbitrarily seeks what has value to him in the earth, but has no idea where it is, and true wisdom is much more elusive – man must come to God to obtain it.

Despite all man's derived knowledge, hoarded resources, and technological developments, he still cannot discover or buy for himself the best treasure of all, wisdom (vv. 12-19). Job will ask two questions twice to emphasize his point and the theme of the chapter: *"But where can wisdom be found? And where is the place of understanding?"* (vv. 12, 20). Job reasons that these two precious virtues cannot be bought with precious metals or gems and cannot be known by the sea, or even the powers of destruction and death; true wisdom must be received from God (vv. 21-23). This is why the Lord Jesus said that *"narrow is the gate and difficult is the way which leads to life, and there are few who find it"* (Matt. 7:14). In fact, the road which leads to salvation was so narrow that only He knew the way: *"I am the way, the truth, and the life. No one comes to the Father except through Me"* (John 14:6). He is God's way and if we want to know God we must come to Him through Christ. Why? Job tells us why: because only God is omnipresent and omniscient (v. 24) and only God is omnipotent over the forces of natures, such as rain and lightning (vv. 25-26). God alone sees, declares, prepares, and searches out all things (v. 27). So, *"Where can wisdom be found?"* The only answer is in God through Christ.

As Job speaks of God's powerful control of nature, he informs us that the air we breathe has weight: *"For He looks to the ends of the earth, and sees under the whole heavens, to establish a weight for the wind, and apportion the waters by measure"* (vv. 24-25). It was not until after Italian physicist Evangelista Toricelli constructed the first barometer in 1643 that atmospheric pressure was measured and understood. Torricelli also noted that small changes in the mercury's height in his barometer directly correlated with changing weather conditions.[58] He had proven what the Bible stated some 3,500 years ago to be true; the air above us exerts a pressure on us because air has mass.

Job concludes that there is only one possible answer to his posed questions: "Only God possesses true wisdom and understanding." In a roundabout way, Job was implying that his friends were void of these. With Solomon-like language (e.g., Prov. 1:7, 9:10), Job sums up what the true nature of wisdom was as pertaining to humanity: *"Behold, the fear of the Lord, that is wisdom, and to depart from evil is understanding"* (v. 28). His associates were thus rebuked for their self-induced and cruel conclusions about Job. If they possessed wisdom, then they would fear the Lord and be still, and refrain from speaking mistakenly on God's behalf. However, we wonder why Job did not consider his own conclusion; if he had, he might have submitted to God's providential dealings (i.e., His mysterious wisdom at work, which is beyond human understanding). How does one know when the fear of God is absent from the human heart? When man's estimation of himself and his self-willed doings increase. The outcome of such primitive pride ultimately results in folly and suffering.

The application of Job's rebuke has far-reaching ramifications, even to us living in the Church Age. Do we speak wrongly about the Lord or teach others something other than what God has said in His Word? Teaching the Word of God is both a tremendous privilege and a great responsibility that ultimately has accountability with God. Regarding this reality, James warned, *"My brethren, let not many of you become teachers, knowing that we shall receive a stricter judgment"* (Jas. 3:1). When a teacher opens the oracles of God to speak, he speaks for God. When an individual perverts the Word of God through traditions of men, vain philosophies, flawed musical lyrics, or by ignorance, he has misrepresented God and slandered God's name. Consider Paul's message to Timothy:

> *If anyone teaches otherwise and does not consent to wholesome words, even the words of our Lord Jesus Christ, and to the doctrine which accords with godliness, he is proud, knowing nothing, but is obsessed with disputes and arguments over words, from which come envy, strife, **reviling**, evil suspicions* (1 Tim. 6:3-4).

"Reviling" in the passage is translated from the same Greek word normally rendered "blasphemy." An individual who teaches, speaks, or sings false doctrine commits blasphemy against God because he or she perverts truth, thus causing God's holiness and perfection to be diminished and/or distorted in the minds of those listening. Job's friends wrongly spoke for God and He will later hold them accountable for their blasphemy, just as He will for everyone who erroneously opens God's Word and misrepresents the Lord (1 Tim. 1:20).

Meditation

> To choose to suffer means that there is something wrong; to choose God's will even if it means suffering is a very different thing. No healthy saint ever chooses suffering; he chooses God's will, as Jesus did, whether it means suffering or not.
>
> — Oswald Chambers

Job: Past Glory and Present Humiliation
Job 29-30

Having concluded his final rebuke of his three companions with unshakable confidence, defense attorney Job anticipating his day in the supreme court of heaven, prepares his closing arguments (Job 29-31). Overcome by nostalgia, Job first reviews his past greatness (Job 29), then he describes his present miserable situation (Job 30), and lastly, he decrees his innocence (Job 31). All this was to apparently convince God that He had acted unjustly against His faithful servant.

Job 29 is one of the great "I" chapters of the Bible (the pronoun being found nineteen times). Ecclesiastes 2 is Solomon's "I" chapter of *self-gratification*. Romans 7 is Paul's "I" chapter of *self-condemnation*. In Job 29, Job engages in *self-glorying*. F. B. Hole explains how this chapter will play an important part in Job's later *self-judgment* and restoration:

> But this chapter records how Job was permitted to let himself go, and sing his own praise, and thus reveal to us the self-righteousness and self-conceit which had lain deep down within him, hidden from all eyes but God's. To bring this to light, and to bring Job himself to judge it, and to judge himself in the presence of God, was the object God had in permitting Satan to bring these extreme testings upon him.[59]

Earlier Job had proclaimed, *"I was at ease, but He* [God] *has shattered me"* (16:12). Job had a happy and prosperous life before God had struck him with an abrupt series of calamities, that took all his wealth, his children, and good health away. Now, months later, Job's intense misery continued without any reprieve (29:2). He reminisces of pleasant days of light and blessing, when he had vast prosperity, his children about him, and when the people honored his leadership and respected his judgments (29:3-11). Those were the days when his God was with him.

Job boasted that he was clothed with practical works of righteousness, and justice was a crown to his head (29:14). He watched over, defended, and supported the weak, the orphan, and the widow against the wicked; this was a tit-for-tat refute of Eliphaz's previous charge (22:6-9). As a brave shepherd, Job had rescued the poor and helpless from the jaws of the wicked who desired them as prey; consequently, Job's goodness was appreciated by all – his benefactors rejoiced in their deliverance (29:12-13, 15-17). Roy Zuck explains that Job fully expected God's abundant blessing to continue (29:18-20): "with his living a long life (days like the sand) of stability (roots), prosperity (dew), and honorable reputation (glory), with perennial strength (pictured by a new bow)."[60] Indeed, God had blessed him, and he had every reason to believe that his fame and affluence would continue until he experienced a peaceful death (i.e., like a bird nestled "in his nest").

How did Job come to this conclusion? Job believed he would have a prosperous and peaceful life because he had used his wealth and influence to help others. Yet, he did not see the fallacy of his own logic. He was connecting God's immediate blessing on earth with his good works, but confronting his friends' view that the wicked were immediately punished for their evil deeds. From a philosophical point of view, both mindsets allow God to be controlled by human behavior, which is obviously not true.

Besides justifying himself before God, Job also further rebukes his three companions: Previous to his calamity, Job's counsel had been welcomed by everyone, his smile refreshed the hearts of the people, like a spring rain to parched ground, and his countenance comforted the mourners (29:21-25). But his miserable comforters had not done so for Job; rather their foolish indictments had only added to his distress.

In contrast to pondering his past glory in chapter 29, Job bewails his present wretched situation in chapter 30. We learn in this chapter that Job was now a social castaway and subject to public mockery and ill-treatment. He no longer held a position of prominence or respect in his community. Rather, he was despised, and even teased by the children of detestable drifters. These men were the outcasts of society and scavenged for their food. Job concluded that these vagabonds were

The Beginning of Wisdom

not even fit to assist his dogs in watching over his sheep, but now their children mocked Job as if he were the scum of the earth (30:1-8). Because he had no strength to protect himself, Job felt threatened by these young urchins who insulted, tripped, and taunted Job; they also blocked his path and spit on him (30:9-15). William Kelly observes that presently Job is more rattled by these juvenile hooligans than by the tart accusations of his three companions:

> There is no reference to his three friends now. He is looking really at this tremendous trial that afflicted his body, and that exposed him to all this disrespect and contempt of the very lowest creatures on the face of the earth.[61]

Besides the emotional pain of being despised and feeling insecure and helpless, Job's physical health was deplorable. He had endured endless days of a painful flesh-rotting disease, but especially during nighttime hours he felt as if a sword was continuously stabbing his bones (30:16-17). He felt that an inordinate power (either speaking of God himself or possibly his disease) had grabbed him by his clothes and thrown him into mire (30:18-19). He was merely dust and ashes. This expression either described Job's ashen (death-like) skin color or referred to the ashes that covered his body. In either case, Job's bodily appearance better resembled a dead corpse than a living person.

After bemoaning his dismal social status and intense ongoing pain, Job mentions that he felt betrayed, neglected, and even attacked by God unjustly (30:20-21). Surely God saw his dreadful plight and his tears: Why had He not answered Job's pleas for help? Rather, God had been like a cruel and powerful tornado destroying all that Job had and even now threatening Job with death (30:22-23). Not only had God raised His hand against him, but his three miserable comforters had further added to his affliction by blindly accusing him of wrongdoing (30:24-25). Previously, Job had wept and grieved with the distraught and he felt he deserved the same type of helpful support from his friends, but instead he was isolated from real consolers and forced to mourn and weep alone (30:26-31).

When Job says, *"My harp is turned to mourning"* (30:31), he means that he was "tuned to mourning" and that was the only kind of music his soul could play. No matter what our troubles might be, if we choose an inward focus, the outcome of depression is inevitable; however, resolving to lift our empty hands heavenward for help and understanding results in peace. Job had trodden the former path in chapter 30, and instead of humbling himself in God's presence, will endeavor to justify himself one final time in the next chapter.

Meditation

> The ashes of his past joys can give no warmth to his poor, comfortless heart today; they can but feed the flame of that pride which burns all the more brightly amid the ruin of its past.[62]
>
> — Samuel Ridout

Job: Self-Justification
Job 31

In his final attempt to prompt God to change His mind, Job issues a solemn oath of innocence with the added weight of a curse clause. "If" he was guilty of any of the supposed crimes he had been accused of doing, he agreed to be intensely punished. Accordingly, the "if guilty, then…" meaning is stated or implied nineteen times in this chapter (e.g., it is found three times in verse 7). Job will rehash eight specific groups of sins or ill motives that his three companions had previously charged him with committing in order to emphatically assert his innocence.

Job begins by declaring that he had not sensually lusted after younger women: *"I made a covenant with mine eyes. Why then should I think upon a maid?"* (v. 1). This is quite a statement of integrity, which doubtlessly few men could honestly proclaim. Job knew that sinners received a heritage of destruction from the Lord (vv. 2-3). Why then would he ever want to burn with lust for another woman and risk experiencing God's displeasure? Like any of us, Job was flesh and blood; he was not saying that he did not have fleshly impulses, but rather he had chosen not to dwell on lustful feelings. He knew that God was watching his every glance and would recompense immoral conduct (v. 4). Job teaches us that lewd behavior is first conceived in the mind as empowered by a lingering look; therefore, he could not afford the "look." Knowing that what he saw would be what he would think about, and could lead him into sin, he chose rather to make a covenant with God to not start the process (Jas. 1:14). David understood the same deadly scenario and vowed: *"I will set no unclean thing before my eyes"* (Ps. 101:3). May we too make a covenant with our eyes not to look on with favor what we know God disapproves of (Rom. 1:32).

Second, Job denied that he had behaved dishonestly with anyone (v. 5). He had used honest scales and was blameless in his business practices; he had not even contemplated being deceitful (vv. 6-7). To further substantiate his innocence, Job was willing to experience total crop failure and to starve if what he was saying was false (v. 8).

Third, not only had Job maintained a pure thought life concerning younger women (vv. 1-4); he adamantly affirms his sexual fidelity also (vv. 9-12). He was not an adulterer, and was completely blameless in his relationship with his wife (v. 9). Job considered adultery to be such a repulsive crime that he vowed that if anyone could prove that he was guilty of such a sin, his wife should "grind" for another man and let her be sexually abused by other men (vv. 10-11). The act of grinding may either have a sexual connotation in agreement with the latter portion of the verse or refer to performing menial tasks, such as grinding grain for another man. Furthermore, if he was guilty of adultery, he believed God would destroy all that he had (v. 12). Given that God knows all things, the only reason Job would readily accept such harsh consequences was that God knew that he was innocent of adultery.

Fourth, Job affirmed the fair handling of his servants (vv. 13-14). Job realized that ultimately he would be accountable to his Creator for the mistreatment of his servants (v. 15). Furthermore, Job discerned that the personage of his servants was just as precious to the Lord as he was, each one being a unique creative act of God in the womb (Ps. 139:13-14).

Fifth, Job directly rebuffs Eliphaz's charge that he had oppressed the poor and neglected the needy (22:7-9; 31:16-23). Job had not hoarded his food, but willingly shared it with orphans, widows, and others in need (vv. 16-18). If Job noticed anyone lacking clothing to keep warm, he supplied wool clothing even if they were unthankful for his generosity (vv. 19-20). Nor had Job abused orphans in the gate of the city (i.e., legal action in court) as he knew that would result in God's ruling against him (vv. 21-23). If he had done so, Job said let his arm fall off, thus, again implying his virtue in the matter!

Sixth, Job addresses the accusations that he had trusted in his wealth (22:24), rather than in the Lord, or had committed the more blatant sin of misplaced devotion – idolatry (vv. 24-28). He had not been enticed to worship false gods or creation itself (i.e., to kiss his hand toward the sun or the moon). With another oath, he denies ever rejoicing in his wealth, or blessing himself for his accomplishments, or engaging in any form of animism, that is, revering creation. Job knew that such offenses would reap God's displeasure.

Seventh, Job denied delighting in the demise of his enemy; in fact, he was known for his hospitality of strangers, not just caring for his own house and servants (vv. 29-32). He validated this statement with another oath and welcomed God's cursing if his declaration was not true. Adam had hid his transgression, but Job had nothing to conceal; surely everyone would already know whether or not Job was a hypocrite; if so, they would have previously scorned him (vv. 33-34). Job never said that he was not a sinner, but rather his sins were not hidden; he had no unconfessed sin as demonstrated by his frequent atoning sacrifices offered to God in chapter 1.

Job felt that no one was listening to his viewpoints; certainly his three companions were not. So, like a defendant in court, Job rests his case, signs his petitions, and asks God, his "Adversary" or "Accuser," to reconsider the evidence and pardon him (vv. 35-36). Job's boldness here is astounding – he actually believed he would refute any incriminating evidence that God might have against him and overturn God's unjust sentence against him (v. 37). Only an innocent believer who knows the character of his God could be so pretentious, or else a delusional man ridden by guilt, but Job's well-articulated arguments defy the latter possibility.

The final charge that Job denies is that he had withheld wages from his servants or put undue hardship upon those he had hired to work his fields (vv. 38-39). Job says that if he were guilty of these offenses, the very ground that his servants labored on would cry out to heaven to accuse Job. To again assert his blamelessness in the matter, Job said that if these accusations were true, let his wheat fields grow thistles and his barley fields produce weeds (v. 40). Obviously, if his whole land was overrun with noxious weeds, Job would lose much more income than he had ever gained by cheating his servants.

Job's long dissertation concludes by silencing his critics and challenging God to break His silence and reconsider His case against Job. However, as shown in Job 1 and 2, God was Job's protector and advocate against spiritual wickedness in high places. Regrettably, Job perceives God's actions wrongly and is incited to defend himself, when no defense was necessary. By vindicating himself through glorying, he has admitted to doing a better job of ensuring justice on the earth than God has. The devil failed to cause Job to directly sin with his lips (1:22), but he was able to use Job's companions to accomplish what he could not, that is, to waste time in unprofitable glorying and to cast doubt on the character of God. We are thankful that these are not Job's final words in the book, for after his humility and brokenness are achieved, the praise of God will constrain his lips.

What application can we derive from Job's response to false accusations? If the devil cannot solicit Christians to sin, he may use someone else to pull them into worthless activities. If we abandon the "best" for the "good," or the "good" for the "permissible," we have erred. For example, if we are lured from our God-sanctioned ministry to defend ourselves against false accusations, Satan gains a victory because the work of God is neglected and the disunity that results is a poor presentation of God's holy character. The lost masses of humanity need to see Christ in His people, not more of what they are accustomed to enduring.

May each believer consider their conduct and be able to look beyond the visible realm to the real battle that is raging in heavenly places. In the balances of eternity, there is much more at stake presently than our creature comforts, our personal rights, our family reputations, or being proven innocent of wrongdoing. It is only through obedience, submission to authority, and brokenness that we experience reviving power and God's protection:

> *For thus says the High and Lofty One who inhabits eternity, whose name is Holy: "I dwell in the high and holy place, with him who has a contrite and humble spirit, to revive the spirit of the humble, and to revive the heart of the contrite ones"* (Isa. 57:15).

> *He who dwells in the secret place of the Most High shall abide under the shadow of the Almighty* (Ps. 91:1).

Hence, every satanic device employed against the believer affords him or her an opportunity to draw near to God and experience the wonder of His fellowship and the power of His deliverance. These wonderful blessings are lost to some degree when we withdraw from the intimate, secret place of the Most High to defend ourselves, or worse, resort to the same debased behavior of our oppressors. Carnality opposed in the flesh can only have one outcome – more carnality: *"the wrath of man does not produce the righteousness of God"* (Jas. 1:20).

The Beginning of Wisdom

In a few chapters, God will make Job aware of his folly and he will repent; may we learn from his experience and not repeat the same error.

But for now Job concludes his emphatic defense – *"the words of Job are ended."* He would not concede his integrity. Job was utterly convinced that everyone was wrong about him, yet, there was something still wrong in Job; it just was not what his friends were saying. Job had taken great pleasure and pride in what the Lord had bestowed to him in grace. Now, when thoroughly challenged by lack, his thoughts centered in what had been lost, rather than to humbly look to the One who had freely provided and abruptly taken away. He should have been filled with wonder, as to why God would have treated any descendant of rebel man with such liberal favor. But Job thought of himself and not of God – this is what we are prone to do in troublesome times.

Meditation

> We all know people who have been made much meaner and more irritable and more intolerable to live with by suffering: it is not right to say that all suffering perfects. It only perfects one type of person – the one who accepts the call of God in Christ Jesus.
>
> — Oswald Chambers

Elihu: Listen to My Anger
Job 32

The ongoing debate which has spanned twenty-nine chapters has exhausted everyone (including us) and can progress no further. Job's associates remain silent after Job's eloquent and prolonged defense, yet they remain unconvinced of his innocence (32:1). God's righteous character has been somewhat slurred by foolish and wordy rhetoric, and the perplexing quandary of Job's suffering remains unresolved. All this to say that the appropriateness of Elihu's entrance at this juncture in the narrative is quite needful and, as Samuel Ridout suggests, even masterful:

> If the book had closed at this point, we would have had more difficulties raised than settled, and unbelief would have lurked among the grand but melancholy shades of the controversy, as it does to this point. On the other hand, if God had spoken directly, revealing Himself in majesty and power, as in the following division, the transition would have been too sudden, and Job's fear of being terrorized by His glory might have been justified. Elihu therefore fits exactly into his place, giving another illustration of the divine authorship and perfection of the book. He addresses ... the moral manifestation of God, the display of His character, thus leading us out of the conflict of human thought on the one side, and preparing us for the right view of the "Faithful Creator" on the other.[63]

Elihu was a younger man who had been present during much or all of the previous discussion, but had remained quiet to show honor to his elders (32:4, 6, 11). He initially thought that *"Age should speak, and multitude of years should teach wisdom"* (32:7), but then concluded, *"Great men are not always wise, nor do the aged always understand justice"* (32:9). Sensing that the four older men were talked out, and being angered by their vain arguments, he decided to respectfully insert

The Beginning of Wisdom

himself into the dialogue (32:5, 15-17). Elihu will answer Job in a different way than his three counterparts had, as he did not feel that it was necessary to waste time countering Job's personal attacks (32:14). This noble resolution was never tested though, as Job did not answer Elihu.

Incidentally, Elihu was a Buzite. Buz was the second son of Nahor, the brother of Abraham (Gen. 22:20-21). This distant family connection with Abraham may explain the monotheistic understanding that all the characters in the story possess. For example, the Midianites were descendants of Abraham and also believed in one God, the Creator of all (Ex. 18:9-12).

The first five verses of this chapter, the only prose in the book other than the Prologue and Epilogue, explains why Elihu was angry and also provides a concise summary of his long-winded speech. Did Elihu have the right to be angry? The answer to this question is, "yes." He was distraught with Job because *"he justified himself rather than God"* (32:2), and he was agitated with Job's three friends *"because they had found no answer, and yet had condemned Job"* (32:3). Elihu, whose name means "my God is He," or "the God of him" will live up to his name. He is the son of *Barachel*, denoting that "God blesses" and God will do just that through this young man's speech.

The more challenging question is what Elihu would accomplish in his anger. Would he resort to the self-exalting behavior of rage (venting unclean anger to feel better) or resentment (internalizing it and becoming bitter)? No, Elihu chose to serve God by his anger and attempt to reprove and enrich the lives of others – he is not internally focused in his behavior. The Greek word translated "indignation" four times in the New Testament is *aganakteo*, which means "to be greatly afflicted or displeased," or in the figurative sense, "indignant." The Lord Jesus experienced this type of anger (e.g., Matt. 20:24; Mark 10:14). In the Old Testament, God has righteous indignation against the wicked (e.g. Deut. 29:28; Isa. 34:2).

To not be angry over the matter of sin – is sin. Hence, Elihu was rightfully angry and also chose to correctly express it through righteous indignation. Anger is an emotion that can lead us into sin, or to honor God and serve others. When our anger is prompted for a present, righteous purpose, such as the righteous provocation of God's character and name, this type of anger has a positive benefit. We do well to heed

Elihu's example and also Paul's instruction, *"Be angry and do not sin"* (Eph. 4:26).

Elihu surmises that Job's friends had not spoken for God, nor had they proven Job wrong; therefore they could not claim to be wise (32:10). Rather, he suggests that they had been poor listeners and had neglected to answer Job's specific statements. Elihu reminds them that only God can accurately reprove Job and defeat his statements (32:13). It is noted that when God reproves Job's friends in Job 42, Elihu's name is never mentioned. As we will see, he was not perfect in his speech, even a bit pompous at times, but his motives for addressing Job and his reflections of God were honorable.

Much of Job 32 is Elihu's own rationale as to why he has the right to speak to his elder brethren and why they should heed his words. Wisdom was not necessarily constrained to years of experience, for Elihu knew that God provided the human spirit with understanding of things hard to naturally comprehend. The young Buzite feels that God has given such insight into Job's trial, and is, in fact, full and ready to explode with a message they needed to hear (32:10, 18-19). He further describes his compulsion to speak: *"the spirit within me compels me"* (v. 18). He refers to the human spirit (the God-conscious part of our being) in verse 8 and God's Spirit, the Holy Spirit, in 33:4 and 34:14. It seems likely then that reference to "the Spirit" in verse 18 is speaking of the Holy Spirit and that his prompting to speak is much more than juvenile enthusiasm. Accordingly, Elihu asks them to listen and to consider his counsel, a specific request that he will make of them eight times throughout his monologue (e.g., 32:10, 17).

He will deliver four consecutive speeches to them in the following five chapters: first message (32:6-33:33), second message (Job 34), third message (Job 35), and fourth message (Job 36 and 37). Each of the final three orations is similar in form, in that Elihu makes an appeal to be heard, followed by a quote from Job's speeches to his friends, and then a rebuke of Job's reasoning. Each of his last three speeches also begins with a similar statement, *"Elihu further answered and said"* (34:1); *"Moreover Elihu answered and said"* (35:1); and, *"Elihu also proceeded and said"* (36:1). Elihu's final message is a declaration of the righteousness and majesty of God, which Job has questioned.

Elihu closes his introductory remarks and this chapter by saying he would remain unbiased in his arguments (as he disagreed with both

The Beginning of Wisdom

positions) and would not resort to flattery to try to win over his hearers (32:20-21). He felt that if he resorted to such carnal tactics while speaking for God, God would severely punish him, even take his life away (32:22).

Indeed, Elihu has a more accurate understanding of Job's situation than Eliphaz, Bildad, and Zophar because he has a clearer and higher concept of God. Their God, though mighty in works, was petty and exacting in His relationship with mankind. Elihu suggests that God is not limited by human reasoning or doings, but is completely true to His holy character. While Elihu rightly reproves Job's friends for misrepresenting God, he does fall short of being a genuine comforter to Job; in fact, he accuses Job of wickedness and folly (34:7-8, 35:16).

Meditation

> The wrath of God is as pure as the holiness of God. When God is angry, He is perfectly angry. When He is displeased, there is every reason He should be. We tend to think of anger as sin, but sometimes it is sinful not to be angry. It is unthinkable that God would not be purely and perfectly angry with sin.[64]
>
> — Stuart Briscoe

Elihu: God's Righteousness
Job 33

Elihu's elaborate approach to gain Job's ear is worthy of consideration. First, he is polite, *"Please, Job, hear my speech, and listen to all my words"* (v. 1). None of Job's three associates ever said "please" while speaking to Job. Second, Elihu addresses Job directly by name three times during his five-chapter discourse (33:1, 31, 37:14) and also refers to Job by name another seven times (e.g., 32:12, 14). In contrast, Job's friends never addressed or referred to him by his given name in any of their speeches. Being able to speak to people by name is a necessary aspect of counseling as it shows that you value them as an individual, that is, he or she has worth as a person. Third, listening demonstrates love, and Elihu had listened patiently to Job and his three companions and considered their dialogues respectfully; he now requests the same courtesy (32:4, 10, 33:2).

Fourth, Elihu takes the high ground of truth and sincerity, instead of a self-exalting and self-defensive posture, which serve to demean the character of God (v. 3). Fifth, the young theologian is no respecter of persons – only God's viewpoint matters and he will not employ carnal means to provoke Job to accept his opinion (32:20-22). Sixth, he assumes no position of prominence over Job, but speaks to him on God's behalf as a concerned equal. Like Job, Elihu was also created by God *"from clay"* and had been given life by His Spirit (vv. 4, 6). Seventh, Elihu respectfully offers Job the opportunity to answer his counsel, even to confront it, if he determines that it is necessary (v. 5).

Eighth, the younger man says he will not browbeat Job, but would be his spokesman before God, so that he can offer his defense without fearing divine retribution (v. 7). Ninth, Elihu repeats back to Job what he thought he had heard Job say, to show that he was listening and to offer further opportunity for clarification (v. 8). Though Eliphaz's first speech began with a conciliatory tone, Job's companions' accusatory speeches were overall void of compassion and appreciation. Elihu

The Beginning of Wisdom

shows us that we must use kindness and respect to gain an audience with those we desire to help to think as God does about the particulars of life.

The junior attorney then replays Job's own words back for him to reconsider. Job had claimed: *"I am pure, without transgression; I am innocent, and there is no iniquity in me. Yet He finds occasions against me, He counts me as His enemy; He puts my feet in the stocks, He watches all my paths"* (vv. 9-11). He will reiterate nearly the same list of statements in the next chapter (34:5-9). Roy Zuck compiled a list of Elihu's quotations of Job either declaring his innocence or God's negligence:

In Elihu's First Speech
33:9a   "I am pure" (6:10, 9:21, 10:7, 12:4, 16:17, 31:6).
33:9b   "Without sin" (13:23, 23:11).
33:9c   "I am clean and free from guilt" (9:20-21, 10:7, 27:6).
33:10a "God has found fault with me" (10:6).
33:10b "He considers me His enemy" (13:24, 19:11).
33:11a "He fastens my feet in shackles" (13:27).

In Elihu's Second Speech
34:5a   "I am innocent [righteous]" (9:15, 20, 27:6).
34:5b   "God denies me justice" (19:6-7, 27:2).
34:6a   "I am right" (27:5-6).
34:6b   "I am guiltless" (10:7, chp. 31).
34:6c   "His arrow inflicts an incurable wound" (6:4, 16:13).

In Elihu's Third Speech
35:2   "I will be cleared by God" (13:18, 23:7).
35:3   "What profit is it to me, and what do I gain by not sinning" (21:15).

In Elihu's Fourth Speech
36:23   "You [God] have done wrong" (19:6-7).[65]

Besides demonstrating Elihu's presence during all the previous discussions, the above list also shows that he was a good listener. Elihu's sticking point was that Job had gone too far in proclaiming his absolute innocence and in blaming God for his unfair treatment. Surely, Job knew that God was much greater than man: Therefore why, should

Job expect God to pause and explain His sovereign dealings in His creation to Job (vv. 12-13)?

The point is well-taken, but in fairness to Job, Elihu's exaggerated claim that Job said he was "without sin" (33:9) is not consistent with the context of Job's statements. Job believed that he was not guilty of any grievous sin deserving such harsh treatment. In an attitude of prayer, Job had asked God: *"How many are my iniquities and sins? Make me know my transgression and my sin"* (13:23) and later acknowledged his righteous lifestyle: *"I have kept His way and not turned aside"* (23:11). This is not the same as proclaiming sinless perfection; Job was merely saying he was guilt-free.

Elihu then asserted that God is much wiser than man, so much so that when He does speak, man is often incapable of perceiving the essence of what He reveals (v. 14). This lack of acuity, of course, was not God's fault, but rather a limitation of man. God even spoke to people in their dreams and nocturnal visions to warn them of the consequences of sin and pride, in an attempt to prevent their untimely and violent demise (vv. 15-18).

God also chastens people through suffering for the purpose of bringing them to repentance and to save them from the pit of death (v. 19). For example, if someone is unable to eat because of a lingering punitive illness, a visiting messenger (a true mediator of God) can turn that person back to the Lord before he or she wastes away (vv. 20-23). *"A messenger"* in verse 23 is derived from the Hebrew word *malak*, which is often rendered "an angel" (as it is translated in the Vulgate). It is likely that a wise person who is rightly representing God's position to an afflicted sinner is in view here, rather than an angelic visitor, though the latter is a distinct possibility.

Penitent sinners can be forgiven by God through an acceptable ransom, though Elihu does not explain what the ransom is or how it could be obtained. In such cases, God is able to relieve their sickness, return them to health, and enable them to have a prosperous life (vv. 24-28). After death, repentance is not possible; there is no ransom that can redeem the soul of the deceased, for *"It is appointed for men to die once, but after this the judgment"* (Heb. 9:27). Paul explains that there is only one way that penitent sinners can be ransomed:

> *God our Savior, who desires all men to be saved and to come to the knowledge of the truth. For there is one God and one Mediator between God and men, the Man Christ Jesus, who gave Himself a ransom for all* (1 Tim. 2:3-6).

Elihu was correct: The sinner only has one path back to God and that is through genuine repentance. But what he did not know was by what means God's anger over all human sin would be once and forever satisfied. This *propitiation* would be later supplied through the judgment of His own Son, the Lord Jesus Christ, at Calvary. Christ's own blood paid the full ransom to save us from a desperate condition and a horrible eternity, which then permits us to be profitable servants and to have fellowship with God.

Considering all the benefits of restoration, Elihu considered God's care to be more protective and instructive than purely punitive (the position of Job's three friends). This was the lesson the Israelites would later learn after Moses led them through the Red Sea and into the wilderness of Shur where they went without water for three days (Ex. 15:22). Why did the Lord lead them into such a harsh wilderness experience? Arthur Pink explains the benefits of such a place to a believer:

> God's purpose in leading His people through the wilderness was (and is) not only that He might try and prove them (Deut. 8:2-5), but that in the trial He might exhibit what He was for them in bearing with their failures and in supplying their need. The "wilderness," then, gives us not only a revelation of ourselves, but it also makes manifest the ways of God.[66]

Such would be the outcome of God's dealings with Israel. Each time God's cloud guided the Israelites into adversity, His grace would overcome it. For instance, when water was finally located at Marah, there must have been great excitement, but then the water was found to be too polluted for human consumption. The situation was desperate, but now disappointment only made it worse. Did the Hebrews cast themselves upon the One who had already demonstrated that He could control an entire sea? No, instead they murmured to Moses, which in reality was a disguised complaint against God.

Moses sought the Lord and He provided a solution: *"the Lord showed him a tree. When he cast it into the waters, the waters were made sweet"* (Ex. 15:25). Once the tree was cast into Marah's water, its bitter taste was replaced with sweetness. Not only was the water made fit for drinking, but it produced a sense of satisfaction and enjoyment in all those that drank from it. It is at this moment that the Lord is introduced as *Yahweh-Rapha,* "The Lord Who Heals," and the scene closes with the Israelites then being led to Elim, a place of abundance (twelve wells) and rest (seventy palm trees). This is the lesson that Job would learn: going on with the Lord through wilderness experiences results in our greater appreciation of God and His abundant blessing and peace.

Many of our failures in life can be attributed to having the wrong view of what a wilderness experience is all about. If new converts would realize that they are destined for disappointments, hardships, and persecution because of their identification with Christ, then every provision of God's grace in the wilderness would be answered with joyful praise. But if the new believer starts out on his or her wilderness journey expecting ease and rest in the world, the relentless hardships to follow will be overwhelming. The mental starting-point, then, for all believers, is Marah, or "bitterness." By expecting bitterness in life, God's supplied grace to overcome each difficulty will just seem all the more *sweet.*

Elihu was correct: In the realm of the living, God afflicts to teach and to warn, not to destroy. For a child of God, such care demonstrates God's unconditional love:

> *My son, do not despise the chastening of the Lord, nor be discouraged when you are rebuked by Him; for whom the Lord loves He chastens, and scourges every son whom He receives* (Heb. 12:5-6).

The young orator has accurately stated what upright Job's offenses were. He has also acknowledged that God often communicates His displeasure and desire for repentance through chastening illnesses, dreams and visions, and through His messengers (vv. 29-30). Why does the Lord graciously do all these things? *"To bring back his soul from the pit"* (v. 30). Alfred Barnes explains the meaning of this phrase: "To

The Beginning of Wisdom

keep him from descending to the grave, and to the dark world beneath. He takes these methods of warning people, in order that they may not bring destruction on themselves."[67] God delights much more in provoking repentance and restoration, than invoking wrath and death (Ezek. 33:11).

Having concisely stated the matter, Elihu pauses to see if Job has anything to say; if not, Elihu instructs him to continue his silence, to listen carefully, and to learn wisdom (vv. 31-34).

Meditation

> Any discussion of how pain and suffering fit into God's scheme ultimately leads back to the cross.
>
> — Philip Yancey

Elihu: Job Rebuked for Challenging God
Job 34-35

In his second lecture, Elihu calls for the attention of Eliphaz, Bildad, and Zophar, whom he respectfully refers to as "wise men" (34:1-2). He challenges them with Job's own words (12:11), that is, to test his words as they would taste food to determine its value (34:3-4). Then, Elihu refers to Job's claim that God had unjustly afflicted a righteous man (34:5-6). The junior prosecutor wrongly sides with Job's three companions in accusing Job of sinning against God, carousing with the wicked, and for declaring that man does not benefit by revering God (which is not what Job actually said; 34:8-9). It should be no surprise, then, that Job drank scorn like water (34:7). While it is true that Job had wrongly accused God of injustice and therefore wondered what advantage there was in living righteously, Elihu goes too far in twisting his statements and accusing Job of fraternizing with evildoers; there was no evidence of that.

Having boldly stated Job's offenses against God, he then seeks to reprove Job of these stated sins. Elihu insists that God is not wicked and does not engage in acts of iniquity or injustice, but rather renders to each man according to his ways; otherwise the earth would be in chaos (34:10-12). Creation cannot function independently from God's watchful care, but rather depends on God's wisdom, power, and consistent pure character. If He chose to withdraw Himself from the earth, *"all flesh"* would perish (34:13-15).

Having shown the necessity of God's fidelity in maintaining creation order, Elihu then shows Job the utter inappropriateness of accusing God of wrongdoing (34:16-17). He uses the example of a lesser authority figure, a king (who is known for his impartiality), to illustrate his point: *"Is it fitting to say to a king, 'You are worthless,' and to nobles, 'You are wicked'?"* (34:18). Obviously, the implied answer to both questions is "no;" how much more absurd is it, then, to condemn the perfectly impartial Master of the Universe (34:19-20)?

The Beginning of Wisdom

Kings do err and reap God's swift judgment, for God is eternal, sees all wickedness, and renders justice on evildoers and delivers those they oppress (34:21-28). But because God is sovereign over His creation, He often renders (from man's limited perspective) judgment through bizarre means and at unseasonable times. Yet, ultimately all wickedness will be reckoned with; evil will not be permitted to continue indefinitely (34:29-30).

God is perfectly righteous and just in all His doings and it is wrong for one of His creatures to accuse Him of acting otherwise. Elihu therefore counsels Job to forbear with his suffering and with God's help choose to look inwardly for what he must learn about himself (34:31-32). Stunned that Job would have the audacity to speak to God so brashly, Elihu instructs Job to stop demanding that the all-wise God behave in a way that he, a sinful man, wanted Him to act (34:33-34). The younger man then punctuates all that he has said by directly charging Job with speaking ignorantly, and being rebellious and sinful in his indictments against God (34:35-37).

Elihu's third oration commences with a twofold reprimand against Job (35:1-3): First, for insinuating that he was more righteous than God in his doings. Second, for concluding that the pursuit of righteousness offered man no advantage because he would suffer for well-doing regardless. Using creation for a reference point, Elihu points out to Job that since the heavens and clouds are affixed above man, surely God, who dwells above the heavens, is much higher than man (35:4-5). The reality of the matter is this: man's failures do not thwart God's purposes, nor do man's righteous doings benefit God; God is independently sovereign regardless of what man does (35:6-8).

The proud do not acknowledge that God is their Maker, or that He has given man more understanding than the animals and birds; therefore God ignores their prayers when they hypocritically call on Him for assistance (35:9-12). A distraught David, on the other hand, knew the consolation of God's "songs in the night" (35:10): *"You are my hiding place; You shall preserve me from trouble; You shall surround me with songs of deliverance"* (Ps. 32:7). Indeed, God does comfort those in distress, if they approach Him with humility and in faith. Building on this point, Elihu concludes the chapter with a lovely devotional thought: Though we do not see God, He is completely aware of each person and his or her difficulties; therefore, we should trust Him and not arrogantly question His goodness (35:13-16).

There is a clear distinction between Job and his four interrogators. Job is settled in his faith to wait on the Lord to resolve his difficulty, but his counterparts want Job to get up and do something. However, there is nothing that Job can do to resolve his traumatic problem. Yes, he is impatient to have the trial over – who wouldn't be. Yet he remains desperate for God to do the fixing! When facing insurmountable difficulties in life, every child of God, must learn that there is only one solution – God.

The only reason believers are permitted to continue living on planet Earth is to bring God glory in the way He deems best (Rev. 4:11). Paul puts the matter this way: *"Let each one remain in the same calling in which he was called. ... Brethren, let each one remain with God in that state in which he was called"* (1 Cor. 7:20, 24). If called to do great feats for God remain faithful to that calling. If called to be sick, be sick for the glory of God. If you are in lack, do without and rejoice in God. If called to suffer in righteousness, then do it all to the glory of God – nothing else matters (1 Cor. 10:31). It is faithfulness to our calling that delights the heart of God, and enriches our own lives as we experience His presence.

Meditation

> Thou, Lord, bruisest me, but I am abundantly satisfied, since it is from Thy hand.
> — John Calvin

> If I had not felt certain that every additional trial was ordered by infinite love and mercy, I could not have survived my accumulated sufferings.
> — Adoniram Judson

Elihu: God's Greatness
Job 36-37

Although Elihu shares more accurate insights about the Lord than his three counterparts did, he does go too far in accusing Job of consorting with wicked people. There is also a tone of self-confidence, even cockiness, that is apparent in some of his words. This high-sounding demeanor is quite evident as he begins his fourth and final speech:

> *Bear with me a little, and I will show you that there are yet words to speak on God's behalf. I will fetch my knowledge from afar; I will ascribe righteousness to my Maker. For truly my words are not false; one who is perfect in knowledge is with you* (36:2-4).

Elihu claimed to have a wide range of insights to share and that he was accurately speaking for God, as compared to Job, who had been talking *"without knowledge"* (34:35, 35:16). Whether or not Elihu was applying the assertion of *"the one who is perfect in knowledge"* to himself (as perfectly enlightened by God) or to God directly is arguable, but obviously only the latter option can be correct.

Regardless, Elihu is a bit high on himself, but since the narrative centers on God's righteous servant Job, there is no record of God rebuking Elihu for his mistaken accusations against Job or his pride. Elihu's behavior should remind us to be very careful when speaking on God's behalf. As previously mentioned, speaking for God (i.e., teaching God's Word to others) is both a prodigious privilege and a great responsibility that ultimately has accountability with God (Deut. 13:1-5; Jas. 3:1).

Siding with Job's three friends, Elihu affirms that an all-powerful God who is perfectly just, impartial, and wise causes the wicked to perish, but preserves and blesses the righteous (36:5-6). Job contended that God does not always bring about the demise of the wicked during their lifetime, but would judge them in the afterlife (20:5-29). He also used himself as an example to show that God does permit the righteous to suffer for reasons that are not always apparent to humanity. Elihu did agree with Job on the latter point. God did permit the upright to be oppressed in His purposes, but would also be faithful to amply restore, care for, and exalt them afterwards (36:7). Eliphaz, Bildad, and Zophar did not believe that this was the case (i.e., suffering was purely punitive, not profitable).

However, a careful evaluation of Elihu's viewpoint will show it to be not that much different than Job's companions: Elihu believed that righteous living guarantees God's blessing in life, in the same way wickedness invokes God's wrath. Only Job is able to contemplate God's retribution for sin and reward for faithfulness beyond the grave.

In verses 8-10, Elihu suggests two reasons why God does afflict His people: First, to rebuke them for being strong in themselves and not Him (i.e., self-sufficient and arrogant); second, to punish them for sinful conduct (36:9-10). Pain gets our attention, and God sometimes uses the cords of affliction to bind His people to their beds for the purpose of instructing them (36:8). Some of us are so busy that it is only by such hardship that God can gain our undivided attention.

Elihu contended that those who repent would be restored, blessed, and enjoy a life of contentment, but rebels will experience God's continuing displeasure and eventually death (36:11-12). Job's three comrades assumed that Job was being punished for secret and unconfessed sin. Job argued that he was innocent and upright and did not understand why God had unjustly forsaken him. Elihu, however, is closer to the truth; he believed that Job's affliction was of the Lord to confront Job's pride and assist him to learn humility.

The same sun that melts wax also hardens clay is Elihu's next point. Some resent divinely appointed troubles and unfortunately do not cry out to God for help, at least with genuine motives; these hypocrites die young and in the company of other perverse people (36:13-14). However, God delivers the poor in spirit who listen and obey the instruction of God's messenger – affliction (36:15). In summary, God's reproof may result in the death of the proud or in the deliverance of the yielding (i.e., those who repent and learn humility). Therefore, Elihu counseled Job not to be preoccupied with what he had lost or the fairness of the trial, but rather on what God was trying to teach him through it (36:16-17). Dear believer, take a moment and solemnly muse

The Beginning of Wisdom

on this exhortation – we often have no control of our circumstances, but we can change our attitude towards them. When we willingly permit God to have access and His way in our lives, we often experience an expedient end to what we are supposed to learn (Rev. 3:20).

God was the only one who could control Job's affliction and He wanted to accomplish much more than just end it; He wanted Job to yield to His instruction and to experience His great deliverance and blessing (36:18-19). Accordingly, Job should not yearn for death as an escape for his situation or try to ignore it by fraternizing with sinners; he needed to confess his pride as sin and apologize for finding fault with God (36:20-21). Elihu accuses Job of wasting precious time. He could end his suffering if, instead of being a hypocrite, he would focus his attention inwardly instead of on external matters, which he could not control anyway. In short, Job was not examining his own heart and learning what God wanted to show him about himself.

To assist Job in diverting his mind to think on essential issues, Elihu speaks of the Lord and His mysterious purposes with such exuberant clarity that we must conclude he is inspired by the Holy Spirit. The remainder of his dialogue lacks misguided notions about Job and ascends into high contemplations of the Lord. The eternal and all-powerful God is independent from all else and thus His ways and judgments are perfect and past finding out; therefore, no creature can instruct the Creator or accuse Him of wrongdoing (36:22-26). If Paul had joined the ranks of this ancient ash-heap fellowship, he probably would have added:

> *Oh, the depth of the riches both of the wisdom and knowledge of God! How unsearchable are His judgments and His ways past finding out! For who has known the mind of the Lord? Or who has become His counselor? Or who has first given to Him and it shall be repaid to him? For of Him and through Him and to Him are all things, to whom be glory forever* (Rom. 11:33-36).

Elihu then describes an example of God's irrefutable wisdom and power as seen in nature – the evaporative cycle by which He maintains the seas and waters the earth (36:27-30). Solomon, Isaiah (40:12, 55:10), Job (26:8), and Elihu all describe the evaporative cycle. Solomon wrote, *"All the rivers run into the sea, yet the sea is not full; to the place from which the rivers come, there they return again"* (Eccl.

1:7). Elihu declares, *"For He draws up drops of water, which distill as rain from the mist, which the clouds drop down and pour abundantly on man"* (36:27-28). The hydrologic cycle was not discovered until the late seventeenth century when Pierre Perrault and Edme Marriotte proved that rainwater was sufficient to sustain river flow and Edmond Halley further demonstrated that oceanic evaporation supplied the moisture for rain clouds which supplied river waters.[68] Science has again verified what the Bible described as part of God's creation order thousands of years ago.

Elihu continues to speak of God's awesome nature by describing His handiwork as evidenced in the lightning of a fierce thunderstorm (36:31-33). These creation references are to remind Job of how majestic God is and also how wrong it would be to allege that such a great God was inconsistent (i.e., to have an unjust or malicious character). God's people cannot fully understand His providential care during times of hardship, but they can become more aware of His abounding grace in overcoming them (1 Cor. 10:13).

Continuing to expose the realms of nature as further evidence of God's awesome majesty, Elihu describes the various weather events that are under His sovereign control: gentle rain, downpours, lightning, tornadoes, snowfall, clouds, sunshine, etc. (37:1-5). God's incomprehensible control of the weather demonstrates that He governs man and beast, who can only anticipate what may happen or simply react the best way they can to what does happen. Examples are extreme temperatures, drought, flooding, snowstorms, tornadoes, etc. (37:6-13). Of course, this all points to man's desperate need for God's mercy: *"He causes it to come, whether for correction, or for His land, or for mercy"* (37:13). This is the only time the word "mercy" is found in the book of Job; its usage here is a fitting introduction to God's solution to Job's problem in the following chapters.

The climax of Elihu's dissertation on the majesty of God is his direct appeal to Job: *"Listen to this, O Job; stand still and consider the wondrous works of God"* (37:14). Then, through a barrage of questions Elihu integrates Job's knowledge of nature to demonstrate that he actually knows very little of how God maintains His creation (37:14-23). How were the clouds formed and the skies laid out? Why did he get hot when wind blew from the south? These questions are a preface to the more challenging interrogation Job will receive from the Lord (chp. 38-41). All of which is to prove to Job that he is utterly ignorant of such things. Given Elihu's two dozen references to thunder, lightning, rain, and clouds in Job 36 and 37, one must wonder if there was a storm brewing as the young orator spoke to Job. Perhaps the cracks of thunder and peels of lightning were announcing the Lord coming to personally speak to Job from a whirlwind in the next chapter.

Verse 24 ends Elihu's fourth speech and is not only a concise conclusion of all that he has said, but also provides Job a final challenge: *"Therefore men fear Him; He shows no partiality to any who are wise of heart."* Job could not genuinely revere God, the supreme Creator, if there were self-conceit and pride residing in his heart. God is infinite, and man is finite; how dare Job accuse God of wrongdoing and cast doubt on His holy character! Job remains silent; he does not respond to Elihu's charge with self-vindication as he had previously done with Eliphaz, Bildad, and Zophar.

Perhaps this meant that God had reached Job through the young orator's words and that Job was at least in partial agreement. The Lord Himself visits Job in the next chapter, and furthers the same line of thought-provoking questions that Elihu has initiated in this chapter. This timing suggests that Job's disposition to defend himself had softened and that he was now willing to peer inward as to what the Lord might be teaching him about himself. Roy Zuck provides this concise overview of Elihu's message to Job:

> God's justice should not be questioned or His sovereignty challenged, because His ways are beyond human understanding. According to Elihu, calamities can serve to remove pride and to protect people from more grave difficulties. God, then, is to be worshipped, and not criticized; He is to be extolled, not examined.[69]

Elihu did not perfectly speak for God, as he did accuse Job of associating with the wicked, which suggested that some part of Job's suffering may be for sin. However, Elihu believed the main reason for Job's suffering was educational – Job had pride in his heart that needed to be revealed and repudiated. It is doubtful that any of us have a blameless and upright life that would cause God to boast before Satan, as He did for Job. From a practical standpoint, this means that if God was willing to further refine Job, none of us is exempt from God's instructional care. Elihu had many good things to say, but only God knew perfectly what Job's suffering was all about and only He could help His servant make sense of it.

These are school days for believers, and God will not be satisfied until we bear the moral image of His dear Son (Rom. 8:29). Until we think and act like Christ, affliction is inevitable, and as we do progress in Christ-likeness, suffering is inescapable (2 Tim. 3:12). Why then should believers be surprised by persecution, calamities, illness, and death? There is no escape from hardship, that is, until we are with the Lord (1 Pet. 1:13). Until then, let us remember that apart from His faithful control, suffering in life would be a most miserable existence.

Meditation

> The deep meaning of the cross of Christ is that there is no suffering on earth that is not borne by God.
>
> — Dietrich Bonhoeffer

> The servant of Christ must never be surprised if he has to drink of the same cup with his Lord.
>
> — J.C. Ryle

The Lord: The Divine Interrogation
Job 38:1-38

The Lord Himself personally speaks to Job from a powerful whirlwind; such an ominous presentation signified divine judgment. God would now hold Job accountable for his arrogant, self-justifying accusations against Himself (v. 1). Many of the Old Testament prophets described God's awesome presence or judgment, as a tornadic wind (e.g. Isa. 66:5; Jer. 23:19; Ezek. 1:4). To demonstrate His tremendous power before a depressed Elijah, God used such a wind that ripped rocks to pieces (1 Kgs. 19:1). At the end of his ministry years later, the Lord lifted up Elijah into heaven by a whirlwind (2 Kgs. 2:11).

It is strangely ironic that God's presence is suddenly made known to Job in the same type of mighty wind that previously caused the deaths of all his children (1:18-19), the difference being that God now personally communicates with Job out of the storm. The scene before us is quite unusual; generally speaking people do not continue to suffer in the Lord's presence without experiencing His healing or deliverance. On this point, D. L. Moody observes:

> The only man who ever suffered before Christ was that servant who had his ear cut off. But most likely in a moment afterward he had it on, and very likely it was a better ear than ever, because whatever the Lord does, He does it well. No man ever lost his life with Him.[70]

In keeping with the biblical precedent, Job will not be permitted to suffer much longer, for he is in God's presence. We are most confident that it is God's utmost desire to refine and bless His upright servant Job. The windstorm of Job 1 brought ruin, death, and grief, but this tempest (Job 38-41) will result in Job's repentance, restoration, and abounding joy. Notice that it is not an abstract God who is speaking with His servant, but "the self-existing" One. *Jehovah* has personally appeared to represent His authority in relationship to Job. Except for one reference pertaining to His power over creation (12:9), His personal name, as known to Israel, has not appeared in the narrative since chapter 2.

Given the previous thirty-five chapters of exhausting strife, the Lord's words were welcome relief to Job, even if commencing with a rebuke, *"Who is this who darkens counsel by words without knowledge?"* (v. 2). The Lord then tells Job to brace himself like a man for His questions (v. 3). Standing upright in a tornadic wind would further hinder Job's ability to stand before God in his own efforts; perhaps this physical drama was a part of the spiritual lesson God had for Job.

Job had accused God of being unjust (9:17, 32:2) and unwise (23:3-7, 31:35-37) in dealing with him, so God will now take the place of the inquisitive student and ask Job for instruction. This, of course, is the irony of the dialogue – an obvious scolding of Job's foolish claims. If Job, in his own wisdom, cannot fathom the creation of the world, what right does he have to accuse the One who does have such knowledge of being unwise? Job will not get his requested opportunity to cross-examine God; rather, it will be God that will demand answers from Job. William MacDonald surmises God's interrogation of Job:

> In the questions that follow, God does not give a detailed explanation of the mystery of suffering. Instead He ranges through the universe to give glimpses of His majesty, glory, wisdom, and power. He is saying, in effect, "Before you take it on yourself to criticize My ways, you should ask yourself if you could manage the creation as well as I do." This, of course, can only show Job how powerless, ignorant, insignificant, inadequate, incompetent, and finite he is.[71]

The narrative holds much more significance and urgency than we have previously observed. No longer will we endure the arguments of little men hammering on each other with their puny observations and insights, but rather precise truth as spoken by the unlimited God of the universe. Yet, we wonder why the Lord did not provide clarity on the matter of human suffering and why wickedness was permitted in the world. Why didn't God disclose His previous discussions with Satan to Job, to show that his suffering had a purpose beyond himself? True, the situation glorified God, but that was not the primary benefit to Job from

The Beginning of Wisdom

his ordeal, concludes James Catron: "It was not so important that Job know *why* he was suffering as it was that he learn *how* to suffer. God wants humble submission to Him in every situation in life."[72] Trusting and rejoicing in the Lord, even when it does not make sense to do so, is evidence of true submission. It is this type of active faith (which defies human reason) that pleases the Lord (Heb. 11:6). God's merciful rebuke of four chapters is further proof that Job is a true child of God in good standing with Him. The writer of Hebrews reminds us:

> *My son, do not despise the chastening of the Lord, nor be discouraged when you are rebuked by Him; for whom the Lord loves He chastens, and scourges every son whom He receives* (Heb. 12:5-6).

No true child of God should be a stranger to His chastening hand, for as we will soon see, it is an expression of His eternal love for His children, those His Son bled and died for.

But Job has not reached the spiritual apex of unspotted faith, yet. Hence, Jehovah stoops down to the earth to confront His beloved servant: *"Where were you when I laid the foundations of the earth? Tell Me, if you have understanding. Who determined its measurements? Surely you know!"* (vv. 4-5). These were not questions demanding answers, but to prompt reverent humility. For what man dare answer God anything about His wisdom or doings? Was Job present when the world began? No. Therefore the eternal God, who was, obliges Job with a brief summary before interrogating him on matters of oceanography, meteorology, cosmology, and astronomy.

First, He created the spiritual realm of principalities, powers, and angels. *All* the "sons of God," referring to angelic beings (including Lucifer), shouted for joy when God laid the foundations of the world (vv. 6-7). He brought time and space into existence to form the beginning of what we see, hear, smell, taste and touch. Even *"the morning stars,"* perhaps a poetic personification of Mercury, Venus, and Mars, rejoiced in the beginning of the material world. If all creation groans because of the consequences of sin, then there should be no quandary as to why creation, in its perfection, should acclaim God's glory (Rom. 8:20-21).

Devotions in Job

Expressly referring to the birthing process, the Lord describes the beginning of oceans, seas, and lakes as a baby coming forth from the womb into the world. He fixed boundaries (coastlines) in order to cradle the infant water in its proper place and shrouded it with a covering of clouds (vv. 8-11). Furthermore, God controlled the light cycle of day and night, noting that the wicked are dispersed from their evil doings in the darkness by the dawning sun (vv. 12-15).

Job had questioned God's wisdom for permitting his distress, so, through a series of questions God was going to teach Job about divine sovereignty. In verse 16, God inquires, *"Have you entered the springs of the sea?"* (Job 38:16). These oceanic springs were not discovered until Matthew Fontaine Maury demonstrated their existence in the eighteenth century. However, firsthand proof did not exist until 1977, when Lewis Thomas (*The Medusa and the Snail*) documented that scientists had found springs in the ocean floor off the coast of Ecuador, at a depth of 1.5 miles. It is estimated that 40 cubic miles of hot water pours into the Earth's oceans each year from these oceanic vents – "hot springs."[73] Obviously, Job had not entered these springs; in fact, he did not know of them, but God did and had complete control over them. The point being that if God had complete control over the oceans and their springs, how could Job question God's dealings concerning one man?

God controlled the day and night, but suggested through questions that Job could not even follow the sun to see where it went after setting, or where the darkness resides after the sun rises in the morning (vv. 19-21). Job had a limited exposure to the solar cycle; he had no idea how the earth rotates around the sun or that the earth spins on its axis. Using irony, the Lord infers that surely the all-wise Job knew about such matters: *"Do you know it, because you were born then, or because the number of your days is great?"* Of course Job was not eternal but had a distinct birth (a beginning), so God was affirming that Job was not present when He set the earth into motion. Nor did Job have any idea as to how God caused rain, frost, ice, snow and hailstones to fall, dispensed lightning, or instigated different wind directions (vv. 22-30).

God then turns His attention to the celestial bodies and poses this question to Job: *"Can you bind the cluster of the Pleiades, or loose the belt of Orion?"* (Job 38:31). We now understand what God was sharing with Job. Within the Taurus constellation is a tight grouping of stars in gravitational lock; they are called "Pleiades." Although many stars are in this cluster (about 440 light years away), only seven are discernable with the naked eye on a clear night; sometimes these are referred to as the "seven sisters" or "seven stars" (e.g., Amos 5:8). Just as the Bible states, these stars are bound together; they cannot pull apart from one another. However, the constellation Orion is composed of stars throughout our galaxy, and we know that the Milky Way is expanding. As the years roll by, Orion's belt is literally *letting out a notch*. The answer to God's question to Job was that only God can arrange and control the constellations in such a way that He binds some stars together and loosens others.

Maintaining all the celestial bodies in their proper order was a greater task than just sustaining the earth, so God challenges Job to accomplish some minor terrestrial feat, like calling down lightning or causing it to rain where needed. This request and all the illustrative questions in this chapter were to prove to Job that God had not abused His power and authority, but rather perfectly controlled all things. Job knew nothing about the creation of the world or the management of it. Therefore, it was absurd for such a finite being to charge the One who is sovereign over all things with mismanagement of his life.

In the final three verses of Job 38 and the next chapter, God transitions from questioning Job about inanimate creation to creatures in the animate world.

Meditation

> Let us not be surprised when we have to face difficulties. When the wind blows hard on a tree, the roots stretch and grow the stronger. Let it be so with us. Let us not be weaklings, yielding to every wind that blows, but strong in spirit to resist.
>
> — Amy Carmichael

The Lord: God's Sovereignty Confirmed
Job 38:39-39:30

God has quizzed Job about the dawning of creation and the order established then which continues to govern all things. The Lord has shown His rule over celestial bodies and terrestrial elements, and will directly address His providential care of living creatures.

Interestingly, God did not begin by asking Job how old the earth was, as not even Scripture reveals the answer to that quandary. Biblically speaking, we do know that the earth, as it pertains to man, began a few thousand years ago and was created in six literal days (Gen. 1). What existed before then – we are not told and should not waste time arguing about.

So far, the Lord has probed the disciplines of oceanography, meteorology, cosmology, astronomy; He now will test Job's knowledge of biology. The Lord's further interrogation of Job will demonstrate His perfect design for various creatures and His ability to sustain them in their diverse earthly habitats. His representative list of creatures includes:

- Six animals: the lion, the deer, the wild mountain goat, and the wild donkey (or onager), the ox, and the horse (38:39-41, 39:1-12, 19).
- Five birds: the raven, ostrich, stork, hawk, and eagle (39:13-18, 26-30).
- One insect: the locust (39:20-25).

The Lord provides for the lions in their dens and the raven with its young. Job certainly did not hunt prey to feed even one lion, let alone all lions; lions were dangerous, so he wisely kept clear of them. God programmed each creature with instinctive protocol to ensure procreation and propagation. He alone knows all the intricate details of their gestation periods, birthing habits, migratory patterns, etc. – Job had no understanding of these things (39:1-4).

Some animals were designed to be domesticated and serve man (e.g., horses), and others to roam free, such as the wild ox who could not be trusted to pull a plow or cart (39:9-12) and the wild donkey, which roamed free in the wilderness searching for any green thing to eat (39:5-8). The point being that by design, the Lord is able to sustain wild donkeys even in a wasteland environment.

The diversity of God's design in creation is self-evident. The ostrich, for example, has an unusual wing design which does not enable it to fly, and she lays her eggs in vulnerable places on the ground, yet, despite her apparent foolishness towards her young, she can still outrun a horse and its rider (39:13-18).

The horse, which snorts with terror, is quite different than the ostrich, or the locust which is easily frightened (39:20). The war horse is a powerful animal that can cover vast distances swiftly; it bravely charges into battle despite the clashing of combatants, the blasting of trumpets, and the sights of glittering spears and javelins (39:19-25). The Lord then speaks of the migratory patterns of the hawk, which He prompts to fly south. Furthermore, He taught the eagle to fly, to nest in rocky crags, to spy out prey from a distance, and to teach its young to hunt for food in the same way (39:26-30).

God's majestic wisdom is obvious in all these matters of life – God's creation is well-ordered and cared for by its Designer and Sustainer. But since Job had accused God of being unwise in dealing with him, God sarcastically asks Job, *"Have you given the horse strength? Have you clothed his neck with thunder [a mane]?"* (39:19). *"Does the hawk fly by your wisdom, and spread its wings toward the south? Does the eagle mount up at your command, and make its nest on high?"* (39:26-27). Job is speechless and rightly so! God will conclude His first speech to Job in the first two verses of the next chapter, in the same way He began, with a rebuke and a challenge.

Meditation

It is important to receive God's arrangement in the circumstances. This arrangement is the discipline of the Holy Spirit. To escape God's arrangement just one time is to lose an opportunity to have our capacity enlarged. A believer can never be the same after passing through suffering.

— Watchman Nee

The Lord: More Questions
Job 40-41

The Lord finishes His first dialogue with Job with a rebuke and a challenge: *"Shall the one who contends with the Almighty correct Him? He who rebukes God, let him answer it"* (40:2). The "one who contends" refers to Job. He had previously said that God contended with him (10:1-2, 23:6), but paradoxically God turns Job's words around on him – in reality, he was the one contending with God. Since Job had charged God with wrongdoing, he should now answer God's questions, if he is so wise and awesome.

After listening to the barrage of questions to challenge his bold assertion (i.e., that God lacked wisdom in his situation), Job utters a brief response: *"Behold, I am vile; what shall I answer You?"* (40:4). In his previous self-confidence, Job had invited God to summon him to His courtroom so he could defend himself and be acquitted (10:2, 13:22). However, after learning of his own insignificance before the Master of creation, a more contrite Job acknowledges that he is incapable of defending himself before God. He will go no further in doing so, but rather will place his hand over his mouth and remain silent (40:5).

Meekness and silence are not the same as repentance and restoration, so the Lord will fire another volley of questions at Job in a second speech. If the Lord is not satisfied with anything less than genuine repentance and repudiation of sin, then we should not be either. Remorseful crying or regretful outcome is not the same as accepting full responsibility for one's wrong behavior. For example, the tears of profane Esau were misleading: He was sorry that he lost the birthright blessing, but not for his petty view of it earlier when he sold it for one meager meal when he was hungry (Heb. 12:16-17). Those counseling a wayward believer must be motivated by genuine love (i.e., what is in the best interest of that individual). Embracing an appeal of sympathy apart from reason will often leave us holding hands with the devil. If we neglect dealing with the true reality of the situation, we effectively diminish God's favor and blessing on the outcome.

Thankfully, the Lord knew Job's heart and that there was more to be accomplished. He likewise knows what is within us; consequently, on this side of glory, all believers are works in progress. But we have an incredible advantage that Job did not – the revealed Word of God and the indwelling Spirit of God to affirm, guide, and convict us of what attitudes and behavior please the Lord.

The Lord, again speaking from a whirlwind, repeated verbatim His former challenge to Job to brace himself like a man and to answer His questions (vv. 6-7). Having already dealt with Job's claim that He lacked wisdom, God now takes up Job's assertion of His injustice, even asking Job, *"Would you condemn Me that you may be justified?"* (v. 8). The reality being that Job had carelessly accused God of acting imprudently to justify himself. Jim Catron outlines the main points of the Lord's second message to Job and explains God's satire and objective:

> So in ironical language, God challenged Job to play God for a day (40:8-14): "Let us see how you will handle the governing of the world." Job must clothe himself with divine attributes and assume divine power (40:9-10). Job was challenged to fulfill the ministry of a judge, of humbling the proud and destroying the wicked. If he could do this successfully, then God would confess that Job is self-sufficient (40:11-14). To narrow it down, God said, "Let's see what you can do with just two animals, the Behemoth (40:15-24) and the Leviathan (41:1-34)." Why, Job doesn't have either the strength or the wisdom to govern these two animals, let alone the universe. Job's inability to govern the universe makes him inadequate and unable to criticize God's actions as ruler either of the universe or of Job personally (9:17).[74]

The Lord wondered if a mortal, like Job, had a strong enough arm to contend with Him (v. 9). Was Job able to arm wrestle the Creator of the universe and win? Absolutely not! How reasonable then was it for Job to suggest that God had abused His power and authority? For someone to get their own way by opposing another person meant that they were at least equal or better than the other person. The Lord reminds Job that he has no such equality and therefore cannot do the great things that He does.

Job had questioned God's punishment of the wicked, so the Lord asks Job if he is able to properly punish the wicked (40:11-13). If he could, then Job could adorn himself with majesty and splendor, and array himself with glory and beauty and he would have God's esteem. But, if that were the case, should not Job be able to save himself from adversity (vv. 10, 14)? The point being that anyone powerful enough to legitimately resist God should be able to take care of his own problems.

The remainder of God's second message to Job centers in the discussion of two of His creatures: the behemoth (40:15-24) and the leviathan (Job 41). These were not mythical, but rather living animals that God had made. Rather than asking Job to play God and control all the planets and the stars, He greatly minimizes the assessment test: "Job, here is your opportunity to prove your power: just control these two animals, if you can!" William MacDonald summarizes what we know about the first animal, the behemoth, from the text:

> God presents the behemoth as the first of His ways, that is, as Exhibit A in the animal kingdom. Although we cannot identify it with certainty, we know that it is herbivorous, amphibian, and exceedingly powerful. It rests in shady, marshy areas and is not easily intimidated. ... The behemoth is sometimes identified with the hippopotamus, and some translations, such as the Louis Segond translation in French, actually put that animal in the text. But by no stretch of the imagination can the hippopotamus be called "the first of the ways of God" – an elephant or mammoth might merit that epithet, but hardly a hippo. ... Some Christian scientists are now convinced that the behemoth must be an animal now extinct, or perhaps found in some remote parts of the African jungle. In fact, a reptile of the dinosaur type does fit the description very closely.[75]

Certainly, the short stubby tail of the hippo hardly aligns with the description of the behemoth's tail, which is *"like a cedar"* (40:17), nor does the hippo's size merit the accolade that it *"drinks up a river"* (40:23). Since there is not such a creature known to be alive on earth today, the behemoth probably went extinct long ago. Nonetheless, Job knew of this enormous brute among God's creatures and agreed that he could not control it.

Since Job could not best the behemoth, the Lord lessens the challenge a bit more by asking Job if he can at least control the leviathan (Job 41). Where the behemoth was primarily a land-dwelling creature, the leviathan is mostly aquatic. The identity of this creature is also debated, but given its description, many believe that it is a reptile and probably a Nile crocodile. He is too strong to catch with hook and line (41:1-2) and his armor-like exterior is resistant to harpoons and spears (41:7, 15-17). The leviathan cannot be tamed and made into a household pet, nor sold as merchandise since he is seldom captured, and furthermore, he is not considered a delicacy to eat (41:3-6). The very sight of this fierce beast discourages anyone from meddling with him (41:8-9).

The Lord abruptly interrupts His description of the leviathan to ask a pertinent question of Job and, in application, of humanity in general: *"No one is so fierce that he would dare stir him up. Who then is able to stand against Me? Who has preceded Me, that I should pay him? Everything under heaven is Mine"* (41:10-11). This is the main point of God's second message: If Job is unable to vanquish even a fellow creature, how much more ludicrous is it for him to aspire to be wiser and more powerful than his Creator, who controls all His creatures? If Job respected and feared the leviathan, which he could not govern, how much more should he revere and be in awe of the eternal God who made the leviathan.

In His first message, God began by speaking of His control over the timid and non-threatening creatures, such as deer and ravens, but he concludes His second speech by choosing powerful and terrifying creatures to better illustrate His own majesty and splendor. Returning to the description of the leviathan, we learn that he is a powerful beast with armor-like scales; his mouth is a vise and his sharp teeth are vicious (41:12-17).

The Lord describes the eyes, mouth, and nostrils, and even the sneezes of the leviathan with poetic language to better depict his terrifying appearance (41:18-25). Because of the leviathan's stout protective exterior, even the strongest hunters with their metal swords, darts, and spears would not dare to confront him (41:26-29). The underside of the leviathan is so jagged that when it traverses through the mud it leaves a trail similar to the spikes of a threshing sledge (41:30). When aroused, the leviathan whips the water into a boiling pot of fury which then dissipates into a foamy wake (41:31-32). The Lord says that *"on earth there is nothing like him, which is made without fear"* (41:33). Besides the leviathan's fearless nature, a hyperbolic tribute is employed in the last verse to emphasize the beast's supremacy in the wild; he is called *"king over all the children of pride"* (41:34).

Job obviously could not control the behemoth or the leviathan; therefore, he had no righteous claim to challenge God's justice in ruling over His creation. Thankfully, Job's response to this second message is one of complete repentance; he acknowledges God's comprehensive sovereignty over everything (42:1-6). God had accomplished what He desired in Job's life and, thankfully, the trial was over. It was now time to restore, heal, refresh, and bless His upright servant Job.

Meditation

> The breaking of the alabaster box and the anointing of the Lord filled the house with the odor, with the sweetest odor. Everyone could smell it. Whenever you meet someone who has really suffered, been limited, gone through things for the Lord, willing to be imprisoned by the Lord, just being satisfied with Him and nothing else, immediately you sense the fragrance. There is a savor of the Lord. Something has been crushed, something has been broken, and there is a resulting odor of sweetness.
>
> — Watchman Nee

Job's Confession, Prayer, and Blessing
Job 42

Job is utterly overwhelmed by God's intense interrogation. He has had enough! He has come to the end of himself. After the Lord concluded His first discourse, Job confessed his own finiteness and agreed not to challenge the Lord further (40:3-5). But that was not far enough. Job was not yet repentant, so God continued to question him. In this chapter, Job confesses not only his low position before God, but also God's complete sovereignty: *"I know that You can do everything, and that no purpose of Yours can be withheld from You"* (v. 2).

The Lord had begun His dialogue by asking, *"Who is this who hides counsel without knowledge?"* In response to this question, Job readily admits that he did not have knowledge of things too wonderful for him to comprehend (vv. 3-4). Previously, Job had heard about the Lord, but His appearance and words had overwhelmed him and brought him to utter brokenness: *"Therefore I abhor myself, and repent in dust and ashes"* (vv. 5-6). Job now valued fully both the greatness and the mercy of God. God had demonstrated how much He valued Job by personally visiting him and reproving him in holy love, despite the cares of the universe. The months of perceived futility produced its desired fruit of repentance (7:3). The fact that Job was willingly broken before the Lord – that his heart had the capacity to be penitent rather than bitter and resentful – proves that his standing with God was never in question. He was not a hardened sinner as his friends conjectured, but a pliable believer homeward bound.

God's lengthy dialogue with Job lasted four chapters; in contrast, His reprimand to Eliphaz for misrepresenting Him was terse and blunt:

> *My wrath is aroused against you and your two friends, for you have not spoken of Me what is right, as My servant Job has. Now therefore, take for yourselves seven bulls and seven rams, go to My servant Job, and offer up for yourselves a burnt offering; and My servant Job shall*

pray for you. For I will accept him, lest I deal with you according to your folly; because you have not spoken of Me what is right, as My servant Job has (vv. 7-8).

This rebuke was assigned to Bildad and Zophar also. All three men were to present their burnt offerings before Job, the one that they had brutally afflicted with their erroneous and self-exalting counsel. They had sought to defend God, but God now puts them on the defensive and only Job's mediation can save them. This demonstrated that Job, the one they had pitilessly attacked and accused of wrongdoing was highly esteemed and accepted by God.

Our carnal minds enjoy envisioning the humiliation of these three men: making that long journey while leading their animals for sacrifice and then having to present themselves on bended knee before Job to beg for his forgiveness. We think, "You proud, self-righteous, ignorant men – you deserve much worse – you are getting off easy." But then we remember how many times we have pointed the same Pharisaical finger at others without discerning proper motives or knowing the facts. Thank God for His mercy and thank God for giving saints the will to pray for us even after we have hurt them. Job did pray for his three friends, though they never once prayed for him. Through Job's intercession, God's judgment against them was averted. At the same time that his friends were forgiven, Job was also cured of his gruesome and debilitating disease. The fact that Job was healed when he prayed for those who had hurt him demonstrates a valuable principle for the Lord's people to heed, one that Abraham himself also learned.

In Genesis 20, Abraham prayed to God for Abimelech's healing, and God answered Abraham's prayer – He removed the Gerarites' inability to have children. An amazing thing transpired as Abraham prayed for those who had mistreated him – he experienced healing also. When God opened the wombs of Abimelech's women, he also opened the womb of Sarah. This is the same wondrous discovery Job experienced: *"And the Lord restored Job's losses when he prayed for his friends. Indeed the Lord gave Job twice as much as he had before"* (v. 10). Do you want emotional healing in your life? Pray for those who persecute you, forgive (release) them of their wrongs against you, and you will set a prisoner free only to realize that you were the one taken captive by your own hardened heart.

The Lord taught, *"If ye forgive men their trespasses, your heavenly Father will also forgive you; but if ye forgive not men their trespasses, neither will your Father forgive your trespasses"* (Matt. 6:14-15). In light of the debt of sin we have been forgiven by God, how can we not extend to others our forgiveness for lesser offenses (Eph. 4:32)? To forgive (i.e., to release to God's control) liberates the heart for free expression of love through service again. Those who hold grudges must realize that the root of bitterness that is festering in their own heart will affect every relationship they have, including their fellowship with the Lord.

The Lord again taught, *"Love your enemies, bless them that curse you, do good to them that hate you, and pray for them which despitefully use you, and persecute you"* (Matt. 5:44). Have you ever tried to pray to God while you were angry? It doesn't work. As we pour our hearts out to the infinite Creator, our hearts become humbled and softened. Prayer is transforming! We may start by asking the Lord to "stomp 'em," but as we continue to pray, we are overtaken by the hurt and pain that the offending party is inflicting on themselves, their family, the Church, and Christ. Suddenly, our pain does not seem so great when looking at the big picture. Next time you are offended by someone, try praying for them – prayer really softens the unforgiving heart. Then, as in the day of your salvation, the healing that comes with forgiveness will be yours afresh.

Furthermore, when Job prayed for his friends, the Lord restored Job himself. In the process of time he had twice as many sheep, camels, oxen, and female donkeys as Job previously possessed (vv. 10, 12). Job had lived an isolated and miserable existence without comforters; now all Job's kin and friends fellowshipped with him; each one brought gifts of silver and gold to Job to demonstrate their appreciation and love for him (v. 11). We might wonder where they were before, when Job needed them most. Whatever the reason for their neglect, they now knew that Job was approved of God and the power of God rested on him. It is not likely that all these thousands of animals just suddenly popped out of the ground one morning, but rather Job used the gifts of his family and friends to purchase the livestock he needed. Truly, Job's wealth was found in those who loved him.

It is the same for believers in the Church Age. For every person who persecutes a believer, the Lord promises that there will be a

The Beginning of Wisdom

hundred more to lend him or her a helping hand (Matt. 19:29). Christian love is a powerful weapon against the enemy, for it practically conveys the gospel message to the lost. The Lord Jesus told His disciples: *"By this all will know that you are My disciples, if you have love for one another"* (John 13:35). The love of the saints is a rich heritage; may we always value each other above things. Job's recovery took time and it was accomplished by a communal effort of love. Today, we thank the Lord for all the gracious benefits of a loving community of saints in the local church.

The Lord bestowed on Job seven additional sons and three beautiful daughters; whether these came from his wife mentioned previously is doubtful, but not impossible (v. 13). Scripture records the names of Job's fair daughters to further substantiate their exceptional attractiveness: Jemimah, "the dove," Keziah or "cassia," a fragrant sweet cinnamon spice, and Keren-Happuch, "horn of eye paint" (v. 14). These three daughters also received an inheritance with their brothers, which was quite unusual in ancient times. The act may have been criticized by others, especially his sons who were losing a share of the inheritance. Like Caleb, who gave an inheritance to his daughter Achsah centuries later, Job was a man of faith who enjoyed blessing others with what God had given him. Such generosity is a prelude to the gospel message of Jesus Christ which offers the gift of salvation and the same eternal inheritance to anyone who will trust in Him for salvation:

> *For you are all sons of God through faith in Christ Jesus. For as many of you as were baptized into Christ have put on Christ. There is neither Jew nor Greek, there is neither slave nor free, there is neither male nor female; for you are all one in Christ Jesus* (Gal. 3:26-28).

Furthermore, Job's daughters were more beautiful than any women of that land, which meant, to those who esteemed such things, that Job had God's stamp of approval. Their beauty would be compensation for Job's own body left disfigured and scarred by his disease.

God blessed His servant Job's latter years, more than his previous years. Job lived another 140 years after his restoration, and died a full man, having seen his posterity unto four generations (i.e., even his great great grandchildren; v. 15). Jewish tradition suggests that Job was seventy years of age when the events of this book occurred; thus God added a double portion of years to his life. If Job was *"blameless and upright, and one who feared God and shunned evil"* at seventy (1:1), what kind of holy spectacle of a man was he after being refined and blessed for another 140 years?

Epilogue

Scripture shows us that God permits both believers and non-believers to suffer the consequences and punitive reimbursement of their sins. However, this was not the case for Job; he was an upright man and his friends were rebuked by God for saying that Job was suffering because of his sin (1:8, 42:8). Yet, God permitted an extreme trial in Job's life to reveal a proud superiority that resided deep in his own heart. Once Job understood that his self-justification and self-defense were at God's expense (i.e., he was defaming God's character), he repented and was blessed by God. God definitely judges sin, but that is not the key lesson from the book of Job. Rather, the child of God must trust in God's perfect character, sovereignty, and foreknowledge, and choose to worship Him in all circumstances, even when His ways make no sense at all to us.

God permitted suffering in Job's life as an educational tool to better him and make him more useful. J. N. Darby summarizes why a good and gracious God sometimes permits such heavy affliction in the lives of His servants.

> Mark the perfect and faithful care of God, from whom (whatever may have been the malice of Satan) all this proceeded, because God saw that Job needed it. We observe that it is God who sets the case of Job before Satan, and that the latter disappears from the scene, because here it is a question of his doings on the earth, and not of his inward temptations. Further, if God had stopped short in the outward afflictions, Job would have had fresh cause for self-complacency. Man might have judged that those afflictions were ample. But the evil of Job's heart consisted in his resting on the fruits of grace in himself, and this would have only increased the good opinion he had already entertained of himself: kind in prosperity, he would have been also patient in adversity. God therefore carries on the work, that Job may know this himself.[76]

Clearly, then, the upright are not exempt from suffering, but rather God manipulates the hardship of His people to better them. C. I. Scofield suggests that the reasons why the Lord's people are permitted to suffer are partially explained by the beneficial purposes which are accomplished:

1. Job's experiences opened his eyes more fully to the ineffable holiness of God (42:5), leading him thereby to self-knowledge and self-judgment (40:4, 42:6).
2. The sufferings of Job are shown to be corrective rather than penal, being used of God to test and refine his character (23:10).
3. The outcome demonstrates that by God's grace His people trust and serve Him because of what He is, not as a mere return for temporal benefits (13:15).
4. Such experiences, as interpreted here by divine inspiration, reveal the ultimate triumph of a wise and loving God in His unseen contest with Satan over the souls of men (chps. 1-2).[77]

In short, all that happened to Job was for his good; through suffering and God's rebuke, he became more aware of his own depravity and better acquainted with God's greatness. Through his sorrowful experiences he and others were refined and blessed, Satan was shamed, and the name of God glorified! This begs the question, What might God accomplish through our sufferings, if we humbly yield to Him?

The mystery of human suffering is not fully explain in the book of Job; however, we know that all suffering has its root in sin, the fall of man, and that God chooses to control the outcome of sin to accomplish His purposes. Satan is permitted to strike God's people with sickness and calamity, but only as God permits (Job 1-2; 2 Cor. 12:7). Thus, we may safely conclude that any beneficial outcome of human misery is evidence of God's merciful intervention in a sin-cursed world. Without God, suffering would be a most miserable and intolerable experience because there would be no purpose in it. With God, as He reckons eternal matters, only good can come from our adversity, though we often cannot comprehend this wonderful truth: *"And we know that all things work together for good to those who love God, to those who are the called according to His purpose"* (Rom. 8:28). God is good and does good.

Meditation

Many men owe the grandeur of their lives to their tremendous difficulties. ... There are no crown bearers in heaven that were not cross bearers on earth.

— Charles Spurgeon

Psalms

Psalms

Introduction

The book of Psalms was Israel's national hymnbook. The title is from the Greek word *psalmos*, a poem normally sung with musical accompaniment. The Hebrew psalms, or songs, encouraged scriptural memorization and meditation, and enhanced the Jews' worship of Jehovah. Psalms that were to be sung by the entire congregation were called hymns (e.g., Ps. 105). Accordingly, the book of Psalms contains the vibrant prayers and joyful praise of the Jewish people.

Though its poetry is ancient, its contents have been a timeless source of encouragement, wisdom, and inspiration for all of God's people down through the ages. In fact, no portion of Scripture is more frequently cited by the Holy Spirit in the New Testament than Psalms, thus affirming its inspiration. This book is comprised of one hundred and fifty individual psalms covering a vast range of topics and personal experiences. This ensures that every child of God will benefit from reading and meditating on the psalms. As you study the character, attributes, and feats of God as He interacts with His covenant people, you too will be motivated to praise and worship God along with the psalmists.

Purpose

The wide variety of psalms naturally conveys a broad diversity of purpose. Some songs are a historical review to remind the Jewish nation of their ongoing dependence on Jehovah. Others are prophetic in nature, or poems ascribing praise to God, or personal songs relating to specific events. For instance, fourteen of David's psalms relate to personal events (often distressing situations) which occurred in his own life, such as when he fled Jerusalem during his son Absalom's rebellion (e.g., Ps. 3). Although David often requested divine deliverance, his poetry expresses a resolute confidence in God's character and faithfulness despite his situation. David knew God's help would come, but in His best timing – this realization encourages us to trust God in the same way.

Some of David's writings are prophetic in nature, such as Psalm 22, which foretells the death of the Jewish Messiah by crucifixion. The majority of David's psalms are fervent prayers either asking for the Lord's assistance, or praising Him for His abiding presence, or acknowledging God's faithfulness and goodness to him and the Jewish nation. Other writers capture this same tenor, though the specific focus of each psalm is unique.

Leviticus was Israel's worship manual, but Psalms was their national hymnal. Psalms is comprised of a wide assortment of hymns, such as *hymns of victory* (e.g., Ps. 68), *hymns of procession* (e.g., Ps. 24), *songs of Zion* (e.g., Ps. 48), and *hallelujah choruses* (e.g., Ps. 146). Some psalms were to be sung congregationally (e.g., Ps. 75), but others were an individual's song of lament (e.g., Ps. 4) or thanksgiving (e.g., Ps. 18). Some were temple liturgies sung during times of public worship (e.g., Ps. 15), and yet others, like Psalm 128, were spoken by a priest to pronounce a blessing on those listening. In summary, the application of the poems in *Psalms* is quite diverse. Perhaps the Hebrew title of the book, *Sepher Tehillim*, meaning, "Book of Praises" best describes the purpose of the entire book – praises to God!

Divisions and Formation

Psalms is the longest book in our Bibles. Both the Hebrew and Protestant Canon contain one hundred and fifty psalms; the Orthodox Canon includes one additional song (Ps. 151). The psalter is actually the combination of five separate books. It is unknown when these five books were arranged; perhaps the divisions were purely arbitrary for liturgical reasons (i.e., smaller scrolls would be more easily handled by worshippers than one large one). Each book concludes with a doxology (praise to God). While the psalms themselves are divinely inspired, the book divisions were humanly devised. The five separate books are comprised of the following individual psalms:

Book One: Psalms 1-41
Book Two: Psalms 42-72
Book Three: Psalms 73-89

Book Four: Psalms 90-106
Book Five: Psalms 107-150

After individual psalms were composed, many were gathered into small collections before being arranged in the five different books. For instance, Psalms 120-143 are known as the *Psalms of Ascent* or *Psalms of Degrees* which the Jews sang while en route to Jerusalem to keep the feasts of Jehovah. Psalms 146-150 were a collection referred to as *Praise Psalms*. The psalms authored by David were commonly referred to as *David's Psalms*. Some of this collection was clearly available in the days of King Hezekiah, who reigned three centuries after David, as he commanded the Levites to sing the psalms of David and Asaph to the Lord (2 Chron. 29:30).

It is unknown who gathered the various smaller collections into separate books and then assembled the final Book of Psalms. Some believe that this was accomplished by the post-exilic scribe Ezra in the fifth century B.C. What is known is that the Holy Spirit not only inspired the original works, but also ensured what was to be collected and preserved for our benefit.

Date and Historical Setting

The oldest psalm (Ps. 90) was written by Moses in the fifteenth century B.C. The contents of Psalm 137, which mentions the destruction of Jerusalem, pertain to post-Babylonian exile experiences of the Jewish people. This means that Psalm 137 was likely written a short time after 538 B.C. Psalms 107 and 126 thank the Lord for rescuing and bringing the Jewish captives back into the land of Israel; hence, these too may have been written after the Babylonian exile. Because of its literary sophistication and unique scholarship, it is possible that Ezra wrote Psalm 119 a as teaching tool for post-exilic Jews; however, others believe that David penned this song. In any case, the vast majority of the psalms were written during the glorious reigns of King David and his son Solomon, about five centuries after Moses penned Psalm 90 and more than four centuries before the Babylonian captivity.

Authorship

For many psalms, an ancient Hebrew superscript introduces us to its historical context and writer by such phrases as "A Psalm of David" (e.g., Ps. 15), or "A Psalm of Asaph" (e.g., Ps. 79). Asaph was David's choirmaster in the temple (1 Chron. 16:4-7). In some cases the superscript indicates the instrumental accompaniment for the psalm (e.g., Ps. 5) or an alternate tune that it might be sung to (e.g., Ps. 57). In our English Bibles these introductions are usually printed in a smaller font to introduce the Psalm, but in the Hebrew Bible the superscripts are the first line of text in the Psalm.

Some have questioned whether these introductory superscripts can be trusted. However, their historicity is notably ancient, and sometimes the internal evidence within the psalms confirms their reliability. There are, for instance, superscripts that refer to incidents in David's lifetime which are not recorded in the books of Samuel or Chronicles. Psalm 60 serves as a good example; its superscript reads: "When he [David] fought against Mesopotamia and Syria of Zobah, and Joab returned and killed twelve thousand Edomites in the Valley of Salt." It would be quite odd for some post-exilic scribe to add this type of detailed information to the Hebrew text centuries later, without any historical basis for doing so. This information is more likely to have been attached to the original song. It is also noted that the Lord Jesus and His apostles referred to the authorship information contained in these superscripts on several occasions, thus proving their trustworthiness (e.g., Luke 20:42).

When a psalm does not have a superscript, its authorship may sometimes be discerned through textual observations. For example, Psalm 10 has no superscript, but because it is surrounded by psalms that are accredited to David, and because Psalm 10 continues the theme of Psalm 9, most scholars believe David wrote both psalms. In fact, it is possible that both were originally the same psalm. Another way to identify authorship is to note a particular style or a repetitive phrase that is peculiar to a particular writer in other psalms for which the authorship is known. For instance, David is the only psalmist who refers to himself as "your servant" when speaking directly to Jehovah; the one exception being that Ethan refers to David as "your servant" (i.e., "the Lord's servant") in Psalm 88. This is why the rabbis of the Talmud and Midrash contend that David wrote Psalm 119, as the phrase "your servant" occurs thirteen times in that psalm. This type of evaluation is not conclusive, but does confirm valid candidates for authorship.

The most prolific author of the psalms was David, writing seventy-three of the one hundred and fifty psalms. Besides David, other known writers of psalms include: Asaph, Ethan, Heman, the Korahites, Moses, and Solomon. As the Korahites were Levitical singers at the temple, they may not have actually composed the psalms; rather, these may have been dedicated to them, or provided to them to publicly perform. The authorship breakdown is as follows:

Asaph: 50, 73-83 (12 total)

David: 3-32, 34-41, 51-65, 68-70, 86, 101, 103, 108-110, 122, 124, 131, 133, 138-145 (for a total of 73)

Ethan: 89

Heman: 88 (joint authorship with the Korahites)

Korahites: 42, 44-49, 84-85, 87-88 (11 total)

Moses: 90

Solomon: 72, 127

Unknown: 1, 2, 10, 33, 43, 66-67, 71, 91-100, 102, 104-107, 111-121, 123, 125-126, 128-130, 132, 134-137, 146-150 (50 total)

In summary, the authorship of one-third of the psalms is unknown. This fact did not prevent their canonization, as the authorship of other books in the Bible is also unknown. The inspired character of these psalms is obvious and their proven historicity is well-established. While it is more difficult to enter into the emotional nature of the poem without knowing the personal circumstance that provoked its composition, the messages contained within these psalms will bless the reader and exalt the Lord.

Psalm Types

Because the Psalms contain such a wide variety of experiences and sentiments, classifying them is a difficult task. This undertaking is further compounded by the fact that, regardless of the method of identification, many can be categorized under multiple headings. Generally speaking, psalms can be classified into four main categories: hymns of praise, songs of lament, songs of thanksgiving (*todah*), and specialized psalms. It suffices here to briefly describe the most common types of psalms and note their placement within the canonized collection.

I. Hymns of Praise

These are hymns of descriptive praise, some of which conclude with a doxology. Based on God's character as revealed through previous actions of grace, the writer assumes Jehovah's continued faithfulness and hence offers praise. A doxology is a call for worshippers to praise God in an abstract way (i.e., no specific reason is mentioned). True worship focuses on who God is inherently and seeks to understand why He does what He does. In this sense, the Hebrew hymns accomplish more than just expressing delight in God and exalting His name – they also affirm confidence in God's holy character. It is important to thank God for His many blessings to us, but these praise hymns go further to joyfully celebrate who God is.

Includes: Psalms 8, 19, 33, 66-67, 95, 100, 103, 104, 111, 113-114, 117, 145-150.

II. Songs of Lament
Communal

Psalms of Lament are the most common type of psalm; some are communal in focus, while others are of a personal nature. In the former category, we see something (a natural disaster, rampant disease, or the oppression of a foreign foe), that prompts the writer to express feelings of sorrow, misery, and helplessness to Jehovah. The psalmist normally affirms trust in the Lord and petitions Him for deliverance. The writer often concludes the psalm by promising allegiance and worship, and ends with a note of praise.

Includes: Psalms 12, 44, 58, 60, 74, 79-80, 85, 90, 94, 123, 126, 129.

Imprecatory
An imprecatory psalm is more than a mere lament, as the writer pleads with God to invoke justice and retribution on his or the nation's oppressors. While this type of prayerful expression is not affirmed by the apostles during the Church Age, we realize that these psalms were composed during the dispensation of the Law – and the mentality of "eye for eye and tooth for tooth" governed the Jewish society. William MacDonald puts the matter this way: "The imprecatory Psalms express a spirit that was proper for a Jew living under the Law, but not proper for a Christian living under grace. The reason these Psalms seem harsh to us is because we are viewing them in the light of the New Testament revelation."[78] No doubt these psalms will be a source of comfort to the Jewish remnant in a future day as they plead with the Lord to be delivered from the brutality of the Antichrist.
Includes: Psalms 35, 69, 83, 88, 109, 137, 140.

Penitential
These psalms are a type of lament in which the writer's sorrow over sin and the subsequent joy of forgiveness and restoration with God are expressed. These writings are profitable in evaluating the cause of sin, to warn against sin, to identify the damages of sin, and to highlight the means of restoration. It is generally agreed that there are seven penitential psalms, though some have diverse application.
Includes: Psalms 6, 32, 38, 51, 102, 130, 143.

Personal
Faced with an overwhelming situation, the psalmist cries out to God for help and deliverance. The writer did not want to surrender to a defeated life, but rather desired to see the glory of God's salvation. David encountered many such circumstances during his life; accordingly, he wrote several psalms seeking Jehovah's assistance. These songs encourage us to follow David's example and to trust the Lord during those inevitable storms of life.

The Beginning of Wisdom

Includes: Psalms 3-7, 9-10, 13-14, 17, 22, 25-28, 31, 36, 39, 41-43, 52-57, 59, 61, 64, 70-71, 77, 86, 89, 120, 139, 141-142.

III. Songs of Thanksgiving
Communal and Personal

These songs recognize God's past or present faithfulness to deliver His covenant people from oppression or some other distressful circumstance. Some songs have a communal focus while others are expressions of an individual's thanksgiving for receiving divine assistance. A psalm of thanksgiving (*todah*) normally concludes with a chorus of joyful praise which not only thanks God for the good that He does, but also affirms His personal goodness.

Includes:
Communal Psalms – 65, 67, 75, 107, 124, 136.
Personal Psalms – 18, 21, 30, 32, 34, 40, 66, 92, 108, 116, 118, 138.

Special Types of Thanksgiving

Two special types of thanksgiving psalms are worthy of mention: *historical salvation psalms* and *songs of trust*. The message of the *historical salvation psalm* relates to God's past covenants and dealings with the Jewish people, such as their national commencement and the Egyptian exodus experience. The writer encourages his Jewish countrymen not to forget God's proven faithfulness, even during times of national discipline, and to continue trusting the Lord during future hardships. The *song of trust* builds on some notable experience with God to express thankfulness and general praise in a hymn-like fashion.

Includes:
Historical Salvation – Psalms 105-106, 135-136.
Songs of Trust – 11, 16, 23, 27, 62, 63, 91, 121, 125, 131.

IV. Specialized Psalms
Ascent

The *Songs of Degrees* or *Ascent* were sung by pilgrims traveling to Jerusalem to observe various feasts and holy days and perhaps by the Jews returning from their Babylonian exile in the sixth and fifth century B.C. These psalms of prayer, petition, praise, and

thanksgiving were sung at various points in the journey to Jerusalem, such as at their first glimpse of the holy city, or upon arriving at the entrance of the temple.
Includes: Psalms 120-134.

Liturgical

A sizeable group of psalms were uttered or sung during Jewish feasts and festivals, or during other special temple services. Songs of Zion, covenant psalms, royal psalms, enthronement psalms, and temple liturgies were all liturgical psalms used in public worship. Songs of Zion might speak of the refuge of God's holy mountain, or to lament its ruin, or to rejoice in the future day that God's glory will shine out from it and fill the earth. Covenant psalms recall God's faithfulness to keep past covenants pertaining to the Jewish people and, in some cases, petition God to continue to do so. The focus of the royal psalms is Israel's anointed king, though not named specifically; these refer to kingly activities such as coronations, marriages, and warfare. On the other hand, enthronement psalms celebrate God's sovereign rule over all of creation and contain expressions of descriptive praise, such as *"the Lord reigns;"* He is *"the great King,"* who *"comes to judge."* The common factor in both categories of psalms is the use of the royal image, yet the imagery of an earthly king and the Lord's rule over all things is quite distinct. Temple Liturgies were used to celebrate various festivals in Jerusalem.
Includes:
Songs of Zion – 46, 48, 76, 84, 87, 122.
Covenantal Psalms – 50, 78, 81, 132.
Royal Psalms – 2, 18, 20-21, 29, 45, 72, 101, 110, 144.
Enthronement Psalms – 47, 93, 95-99.
Temple Liturgies – 15, 24, 68, 82, 95, 115, 134.

Messianic

Throughout Old Testament Scripture, Jehovah provided His covenant people with a detailed prophetic portrait of their coming Messiah. God wanted His covenant people to recognize the true Messiah when He appeared to them. The Lord Jesus not only confirmed that the Law and prophets foretold of Himself, but that

The Beginning of Wisdom

the book of Psalms prophetically spoke of Him as well (Luke 24:44). The difficulty of evaluating potentially messianic psalms is distinguishing the personal and spiritual experiences of the writer from those which are a prophetic reference to Christ. The latter is affirmed by New Testament quotations of the psalm being prophetically fulfilled. For instance, both Peter and Paul quoted Psalm 16, which relates to the resurrection of the Jewish Messiah, and affirmed that the Lord Jesus Christ had fulfilled that prophesy (Acts 2:25-28, 13:35).

Additionally, there are a few psalms which are not labeled as "Messianic Psalms" but clearly have messianic applications. For example, Psalm 78:2 foretells that God would speak to the nation through parables to reveal the dark sayings of old. Matthew confirms that Christ's ministry to Israel was marked by parabolic teaching, thus fulfilling the psalmist's prophecy; yet, the psalm does not relate specifically to the Jewish Messiah, but to God Himself (Matt. 13:35).

There are sixteen psalms that are generally acknowledged as being messianic in nature, that is, all or part of that psalm prophetically speaks of Christ. Sometimes an entire psalm applies to Christ (Ps. 22; 110), while other times it is only a few verses (Ps. 40:6-10), and on some occurrences only one verse (Ps. 41:9). T. Ernest Wilson organizes these psalms in chronological order as each pertains to aspects of Christ's first and second advents:

> Psalm 2 is an introduction to the whole collection, giving a prophetic outline of the official glories of the Messiah. Psalm 40 refers to His incarnation; Psalm 22 to His crucifixion; Psalm 16 to His resurrection. In our exposition we shall follow the chronological order in the life of our Lord. There are sixteen Messianic psalms and we shall consider them in the following sequence: (1) Psalm 2: The Official Glory of the Eternal Son; (2) Psalm 40: The Incarnation; (3) Psalm 91: The Temptation; (4) Psalm 41: The Betrayal; (5) Psalm 22: The Crucifixion; (6) Psalm 69: The Trespass Offering; (7) Psalm 16: The Resurrection; (8) Psalm 68: The Ascension; (9) Psalm 45: The King-Bridegroom; (10) Psalm 24: The King of Glory; (11) Psalm 110: The Priest-

King-Judge; (12) Psalm 8: The Last Adam; (13) Psalm 72: The Millennial Reign; (14) Psalm 89: The Davidic Covenant; (15) Psalm 102: The Unchangeable One; and (16) Psalm 118: The Headstone of the Corner.[79]

Includes: Psalms 2, 8, 16, 22, 24, 40, 41, 45, 68, 69, 72, 89, 91, 102, 110, 118.

Wisdom
The Jewish people desired to rightly apply divine revelation to daily living. While more emphasis is placed on wisdom in the book of Proverbs, several psalms are also instructive in nature. James Catron suggests that wisdom psalms primarily focus on two important questions:

1. What is the relationship between godliness and reward?
2. How does God handle people in sin?[80]

Certainly, these questions would be profitable for God's people to consider in any age.
Includes: Psalms 1, 19, 36, 37, 49, 73, 112, 119, 127, 128, 133.

Psalm Formats

Alphabetical
This type of psalm uses an alphabetical acrostic in its presentation. Psalm 119 is the most familiar example; it is divided into twenty-two sections, one for each letter of the Hebrew alphabet. Each section contains eight verses with each verse in the section starting with the particular letter being emphasized in that portion. The first eight verses begin with the first letter of the Hebrew alphabet, *aleph*, and the next set of eight verses commence with the second letter, *beth*, and so forth. Some believe this format was used to enhance memorization, while others believe it assisted Hebrew children in learning their alphabet.

Conclusive
In this subset of psalms, the composer has evaluated a personal experience and has arrived at some conclusion pertaining to it, which is usually stated in the introduction. The writer then proceeds to explain both how he reached his conclusion and its application. David follows this format in Psalm 32.

Contrastive
This format supplies a contrast (usually between two things, philosophies, or characters), to emphasize the wisdom of doing what is God-approved and refraining from what is not. Psalm 1 is a classic example of a contrastive psalm. It compares the way and destiny of the godly man, who is blessed and fruitful, and those of the ungodly, which are worthless and disapproved.

Dramatic
This song reads like a play in which several speakers are dramatizing an event or situation to highlight its significance. The framework of Psalm 2 features six different speakers and is a good example of a dramatic psalm.

Petition
Most of the petition psalms follow a similar format: an acknowledgment of the trial, a recognition that God is greater than the distressful or challenging situation, and an awareness that He is more than able to deliver the writer, or the nation, from it. David wrote several such psalms (e.g., Ps. 3).

Repetitive
A repetitive psalm announces the main theme in the introduction and then reworks this motif using illustrations or similar expressions. As an example, Psalm 136 emphasizes that *"the Lord's mercy endures forever"* in each of its twenty-six verses.

Deriving Application
The psalms were penned during the dispensation of the Law and directly relate to the interaction of the Jewish people with Jehovah. It is understood that the Law was to show the Jewish nation their sin (Rom.

3:20) and to point them to their Savior, Christ (Gal. 3:24). Because the blood of animals could not provide propitiation for sins, nor could any Jew keep the Law, that system, having served its purpose, was replaced by God with a New Covenant which could save (2 Cor. 3:6-18; Heb. 8:8). Accordingly, William Kelly notes both the importance of Psalms to Christian living and the dangers of dispensational misapplication:

> There is no part of scripture more ... important for the believer to understand by divine teaching, so as on the one hand to enjoy truth needful, fertile, and strengthening for the affections, and on the other hand to keep clear of mistaken applications which might darken and even destroy all right sense of our proper relationship as Christians. [For example,] one plain evil result of what is miscalled spiritualizing is the handle it gives to the Judaizing or superstitious. If Judah and Israel, if Zion and Jerusalem, point to the church, men logically infer that the righteous destruction of the enemies, the wicked, etc., warrants the office of the unchristian and unholy Inquisition, and the punishment of heretics even to death. ... Thus uniformly earthly judicial righteousness is the atmosphere, not heavenly grace according to which the Christian is called now to feel, and pray, worship and walk.[81]

In summary, musing on the Psalms will provide Christians encouragement, devotional inspiration, and wisdom for godly living. Yet, we understand during the Church Age the indwelling Holy Spirit cannot be taken away from true believers (Ps. 51:11), and that we are to love and pray for our enemies, rather than pleading with God to destroy and eternally condemn them (Ps. 69:28). Such imprecatory aspirations do not conform to the example and teachings of the Lord Jesus or His apostles. Studying Psalms within its proper dispensational context permits us to appreciate both Old Testament and New Testament truth.

> We have now before us one of the choicest parts of the Old Testament, wherein there is so much of Christ and His gospel, as well as of God and His law, that it has been called the summary of both Testaments.
> — Matthew Henry

The Beginning of Wisdom

The Exploits of David

David is the main contributor of Psalms and many of his poems were composed during distressing circumstances. A greater understanding of these arduous experiences will enable us to better appreciate how David lived a blessed life amidst them. The following table summarizes in chronological order the main events in David's life – dates are approximate and represent a best fit with the biblical record.

Date (B.C.)	Events in the Life of David
1040	Born
1025	Kills Goliath at about 15 years of age (1 Sam. 17:33)
1025	Dwells with Saul in Gibeah (1 Sam. 18:2)
1018	Begins fugitive years around the age of 22 (1 Sam. 21)
1010	Saul dies; at 30, David rules from Hebron (2 Sam. 5:4)
1003	David is made king at Jerusalem (2 Sam. 2; 5:1-3)
1001	Sins with Bathsheba (2 Sam. 11-12)
999	Solomon is born (2 Sam. 12:24)
979	Absalom's rebellion and death (2 Sam. 15-18)
972	Begins to gather temple materials (1 Chron. 17, 29)
970	David dies at 70, Solomon is king at 29 (1 Chron. 22:5)

After David slew Goliath around the age of fifteen, he dwelt in Saul's palace at Gibeah for about seven years (1 Sam. 17:45-18:2). From the age of 22 to 30, David was either on the run from King Saul or was dwelling among the Philistines in Ziklag (1 Sam. 27:7). In his fugitive years during Saul's reign, David wrote several psalms, ten of which address this crisis directly; the likely order of these poems would be: 7, 59, 56, 34, 52, 63, 54, 18, 57, and 142. In all, Saul made thirteen recorded attempts on David's life. Unfortunately, while dwelling at Ziklag, David lapsed spiritually and engaged in gruesome covert raids on villages; there is no evidence that David composed any psalms during this time. At the age of thirty (after Saul's death) he began to reign over Judah in Hebron. Seven years later he captured Jerusalem from the Jebusites and was subsequently anointed king over all the tribes of Israel (2 Sam. 5:1-3). He ruled over God's people for a total of forty years before dying at the age of seventy (2 Sam. 5:4).

It is evident from David's writings that the man after God's own heart (1 Sam. 13:14) frequently suffered a broken heart. He was often despised, plotted against, slandered, and persecuted for doing the will of God. Many sought to kill David; yet, through each challenging situation he found the Lord to be a faithful Refuge of peace, an unmovable Rock of strength, and a mighty Fortress of protection. David proves that those who suffer patiently with the Lord in righteousness know more about God's true nature than those who do not.

> The most valuable thing the Psalms do for me is to express the same delight in God which made David dance.
>
> — C.S. Lewis

Selah

The psalmists often insert the Hebrew word *selah* to emphasize an important statement or to conclude their song. The best equivalent meaning of *selah* in the English language would be "pause and think about it!" As the reader meditates on each psalm, why not take an extra moment to pause and ponder the text when prompted to do so? This response will require discipline, but will certainly enhance our thoughts of praise and worship towards God and also assist us to better live for Him.

> The Psalms are like a general hospital for souls where we might each select the medicine for our own disease.
>
> — Martin Luther

Devotions in Psalms

Book 1

Book 1 contains the first forty-one psalms; all but the first two were written by David. The author of Psalms 1 and 2 is unknown.

Psalm: 1   **Type: Wisdom**   **Author: Unknown**

Two Men and Two Destinies

Psalms is the only book in the Bible which begins with the word "Blessed." Psalms 1 and 2 are linked together in the Hebrew Bible and form a fitting introduction to the entire collection. Psalm 1 commences with a beatitude and Psalm 2 concludes with one. In an ideological sense, Psalm 1 upholds the moral glory of Christ, while Psalm 2 presents His official glory associated with His exalted position. Psalm 1 is rightly placed to introduce the entire collection as it poses a contrast between the ways of the wise and the foolish; the former is blessed of God, while the latter is judged. J. G. Bellett comments on the lovely tenor of Psalm 1:

> This psalm is very soothing to the soul. It is the godly man in the care and leading of God, whom we see before us. No other intrudes to disturb the rest and security of the righteous one; but on he goes, in his proper undistracted path, to his reward.[82]

The Hebrew triad is repeatedly employed to fully develop this contrast; a blessed man does not: walk in the counsel of the ungodly, stand with sinners, or sit with scoffers; rather, he delights in God's law, meditates continually on it, and (consequently) is blessed by God. Accordingly, the wise man is fruitful and prospers in all his doings; he

The Beginning of Wisdom

is likened to a flourishing tree planted by a river. In contrast, the ungodly are like worthless chaff blown from the threshing floor; they will be judged, and will not be numbered with the righteous. The last verse summarizes the entire psalm. God knows *"the way of the righteous"* and *"the way of the wicked";* He will bless those who stand with Him, and those who do not will perish.

Psalm: 2   Type: Liturgical – Royal/Messianic   Author: Unknown

Christ – God's Coming King

This messianic psalm is quoted seven times in the New Testament. The first three verses express the psalmist's amazement that the nations would plot against God's *"anointed,"* a rebellion sure to fail. This poem prophetically refers to both of Christ's advents. Acts 4:25-28 confirms that this psalm was partially fulfilled by the crucifixion of Christ, which concluded His first earthly sojourn. The remainder of the Psalm will be fulfilled when the nations become His inheritance and He rules over them with a rod of iron (vv. 8-9).

God's reply to the rage of the nations is in verses 4-6: the nations shall suffer the disdain and indignation of God, for His King will sit on the throne in Zion and rule over them. Zion is mentioned forty times in Psalms and here it speaks specifically of the temple area in Jerusalem – this is where God will install His King. Hamilton Smith notes that the Spirit of God poses human-related notions within the poem, such as mocking laughter, to cause us to better understand God's contempt for haughty rebels:

> From a world in revolt we pass to the calm of heaven to learn God's thoughts of man's vain efforts. The great men of the earth – its political leaders, its scientists, its philosophers – may combine to cast off all recognition of God, but, unmoved by all their efforts the Christ of God "sits in the heavens," and holds man's revolt in derision. Men rage on earth; God laughs in heaven. Human ideas are employed to convey to us heaven's contempt of man's folly.[83]

In verses 7-9, God the Father issues four decrees to reveal His Messiah to the nations. First, God's own Son will be the One to experience coronation. Second, after completing His redemptive work, He would undergo bodily resurrection and then be exalted by the Father to the highest position of prominence (Acts 13:32-34). Third, all the nations of the earth will be His inheritance. Fourth, He will reign over the nations in righteousness and enforce His rule with a rod of iron; no evil will be permitted to tarnish His glorious kingdom.

The final three verses relate to the Holy Spirit's work to reconcile sinners to the Savior. Given God's revelation of His Son in the previous verses, humanity would be wise to fear and serve Him. They should willingly choose to *"kiss the Son";* the Aramaic word *bar* is rendered "son," a term the Gentiles would understand to mean "the rightful heir." Ultimately, every individual must decide whether they will respect the One God loves and honors, or be wise in their own conceit. As shown in Luke 7:38, a kiss was a sign of true repentance. Blessed are those who humble themselves before God, repent of their sins, and please God by honoring His Son – the Savior and King of the world and the One who will inherit all things.

Psalm: 3   Type: Lament – Personal   Author: David

Gazing Heavenward – The Lord Sustains

David penned this psalm while fleeing from his rebel son Absalom, who sought to take his father's throne and life. This was a most distressing time for David; moreover, he was concerned for the welfare of all those who had fled with him from Jerusalem. In addition, David's foes were saying that there was no hope of deliverance for him (v. 2). David confronted this notion by declaring that God was his "shield" (i.e., protector) and the "lifter" of his head. Though surrounded, David knew he would be sustained by the Lord. It is our natural tendency to hang our heads in discouragement during difficult trials; David chose to peer heavenward and to watch and wait for his deliverance. Consequently, David could lie down in peace each evening and enjoy sleep. God had confirmed a covenant with him; therefore, David knew the Lord must sustain and protect him, no matter how bleak the situation appeared. In fact, the Lord had already delivered David from his enemies many times. Hence, he could beseech the Lord to bless him again by smiting his enemies. The betrayal of a loved one is one of the deepest emotional wounds to suffer, but as William Kelly reminds us, the Lord Jesus uses such lingering pain in our own lives so that we may better identify with Him, and learn to trust Him:

> No enemy is so trying as the traitor in the midst of God's people; and the nearer to the king, the more of pain, sorrow, and shame. The king also had known more than one profound humiliation, never one so heart-breaking, yet so public, as this. But in him it was far from being unalloyed; in Christ it was in every sense purer and deeper sorrow. His Spirit operates so that His own may unaffectedly and without presumption make His words theirs.[84]

David teaches us to exercise a deliberate confidence in God's character even when our emotions are prompting us to do otherwise. Rejoicing in the Lord during desperate circumstances honors the Lord and delivers our minds from the grip of depression (1 Thess. 5:16).

Psalm: 4   Type: Lament – Personal   Author: David

Lie Down in Peace – Secure in the Lord

The structure and expressions in Psalm 4 are similar to Psalm 3, which means David may have written it during the same crisis. David begins the psalm by calling on God to respond to his prayer for deliverance, and then he warns his enemies that they would be foolish to sin against God by ill-treating him. David was in God's protective care (v. 3). This realization allowed him to rejoice in the presence of his foes and rest peacefully in the Lord (vv. 7-8). Instead of slandering David's character and spreading lies about him, David exhorts his enemies to consider their ways, to cease sinning, and to put their trust in God (vv. 4-5). As William MacDonald suggests, "Prosperity does little for us, but adversity produces growth and maturity."[85] The pressures in David's life only served to spiritually enlarge his heart to beat for the Lord.

Devotions in Psalms

Psalm: 5   Type: Lament – Personal   Author: David

A Prayer for Guidance in Righteousness

David twice declares that his first conscious thoughts each morning were directed to the Lord in prayer (vv. 1, 3). David was entreating the One who hated iniquity and would destroy evildoers (vv. 2, 4-6). Because David had experienced God's mercy, he could joyfully approach the house of God (the tabernacle at that time) to worship the Lord (v. 7). Because David's heart was right with the Lord, he could eagerly request divine guidance in righteousness; he wanted what God wanted (v. 8). With his present adversity in mind, David more urgently petitioned God to judge his oppressors, who indulged in flattery and deceit in order to work evil against him (vv. 9-10). In closing, David acknowledges that he can joyfully sing, knowing God blesses and protects the righteous, that is, those who love Him and reverence His name (vv. 11-12). A millennium later, Paul would remind the believers in Rome of this same truth: *"We know that all things work together for good to those who love God, to those who are the called according to His purpose"* (Rom. 8:28).

Psalm: 6   Type: Lament – Personal/Penitential   Author: David

A Plea for Mercy

This is David's first penitential psalm. There is no information within the psalm to tie it with any specific situation in David's life. Apparently, David had sinned against the Lord in such a way as to prompt severe divine chastening; he was suffering from a life-threatening illness or perhaps an injury that brought him to the brink of death (v. 1). Having tearfully besought the Lord in prayer, David was confident he would be healed from his agonizing physical condition (vv. 2-3). In verses 4-5, David poses two reasons God should heal him. The first is His unfailing love, which David had repeatedly experienced. The second is that if David died, he would not be able to praise God from the grave (that is, he could not praise Him in His sanctuary, the tabernacle). Suffering physically, David expresses his anguish to the Lord – if he died his enemies would gloat that they were actually God's chastening rod to administer justice (vv. 6-7). However, David was confident God had heard his prayers and could thus command his enemies to depart from him. David knew the Lord's faithfulness and was therefore quite sure that He would put his enemies to shame and grant him full recovery (vv. 8-10).

Psalm: 7   Type: Lament – Personal   Author: David

A Prayer for Deliverance

This psalm was likely written before David's enthronement and during the time he was being relentlessly hunted by King Saul. The Hebrew superscription ties this poem to David's experience with Cush the Benjamite. This man is not referred to elsewhere in Scripture, so we have no specific timeframe with which to associate the song, but apparently Cush was slandering and opposing David. David desperately needed the Lord to *"rescue"* him; he likened his enemies to a lion about ready to tear its prey (v. 1). Though his enemies were saying David had *"done evil,"* David asserted his innocence before the Lord (vv. 3-4). He therefore asked the Lord to vindicate him in such a way as to substantiate his integrity (vv. 6-9). David then proceeds to describe the means in which the righteous Judge, who is always angry over sin, affects justice on the wicked (vv. 10-11). He prepares His judicial decrees in much the same way a soldier readies his sword, bow, and arrows for warfare (vv. 12-13). He traps the wicked in their own lies, deceit, and devices, and then reimburses them with their own evil intentions (vv. 14-16). Although not yet delivered, David confirms his trust in his righteous Lord by vowing to praise Him for His future exoneration (v. 17).

Psalm: 8   Type: Praise/Messianic   Author: David

Human Authority Will Declare God's Glory

This messianic song relating to human authority is quoted four times in the New Testament. "God is indescribably great," writes

William MacDonald. "Man, by contrast, is pathetically tiny. Yet God has conferred tremendous glory and honor upon man. The wonder of this fact brings forth an eloquent gasp from David."[86] David ponders God's wondrous design for man before human sin plunged the earth into chaos and humanity into ongoing rebellion. David initiates and concludes the psalm by referring to the majestic name of God. The Creator is alone in majestic grandeur – His glory is high above the heavens (v. 1). David is utterly amazed that a God of such majesty would select mankind to represent His authority on earth and be administrators of His dominion. Even feeble children and infants represent the authority of God on the earth (v. 2). It is noted that the Lord Jesus referred to a portion of verse 2 to reprove the Pharisees and to declare Himself as the Son of David during His triumphant entry into Jerusalem (often referred to as "Palm Sunday" by Christendom). This event occurred a few days prior to His crucifixion (Matt 21:16).

David's rhetorical questions in verse 4 are used to express his great quandary: why would the Creator of the moon, stars, and all the heavens, have such a fervent interest and passion for the welfare of finite man? Why would God bestow such dignity and honor to humanity, who was created with less status and power than the angels (v. 5)? The writer of Hebrews quotes this psalm (Heb. 2:6-8) to contrast the first Adam's failure to represent God on the earth with the obedience of Christ, the Last Adam (1 Cor. 15:45-47). The writer of Hebrews continues to explain that, to repair the damage of the first Adam, the Son of God had to venture from heaven to become a man and experience death for everyone born of the first Adam (Rom. 5:12; Heb. 2:9). Christ willingly humbled Himself to assume a position in Creation far inferior to His divine personage for the purpose of suffering God's judicial penalty for sin, death (Rom. 6:23; Phil. 2:6-8). Thus, in Christ, redeemed humanity would achieve the exalted destiny in creation that God had originally purposed.

Some 3000 years ago David referenced *"the paths in the sea"* (v. 8). This verse prompted nineteenth century naval officer Matthew Fontaine Maury to explore the oceans for prevailing sea currents. After circumnavigating the world from 1832 to 1836, he published the first textbook on modern oceanography, *The Physical Geography of the Sea and Its Meteorology*. Maury did indeed find *"paths in the sea,"* pioneered the science of oceanography, and revolutionized the trade routes for sailing ships. It is somewhat ironic, then, that a psalm pertaining to human earthly authority actually prompted man to explore, discover, and better exercise his God-given capacity.

Psalm: 9   Type: Lament – Personal   Author: David

Praise to God for Vanquished Enemies

This poem is an acrostic which is based on the first half of the Hebrew alphabet; Psalm 10 is likewise arranged, but uses the remaining half of the alphabet. In this song, David thanks the Lord for delivering him from his enemies and vindicating his name. David's inward understanding of God's righteous and just character becomes an outward expression of praise in this psalm. He concludes that God does and will punish the wicked. Although Psalms 9 and 10 may have been the same song originally, Allen Ross explains why each should be considered to be a complete poetic expression, though their messages are certainly complementary:

> Psalms 9 and 10 may have originally been one psalm, as they are in the Septuagint. They are connected by their form in the Hebrew, for nearly each stanza (approximately every other verse) begins with a successive letter of the Hebrew alphabet. Also, the two psalms have similar wording. For example, "in times of trouble" is found in 9:9 and 10:18, and in only two other passages in the Psalms. Also, each of the two psalms closes with an emphasis on mortal men (9:20; 10:18). Finally, each psalm mentions "the nations" (9:5, 15, 17, 19-20; 10:16). Yet there is warrant for the two psalms being separate. Psalm 9 is a triumphant song of thanksgiving, while Psalm 10 is a complaint and prayer over godless men in the nation. Because Psalm 9 is complete in itself, it is better to regard Psalm 10 as a related psalm.[87]

The main theme of verses 1-12 is that the Lord is true and is the eternal Judge of all those guilty of unjust cruelty. David delighted in proclaiming the wonders of God's vengeance against his enemies: He had driven them back (v. 3), rebuked them, and destroyed their cities (v. 5); the Lord had even blotted out their names from remembrance (v.

6). David lauds the eternal and righteous judgeship of the Lord; He is no respecter of persons in issuing retribution for evil (vv. 7-8). Hence, David invited the oppressed to put their trust in the Lord and to hope in Him alone (vv. 9-10). The Lord was David's "Refuge" – a secure resting place for the weary. David testified in praise that God's retribution against evildoers and vindication of the righteous was sure (v. 11). He concludes by proclaiming the Lord is a reliable solace to the ill-treated and He will not forget the cries of the brokenhearted (v. 12).

In verses 13-20, David turns from praising God for His past deliverance to pleading with Him for assistance in overthrowing his persecutors, as some were threatening David with death (v. 13). David desired to have further cause to praise the Lord *"in the gates of the Daughter of Zion"* (presumably the tabernacle in Jerusalem; v. 14). He was confident that those wicked nations, who were not mindful of the Lord, would be judged; a grave was their destiny (vv. 15-18). The psalm concludes with the prayer that all men would understand the inevitable righteous judgment of God upon the wicked and that God would uphold those who trust in Him (vv. 19-20).

Psalm: 10   Type: Lament – Personal   Author: David

A Plea to Judge and Deliver

David wrote a bold inquiry as to why God seemed to be aloof and unconcerned with the plight of the afflicted: why does God permit the wicked to triumph over the righteous at all? David then provides a vivid character sketch of the wicked and what they do. Seemingly, David is making a case to prompt God's overdue judgment. He begins with the character of the oppressor, who is proud; persecutes the weak (vv. 2, 8); boasts and applauds coveting (v. 3); possesses a haughty countenance and Godless thinking (v. 4); has grievous ways (v. 5), an obstinate rebel heart (v. 6), and a mouth full of cursing; and is prone to deceit, fraud, and vanity (v. 7). The behavior of the oppressor is also addressed; he ambushes the poor, persecutes the weak, and murders the innocent (vv. 2, 8-10). Since God did not render immediate help to his victims, the evil oppressor surmised he would not be punished. Either God did not see his crimes, had forgotten them (v. 11), or was simply

The Beginning of Wisdom

unconcerned about his evil deeds (v. 13). Did not such a wicked disposition deserve God's judgment? Why would God allow someone to think they could get away with such atrocities? David thus pleads for the Lord to render judicial punishment on the wicked (v. 12). The imagery invoked in verse 15 of breaking one's arm meant that David wanted the Lord to confiscate all of the oppressor's strength. The poor, the humble, and the fatherless deserved God's help because they had put their trust in Him (vv. 14-18).

William Kelly notes the link between Psalms 9 and 10, and their uniform conclusion:

> This untitled psalm, dependent on the preceding one of which it is the supplement, is occupied with the wicked internal enemy that hates and afflicts the righteous Jew. As Psalm 9 looks at the Gentile oppressors generally as the object of Jehovah's judgment at the close, so this details the enemy within, though it binds up with the expected judgment the perishing of the nations out of His land (v. 16) when Jehovah is King forever. It is more special. Both run to and converge on the end of the age.[88]

Whether the enemy is within or without, or offenses were past or present, the Lord will judge all those who oppress His people! It may seem as if the Lord is silent to a particular injustice, but there is a coming day when He will render unto every man his just due.

Psalm: 11   Type: Thanksgiving – Song of Trust   Author: David

The Lord Is My Refuge

Although the historical setting which precipitated this psalm is unknown, the intensity of its tone indicates David was in the midst of a life-threatening situation. When faced with imminent peril, our natural tendency is to fly like a bird to a safe mountaintop, rather than to put our trust in the Lord (v. 1). David scoffs at the fainthearted suggestion that he should flee from danger, and rather declares the Lord is his Refuge. Verse 2 suggests the wicked were on an evil mission to slay the righteous. The temptation of the righteous is to imagine the worst outcome when the foundations of law and order (those representing

God's authority) are jeopardized (v. 3). But this was not David's view; his trust was in the all-seeing One whose throne was in heaven and who could not be corrupted or threatened by the wicked (v. 4). Faith that is not tested will not be trusted, so God does examine (i.e., He tests and refines) the righteous; however, He opposes the wicked and all who love violence (v. 5). The latter were destined to receive a cup of fiery indignation (v. 6); however, the upright, those who trust the Lord, will behold the Lord's glory in heaven (v. 7). David was able to rise above his outlook of doom and gloom by maintaining a steadfast "up-look" on the One who is in control of all things.

Psalm: 12   Type: Lament – Communal   Author: David

God's Pure Word Thwarts Wicked Speech

David laments that, from his perspective, there seemed to be few godly (that is, covenant obeying) people in Israel (v. 1). He then contrasts the deceitful words, the flattering lips, and the vain ways of a culture ignoring God's rule (v. 2) with the untainted purity of God's Word (v. 6). His confidence is in the latter and, therefore, he prays God would cut off the lying lips and the proud tongues of evil collaborators (vv. 3-4). How foolish these double-minded and godless people were to think they could achieve all their goals through politicking lies and oppressing the weak. David calls on the Lord to end their proud legacy and to deliver those they exploited (v. 5). In conclusion, the righteous should trust in God's perfect and unchanging promises – He will judge proud and deceitful individuals who pervert the truth in an attempt to accomplish their own self-seeking agendas (vv. 7-8). While the exact historical event relating to this psalm is unknown, it is general enough to fit several challenging episodes in David's life, and likely ours too.

Psalm: 13   Type: Lament – Personal   Author: David

Waiting on the Lord

When unjust suffering continues day after day without any sign that relief is forthcoming, the child of God is likely to cry out to the Lord,

"How long, O God?" David does so four times in the first two verses through a series of rhetorical questions which seemingly are to motivate God to respond favorably. David's heart was filled with sorrow as he wrestled inwardly with his thoughts and outwardly against his adversary (v. 2). Had God forgotten him? Why was God ignoring him (v. 1)? David desired God to illuminate his mind with divine wisdom and insight concerning his situation, and to spare his life, lest his enemies gloat over his demise (vv. 3-4). Yet, the psalmist knew his enemies were fighting a losing battle, for they were challenging God's unfailing mercy. Having full assurance that God had heard his prayer, the song concludes with joyful praise to the Lord for the deliverance to come and for His abounding goodness. Waiting on the Lord for relief often feels like a heavy weight. While David could not change his pressing circumstances, he found that a joyful, trusting heart cannot be crushed by them.

Psalm: 14   Type: Lament – Personal   Author: David

Oh, Foolish Atheist – Part 1

Only twice in the Bible are the thoughts of a fool recorded for us to consider (Ps. 53:1, a second version of Ps. 14, is the other reference). Why does the atheist declare, *"There is no God"* (v. 1)? The real reason is so that he or she can willingly pursue a life of sin, that is, to live in such a way that shuns God's Word and authority. Because the atheist does not want there to be a God, he denies God's existence. In Romans 3, Paul refers to Psalm 14:2-3 in order to reinforce the conclusion that was carefully developed in Romans 1 and 2: *naturally speaking*, no one seeks after God, understands His righteousness, or can continue in well-doing (Rom. 3:10-12). When the Lord peers down from His heavenly throne to examine humanity, He finds that there is no one who perfectly does what is right, and that most are unconcerned about their spiritual condition before God. Paul rightly concludes, *"We all have sinned and fallen short of the glory of God"* (Rom. 3:23). If man could keep God's Law, he would be justified before God (Rom. 2:11-13), but it is self-evident no one can approach God this way;

rather, man must be justified through faith by the One who did meet all the demands of the Law – Christ (Rom. 3:26-28).

Having introduced the foolishness of atheism, David alludes to its outcome: divine retribution. The audacity of the atheist to think he could devour God's people (those justified in Christ) without invoking any consequences was astounding to David (v. 4). The wicked did not realize the Lord was with His people in their sufferings and, thus, they would be totally surprised and filled with dread when their judgment did come (v. 5). While it is true the wicked may frustrate and inflict God's people for a time, they will learn one day that the Lord will vindicate all who seek Him for a refuge (v. 6). David closes the song by expressing his yearning for the Kingdom Age, when God's covenant people will be delivered from hostility, the wicked will be judged, and righteousness will reign in Zion (v. 7).

Psalm: 15   Type: Liturgical – Temple   Author: David

Who May Abide With the Lord?

The psalmist already knew the answer to his question concerning who would be permitted to commune with God and to abide with Him in His holy habitation (v. 1): those who walk uprightly and do works of righteousness. To "walk uprightly" means to have blameless conduct before the Lord. Whereas the previous psalm alludes to positional salvation, the focus of this psalm is how to maintain fellowship with God, the great privilege of all those justified by faith in Christ. John declares the same truth David affirms in this Psalm: *"God is light and in Him is no darkness at all. If we say that we have fellowship with Him, and walk in darkness, we lie and do not practice the truth"* (1 Jn. 1:5-6). David then provides a character sketch of the person who enjoys walking with God in the light of revealed truth. This individual speaks honestly and sincerely; he or she does not gossip, slander, or harm another through malicious speech. Those who desire to abide with the Lord do not esteem evildoers or their vile ways, but rather extend honor to those who fear the Lord (v. 4). The righteous will keep their commitments even though it may cost them loss to do so; they will not take advantage of the impoverished who must borrow money, nor will they accept bribes against the innocent (v. 5). In summary, those who are justified by faith have the opportunity to fellowship with God to the degree they choose to submit to God's revealed truth. David declares that those who do will not be easily shaken in their minds during challenging times, for they are secure in the Lord and blessed by Him forever (v. 5).

Psalm: 16   Type: Thanksgiving – Song of Trust/Messianic
Author: David

The Lord Is My Portion

David summarizes the entire psalm in his opening decree: *"Preserve me, O God, for in You I put my trust"* (v. 1). In the first eight verses David details how he came to know the Lord as His full "portion" in life; in the last three verses he explains why he could joyfully trust the Lord in the face of death. Jehovah was David's inheritance; apart from Him nothing had value or importance (v. 2). Consequently, while on earth, David enjoyed fellowship with *"the excellent ones"* (other righteous believers), who felt the same way he did about the Lord (v. 3). Companionship with these faithful saints was wonderful! On the contrary, David was determined not to commune with those who honored or served false gods (v. 4). Why? Because God had bestowed David with the best inheritance he could have ever imagined, Himself. This meant David was experiencing the best possible life, a life of full gratification in the Lord (vv. 5-6). While considering the Lord as his abundant portion, David is prompted to praise the Lord for His counsel and instruction, which had safely guided him through previous calamities (v. 7). Because of the Lord's presence and strong hand, David was confident he would stand firm in His faith despite the attempts of his enemies to extinguish his life (v. 8).

David was confident God would preserve his life and that his body would not see decay in the grave *at that time* (vv. 9-10). Both Peter and Paul quoted David to confirm that there was a prophetic meaning to his statement relating to the future resurrection of Christ, the Holy One of Israel (Acts 2:25-28, 13:35-37). Clearly, these verses transcend David's own experience, for his body did see corruption (his tomb is still in Jerusalem today). In David's situation, God granted him deliverance from his enemies, but he could not escape death; it was inevitable. However, as it concerns Christ, this passage promises a glorious resurrection from death; therefore, as Hamilton Smith suggests, the entire psalm can be seen as tracing Christ's life of faithful obedience which led Him into a solitary grave:

> Psalm 16 is a prophetic description of the Lord Jesus in His lowly path through this world. He is viewed not in His divine equality with God, though ever true, but in the place of perfect dependence as the servant of Jehovah. It presents the inward life of faith before God, rather than the outer life seen before men. It is a life that has God for its object, so that it is a life lived to God, as well as before God.[89]

The New Testament attests to the resurrection of Christ, speaking of this spectacular event over one hundred times. Paul proclaims that without His resurrection we would not have eternal life or, by extension, hope (1 Cor. 15:12-19). Thus, both the cross and the resurrection of Christ compose the gospel message today (Rom. 10:9; 1 Cor. 15:3-4). Without Christ's resurrection, saints would just be forgiven dead people with no hope of living for Christ now or having a future heavenly life with God. But this was not David's confidence; he understood there was a *"path of life"* which permitted a glorious and joyful entrance into the eternal presence of God (v. 11). Likewise, believers can be confident death will never sever their fellowship with God (2 Cor. 5:8). Death has been conquered and its Victor is exalted and enthroned in heaven (1 Cor. 15:54-57).

Psalm: 17   Type: Lament – Personal   Author: David

Reliance on the Lord

David affirms his integrity before the Lord and also his desire to be present with the Lord in His glorious kingdom. The crisis presented in this psalm was that David was surrounded by enemies who sought his life and who only cared about temporal affairs (v. 14). Allen Ross notes the change in tenor from Psalm 16 to Psalm 17:

> The psalm is similar in many ways to Psalm 16, but there is a major difference. In Psalm 16, David was aware of danger in the background, but his faith encouraged him not to fear. In Psalm 17, however, the danger was pressing in on him, so help from the Lord was urgently needed.[90]

The urgency of the situation is felt in the first verse; note David's threefold request: *"Hear a just cause," "Attend to my cry,"* and *"Give ear to my prayer."* In verses 2-5, David asks the Lord to examine and confirm his integrity, to vindicate him, and to protect him from his proud, evil oppressors. The basis for such a prayer is revealed in verses 6 and 7; God extends His loving-kindness to those who put their trust in Him. David had experienced God's faithful love and employs two figures of speech to describe it: *"the apple of Your eye"* and *"the shadow of Your wing"* (v. 8). The first expression speaks of intimate companionship and the latter of security and protection. David then describes the wicked nature of his oppressors in attempt to further motivate the Lord to execute action against them (vv. 9-12). While the wicked he encountered had only a portion in this life (i.e. the enjoyment of temporal benefits), David lived for eternity and heavenly rewards (vv. 13-14). Those who live for today deserve destruction, but the righteous live in grace, are satisfied with the Lord's goodness, and long to see His face (v. 15). It is hard for the righteous to suffer for the sake of righteousness now, but in the grand scheme of eternity, it will always be the best decision to do so.

Psalm: 18   Type: Thanksgiving – Personal/Liturgical – Royal
Author: David

The Warrior-King at Rest

The Hebrew superscription of this psalm identifies the author (David), and his reason for writing: to acknowledge the Lord had delivered him from all his enemies, including Saul. It is noted that this psalm, with some variation, is also recorded in 2 Samuel 22. David begins by expressing his love for the Lord and declaring what the Lord is to him: his Rock, Fortress, Refuge, Shield, Stronghold, and Horn of Salvation (vv. 1-3). In verses 4-19, David poetically describes how he was in the clutches of death many times, but the Lord intervened and delivered him from his enemies. Why did God rescue David? He suggests that God honors those who humbly walk in His ways and refrain from the filth of the world, but opposes the arrogant and perverse (v. 26). Accordingly, David received the Lord's help because he had walked in righteousness and maintained his integrity; he had clean hands before the Lord (vv. 20-29). The panoramic view of all God's goodness prompted David to praise God for His faithfulness and to thank Him for all His splendid benefits (vv. 30-50).

William MacDonald notes that verse 49 is quoted in Romans 15:9, where it is directly applied to the Lord Jesus. For this reason he suggests the entire psalm is a fitting overview of Christ's victory over sin, death, and the devil: "It describes graphically His death, resurrection, exaltation, Second Coming and glorious kingdom. Nowhere else in the Bible are we given such a vivid account of the tremendous battle that took place in the unseen world at the time of our Savior's resurrection."[91] Whether it speaks of David or the Lord Jesus, from this psalm's point of view the ominous days of war are past, and the warrior-king now enjoys peace and the victor's song.

Psalm: 19   Type: Praise/Wisdom   Author: David

Divine Revelation Should Prompt Cleansing

The majestic nature of God as revealed in creation (vv. 1-6) and the specific revelation of His Word (vv. 7-11) prompted the psalmist to examine himself. From a scientific standpoint, verse 6 informs us that the Sun has a circular path of motion. Skeptics once asserted these verses were incorrect; the sun doesn't travel on a circular path – it's just the planets that do. However, we now know the sun moves in a "circuit," or circular course through space, at speeds approaching 600,000 miles per hour within one of the spiral arms of the Milky Way Galaxy. Furthermore, the Milky Way is hurtling through space at an estimated speed of 2,000,000 miles per hour.[92] Science is in agreement with Scripture.

In the same way the sun dominates the day, the Law was foremost in the Old Testament in declaring God's will to man (v. 7). Verses 7-11 confirm that God's Word and His work are a direct reflection of His character; that is, they are what He is: perfect, sure, right, pure, clean, true, and righteous. In this psalm the works and the Word of God are shown to have two qualities, says J. G. Bellett; they glorify God and bless the creature:

> This is the meditation of a true worshipper of God, honoring Him both in His works and His word. The Gentiles should (but did not, Rom. 1) have known God from His works, and Israel should (but did not, Rom. 2) have kept His word or His law. The true worshipper here, therefore, condemns both, and glorifies God in His two great ordinances or testimonies. [93]

David considered it a joy and a privilege to know and keep God's commandments; doing so revives the soul and makes one wise in righteous living (vv. 8-9). To him, God's statutes were more precious than gold, sweeter than honey, and ensured a prodigious reward if obeyed (vv. 10-11). David's self-examination resulted in the confession of willful sins, asking forgiveness for hidden sins, and beseeching God to preserve him from committing future transgressions (vv. 12-13). Light and darkness cannot exist together and David, illuminated by divine revelation, desired to be blameless before the Lord so that his praise would be accepted by his *"strength"* and his *"Redeemer"* (v. 14). May all God's people have the same wise passion!

Psalm: 20   Type: Liturgical – Royal   Author: David

A Plea for Victory

Before venturing into battle, the king, also the psalmist, first went to the sanctuary (this would be the tabernacle in David's day) to offer sacrifices and to pray for preservation and victory. There he was accompanied by a congregation who in unison petitioned the Lord to prosper the king's battle strategy and to grant his request for conquest (vv. 1-4). Since the congregation was gathered at God's dwelling place, they corporately asked for *"help from the sanctuary"* on the king's behalf. The entire community then confirmed their confidence that the Lord would answer the king's prayer and also their anticipation of ecstatically praising God on his return from battle (v. 5). The king himself, David, then expresses his own confidence in the saving power of God's right hand, rather than the devices of war (vv. 6-7). Because of the reputation of God's name and His unchanging character, David anticipated a great rout of his enemies (v. 8). The congregation then repeated their initial request to save the king in battle (v. 9). While believers in the Church Age are not called to engage in armed religious conflict, all those clad in spiritual armor who wield the Sword of the Spirit as they storm the gates of hell with the gospel of Jesus Christ will be refreshed by this psalm.

Psalm: 21   Type: Liturgical – Royal   Author: David

God Preserves the King

This psalm is similar both in construction and content to the previous psalm and apparently is an expression of thanksgiving by the congregation for answering their prayers to preserve the king in battle. The historical setting of this psalm may have been David's victory over the Ammonites and Syrians (2 Sam. 10:14-19). The returning king praises the Lord for displaying His majestic power in battle and for granting him the desire of his heart – the preservation of his life and a complete triumph (vv. 1-6). David affirms the reason his prayer was granted was because he fully trusted in the unfailing love of the Most High (v. 7). The king is then addressed by the congregation, who state they knew he would be completely victorious over his enemies because he trusted in the Lord (vv. 8-10). They realize God would grant him future victories for the same reason, despite the ongoing efforts of David's enemies to overcome him. The congregation declares they will sing praise to God alone for flexing His might and power on behalf of their king (vv. 11-12).

Psalm: 22   Type: Lament – Personal/Messianic   Author: David

Calvary – The Good Shepherd Suffers

We now have arrived at the most important Psalm trilogy in our Bibles: the shepherding series of Psalm 22, 23, and 24 which foretells the then future work of the Lord Jesus in relationship to those He would save. In Psalm 22, the Lord is presented as the *"Good Shepherd"* who lays His life down for the sheep at Mount Calvary (John 10:9-11). In Psalm 23, the ongoing sanctifying work of the Lord Jesus is pictured, as He faithfully leads His sheep through the valley of shadows and provides for all their needs. The writer of Hebrews highlights this continuing ministry of the Lord Jesus, the *"Great Shepherd"* (Heb. 13:20-21). Finally, Psalm 24 speaks of the Lord gathering up His people to Mount Zion, speaking of the heavenly city. This shepherding ministry of Christ is acknowledged by Peter; He is the *"Chief Shepherd"* who will return and gather His sheep to Himself (1 Pet. 5:4). This is speaking of the return of Christ to the air to "snatch away" from the earth all those who are His sheep. This trilogy, then, speaks of the death, burial, resurrection, and exaltation of Christ.

T. Ernest Wilson observes there are actually four psalms (Psalm 22 being the first) that foretell the death of Christ, but these do so from different perspectives:

Psalm 40 is the burnt offering – God's purpose.
Psalm 22 is the sin offering – the passion.
Psalm 69 is the trespass offering – the penalty.
Psalm 118 is the peace offering – the prophetic program.[94]

As David laments his own situation in this poem, the Spirit of God seizes David's pen to interject prophetic details pertaining to the future sufferings of the Messiah. Though it is David's poetry, William Kelly notes whose voice is really heard throughout the psalm:

Such is this wondrous psalm; the sufferings that pertain to Christ, and the glories after these. No voice is heard throughout but Christ's; none could be with His atoning cries to God, though we may join in praising God and the Lamb, and we are assured that the truth that He was alone in those sorrows is the guarantee of that efficacious work, whereby all our evil is annulled and we stand in His acceptance as believers in Him who contrasts Himself with those before Him that cried and were heard.[95]

Hence, the psalm may be divided into five main sections: the sufferings of Christ in relationship to God (vv. 1-6), to man (vv. 7-18), and to Satan (vv. 19-21), and a preview of the Lord's resurrection (vv. 22-25), and His future Millennial Kingdom (vv. 26-31). In all, ten specific prophecies can be identified within Psalm 22 as being fulfilled by Christ at Calvary; clearly, these do not literally apply to David.

Psalm 22 Prophecies Pertaining to Calvary	OT Reference/NT Fulfillment
"My God, My God, why have You forsaken Me?"	Ps. 22:1/ Mark 15:34
Time of darkness	Ps. 22:2; Amos 8:9/ Matt. 27:45
Mocked and insulted	Ps. 22:7-8/ Matt. 27:39-43, 45
Scoffers to mock: "He trusted in God, let Him deliver Him"	Ps. 22:8; Ps. 31:14-15/ Matt. 27:43
Be thirsty during execution	Ps. 22:15/ John 19:28
Hands and feet pierced	Ps. 22:16/ Matt. 27:31, 35
Stripped of clothes	Ps. 22:18/ Luke 23:34
Soldiers cast lots for outer coat	Ps. 22:18/ Matt. 27:35; Mark 15:24
Soldiers divided inner garment	Ps. 22:18/ Matt. 27:35; Mark 15:24
Committed Himself to God before dying	Ps. 22:20-21/ Luke 23:46

Although David felt that his tearful pleas for deliverance were not being heard, he chose to trust in the Lord who had clearly answered the prayers of his forefathers during grueling times (v. 4). Hence, David's distress from oppressive enemies is used as a backdrop to better assist our understanding of how the Savior felt during the unfathomable anguish of Calvary, while His faith in God the Father was unshaken. The Lord Jesus quoted verse 1 from the cross to affirm that while acting as our Sin-bearer, His fellowship with His Father had been severed. Christ was made *"the reproach of men and despised by the people"* and *"a worm"* (v. 6). "Worm" is translated from the Hebrew word *tolaath*. The *tola* worm was smashed to yield a scarlet colored dye; this pictures the humble servant nature of Christ and how He was crushed to produce the blood of our redemption.

God answered David's prayer for deliverance. He did again praise the Lord in the congregation of his brethren (v. 22), but the Lord Jesus was not delivered in this way – in the will of God, Christ had to die. The only means by which the Lord Jesus could fulfill this prophecy after being crucified was to be raised from the dead; the fulfillment of this prophecy is recorded in John 20:17. He procured propitiation for our sins at Calvary and secured our eternal life through His resurrection; thus, the meek (those who humbly receive Christ) will be satisfied and be able to praise God in His heavenly abode forever (v. 26). In fact, in a coming day, the entire world will turn to the Lord; everyone will worship and serve Him (vv. 27-31). We understand this to refer to the Millennial Kingdom of Christ. Psalm 22 stands out among all other psalms in respect to foretelling the then future sufferings of the blessed Savior.

Psalm: 23   Type: Thanksgiving – Song of Trust   Author: David

The Vale of Shadows – The Great Shepherd Leads

This psalm is probably the most memorized psalm and likely the most cherished poem in all of literature. It has been a solace to many during times of trial, profound grief, and impending death. The Lord is portrayed as the Shepherd who gently leads His sheep in their heavenly pilgrimage during their earthly sojourn. With Mount Calvary (Ps. 22) on one side and Mount Zion (Ps. 24) on the other, the Lord guides His people through the threatening Valley of Shadows (Ps. 23) that lies between these mountains. Those in His care will: not lack (v. 1), enjoy tranquility of mind (v. 2), know the path of righteousness (v. 3), experience divine comfort (v. 4), ultimately triumph over their enemies (v. 5), and benefit from the Lord's communion, goodness, and mercy forever (v. 6). All believers must travel through this ominous course before ascending Mount Zion in glory. While the path of righteousness through the Valley of Shadows will be difficult, it is good to remember that it is in the valley and not on the mountaintops that fruit-bearing occurs. The insults and the threatenings now levied on a righteous life are mere flittering shadows which fade with the setting sun. Shadows may scare us, but they have no power to hurt anyone. It is only when we have a diminished opinion of the Great Shepherd that the enemy's suggestions (or shadows) gain a foothold in our minds.

Psalm: 24   Type: Liturgical – Temple/Messianic   Author: David

Mount Zion – The Chief Shepherd Reigns

The ascension of Christ is referenced some twenty times in the Gospels and in Acts to document the prophetic fulfillment of this psalm. The Lord created and established the earth; He thus reigns supreme over creation from His holy hill (vv. 1-2). Although Satan wanted to *"ascend to the hill of the Lord"* (v. 3) and reign as God, his pride was judged and he lost his privileged status as a covering cherub (Isa. 14:12-15; Ezek. 28:12-17). Only those with clean hands and a pure heart may be with the Lord in His holy dwelling place (vv. 3-4). Initially, this spoke of the glorified Savior alone, but after His redemptive work the reference could be expanded to all those who have been justified and glorified in Him (vv. 5-6). The Lord Himself, in communicating with the sentinel posted at the everlasting gates of glory, announces both of His return entrances to heaven (vv. 7, 9). The first entrance was as Calvary's Victor, *"the Lord mighty in battle."* At the cross Christ triumphed over Satan, the prince of the world (v. 8; John 12:31-32). He entered heaven alone at this time and *"sat down on the right hand of the Majesty on high"* (Heb. 1:3; Rev. 3:21). Later, He eagerly departs from this high station to again return to the earth (i.e., to the air above the earth) to gather up His saints (v. 9; 1 Thess. 4:13-18). Thus, at His second return entrance into heaven He will not be alone; He is *"the King of Glory – the Lord of hosts"* (v. 10). This shepherding trilogy from Psalms shows that resurrected saints return to heaven with Christ and are not raptured at the end of the Tribulation Period to merely accompany Christ from the air to the earth to establish His kingdom, as some suggest.

Psalm: 25   Type: Lament – Personal   Author: David

Defend, Guide, and Pardon

This psalm is a lovely meditation on the nature of God that should prompt us to humbly confess our sin and to seek God's instruction and forgiveness in prayer. The entire poem is an acrostic, as each of the twenty-two verses begins with a successive letter of the Hebrew alphabet (though one letter is omitted and another is used twice). David could earnestly seek the Lord because he knew those who did would never be put to shame; David's enemies had no such hope (vv. 1-3). David prayed that God would show him the right way and teach him the path of truth, and that God, in His tender mercy, would not remember (act on) the sins of David's youth (vv. 4-7). The request for both enlightenment and pardon is reiterated two more times in verses 8-22. Having complete confidence in the character of God, the psalmist concludes his prayer with a request that Israel would also be delivered from all her enemies (v. 22). In Psalm 25, David teaches that if we want the Lord's guidance and help in life, we need to be honest with Him about our sin.

Psalm: 26   Type: Lament – Personal   Author: David

Integrity Should Be Rewarded

The exact setting of this psalm is unknown, though it stems from the fact that, unlike many in his day, David had an upright heart and he worshipped only Jehovah. In Psalm 26, David asserts his integrity (vv. 1-3), provides evidence of it (vv. 4-8), and then petitions the Lord to deliver him from the fate of the sinner because of his uprightness (vv. 9-12). David claims that his walk (personal testimony) is marked by moral integrity, adherence to the truth, and unwavering trust in the Lord; he asks the Lord to validate these assertions (vv. 1-3). David claims to be upright, not sinless. He identifies with worshippers of Jehovah and keeps himself separate from sinners (vv. 4-5). He offers worship at God's sanctuary with clean, innocent hands and with complete sincerity – David loved to praise the Lord (vv. 6-8). Based on his integrity, David asks the Lord in verses 9-11 to be merciful to him and ransom his life and not prematurely end it, as was often the case with flagrant sinners (e.g., those who murder, deceive, and take bribes). David wrote this poem with full assurance the Lord would answer his prayer, and thus he promises to continue praising Him in the congregation of His people (v. 12).

Psalm: 27 Type: Lament – Personal/Thanksgiving – Songs of Trust   Author: David

Seeking and Waiting on the Lord

Initially, David expresses a sincere confidence that the Lord will deliver him from his enemies. The Lord was his light (i.e. the One who illuminated the truth in his mind), his salvation from harm, and the strength of all his exploits (vv. 1-3). David yearned to commune with the Lord; in this composition, he conveys a desire to remain in God's earthly sanctuary (i.e., the tabernacle) at all times (v. 4). Being in God's presence further ensured David's safety; thus, he assertively declares he will triumph over his enemies and will continue to sing joyful praises to God (vv. 5-6). However, there is a mood change in verse 7 which introduces an anxious tone to David's petition; apparently, he did not feel the Lord's help was being provided in a timely manner. He pleads for the Lord not to forsake him and to continue to comfort and to assist him during perilous times. David's expression certainly reminds us of the innermost thoughts of the Lord Jesus as He was agonizing in prayer in the Garden of Gethsemane just hours before His arrest and crucifixion. While the mission of redemption could not be averted, the Father did send an angel to minister and comfort His Son (Luke 22:43).

Jehovah had instructed the righteous to seek His face in prayer during onerous occasions, and that was what David was doing; he thus expected God, his Helper, to respond (vv. 8-9). David was confident that though his own parents might forsake him, God never would (v. 10). Accordingly, David wanted God to teach him the right way to go, so that his enemies would not be able to ambush and destroy him (vv. 11-12). The song concludes with an affirmation of confidence in God's protection and a firm resolve to wait for the Lord's deliverance (vv. 13-14).

Psalm: 28   Type: Lament – Personal   Author: David

God Hears and Blesses

In a more urgent tone than Psalm 26, David earnestly pleads with the Lord not to let him die with the wicked and deceitful hypocrites when they would be justly overthrown (vv. 1, 3-4). God's mercy and assistance were anticipated because David had sought God in genuine brokenness and in tears (v. 2). David could proclaim to others that God had heard his prayers and was confident that Jehovah would both deliver him from murderous schemes and judge the wicked (vv. 5-6). The Lord was David's Strength and Shield, a Mighty Fortress to His anointed (speaking of King David), and therefore was deserving of praise (vv. 7-8). The psalm ends with the psalmist requesting that God would sustain His people through all their difficulties and tribulations (v. 9).

Psalm: 29   Type: Liturgical – Royal   Author: David

God Rules Over Creation

Psalm 29 stresses the awesome power the Creator possesses over all His creation. Thus, the phrase *"give unto the Lord"* occurs three times in this climactic poem which crescendos by calling on all creatures, including *"the mighty ones"* (i.e., angels), to worship the Lord in the beauty of holiness (v. 1-2). Allen P. Ross supplies this summary of the psalm:

> David witnessed an awesome thunderstorm moving across the land of the Canaanites, and attributed it to the power of the Lord. He called on the angels to glorify Him who sits as King forever over nature. Psalm 29 is a polemic against pagan beliefs in false gods who were credited with being responsible for storms.[96]

A devastating storm apparently blew inland off the Mediterranean Sea (vv. 3-4). As the tempest progressed eastward, gusts of wind snapped the cedars of Lebanon, forked lighting streaked across the sky like flames of fire, leaves were stripped from trees, and deafening claps of thunder shook the mountains of Lebanon and Sirion and even the Desert of Kadesh (vv. 5-9). Instead of complaining about the weather, as people often do, David is prompted to praise God's awesome power as illustrated by it. Seven times David likens *"the voice of the Lord"* to the majestic happenings of this powerful storm. Witnessing the awesome power of God in creation should cause everyone to honor and worship Him in His temple. David concludes that the Lord reigns as King forever and because He is sovereign over creation, He is quite able to bless His people and grant them peace (vv. 11-12).

Psalm: 30   Type: Thanksgiving – Personal   Author: David

Praising God for Chastening and Deliverance

The Hebrew superscript reads: "A Psalm and Song at the dedication of the house of David." It is not likely that David is dedicating his place of residence to the Lord; rather, what is in view is probably the future site of the temple his son Solomon would build and the materials for the project (1 Chron. 22:1-6). The temple was built on the threshing floor of Araunah, where the disciplinary plague was stayed by David's burnt offering to the Lord. Because of stubborn pride (v. 6), perhaps relating to his census of the nation of Israel (1 Chron. 21:26), David was severely disciplined by the Lord (v. 7). In response, David humbly besought the Lord in tears and sackcloth for forgiveness and restoration (vv. 8-11). With his chastening behind him, David could now praise the Lord for preserving his life, not permitting his enemies to triumph over him, and for healing him, probably of a physical illness, but certainly of emotional distress (vv. 1-3). He could now sing to the Lord with other saints concerning His righteous and holy ways (v. 4). God is slow to anger and quick to forgive; accordingly, David's remorse and weeping had been for a short season and now were replaced with joyful praise (v. 5). Divine chastening is a confirmation of God's love for His erring children:

My son, do not despise the chastening of the Lord, nor be discouraged when you are rebuked by Him; for whom the Lord loves He chastens, and scourges every son whom He receives (Heb. 12:5-6).

David understood this fact and was moved to praise God, the One who heals better than humanly derived medicine can (v. 12). God had dealt righteously and mercifully with David, and he was richer for it – and so are we.

Psalm: 31   Type: Lament – Personal   Author: David

The Lord – A Mighty Fortress

We come to yet another psalm in which David laments his distressing circumstances and pleads for divine assistance and preservation. Through each challenging episode of his life he found the Lord to be a faithful Refuge, an unmovable Rock, and a mighty Fortress (vv. 1-2). Accordingly, David affirms his confidence that the God of truth will redeem him and lead him out of danger again (vv. 3-5). David knew God loved him and he already knew the outcome of his prayer, so he could expectantly praise God for his forthcoming deliverance (vv. 7-8). He also could express his disgust for those who ignorantly embrace useless idols because they would not find help during life's calamities (v. 6). After David laments his present danger (vv. 9-13), he prays for rescue (vv. 14-18), and then concludes the psalm by praising the Lord for His goodness (vv. 19-23). Because David had repeatedly found the Lord to be both loyal and kind, he could encourage others (including us) to love the Lord, to be strong in the Lord, and to hope in Him alone (vv. 23-24). This was the example of the Lord Jesus who, in perfect faith, moments before His last breath could say, *"Father, 'into Your hands I commit My spirit'"* (v. 5; Luke 23:46).

Psalm: 32 Type: Thanksgiving – Personal/Penitential
Author: David

Rejoicing in God's Forgiveness

The content of this composition indicates David had been divinely chastened, then forgiven, though the Hebrew superscript does not inform us of the particular sin. The circumstances and tenor of this psalm seem quite different than Psalm 30, where David's discipline was for pride (perhaps pertaining to the numbering of Israel). While remorseful for past transgressions, the main theme of this poem is the joy of being forgiven and restored to God after His discipline had ceased. It is likely, then, that this psalm follows on the heels of Psalm 51, which pertains directly to his adultery with Bathsheba and the murder of her husband Uriah (2 Sam. 11).

Although he could not know specifically how God could forgive him, for the Law demanded that murderers and adulterers be put to death, David knew by faith that His transgressions were forgiven, his sin was atoned for, and his iniquity was no longer imputed to him (vv. 1-2). David recalls the time he was silent in his sin and under God's heavy hand: he groaned deep in his bones day and night, he grew old and his vitality dried up as crops in a long summer's drought (vv. 3-4). The way out of this pitiful spiritual condition was to confess his sin and ask for forgiveness (v. 5). Given the outcome of his experience, he counsels others (v. 6) not to linger in the denial of sin, but to get right with the Lord while He may be found, rather than be overwhelmed by the mighty waters (i.e., correction by calamity). Having confessed his sin, David had grown to appreciate the Lord as his Hiding Place – God is a Refuge to those who trust in Him (v. 7). Others are instructed to submit to the Lord, rather than to force His chastening hand upon them; those who do will experience his abiding love, and be able to praise God unhindered (vv. 9-12). David had learned that he must choose to be in intimate fellowship with the Lord in order to be guided by His eye in the way he should go (v. 8). When in face-to-face communion with God, what we should do is what He delightful looks upon in favor.

Psalm: 33   **Type: Praise**   **Author: David**

Rejoice in the Lord!

Although there is no Hebrew superscription for this psalm, the Septuagint ascribes it to David, who summons the righteous to praise the Lord for the reliability of His word and His righteous works (v. 6). It is fitting for God's people to joyfully praise the Lord in song as accompanied by musical instruments skillfully played (vv. 2-3). The heavens and the earth were framed by God's righteous word, and man who benefits from God's goodness should stand in awe of the Lord and not resist His rule (vv. 4-11). David delighted to be a part of God's chosen people, God's representatives among the nations (v. 12). No one could escape God's all-seeing eye; He was aware of all human deeds and even the motives prompting them (vv. 13-17). David surmised that this divine perception benefitted those who chose to revere the Lord and to rejoice and hope in Him – they would be delivered from death and be preserved in life by their Help and Shield, the Lord (vv. 18-22).

Psalm: 34   **Type: Thanksgiving – Personal**   **Author: David**

The Lord Delivers the Righteous

David fled to the Philistine-controlled border town of Gath to escape King Saul's jealous rage. His victory over Goliath had gained David notoriety among the Philistines, which prompted his arrest. According to the superscription, this psalm was written after David escaped from Abimelech (Achish by name) after feigning insanity; he then hid in the cave of Adullam (1 Sam. 21:10-15). However, it is not his resourceful scheming that David boasts in, but rather how God answered his prayer and controlled the situation to preserve his life and secure his freedom (vv. 2, 4). David hoped his passion to praise God *"at all times"* in this matter would prompt all the afflicted to seek the Lord's help, so that they might add their praises to his (vv. 1, 3), experience radiant joy, and not suffer shame (vv. 5-6). Hamilton Smith observes that the first three verses identify the theme of the psalm:

The godly man blesses the Lord, boasts in the Lord, and exalts the Lord, and does so *"at all times."* This praise at all times is the distinguishing thought in the psalm. It is easy to praise the Lord when circumstances are favorable, when there are no fears to assail and no clouds in the sky; when there are no troubles to crush, nor dangers to confront. To bless the Lord "at all times" – in dark days or fair – is an experience that can only be known by the saint with a broken and a humble heart (v. 18). It is this that the psalm so touchingly unfolds.[97]

All those who trust in the Lord for protection will be able to *"taste and see that the Lord is good"* (vv. 7-8). David proclaims, *"The eyes of the Lord are on the righteous, and His ears are open to their cry"* (v. 15); He will deliver them from trouble (v. 19); none shall be desolate (v. 22). The righteous are those who fear the Lord (vv. 9-11), keep their tongues from evil (v. 13), serve others, and seek peace (v. 14). In contrast, the wicked shall be ensnared by their evil devices (v. 21), cut off from the earth, and not remembered (v. 16). David wanted the righteous to rest in God's sovereign protection. During our earthly sojourn there will be suffering for those who live for the Lord (2 Tim. 3:12) but, as David reminds us, *"The Lord is near to those who have a broken heart, and saves such as have a contrite spirit"* (v. 18). Amen.

Psalm: 35   Type: Lament – Imprecatory   Author: David

A Prayer for God to Judge

David's enemies had no valid reason for warring with him; therefore, he urgently pleads with the Lord to *"fight against those who fight against me"* (v. 1). Invoking his imagination, David poetically requests the Lord take up shield, buckler, spear, and battle-axe and stand directly in the path of his approaching oppressors as his frontline defense (vv. 2-3). The Angel of the Lord (a theophany of Christ) was his Champion to cast his enemies aside as wind clears a threshing floor of worthless chaff (vv. 4-6). David then laments the unjust hatred of his adversaries – they had repaid evil for good and mocked him in his distress (vv. 11-17). However, David was determined to publicly praise the Lord when his prayer for deliverance against those who hated him without cause was answered (vv. 18-19). Jehovah is a righteous God

The Beginning of Wisdom

and it is on this basis David pleads for justice to be served to those who had mocked, falsely accused, slandered, and wrongly striven with him (vv. 20-21). The psalmist pleads with the Lord to no longer be silent, but to rise up and exonerate His servant (vv. 22-26). David's confidence in the Lord to vindicate him is declared in his concluding prayer, which anticipates all who would stand with him to praise and exalt the Lord continually: *"Let the Lord be magnified, Who has pleasure in the prosperity of His servant"* (v. 27).

David's imprecatory prayers in this psalm and Psalm 71 are similar to Nehemiah's when he called on God to judge those who opposed his wall-building effort (Neh. 4:4-5), and also to what is uttered by the martyred dead in heaven during the Tribulation Period (Rev. 6:9-11). While Scripture does record the prayers of the righteous pleading for immediate wrath upon their enemies, this protocol is not endorsed during the Church Age. In the Age of Grace, Christians should desire their adversaries experience God's grace and be saved, not destroyed. Though the Lord Jesus and Stephen suffered at the hands of their oppressors, both prayed that God would not judge at that time those who had ill-treated them (Luke 23:34; Acts 7:60). The Lord instructed His disciples, His apostles in the Church Age, to pray for and show love to their enemies; perhaps some would repent and be saved (Luke 6:27-35). Such kindness demonstrates God's love in action and can soften the hardest of rebel hearts. Thus, Christians are not to seek the destruction of their persecutors, but are rather to pray for their salvation. Believers are to overcome evil deeds by reflecting Christ in generous acts of righteousness (Rom. 12:19-21).

Psalm: 36   Type: Lament – Personal   Author: David

No Mercy for the Wicked

This psalm contrasts the lifestyle, character, and demise of the wicked with that of the righteous who are recipients of God's mercy. David received understanding concerning the sinfulness of the wicked: they do not fear the Lord and therefore engage in evil without remorse. The wicked become so proficient at soothing their own consciences that they can continue in deceptive speech and licentious deeds during the daytime, and plot evil at night (vv. 2-4). In contrast to the evildoers who surrounded him, David found meditating on the character and attributes of God comforted his soul. David had experienced God's faithfulness, mercy, and enduring love, and therefore thoroughly trusted God's righteous and just character which, in his view, ensured the preservation of both man and beast (vv. 5-6). This understanding should prompt all men to trust in the Lord so that they too might be protected and be blessed with light and life (vv. 7-9). David concludes by acknowledging God's loyal love and by asking the Lord to preserve his integrity from the influences of the proud, who were destined to be destroyed (vv. 10-12).

Psalm: 37   Type: Wisdom   Author: David

Trust in the Lord

Like Psalms 25 and 119, this song is arranged as an acrostic; every other verse starts with a successive letter from the Hebrew alphabet. Sometimes it seems as though the wicked are flourishing in life and prevailing over God's people. A now elderly David encourages the righteous to trust in the Lord and not to envy or fret over evildoers; their doom is guaranteed (vv. 1-3). Rather, believers are to commit their way to the Lord, to delight in the Lord, and to seek Him in prayer so that they may receive the yearnings of their heart (vv. 4-6). Those who do not choose to rest in the Lord will be prone to sin in their anger, *"but the meek shall inherit the earth"* (vv. 8-11). Though the wicked plot against the righteous, God laughs at their conniving, selfish ways and perverted schemes; all they do will amount to nothing and, in the end, they will perish (vv. 12-22). In contrast, the righteous are better off having little in life with the Lord's blessing; such have a tremendous inheritance which will never be lost (vv. 16, 18, 22). In fact, the Lord promises particular blessings to the righteous: divine protection, sufficient food, His abiding love, and wisdom from His Word (vv. 23-31). The exploits of the wicked cannot thwart God's power to preserve the righteous, nor gain a reprieve from judgment – though it may seem like they are prospering, the wicked shall perish (vv. 32-38). David reminds us that the Lord is a reliable Refuge and Salvation and that there is no reason to agonize over or envy those destined to destruction (vv. 39-40).

Psalm: 38   Type: Lament – Penitential   Author: David

Godly Sorrow Prompts Repentance

Suffering severely under the chastening hand of the Lord, David petitions the Lord to temper His anger with mercy and to pardon him for his offense (vv. 1-2). David did not attempt to hide his sin, but readily confessed his foolishness; he was emotionally miserable night and day, and was also suffering from a debilitating illness because of his transgression (vv. 3-8). David's pitiful state, brokenness, and deep sighing were fully visible to the Lord (vv. 9-10). In his distress, many of David's friends had abandoned him, and his enemies were speaking evil of him and plotting against him (vv. 11-12). Rather than listening to or speaking against his enemies, David acted like a deaf-mute; his trust was in the Lord alone to deliver him from his oppressors (vv. 13-16). The psalmist does not deny his sin, nor suggest his suffering is unjust; rather, he confesses the transgression before the Lord and pleads for God to rescue him from his vicious enemies who plan his destruction (vv. 17-20). The situation was desperate, God's discipline had served its purpose, and David now entreats the Lord not to forsake him, but instead be his Savior (vv. 21-22). William Kelly suggests this psalm will not only encourage the repentant Christian who has experienced God's chastening, but it will also comfort the restored Jewish remnant at the Lord's Second Advent:

> Indeed, without questioning the peculiar comfort it will prove to the godly Jew when awakened in the latter day to feel its value, it is most suitable to the Christian suffering under the chastening hand of the Lord for folly and sin. Then is the time to cherish confidence in Him, as the Christian may do even more deeply and dropping all thought of enemies save of a spiritual kind. We can cry even then, Abba, Father.[98]

David teaches us to not ignore sin, but to confess it to God, and to not complain about His just recompense for our stupidity. Such

Devotions in Psalms

repentance should never be repented of, for restored fellowship with God should be cherished (2 Cor. 7:10).

Psalm: 39   Type: Lament – Personal   Author: David

Human Frailty

This poem continues the theme of the previous psalm; though the imminent threat from his enemies had passed, David was suffering a prolonged illness that had brought him to the brink of death. The experience had taught him the frailty of his own body and the brevity of human life in general (vv. 4-6). This realization caused David to carefully consider his speech – though his enemy's gossip and slander angered him, he did not want to sin with his tongue (vv. 1-3). Hence, David laments his agony, and pleads with the Lord to end his chastening and to restore his physical health so that he might live out his remaining days in peace (vv. 8-11, 13). The closing prayer petitions God to honor his tears of repentance and to not treat him as a stranger (v. 12). David affirms his guilt before the Lord, but also casts himself completely on the Lord, his Hope, for mercy and restoration (v. 7). May we also remember that life is too short to waste it away in sin!

Psalm: 40   Type: Thanksgiving – Personal/Messianic
              Author: David

God Gives a New Song

In appreciation for being richly blessed, David commits himself as a living sacrifice to the Lord in this song (vv. 1-10). David begins by informing the congregation God had wonderfully rescued him from a terrible situation, which he likens to being pulled out of a slimy pit and set on a secure rock; consequently, he had a new song of praise in his heart (vv. 1-3). He advises those listening that God's marvelous benefits designated for His people are innumerable; hence, if they want to experience God's blessing, they must trust in Him completely (vv. 4-5). David realized that, through his sufferings, the glory of God was being shown to others. He then concluded God was more interested in him than the animal sacrifices he offered (v. 6). In response to this awareness, David was going to live for the Lord, which meant doing the will of God as declared in the words of the scroll (vv. 7-8).

Though the text is an expression of his own dedication, David prophetically wrote of the One who would willingly come in obedience to God and sacrifice Himself, thus fulfilling the significance of the Levitical offerings. The blood sacrifices and meal offerings of Leviticus righteously accommodated the inflexible holiness of God, as declared in the Law, such that grace in its purest form could coexist together with holiness in peaceful bliss. These offerings foreshadowed what the Lord Jesus Christ has now accomplished at Calvary for all believers:

> *Sacrifice* [zebach] *and offering* [minchad] *You did not desire; My ears You have opened. Burnt offering* [olah] *and sin offering* [chataah] *You did not require. Then I said, "Behold, I come; in the scroll of the book it is written of me. I delight to do Your will, O my God, and Your law is within my heart"* (vv. 6-7).

The Hebrew words employed in Psalm 40 directly relate to all the Levitical offerings: *zebach* pertains to the *peace* offering, *minchad* to the *meal* offering, *olah* to the *burnt* offering, and *chataah* to the *sin* offering. Although distinct, the sin and the trespass (*'asham*) offerings were often connected together (Lev 7:7), as in this psalm. The writer of Hebrews quotes from Psalm 40 to confirm Christ's sacrifice at Calvary on behalf of humanity was a direct fulfillment of David's prophecy (see Heb. 10:5-7). God the Father did not want us to miss the link between the willing Servant and the suffering Son of God.

A comparison of Psalm 40 and Hebrews 10 clearly reveals that the One who had His ear opened to be marked as a servant in Psalm 40:6 is the same One who offered His entire body, indeed His life, to God (John 10:11), and fulfilled the complete meaning of all five Levitical sacrifices. For this reason, we read in the New Testament:

> *And walk in love, as Christ also has loved us and given Himself for us, an offering and a sacrifice to God for a sweet smelling aroma* (Eph. 5:2).

Devotions in Psalms

> *But this Man, after He had offered one sacrifice for sins forever, sat down at the right hand of God, from that time waiting till His enemies are made His footstool. For by one offering He has perfected forever those who are being sanctified* (Heb. 10:12-14).

In summary, the Lord Jesus Christ is the faithful One who was fully dedicated to doing the will of God unto death and thus fulfills all that the sweet and non-sweet savor offerings symbolize.

The tone of the psalm transitions in verse 11 to one of urgent prayer for deliverance. David had many troubles, which he felt were a direct consequence of his sins (vv. 11-12). He reminds the congregation that the praise and worship of God is the ultimate objective of doing God's will. This he does by acknowledging God's holy character and wondrous attributes (vv. 9-10). David concludes the psalm by repeating an urgent plea for immediate rescue from his enemies and then explains why: he desires that the righteous will be moved to praise the Lord with him when divine intervention does occur (vv. 13-17). The highest calling of a believer is to be a living sacrifice for Christ, which means separation from worldliness and full consecration to Christ (Rom. 12:1-2).

Psalm: 41   Type: Lament – Personal/Messianic   Author: David

Blessed Is He Who Gives to the Poor

This psalm may well be the sequel of Psalm 39, as David recounts a previous prayer for divine retribution against those who had deceitfully spoken against him during his long illness, which he considered the result of divine chastening for personal sin (vv. 4-10). In contrast to these betrayers, the psalmist instructs the congregation not to take advantage of the weak, but to extend kindness to the needy; those who do will obtain the Lord's favor (v. 1). This includes protection from enemies and sustaining care when suffering from infirmities (vv. 2-3).

Verse 9 may refer to the betrayal of David's trusted counselor Ahithophel during the rebellion of Absalom, David's son (2 Sam. 17:1-23). On the eve of His crucifixion, the Lord referred to this verse, which states, *"Even my own familiar friend in whom I trusted, who ate my bread, has lifted up his heel against me,"* which foretells the betrayal of Judas, one of His disciples (see Mark 14:18-21). However, we note Christ never called Judas a familiar friend or trusted him. Although David likely had his own trusted friend, Ahithophel, in mind when he penned these words, they have a greater fulfillment in the life of Christ. Since the Lord Jesus knew from the beginning that Judas would betray Him (John 6:70-71), He only referenced the portion of the verse which was messianic in nature. This ensured the betrayer would be properly identified when the Lord Jesus, the host of the Passover feast, passed Judas the sop in fulfillment of this prophecy (John 13:18-19). Although David had prayed for God to judge his treacherous foes, the Lord repeatedly showed kindness to Judas, even calling him "friend" in the Garden of Gethsemane just before His own arrest (v. 10; Matt. 26:50). At His First Advent the Lord came to seek and to save the lost, not to condemn sinners.

Turning from the congregation, David directly addresses the Lord to acknowledge He had delivered him from his enemies, which David felt was an endorsement of his own integrity. Book 1 then closes with a doxology: *"Blessed be the Lord God of Israel from everlasting to everlasting! Amen and Amen"* (v. 13). While the first book in the Bible ends with a coffin in Egypt, picturing the aftermath of sin (i.e., man is spiritually dead in the world), the first book in Psalms ends with the hope of resurrection – God's people in His presence forever!

Book 2

Book 2 includes Psalms 42 through 72. David wrote twenty of these psalms (Psalms 51-70). Seven are ascribed to "the sons of Korah" (Psalms 42, 44-49), which may mean they authored these poems or it may indicate these songs were dedicated to them and performed by them. The authors of three psalms are unknown (Psalms 43, 67, 71), one was written by Asaph (Ps. 50), and one was composed by Solomon (Ps. 72). The main theme of the second book is redemption.

Psalm: 42   **Type: Lament – Personal**   **Author: Korahites**

Yearning for God

Many of the ancient Hebrew manuscripts combine Psalms 42 and 43 as a single poem. The composition of these psalms seems to confirm this, as the same refrain in Psalm 42 (vv. 5, 11) is repeated in verse 5 of Psalm 43. The psalmist begins Psalm 42 by expressing his deep yearning for God and concludes with the joyful expectation of communing with God in Psalm 43. A simile is employed in the first two verses: just as a deer requires drinking water to survive, the parched soul of the psalmist desperately required communion with the living God to be revived (vv. 1-2). Apparently, civil affairs had kept him from worshipping the Lord at the tabernacle (or temple); thus, his enemies had been relentlessly taunting him with such questions as, *"Where is your God?"* (vv. 3-4, 10). By posing the rhetorical question in the refrain, *"Why are you cast down, O my soul?"* (vv. 5, 11), the psalmist encourages himself not to be downhearted. His hope was in the Lord and he fully anticipated the opportunity to praise the Lord again at His dwelling place among His people – Jerusalem. The second stanza commences with the psalmist lamenting his situation; he was far from home and his enemies were ruthlessly pounding him like billowing waves on the hull of a ship (v. 7). He preferred to be with the Lord on Mount Zion rather than in the far north on Mount Mizar, which is a peak in the Mount Hermon range (v. 6). Yet, the psalmist was convinced of the Lord's abiding presence (i.e., he was enjoying God's love by day and soothing songs at night), and sure that He would rescue him (v. 8). Before repeating the refrain again in verse 11, the psalmist attempts to motivate the Lord to quickly answer his prayer by reminding the Lord that he was suffering physically and emotionally under the constant oppression of his foes (vv. 9-11). This poem crescendos and concludes in Psalm 43.

Psalm: 43 **Type: Lament – Personal** **Author: Unknown**

Hope in the Lord

This poem is likely the third stanza of the previous psalm. The psalmist petitions the Lord to hear his cause and to render action against his deceitful and wicked enemies so that he can return to Jerusalem (v. 1). He knew God was his solace and stronghold, but why did God continue to allow his enemies to hound him – had God rejected him (v. 2)? The psalmist confirms that God would safely lead him back to Jerusalem through divine understanding and guidance from God's Word (v. 3). Before repeating the refrain a final time (v. 5), the psalmist affirms his vow to joyfully praise the Lord in Jerusalem after his rescue is complete. The psalmist teaches us that communion with the Lord and hope in His goodness during strenuous circumstances will prevent us from slipping into despair.

Psalm: 44 **Type: Lament – Communal** **Author: Korahites**

A Prayer for National Deliverance

The Jewish nation was in a quandary: they were faithful to Jehovah, who had miraculously established their forefathers in Canaan against a vast enemy, so why were their nemeses prevailing against them now? William MacDonald writes, "The pain of defeat is made more bitter by the memory of former victories, and we never value our fellowship with God so much as when His face seems to be hidden from us."[99] Based on Jehovah's past faithfulness, the nation confirms their confidence in Him, not their own military strength, to overcome their enemies (vv. 1-8). Despite their long history of divine assistance, the Jewish nation had recently suffered a humiliating defeat, which had caused them to be scattered like threatened sheep, to be sold as slaves, and to be reproached by their enemies (vv. 11-16).

The Jews surmised that this loss occurred because Jehovah was no longer fighting with them (vv. 9-10). They could not reconcile this fact because they had remained loyal to Jehovah; indeed, this was the very reason they were in conflict in the first place (vv. 17-20). Certainly the

Lord knew they had not worshipped other gods, so why were they being led like lambs to the slaughter (vv. 21-22)? The psalm concludes with this question yet unanswered, but with the nation still affirming their trust in the Lord, who hopefully would arouse and deliver them from their miserable and shameful oppression (vv. 23-26). When adversity looms, may we too have confidence in the faithful character of God and the courage to pray: *"You have cast us off and put us to shame...In God we boast all day long, and praise Your name forever"* (vv. 9, 8). May we also have the ability to rejoice in whatever our lot may be, *"Giving thanks always for all things to God the Father in the name of our Lord Jesus Christ"* (Eph. 5: 20).

Psalm: 45   Type: Liturgical – Royal/Messianic   Author: Korahites

The Splendor of the King

This royal psalm is designated as *"A Song of Loves"* by the Hebrew superscript and celebrates the wedding day of the mighty king. The writer's heart so overflowed with this noble theme, the majesty of the king, that his pen could not be constrained (v. 1). The king's surpassing character and gracious words indicated he was blessed of God (v. 2). The psalmist anticipated that his mighty king would demonstrate his valor by upholding truth, humility, and righteousness as he rode into battle; he would therefore achieve stunning victories among the nations (vv. 3-5). The writer employs the Hebrew *elohim*, a plural noun normally translated "God" in the Old Testament, to acknowledge that his king is God's representative on the earth. Although not often rendered in this fashion, *elohim* is used elsewhere in the Old Testament to identify just and honorable representatives of God's authority (Ex. 21:6; Ps. 82:1).

Because the king loved righteousness and hated wickedness, God would bless him with great joy and an everlasting throne (vv. 6-7). The writer of Hebrews quotes verse 6 to substantiate its messianic connotations: God the Father addresses His resurrected Son as God, and rewards Him with an everlasting kingdom and the highest station possible in glory (Heb. 1:8-9). The Son had faithfully completed His divine mission in righteousness. Previously, God had promised David that one of his descendants would sit on an everlasting throne (2 Sam. 7:16) – Jesus Christ is that descendant (Matt. 1). Presently, the Lord Jesus resides on His Father's throne in heaven, and though He does have the title deed to His kingdom, He will not return to the earth to establish it until the Church Age, or the fullness of the Gentiles, is complete (Rom. 11:25; Rev. 3:21).

The royal attire of the king on his wedding day was perfumed with myrrh, aloes, and cassia. The ceremony would take place in ivory palaces, with *"stringed instruments"* garnishing the festive atmosphere with joyful music (v. 8, NASV). The closing scene is described: the king's queen, adorned with gold from Ophir, is seen standing with him at his right side; the king's daughters, also present, receive honor on this merry occasion (v. 9). The psalmist then reminisces on a moment just prior to the bride's appearance for the ceremony. Knowing the king's desire and delight in his new queen, the poet counsels her to faithfully honor and adore him (vv. 10-11). In doing so, she would be blessed with a gift from Tyre and have the praise and blessing of the people (v. 12). The writer then describes the moment of her presentation to the king; she is escorted by bridesmaids, and is adorned with gold and a beautifully embroidered gown (vv. 13-15). The song closes with the prediction that the marriage union will be blessed with many sons, who will be princes in the land, thus ensuring the king will be remembered throughout the nations for generations to come.

This glorious panorama prophetically relates to Christ's Second Advent to the earth when He will again be spiritually unified with the nation of Israel and both will be honored by the nations. This commences directly after the conclusion of the marriage supper of the Lamb in heaven (Rev. 19:7-16), which is enjoyed by Christ with glorified believers (the Church, and perhaps Old Testament saints). There is the question of who is represented by the queen of this psalm. Certainly, the Lord told parables that present the Church as His heavenly bride, though the restored adulterous nation of Israel cannot be ignored. For example, one parable (Matt. 25:1-10) speaks of the bridegroom (Christ) returning to earth with his heavenly bride, who then is joined by patiently waiting, Spirit-filled virgins (the revived Jewish nation). Yet, Psalm 45 is Jewish in focus, and thus the prophetic emphasis is on the future restoration of Israel, the once adulterous wife of Jehovah (Ezek. 16:15-38; Jer. 3:8). With this understanding,

Hamilton Smith suggests the nations ruled by Christ during the Kingdom Age are the *"King's daughters,"* who will do homage to the King, and that the new Queen is indeed the revived nation of Israel (v. 9):

> The place of honor will be reserved for restored Israel, brought before us under the figure of the queen standing at the right hand of the King (Isa. 54:5; Jer. 3:1; Hos. 2:19-20). The psalmist, using the figure of a bride, calls upon restored Israel to consider the new relationship upon which the nation is entering, and to forget the sorrowful past with all its failure and unfaithfulness to Jehovah (vv. 10-12).[100]

It is the writer's opinion that in the eternal state previous distinctions such as Old Testament saints, the Church, Tribulation saints, the nation of Israel, etc. will be remembered, but not emphasized. These distinctions served God's purposes in time while He was unfolding His great plan of salvation in various stages, but will not be significant throughout eternity (1 Cor. 15:26-28; Rev. 21:24-27, 22:1-5). In a general sense, the Bride of Christ after the Kingdom Age refers to all the redeemed. However, the prophetic focus of this psalm is the establishment of Christ's future kingdom, His restoration with the Jewish nation, and His fulfillment of the Abrahamic covenant to bring Israel into their earthly inheritance. Regardless of a passage's dispensational emphasis, the future of every believer is quite exciting; truly it can be said that with Christ, we will live "happily ever after." Hence all believers can agree with Paul, *"Looking for the blessed hope and glorious appearing of our great God and Savior Jesus Christ"* (Titus 2:13).

Psalm: 46   Type: Liturgical – Song of Zion   Author: Korahites

God is Our Refuge and Strength!

Although the storms of life may cause God's people to fret or fear, there is no reason for dismay, for the Lord is a safe refuge and bulwark of strength (vv. 1-3). This psalm is included with the songs of Zion because Jerusalem, *"the city of God,"* is central to its theme (v. 4). Jerusalem is where God dwells among His covenant people and thus their safe haven; the city is a fortress of protection against the raging nations (vv. 5-7). The psalmist exhorts his fellow countrymen to observe the Lord's awesome protective power and to then bestow proper praise and honor to the Lord, who will ultimately be exalted by all the nations (vv. 8-10). One so near, so faithful, so mighty, and so certainly destined to be worshipped by all is deserving of trust – *"The Lord of hosts is with us; the God of Jacob is our refuge"* (v. 11).

David Livingstone, a pioneer missionary in the mid-nineteenth century, often suffered terrible physical ailments and life-threatening situations while exploring central Africa and spreading the gospel message among the tribal people of that region. Livingstone's Bible was recovered at the time of his death; it was noticed that he had passed his finger over verses 6 and 11 of Psalm 46 so often that the ink was nearly rubbed off of the page: *"The Lord of hosts is with us; the God of Jacob is our refuge. Selah."*[101] How often those words must have comforted his heart as he ventured through dangerous, insect-infested jungles, so far from his loved ones and from human assistance. Likewise, the Lord's abiding presence was a comfort to Moses, Jeremiah, Isaiah, and Paul in their difficult ministries, and no less so for us also as we strive to faithfully serve the Lord!

Psalm: 47   Type: Liturgical – Enthronement   Author: Korahites

King of the Earth, Sovereign Over All

This enthronement psalm acknowledges the sovereign rule of Jehovah over creation now, and anticipates His future visible reign as the Jewish Messiah over all the earth (vv. 2-4). With these facts in hand, the psalmist solicits all the peoples of the earth to honor the Lord Most High, the Great King over the earth, with the clapping of hands, shouts of joyful praise, exuberant singing with understanding, and jubilant blasts from the trumpet (vv. 1, 5-7). The writer concludes the Lord must be greatly exalted, for He is Sovereign over all and shall gather all His covenant people together when He rules over the nations as the King of the earth (vv. 8-9). For the Lord to have His proper recognition is the noble expectation of His saints (Rom. 14:11; Phil. 2:9-11).

Psalm: 48 Type: Liturgical – Song of Zion Author: Korahites

Glorious Zion

William MacDonald suggests the following scenario as a possible setting for this psalm:

> A foreign invader had come up to the very gates of Jerusalem. Inside, the people were expecting the agonies of a long siege. Humanly speaking, the prospects were bleak. Then the Lord worked a miracle. The enemy saw something that threw them into utter panic. They retreated in terror. Jerusalem was preserved from destruction, and a great wave of praise went up to God. Psalm 48 captures something of the ecstasy of that moment.[102]

This psalm is about Zion (the city of God and the mountain of His holiness) and her majestic Ruler (vv. 1-2). The author is prompted to praise God because He had again shown Jerusalem to be the place of His presence and a refuge for His people during invasion (vv. 3-7). The Lord of heavenly and earthly hosts (i.e., armies) had made Jerusalem safe and secure (v. 8); this was a demonstration of faithful love and unwavering righteousness (vv. 9-10). The writer then invites his countrymen to take a panoramic review of Jerusalem – all of its citadels, bulwarks, and towers were intact! Surely the One who kept them secure would continue to be their guide forever (vv. 11-14). No doubt, as William Kelly surmises, this psalm previews Christ's future rule in Jerusalem, the religious epicenter of the world, during the Kingdom Age:

> The remnant rise in the expression of their faith and can now begin with Jehovah, as they see the vision of Zion in its beauty and glory, and all confederacies confounded, yea, vanished away. It is an advance even on the last. The glory of the king penetrates as it were place and people. So predicted: Isa. 2; 60; Mic. 4; 5; Zech. 14.[103]

After the Church Age is complete, the Lord will again refine and restore His covenant people, the Jews (Rom. 11:25). Clearly, Jehovah cannot be finished with the Jewish nation, for He decreed an everlasting covenant with Abraham's descendants through Jacob.

Jehovah is a covenant-keeping God and He has established irrevocable promises that He must fulfill. In so doing, the vast wonders of divine grace and mercy will be witnessed and appreciated by all who trust in the Lord.

Psalm: 49   Type: Wisdom   Author: Korahites

Wealth Cannot Redeem Anyone

With no regard to social class, the psalmist calls on everyone to consider his wise parable, a conundrum requiring effort to understand, but worthy of evaluation and credence nonetheless (vv. 1-4). The subject matter is then introduced through a series of human observations in verses 5-12. In the first place, prosperity imparts a false sense of security to the wicked; ultimately their wealth cannot redeem their soul, nor the life of another, nor can it prevent death (vv. 5-9). Furthermore, the wicked die and someone else obtains their hoarded wealth and then their body decays in the same way that the carcass of a beast does (vv. 10-12). The psalmist then concludes there is no reason to fear the evil doings of the wicked, for their power and glory are temporary and will fail them when most needed (v. 5).

Accordingly, the doom of the self-righteous and the proud evildoer is assured, while the righteous have the hope of being redeemed from the grave (i.e., resurrection) and being rewarded by the Lord (vv. 13-15). The conclusion is straightforward: it is foolish for God's people to envy the wealth, power, and prestige of the wicked because it is short-lived; these things cannot enter eternity with them, although their shame and condemnation follow them beyond the grave (vv. 16-20). The destiny of the believer in glory is far better than the fleeting splendor of the wicked (vv. 16-20). Paul puts the matter this way: *"For I consider that the sufferings of this present time are not worthy to be compared with the glory which shall be revealed in us"* (Rom. 8:18). Living for the Lord and others, rather than for things and ourselves, is an investment with guaranteed eternal dividends.

Psalm: 50   Type: Liturgical – Covenantal   Author: Asaph

Almighty God Shall Judge

Asaph was the Levitical choir director of the temple singers during David's royal tenure. In this exhortative poem, Asaph will challenge the mindless formalized worship of the Almighty God by reminding his countrymen that they must all stand before Him, the righteous Judge, and be examined in His heavenly courtroom (vv. 1-6). Therefore, they should not forget the Lord or His commandments and offer genuine praise from the heart (vv. 22-23)! Asaph notes that God will judge the wicked because they did ignore and disdain His commandments (vv. 16-21). The Law of Moses and the teachings of the prophets are rooted in two commandments, as the Lord Jesus confirmed: *"You shall love the Lord your God with all your heart, and with all your soul, and with all your mind"* and *"You shall love your neighbor as yourself"* (Matt. 22:37-40).

Asaph reminds his brethren of the divine standard to which they would be held on Judgment Day. Some were apparently counting on their many sacrifices and offerings to earn God's favor, but Asaph reminds his readers anything they offer to God is technically His already, and if it is offered in vain rote or religious hypocrisy it has no value to Him (vv. 7-13). Samuel concisely states this realization: *"Behold, to obey is better than sacrifice"* (1 Sam. 15:22). Asaph affirms when God's people offer Him sincere praise and righteous conduct that He longs to manifest His glory by responding to their prayers, especially those for deliverance (vv. 14-15). This psalm reminds God's people in any dispensation to live holy, to render honest worship, and not to be apathetic or superficial with the Lord, for He will judge such things. Paul echoed this sentiment when he reminded Christians of their accountability to God: *"So then each of us shall give account of himself to God"* (Rom. 14:12).

Psalm: 51   **Type: Lament – Penitential**   **Author: David**

A Psalm of Penitence

The occasion of this psalm is established by the Hebrew superscript: "A Psalm of David, when Nathan the prophet came unto him, after he had gone in to Bathsheba." It is likely Psalm 32, which declares the joy of forgiveness, follows on the heels of this psalm, which pertains directly to David's adultery with Bathsheba and the murder of her husband Uriah (2 Sam. 11). After an entire year of defiance, the prophet Nathan came to rebuke David, who subsequently repented of his sin and was reconciled with the Lord (2 Sam. 12). Under the Law, adulterers and murderers were to be executed, meaning there was no provision to spare David's life, yet he knew the character of God, and thus chose to trust in Him. God is a covenant-keeping God and had made unconditional promises to David; therefore, by faith, David knew there must be an unrevealed means beyond the Law by which the Lord could righteously forgive his capital offenses. This way is now known to be the blood of Christ, which sealed a New Covenant between Jehovah and the Jewish nation (Heb. 8:8). The original covenant, the Law, could not save as no one could keep it; its purpose was to show sin and point sinners to the Savior, Christ (Rom. 3:20; Gal. 3:24).

Having previously experienced the tender mercies and lovingkindness of the Lord, David no longer wanted to bear the heavy burden of his sin, and so he confesses it to the One he had sinned against (vv. 1, 4). With a penitent heart David pleads with the Lord to blot out (or erase) his transgressions, wash away his iniquity, and purify him from his sin (vv. 2-3). David then acknowledges he was born with a nature prone to sin against God's Law; consequently, though he had diligently tried to continue in well-doing, he had failed – he knew that he was a sinner by nature (vv. 5-6). Paul tells us in Romans 2:1-15 that we suffer from feelings of guilt because we have offended our conscience (i.e., we have not obeyed the moral law ingrained within our hearts). Internal guilt and the unexplainable sensation of impending judgment are God's means of proving to us that we need a Savior.

Not only did David desire to be cleansed from his sin and its effects, but he also wanted to again experience full restoration with

God and the joy of his salvation (vv. 7-9). This renewal would include the blessings of a clean heart and the abiding presence of the Holy Spirit (vv. 10-12). David then identifies some of the benefits of being forgiven, including the ability to teach others the pitfalls of sin (v. 14), to sing jubilant praises to God (vv. 14-15), and to offer up the sacrifice of a broken and contrite spirit, which God greatly appreciates (vv. 16-17). Indeed, God only valued burnt offerings when presented with sincere humility and thankfulness (v. 19). David's statement in verses 18 and 19 may be understood as a request for God to prosper Jerusalem's defense against their enemies. However, it seems more fitting to understand his petition in the context of the psalm, which deals with sin and the loss of blessing: that is to say, if the moral defenses of the city faltered (i.e., the enemy of sin was permitted to invade the community), then God's favor would be lost.

Man's moral integrity before God and genuine worship of God are integrally tied to the blessings of God. Having suffered the loss of the latter for a full year, David was determined not to repeat the painful consequences of gross sin again. Paul puts the matter this way: *"For he who sows to his flesh will of the flesh reap corruption, but he who sows to the Spirit will of the Spirit reap everlasting life"* (Gal. 6:8). Sin results in death (separation from God), but yielding to God's Word and His Spirit results in the abundant life (fellowship with God). What is David's message to us? Suffering the repercussions of moral failure is a tragic means of increasing one's resolve to stay intimate with God, yet, through sincere repentance and brokenness, communion with God may be enjoyed again despite our wayward choices.

Psalm: 52   Type: Lament – Personal   Author: David

Judgment of the Deceitful

In this poem, David contrasts his faith in the Lord (and God's resulting favor) with a sinful, treacherous man who receives God's displeasure. The Hebrew superscript identifies Doeg the Edomite as the man in question. Doeg informed King Saul of fleeing David's whereabouts and then murdered eighty-five righteous priests who had innocently assisted David (1 Sam. 21-22). David was astonished that anyone who had so dishonored the Lord could ever boast of his own despicable deeds (v. 1). Doeg loved wickedness and used his deceitful tongue as a sharp sword to devour the innocent (vv. 2-4). David reasoned Doeg would suffer a short life in divine retribution; this would strengthen the resolve of the righteous to trust in the Lord, rather than to pursue ill-gotten riches like Doeg had (vv. 5-7).

The remainder of the psalm contrasts the dishonor and demise of the wicked man in the previous verses with David's blessed status in the Lord. David likens his divine prosperity to a flourishing olive tree, as compared to the wicked who are an evil tare that will be uprooted and burned in divine retaliation (v. 5; Matt. 13:38-40). Knowing God would judge the wicked and that he himself had received God's favor for living righteously served to increased David's resolve to trust in the Lord's mercy forever (v. 8). Doing so meant he would always be able to praise the Lord with the upright (v. 9). David implores the righteous to loathe treachery and its evil devices, and to put their confidence in the Lord's mercy and prevailing justice.

Psalm: 53   Type: Lament – Personal   Author: David

Oh, Foolish Atheist – Part 2

This poem is a version of Psalm 14 in Book 1. Perhaps the minor differences were to accommodate its arrangement in Book 2 to the well-known tune of *Mahalat*. Verses 5 and 6 of Psalm 14 are combined into a single verse (v. 5) in Psalm 53; aside from this, the two psalms are essentially identical. Those who say there is no God may frustrate and inflict God's people for a season, but in a future day the Lord will righteously vindicate all who seek Him for a refuge.

Psalm: 54   Type: Lament – Personal   Author: David

The Betrayed Pleads for Deliverance

King Saul was in hot pursuit of David, supposing if he could but slay David (whom God had anointed king to replace him) that he would retain the kingdom and a dynasty. David penned this poem shortly after the Ziphites had informed Saul of his location. In it, David urgently pleads with the Lord to deliver him from his vicious oppressors because they had no respect for God's name, which represents His person and character (vv. 1-3). The latter portion of the psalm is an expression of David's trust in God, his Helper, to render justice and retribution on his enemies (vv. 4-5). There was no doubt in David's mind that the Lord would grant his prayer, thus, he promised to praise the Lord and offer peace offerings to show his thankfulness (vv. 6-7). Because God is good, His name is also good – David knew that God would judge all those who devalue His name by ill-treating those who treasure it.

Psalm: 55   Type: Lament – Personal   Author: David

A Plea Against a False Friend

If you have ever been betrayed by a close friend, you will be able to relate to David's pain in this psalm. David fully expected to be mistreated and oppressed by his enemies, but for this to come at the hand of a fellow companion, a friend, one together with whom David had worshipped the Lord, was overwhelming (vv. 1-5, 12-14). This trusted companion may have been Ahithophel, who defected from David's ranks during Absalom's rebellion and sided with the conspirators. David wished he had the wings of a dove to fly away to some safe haven far from this threatening tempest and its painful repercussions (vv. 6-8). His betrayers deserved divine retribution because their violent ways and deceitful speech had made the city (likely Jerusalem) full of sorrow, strife, and wickedness (vv. 9-11).

The smooth words and soft allusions of his oppressors cut into David's heart like a sharp sword (vv. 20-21). He made two specific requests; the first was for the Lord to confound their speech in order to prevent further chaos (v. 9). Second, in light of their evil actions, David asked God to inflict them with a death-like sorrow (see Ps. 18:4) or even death itself (v. 15); at the very least, his enemies should only be granted a brief life (v. 23). Though the psalmist loathed this storm of life, he was determined to call on the Lord day and night until deliverance was realized (vv. 16-18). David had full confidence in the righteous and just character of God, and therefore full assurance that his betrayers, who had no fear of God, would suffer (v. 19). What is David's message to all those who have been betrayed by a close friend? *"Cast your burden on the Lord, and He shall sustain you; He shall never permit the righteous to be moved"* (v. 22). The Lord supported David through this hurtful experience and, dear believer, He will likewise render justice on your behalf and will be a solace for your grieving heart.

Psalm: 56   Type: Lament – Personal   Author: David

In God Will I Trust

In this psalm, David expresses his confidence in the Lord to protect him after fleeing from King Saul to the Philistine-controlled city of Gath (1 Sam. 21:10-15). Accordingly, the setting and content of this poem are similar to Psalm 34. The circumstances were life threatening – David was surrounded by his enemies and, at this juncture in time, those loyal to him were few; he therefore cries out to the Lord for mercy (vv. 1-2). At first David acknowledges his fear, saying, *"Whenever I am afraid, I will trust in You"* (v. 3), but after a season of prayer he affirms: *"In God I have put my trust; I will not be afraid. What can man do to me?"* (v. 11). Notice how David flipped the order of his fear and his trust in these two verses to encourage his own heart. This illustrates, as Hamilton Smith explains, the transforming effect prayer has on the believer's thinking, when real faith in a sovereign God is exercised in ominous situations:

> Every day the enemy perverts the words of the godly: with evil intent they consult together and secretly watch his steps, seeking to take his life. In the consciousness that iniquity cannot go unpunished, the soul looks to God to cast down all those who oppose His people. In contrast to the treatment at the hands of the wicked, God counts every step that His people have to take, keeps a bottle for their tears, and a book wherein to record their sorrows. In the consciousness of God's tender care the soul can look for deliverance from his enemies and say with triumphant assurance, "God is for me."[104]

Devotions in Psalms

At first, anxiety and dismay grip our hearts, but as we begin to turn our focus from our circumstances to the One who knows all about them and is in full control of all things, fear is displaced by joy. Sincere prayer causes us to recognize the fact that there is no situation that surprises God or is too hard for Him to work for our good and His glory (Rom. 8:28). Thus, David concluded it did not matter what any mortal man spoke or did against him; God would judge them appropriately (vv. 5-7). David referred to the ancient burial practice of collecting the tears of those in mourning in a small bottle, which was placed in the grave of the deceased prior to burial (v. 8). It is comforting to know God is so intimately aware of our sorrows and righteous sufferings that He keeps a ledger of every tear we shed at such times. Like David, we too can announce, *"God is for me"* (v. 9; Rom. 8:31), praise His name even in times of adversity (vv. 4, 10, 12), and ask Him to guide each footfall so that we do not wander from the path of light and life (v. 13). Such faith can expectantly proclaim, *"You have delivered my soul from death,"* even before we experience God's merciful rescue (v. 13)!

Psalm: 57   Type: Lament – Personal   Author: David

Trusting in God When in Distress

This poem is similar in theme and construction to the previous psalm, but has a more celebratory tone. It was likely written not long after Psalm 56, as the Hebrew superscription notes David was hiding from Saul in a cave when it was penned. Samuel recorded that David hid in two caves: at Adullam directly after escaping from the King of Gath (1 Sam. 22:1; Ps. 56), and at Engedi a few months later when David spared Saul's life (1 Sam. 24:1-3). David visited the cave at Adullam again in the latter years of his life, as it become the base of operation during a military campaign (2 Sam. 23:13). Although David likely hid in other caves during those years he was hotly pursued by Saul, the tone and content of this psalm certainly fits the scenario occurring after David's escape from Gath. Despite his continuing crisis, David composes two stanzas to proclaim His trust in the Lord; each concludes with a refrain of aspiration for God to be exalted in the situation (vv. 5, 11).

Though hiding in an earthly cave, David knew the only safe refuge was under the shadow of God's wing – it is from this safe haven David would plead for mercy until all his calamities had passed (vv. 1-3). The psalm is saturated with metaphoric language; the imagery of a hen protecting her chicks under her wings is employed to speak of David's security in God's presence (Matt. 23:27). David describes his surrounding enemies as prowling lions and ravenous beasts who sought to devour him through military conquest; however, God would exalt Himself through their defeat (vv. 4-5). David's enemies had spread a net and had dug a pit to capture him; he knew God would cause them to fall into it and be destroyed (v. 6). Because David had focused his heart on the Lord instead of fretting over his distresses, he was confident in the outcome and hence vows to sing a victory song to the Lord in the dawning day of liberation (vv. 7-8). He would praise the Lord for His great mercy and truth among the nations (vv. 9-10). The poem concludes with the refrain: *"Be exalted, O God, above the heavens; let Your glory be above all the earth"* (v. 11). Whether in turmoil or in peace, whether impoverished or abounding, may this prayer be the aspiration of God's people.

Psalm: 58   Type: Praise – Communal   Author: David

Depraved Judges to Reap Justice

The psalmist expresses his disgust for officials who did not uphold God's righteousness and standard of justice in executing their offices, but rather exploited the people and promoted violence and corruption (vv. 1-2). From birth, these men had been prone to fraud; they were unconcerned where they spewed their poison and were numb to reproof (vv. 3-5). That is, they were apathetic towards the welfare of the people. Through metaphoric language David calls on the Lord to wipe out the wicked judges in the land; these vicious lions deserved to have their teeth torn out (v. 6). They all should come to a swift end, in the way water evaporates, as a miscarried baby never sees daylight, as brambles are quickly consumed by fire (vv. 7-9). The psalmist is not saying that all miscarried babies result from God's judgment, but rather depraved judges will suffer an untimely end.

Continuing the figurative language, David notes the righteous will rejoice when the honorable Judge over all the earth vindicates His name by terminating all those who misused His authority (vv. 10-11). God instituted human government to teach us submission to His authority, so when those who are representing Him become corrupt, His retribution is severe because His character has been blasphemed (Gen. 9:6; Rom. 13:1-5). James reminds us those who represent Christ on the earth today (i.e., Christians) are to be impartial and just in their treatment of others; those who do not become *"judges with evil thoughts"* (Jas. 2:4). God will avenge the oppressed in His timing; hence, David understood it was better to be mistreated and happy in the Lord than to be numbered with those who tainted the Lord's name through corruption.

Psalm: 59   Type: Lament – Personal   Author: David

God Is My Defense

David fled to his home after barely escaping Saul's javelin and then, as this psalm records, resorted to the throne of grace in breathless haste. Saul sent men to watch David's house with instructions to kill him in the morning, but his wife Michal, Saul's own daughter, helped David escape during the night and delayed Saul's awareness of his getaway until the next morning (1 Sam. 19:10-12). According to the Hebrew superscript, Psalm 59 was penned during this life-threatening scenario, which places it just prior to the events of Psalm 52. David prayed to be delivered from blood-thirsty men, who did not deserve God's mercy because he had done nothing wrong to merit such ruthless hostility (vv. 1-5). His would-be assassins were like snarling dogs prowling about at night; their words were perverse and sharp as swords, yet in their arrogance they did not even think God could hear them (vv. 6-7). God laughs at such ignorance and scoffs at such evildoers; therefore, David knew God would show mercy and preserve his life (vv. 8-10). However, David did not want God to simply slay his aggressors; he wanted justice to be rendered in such a way that they would be publicly humiliated for their evil deeds (vv. 11-12). This manner of retribution would demonstrate to the nations that a God of justice ruled over Israel (v. 13). Despite the threatening posture of his enemies, David was confident he would have further reason to sing praises to God, who was his strength, refuge, and defense. This God is our God too!

Psalm: 60   Type: Praise – Communal   Author: David

Win or Lose, God Is in Control

The Hebrew superscription states this poem was used for teaching purposes and was based on David's military experiences battling the Arameans (Syrians) in the north and the invading Edomites in the south (2 Sam. 8:8-13; 1 Kgs. 11:15-16). At this point in the Syrian war, the main Hebrew army was in the north, which meant David's troops were spread thin in the south where the Edomites launched a surprise invasion. This resulted in terrible Jewish losses; the Jews had been forced to unfurl a banner of retreat (vv. 1-4). David surmised the defeat was from the Lord because He was angry with Israel. Victory is at the hand of God, so David petitioned the Lord, on behalf of those He loved, to turn their divinely-orchestrated calamity into a God-directed triumph (v. 5). Joab was sent south to fend off the Edomites and God did grant a tremendous victory to his forces. Reviewing the entire situation, the psalmist reminds his countrymen of God's previous promise: since all Jewish territories were His, He would ensure Israel's inevitable victory over their enemies (vv. 6-8). It is observed that verses 5-12 are identical to the text of Psalm 108:6-13 to reiterate this conclusion.

Three rhetorical questions are employed to affirm that whether a conflict is won or lost, human strength is futile in thwarting God's design, for He alone is in complete control (vv. 9-11). Hence, David was confident that though the Lord had previously abandoned them in battle, He would for His name's sake ultimately grant them victory over all their enemies (v. 12). When gripped by adversity, let us remember the Lord is in control and all of our hopes rest in Him; thus, we are to *"in everything give thanks; for this is the will of God in Christ Jesus for you"* (1 Thess. 5:18).

Psalm: 61   Type: Lament – Personal   Author: David

The High Rock of Defense

The superscript identifies David as the psalm's author, but no information is provided in respect to his circumstances. There is good internal evidence to suggest Psalm 61 was written during one of David's greatest trials – his son Absalom's rebellion. The king and a handful of his loyal subjects had quickly fled for their lives into the rocky and desolate wilderness east of Jerusalem, but their provisions were low (2 Sam. 15-16). They lodged temporarily in this wilderness until Hushai, David's spy, sent word for them to hurry and cross the Jordan to escape their pursuers (2 Sam. 17). The situation was bleak; they were greatly outnumbered and the people were hungry, weary, and thirsty (2 Sam. 17:29).

There are several Hebrew words in the Psalms rendered "cry," but *rinnah* in verse 1 denotes a shrill sound; the tone of David's prayer was then one of desperation. Perhaps David was inspecting the defenses of their temporary encampment when the Lord drew his sight upward from the surrounding rock formations to his heavenly Rock of defense (vv. 2-3). David knew there was no safer abiding place than in God's presence and he expresses his resolve to remain there forever (v. 4). God had promised David a royal dynasty, so on that basis David prays for God's abiding protection, a lasting heritage of souls loyal to Jehovah, and a prolonged life to serve the Lord (vv. 5-7).

David's prayer demonstrates an unwavering faith in a tremendous God, the One who completely controlled the situation and would ensure the manifestation of His glory in it. Though our challenges are different from David's, C. H. Spurgeon explains the proper outcome of both is the same:

> There are reserved and special things in Christian experience: all the developments of spiritual life are not alike easy of attainment. There are the common frames and feelings of repentance, and faith, and joy,

and hope, which are enjoyed by the entire family; but there is an upper realm of rapture, of communion, and conscious union with Christ, which is far from being the common dwelling-place of believers. We have not all the high privilege of John, to lean upon Jesus' bosom; nor of Paul, to be caught up into the third heaven. There are heights in experimental knowledge of the things of God which the eagle's eye of acumen and philosophic thought hath never seen: God alone can bear us there; but the chariot in which he takes us up, and the fiery steeds with which that chariot is dragged, are prevailing prayers. ... Prevailing prayer takes the Christian to Carmel, and enables him to cover heaven with clouds of blessing, and earth with floods of mercy. Prevailing prayer bears the Christian aloft to Pisgah, and shows him the inheritance reserved; it elevates us to Tabor and transfigures us, till in the likeness of his Lord, as he is, so are we also in this world. If you would reach to something higher than ordinary groveling experience, look to the Rock that is higher than you, and gaze with the eye of faith through the window of importunate prayer. When you open the window on your side, it will not be bolted on the other.[105]

As David became occupied with the exalted Lord instead of his circumstances, he was refreshed in his spirit and was prompted to sing praises to God. When our hearts are overwhelmed, may we also have the faith to lift our eyes from the dismal earthly outlook *"to the Rock that is higher"* (v. 2).

Psalm: 62   Type: Thanksgiving – Song of Trust   Author: David

Waiting on God, My Salvation

The phrase "my salvation" is found four times in this psalm (vv. 1, 2, 6, 7), which is more than any other passage of Scripture in our Bibles. The word "salvation" is derived from the Hebrew *yeshuw`ah*, meaning salvation or deliverance. Like the name "Joshua" (Hebrew: *Yehowshuwa`*), the Greek name for Jesus (*Iesous*) is also derived from two Hebrew words: *Yehovah* (Jehovah) and *yeshuw`ah* (as mentioned previously, this means salvation). As Matthew explains, Jesus' own name expresses His identity; He is literally "God's salvation" for humanity (Matt. 1:21). Peter spoke of Christ when he said, *"Neither is* *there salvation in any other: for there is no other name under heaven given among men, whereby we must be saved"* (Acts 4:12). Although David wrote this psalm without knowing the personal name of His Lord/Savior, we do; consider substituting "Jesus" for "salvation" as you read this poem.

The psalm contains three stanzas of four verses each (verses 4 and 8 both conclude with "Selah" and form sections within the psalm). In this poem, David contrasts the security of trusting the Lord with the uncertainty of human wisdom and might. David had resolved to wait on the Lord, his Rock and Fortress, to obtain salvation (deliverance) from his enemies (vv. 1-2, 5). How ludicrous it was, then, for vain men with lying tongues and evil hearts to attempt to cast him down: did they not know how powerful his God was and that they were sealing their own destruction (vv. 3-4)? In verse 2, David said he would *"not be greatly moved"* by his oppressors because he trusted in God as his Rock and Defense; however, after further consideration he concludes, *"I shall not be moved"* (v. 6). God was not only his Refuge, but His security and salvation were available to all His people if they would only trust in Him and pour out their hearts to Him (vv. 7-8).

Why should God's people put their trust in other humans whose lives are expended in one breath? When weighed on the scales of eternity, human life is insignificant. Simply put, mortal man can do nothing against the eternal God; therefore, it is foolish to oppress others to gain wealth, or to trust in one's riches if wealthy already (vv. 10-11). God will render to everyone just recompense for their deeds; therefore, it would be wise for us to trust in the Lord for mercy and security instead of putting our confidence in human wherewithal, and so meriting His displeasure (v. 12).

Psalm: 63   Type: Thanksgiving – Song of Trust   Author: David

Thirsting for God

The superscript places David in the wilderness of Judah (perhaps fleeing from Absalom); he was consequently separated from the Ark of the Covenant, the appropriate place to worship at that time (2 Sam. 15:24-25). David's soul thirsted for God, and we can empathize – the world is a dry and thirsty abode, but believers find true spiritual satisfaction in communion with God (v. 1). The Hebrew word *shachar* literally means "to dawn" and is translated *"early will I seek you"* (v. 1). Whether David figuratively meant that he earnestly desired the Lord or that he would literally rise at dawn to be with the Lord is unclear, but certainly he was reserving the best part of each new day to be with the Lord. David had experienced the joy of witnessing God's glory and power displayed in His sanctuary, hence he intensely longed to be in the Lord's presence again (v. 2). Though temporarily sojourning in a desolate wilderness, David valued God's companionship more than life-sustaining water or rich foods.

His soul was gratified by praising the Lord for His loving-kindnesses, which he esteemed better than life itself (vv. 3-5). To forget God was death; therefore, David determined to meditate on the Lord during the night watches (v. 6). If he could not be at God's sanctuary, he took comfort in knowing he was still under His wing of protection; the Lord was with him and was his Help (vv. 7-8)! He anticipated that God would utterly destroy his enemies and he would rejoice in the Lord, as would all who were loyal to Him (vv. 9-11). David lived out the exhortation Paul would later give to the Thessalonians regarding joy amidst distressing circumstances: *"Rejoice always, pray without ceasing, in everything give thanks; for this is the will of God in Christ Jesus for you"* (1 Thess. 5:16-18). The joy of the wounded moves the hand of God. Praising God nourishes a hungry soul, and giving Him thanks rejuvenates a parched spirit. Rejoicing is a choice, and one that secures the believer's mind in hope and prompts God to do the impossible (Phil. 1:18)!

Psalm: 64   Type: Lament – Personal   Author: David

A Prayer of Preservation

William MacDonald describes the nature of this psalm: "Two archery contests emerge in Psalm 64. The preliminary event is between the wicked and the righteous (vv. 1-6). The main event is between God and the wicked (vv. 7-10)."[106] The first contest is one-sided; righteous David is outnumbered by the wicked and, although their quivers are full, he has no arrows with which to fight. However, David has a secret weapon – he prays to the Lord for divine preservation from those "workers of iniquity" who were plotting to murder him (vv. 1-2). Because these wicked men had no fear of God, they secretly ambushed innocent David with a volley of arrows (bitter words) and jabs from a sword (a sharp tongue; vv. 3-4). They encouraged each other in their perverse doings and bragged how their evil deeds would go undetected; such conduct demonstrates the deep depravity of the human heart (vv. 5-6).

David, however, was convinced God would ensnare his enemies in their own evil devices and bring them to ruin, that is, the Lord would release His own volley of arrows upon them (vv. 7-8). God is the obvious victor in the psalm's second archery contest. The psalmist is sure when the righteous see God's justice invoked in this matter, they will scorn David's enemies, reverence the Lord, and have further reason to trust Him as their Refuge (vv. 9-10). It is good to remember that though injustice may reign today, tomorrow *"the righteous shall be glad in the Lord, and trust in Him and all the upright in heart shall glory"* (v. 10).

Psalm: 65   Type: Praise   **Author: David**

God's Earth Provides for Man

God is sovereign over His creation and this poem celebrates God's goodness to His people by blessing them with bountiful crops, flocks, and herds (v. 13). Together with Psalm 66, these odes of thanksgiving may have been sung by the congregation at annual harvest celebrations. It is David's conviction that God hears and amply responds to the prayers of those who have received blood atonement for their sins (vv. 1-4). In fact, the One who forms the mountains, controls the oceans' movements, and alternates day with night deserves the reverence of all men; without God, there would be no reason to rejoice (vv. 5-8). It is the Lord who cares for the land; He causes the rain to fall, the grass to grow, and the sown fields to produce grain (vv. 9-11). This abounding fruitfulness is creation's means of lifting up joyful praise to the Creator (vv. 12-13). Man should pause to thank God for His bountiful provisions in nature, and also learn from nature's example: willingly yielding to God's control results in the praise of His glory.

This psalm likely anticipates Christ's Second Advent, when the curses levied on the earth because of human sin will be removed and creation will have its full ability to honor the Lord in abundant fruitfulness (Rom. 8:21-22). A handful of seed casually scattered on a mountaintop will produce a great harvest (Ps. 72:16), longevity of life will be restored to humanity (Isa. 65:20), weapons will be used as agricultural implements (Mic. 4:3), and a spirit of peace and tranquility will rest upon the whole earth (Isa. 11:9). All this and more Christ shall do: *"Even so, come, Lord Jesus"* (Rev. 22:20)!

Psalm: 66   Type: Praise   **Author: Unknown**

All Should Praise God

In this song of thanksgiving the writer and his countrymen praise God for a previous national deliverance as well as for present blessings (vv. 1-12). The writer then concludes the psalm with a personal expression of praise and thanksgiving (vv. 13-20). The Jewish nation had witnessed the wonders of God's might in deliverance from their enemies (v. 3) and through receiving a bountiful land as an inheritance (v. 12). Though they had been refined through repeated testing (vv. 10-11), God had faithfully provided for and protected His covenant people; He deserved their praise (vv. 8-9). In fact, the Jews had witnessed the magnificent power of the Lord many times, such as the crossing of the Red Sea and the Jordan River (vv. 6-7). But the Jews were not satisfied with worshipping God alone; they called on all peoples to examine the evidence of God's awesome feats and to also lift praise and worship to their Creator (vv. 1-2, 4-5).

The writer, who is leading the congregation in praise, addresses the Lord in verses 13-15 before conveying his personal testimony to the congregation in closing (vv. 16-20). The psalmist tells the Lord he will fulfill his vow to offer burnt offerings at the temple because God had delivered him from trouble (vv. 13-15). The writer then declares His praise for God to the congregation. Because he did not regard iniquity in his heart, the Lord had heard his desperate plea for help and delivered him (vv. 16-20). God has invited believers, His children, to come boldly into His presence at the throne of grace in times of need; the psalmist teaches us that we must do so without clinging to sin, otherwise our prayers go unheard and consequently unanswered (Heb. 4:15-16; 1 Pet. 3:7).

Psalm: 67   Type: Praise   Author: Unknown

The Nations to Hear of Israel's God

The psalmist calls on the Jewish nation to praise God for His righteous judgments (v. 4), so they might further enjoy God's blessing (vv. 1, 7); this would permit all nations to witness His saving power (v. 2). The desired result would be that all people would praise God (vv. 3, 5, 7) and be blessed by the Lord: *"then the earth shall yield her increase; God, our own God, shall bless us"* (v. 6). Israel was to be a channel of light and of blessing to the nations; at Sinai, they were commissioned to declare to all peoples that there was only one God, and that by obeying and revering Him, anyone could experience a joyful and prosperous life (Ex. 20:2; Deut. 33:26-29). The writer reasons God must have a way of healing the nations: *"Your way may be known on earth, Your salvation [yeshuw`ah – see commentary on Ps. 62] among all nations"* (v. 2). Indeed, God has now provided the means of healing all people through the redeeming blood of His dear Son. Jesus Christ is the hope of the nations:

Behold, My Servant shall deal prudently;
He shall be exalted and extolled and be very high.
Just as many were astonished at you,
So His visage was marred more than any man,
And His form more than the sons of men;
So shall He sprinkle many nations.
Kings shall shut their mouths at Him;
For what had not been told them they shall see,
And what they had not heard they shall consider (Isa. 52:13-15).

The Beginning of Wisdom

Psalm: 68   Type: Liturgical – Temple/Messianic   Author: David

Triumph and Glorious Ascension

The occasion of the psalm may have been to celebrate David's conquest of the Jebusites, who had controlled Jerusalem for centuries: *"David took the stronghold of Zion (that is, the City of David)"* (2 Sam. 5:7). Then, with great fanfare and festivity (as described in vv. 24-27), David brought the Ark of the Covenant to Jerusalem and placed it within a tabernacle that he had pitched there (2 Sam. 6:17). Jerusalem was now the capital of Israel and the only proper place to worship Jehovah. Allen P. Ross provides this overview of the psalm:

> The psalmist reviewed the history of Israel from the wilderness wanderings to the occupation and conquest of the land. He emphasized God's choice of Zion, which resulted in Israel's taking many Canaanites as captives and the Israelites receiving gifts or spoil from the captives. This is the reason he sang praises: God was marching triumphantly on behalf of the oppressed. David called on others to join him in praising their strong Lord.[107]

To the Jewish mind, the Ark of the Covenant represented God's presence; when the Ark moved, so did God. Whether this scene or another of David's victories resulted in this psalm of praise is unknown; what is certain is that this poem prophetically celebrates Christ's victorious and triumphal ascension to Mount Zion after His resurrection, as verse 18 is loosely quoted in Ephesians 4:11. In that passage, Paul notes many who had been captives of sin and death were now liberated by Christ's victorious work at Calvary, and had also received spiritual gifts from Him. In the Church Age, these liberated captives are being actively blessed and led ever heavenward (Eph. 4:12). Though Psalm 68:18 is applied to the Church in the book of Ephesians, Hamilton Smith explains its application here to the nation of Israel:

> In Christ's place of glory He received gifts for men. In Ephesians the gifts are spoken of in connection with the Church; here in connection with Israel, even though Israel had been rebellious. Thus by His gifts in grace, God secures a people in whose midst He can dwell. In Psalm

22:2-3, we read of Christ forsaken on the Cross, in order that Jehovah might dwell in the midst of a praising people. In this psalm He ascends on high to secure a praising people. Thus they say, "Blessed be the Lord, who daily loads us with benefits, even the God of our salvation."[108]

David prayed God would demonstrate His awesome power by vanquishing the wicked, so that the righteous might continue to rejoice in Him. God merits praise, not only because He is alone in majesty, but because He assists and comforts the oppressed and downcast (e.g., widows and orphans: vv. 4-6). He also deserves the worship of His covenant people for delivering them from slavery, refreshing them in the wilderness, and bestowing them with a land full of milk and honey for a possession (vv. 7-14). In retrospect, God had journeyed with His people all the way from Egypt to Mount Zion, the location He had chosen long ago to be worshipped (Gen. 22; vv. 15-18). So, David bringing the Ark into Jerusalem was truly a long-awaited triumphal entry.

As previously mentioned, this pictures Christ's victorious entrance into heavenly Zion after His resurrection. David praises the Lord for His daily sustenance and protection, and affirms his conviction that because God's presence had entered Zion, their remaining enemies would be conquered (vv. 19-23). Accordingly, David requested God to again exhibit His tremendous power by humbling the surrounding pagan kingdoms in order that they too would recognize the One *"who rides on the heaven of heavens"* resided with His people in Jerusalem. He alone is worthy of praise (vv. 28-35). Ultimately, the latter portion of the psalm will be fulfilled after Christ's Second Advent when He reenters Zion, having triumphed over the Antichrist and his army.

Psalm: 69   Type: Praise/Messianic   Author: David

The Psalm of the Trespass Offering

The previous psalm staged the future exaltation of Christ; in contrast, this psalm speaks of His humiliation and sufferings, the subsequent judgment on His adversaries, and the rescue of His

The Beginning of Wisdom

covenant people in their land. The Holy Spirit often used the deep trials and anguish of righteous David to prophetically express the future emotional anguish of Christ in accomplishing God's redemptive work. This revelation not only prompts our appreciation, but also, as William Kelly observes, shows that Christ's sufferings are the basis for His exaltation (aside from His intrinsic and moral glories, which are also cause for acclaim):

> This psalm tells of His sufferings, though in a way evidently distinct from Psalm 22, where divine abandonment crowns all, as here human evil is prominent and calls for judgment, instead of the grace which is the answer in that psalm. But He was afflicted in all their affliction, as says the prophet. David was the occasion; yet the Spirit of Christ enters into all their wrong-doing, not only to vindicate God but to give expression to the confession of the godly remnant, who will thus pour out their heart in the latter day, when His wrath shall fall on their oppressors and betrayers.[109]

Hence, Christ, who patiently enduring the wrong-doings of men for the glory of God was exalted; this provides an honorable pattern for all God's people to follow (1 Pet. 2:20-21).

In this psalm David urgently pleads with the Lord to deliver him from destruction because he bore the reproach and rejection of his brethren for zealously doing the will of God (vv. 1-18). David knew God was aware of his anguish and mistreatment, and therefore urged the Lord to judge his enemies and blot their names out of *The Book of the Living* to seal their eternal doom (vv. 19-28). Knowing the value of praise, David expressed his confidence in the Lord to protect him and to vanquish his enemies, the end result of which would be praise to God by all who witnessed His deliverance (vv. 29-36).

Concerning *The Book of the Living*, Moses also knew God kept a roster of the names of everyone He would create (Ex. 32:32-33). David refers to this book in verse 28 and then again in Psalm 139:15-16. John also speaks of *The Book of the Living* and assures us that the names of the faithful (true believers) are not blotted out of this book (Rev. 3:5). On the other hand, the names of unbelievers are blotted out of *The Book of the Living* as they die, because they did not receive God's forgiveness for their sins while they were living (Heb. 9:27). This means that when it is reviewed at the Great White Throne Judgment (after the earth's destruction), it will contain only the names of the righteous. *The Lamb's Book of Life* is a timeless, unaltered roster of all the redeemed – all who will be saved throughout time (Rev. 13:8, 17:8, 21:27). *The Book of the Living*, though written before time began, has its fulfillment in time. *The Lamb's Book of Life*, also written before creation, has its verification at the Great White Throne Judgment. Because the names of the lost, when they die, are blotted out of the former book, both books will match at the Great White Throne Judgment; their records will be in perfect agreement. The one shows God's foreknowledge; the other, His record of human responsibility.

This psalm is quoted in the New Testament on seven occasions in direct application to the Lord Jesus Christ, God's trespass offering for us. Under the Levitical system the sin offering was necessary for the *offense of sin*, but the trespass offering was required for the *damages of sin*. The sin offering deals with the guilt of sin; Christ's blood purges the believer's conscience of that. The trespass offering deals with the devastation sin causes and seeks to offer restitution. Through Christ's sin and trespass offering, full restoration of the sinner to God is permitted. Hence, the Lord Jesus, as David prophetically confirms in this psalm, is superbly pictured in the trespass offering as the One who compensates for all the destruction caused by man's sin.

Psalm 69 describes what Christ was to accomplish and suffer as God's trespass offering for us. There may be no other text in our Bibles that so personally reveals the personal anguish of our Lord suffering as God's trespass offering:

Those who hate me without a cause are more than the hairs of my head; they are mighty who would destroy me, being my enemies wrongfully; though I have stolen nothing, I still must restore it (v. 4).

Because for Your sake I have borne reproach; shame has covered my face (v. 7).

Because zeal for Your house has eaten me up, and the reproaches of those who reproach You have fallen on me (v. 9).

Deliver me out of the mire, and let me not sink; let me be delivered from those who hate me, and out of the deep waters. Let not the floodwater overflow me, nor let the deep swallow me up; and let not the pit shut its mouth on me (vv. 14-15).

Reproach has broken my heart, and I am full of heaviness; I looked for someone to take pity, but there was none; and for comforters, but I found none. They also gave me gall for my food, and for my thirst they gave me vinegar to drink (vv. 20-21).

Christ restored all that was lost by Adam in Eden and more. To accomplish this, in His rejection Christ both tasted the gall before being nailed to the cross and drank the vinegar just prior to His death, thus fulfilling the prophecy of verse 21 (Matt. 27:22-50). Having Christ as our trespass offering liberates our minds from the guilt we too experience when we sin against the Lord. The trespass offering served a unique purpose in calling man's attention to the necessity of providing restitution for offenses. Rejoice, dear believer; full restitution for both the offense of sin and its damages has been offered to God on our behalf! As a result, the fellowship with God that was temporarily lost in Eden has been fully restored in Christ: "Though I have stolen nothing, I still must restore it" (v. 4).

Psalm: 70   Type: Lament – Personal   Author: David

Remember and Assist

This psalm is largely a repeat of Psalm 40:13-17. It is an urgent plea for God to remember David, who desperately needed to be rescued from those who sought his life (vv. 1, 5). David was confident God would silence those who had shamed and confounded him by causing them to experience the same (vv. 2-3). This outcome would encourage all to seek and appreciate their salvation in the Lord, and to gladly proclaim: *"Let God be magnified"* (v. 4). Amen!

Psalm: 71   Type: Lament – Personal   Author: Unknown

Help and Hope for the Elderly

The writer confirms he had faithfully served and honored the Lord (his Hope, his Rock, his Fortress, and his Strong Refuge) throughout his life and desired to continue doing so in his autumn years (vv. 1-3, 5-8). However, because of his increasing frailty, he urgently needed the Lord's deliverance from his oppressors (vv. 4, 9-10). These wicked men mocked the psalmist, taunting, *"God has forsaken him; pursue and take him, for there is none to deliver him"* (v. 11). The writer pleads with the Lord not to forsake him in the latter years of his life, but rather to quickly smother his enemies with reproach and dishonor (vv. 12-13). Remembering God's past goodness rekindled the psalmist's hope in the Lord and caused him to rise above his fears associated with old age (vv. 14-21). There is none like the Lord (v. 19), the Holy One of Israel (v. 22), and for that reason the psalmist knew he would be delivered and thus enabled to continue praising God and telling others of His righteous ways. This is the great privilege of all who have been redeemed by *"the Holy One of Israel"* – the Lord Jesus Christ (v. 22; Isa. 54:5; Luke 4:34). Prophetically speaking, this psalm represents the prayer of the afflicted Jewish remnant during the Tribulation Period, who in their old age, so to speak, receive final deliverance through Christ.

Psalm: 72   Type: Liturgical – Royal/Messianic   Author: Solomon

Christ's Glorious Kingdom

King Solomon, the author of this poem, established the most glorious kingdom in Israel's history. His wealth was so vast that silver became like common stones in Jerusalem; his wisdom was coveted by rulers worldwide (1 Kgs. 10:23-27). Though the splendor of his own monarchy was astounding, Solomon foretells an even more spectacular dominion of peace, prosperity, and righteousness – the Millennial Kingdom of Christ (Isa. 11; Rev. 20). The millennial reign of Christ is the theme of Psalm 72 and is a direct answer to the sufferings of Christ at the hands of sinners in Psalm 69, the petition of Christ recorded in Psalm 70, and the restoration of Israel foretold in Psalm 71.

The psalm commences with a request for divine wisdom for the king so he might render prudent decisions that will assist the needy and punish those who exploit them (vv. 1-4). Such a righteous king would rule in prosperity and be remembered and reverenced by everyone for generations to come (vv. 5-7). Even kings from distant shores would gladly pay tribute to such a king and be in subjection to him (vv. 8-11). This ideal king would champion the cause of the poor and be a savior for all the oppressed (vv. 12-14). This ruler would receive gifts and praise from the nations and they would be blessed in turn by him (vv. 15-17). While Solomon's reign was a foretaste of the Messiah's kingdom to come, only He can rule the world in righteousness and utter peace, and only He can remove the judicial curses resulting from original sin in Eden – only the Lord Jesus Christ is the perfect King! There are dozens of Old Testament passages that inform us what to expect during Christ's Millennial Kingdom (not to be confused with *The Eternal State* or *The Day of God*); here are some highlights:

> Isaiah 11: Children play with poisonous snakes, lions eat grass, wolves dwell with lambs, and the whole earth is full of the glory of God.
>
> Isaiah 60: Any nation opposing the Lord will be laid waste (v. 12).
>
> Isaiah 65: Longevity of life will be restored (v. 20).
>
> Ezekiel 36-39: Christ will gather all the Jews dwelling in the nations back to Israel. The Jewish nation will receive a clean heart and the indwelling Holy Spirit so that they can worship their Messiah in Jerusalem.
>
> Ezekiel 40: The millennial temple described by Ezekiel has specific dimensions and is to be erected in Jerusalem.
>
> Zechariah 14: The nations gather against Jerusalem and half the city is conquered. The Lord returns to the earth (splitting the Mount of Olives). The nations opposing Israel are destroyed and Jerusalem becomes the religious center of the world. Any nation that does not come to Jerusalem to worship is swiftly judged.

Zechariah 8: Jerusalem will be the religious capital of the world – all those entering the millennial kingdom will journey to Jerusalem to worship and pray to the Lord. The Jews will be the most esteemed nation on earth.

Psalm 72 is not the only psalm to pertain to the Millennial Kingdom of Christ, says T. Ernest Wilson; Psalms 2, 8, 22, 24, and 95-100 also relate to the future establishment of glory and righteousness on earth.[110] After contemplating the blessings of a righteous king and providing a lovely prophetic portrait of Christ's future kingdom, Solomon concludes the poem (and Book 2) with a doxology (vv. 18-19). The psalmist specifically requests that the entire earth be filled with God's glory, thus ensuring the praise of all men – this prayer will be fulfilled during the millennial reign of Christ.

As a final note, the last verse of the psalm, which reads, *"The prayers of David the son of Jesse are ended,"* relates to an earlier collection of David's psalms; as they are organized in our Bibles, David authored eighteen more psalms after Psalm 72.

Book 3

Asaph wrote eleven of the seventeen psalms in Book 3. Ethan and Heman each wrote one psalm and, like Asaph, were Levite musicians during David's reign. David himself wrote one of these poems while the Korahites are accredited with three.

Psalm: 73   Type: Wisdom   Author: Asaph

A Quandary: Why Do the Wicked Prosper?

Asaph informs us of a personal crisis which nearly caused him to slip from his faith: he knew God was good to the pure in heart who trusted Him, but why did He permit the wicked to prosper (vv. 1-3)? Why did it seem that arrogant, violent people who spewed wicked words, relied on corrupt devices, and turned others from the path of righteousness did not suffer as much as the righteous did (vv. 4-10)? These self-confident evildoers acted as if they owned the world and as if God did not notice their sins (vv. 11-12). Asaph wondered if he had cleansed himself in vain – what value was there in holiness if the righteous continue to experience affliction while the wicked remain unpunished and, indeed, seem to prosper in the world (vv. 13-14)?

This painful dichotomy in Asaph's mind, which he realized was wrong and could be harmful to God's people if shared, was resolved when he sought understanding in God's sanctuary: the destruction of the wicked is sealed; they are not to be envied (vv. 15-17). In God's timing He will cause them to be cast down and suddenly destroyed, and then their lives will seem like a brief dream, one not to be remembered (vv. 18-20). Ignorance had vexed Asaph's soul, but after understanding that the fate of the wicked would be determined by a righteous God, he was able to rejoice in his salvation (vv. 21-22). God was with him, leading him in wisdom, and would receive him into glory in a coming day (vv. 21-24). Asaph concludes the material prosperity of the wicked is temporary and only what is spiritual has lasting value, that is, knowing and being with God (vv. 25-28). When doubts assault our minds, may we remember the eternal perspective: *"My flesh and my heart fail; but God is the strength of my heart and my portion forever"* (v. 26).

Psalm: 74   Type: Lament – Communal   Author: Asaph

Deliverance From Blasphemers

In this song, Asaph cries out to the Lord to remember His covenant people and, as in the past, recompense the blasphemers who had destroyed the sanctuary and the synagogues of God in the land (vv. 1-8). The historical situation he refers to is uncertain, but definitely describes the type of devastation that occurred centuries later during the Babylonian invasion. The psalmist was troubled that there was no prophet who could provide spiritual guidance as to how long this dreadful situation would continue (v. 9), so he appeals directly to the Lord for insight and action by posing three questions:

O God, how long will the adversary reproach? Will the enemy blaspheme Your name forever? Why do You withdraw Your hand, even Your right hand (vv. 10-11)?

Clearly, Asaph wondered why God would allow His temple to be destroyed, but he seems even more disturbed that God was permitting His name to be openly profaned by their invaders. It was one thing to attack God's people, but quite another to publicly reproach God's name. This, as Matthew Henry explains, was Asaph's definitive reason as to why God should punish their aggressors – they were blasphemers:

> As nothing grieves the saints more than to hear God's name blasphemed, so nothing encourages them more to hope that God will appear against their enemies than when they have arrived at such a pitch of wickedness as to reproach God Himself; this fills the measure of their sins apace and hastens their ruin. The psalmist insists much upon this: "We dare not answer their reproaches; Lord, do Thou answer them. Remember that the *foolish people have blasphemed Thy name* and that still *the foolish man reproaches Thee daily.*" Observe the character of those that reproach God; they are foolish. As atheism is folly (Ps. 14:1), profaneness and blasphemy are no less so.[111]

The foolishness of man is never more obvious than when he maligns his Creator. On the basis that God, Israel's sovereign King and Savior, had faithfully delivered His people in the past, Asaph calls on God to respond now (vv. 12-14). The examples given are God's opening the Red Sea as an escape from Pharaoh, crushing the heads of the serpents (perhaps crocodiles), and smiting the Leviathan, a seven-headed mythological monster used here to symbolize Egypt. Certainly the One who causes water to flow from rock and riverbeds to dry up, and who controls the rotation (days and nights) and the tilting (seasons) of the earth can judge foolish blasphemers (vv. 15-18). The Jewish people were like a defenseless dove, so Asaph calls on the Lord to remember the sheep of His pasture and honor His covenant by protecting them from their enemies (vv. 18-23). Those who blaspheme God's name will be punished; let His people continue in righteousness and in faith, lest we ourselves cause His name to be dishonored.

Psalm: 75   Type: Thanksgiving – Communal   Author: Asaph

The Wicked Are Destroyed; The Righteous Are Exalted

The prayer in the previous psalm for God to arise and to plead His own cause (Ps. 74:22) is answered by Psalm 75; ultimately, this will occur at the Second Advent of Christ. On behalf of his fellow countrymen Asaph thanked the Lord for His faithful presence and for demonstrating His wondrous power in righteous judgments, which at times had even rattled the earth (vv. 1-3). God warns the fool to not be foolish and the proud to repent before they experience His fierce indignation; if they rebelled against His authority, they would reap the consequences (vv. 4-6). It is noteworthy that the weight of rebuke in these verses falls heavier on the proud than the fool. At God's appointed time the wicked will have God's full judgment and the righteous shall be exalted; in this surety the psalmist both praises God and warns the proud to submit to God while they still can (vv. 7-10). This psalm reminds us to keep an eternal perspective while dwelling in a temporary world. Let us warn sinners to repent while there is still time and let us not be discouraged when that which is momentary is repulsive and hurtful – God will judge all injustice!

Psalm: 76   Type: Liturgical – Song of Zion   Author: Asaph

A Powerful God Is Praised

By executing powerful judgments on Israel's enemies, the God of Jacob, who dwelt with His people in Jerusalem, had distinguished Himself among the nations (vv. 1-3, 5-6). The One who is more majestic than the mountains cannot be opposed when moved with righteous indignation to protect the meek of the earth; no one can survive His wrath (vv. 4, 7-9). Asaph knew God's awesome judgments were crafted in His sovereign purposes. Such displays of supremacy should prompt two responses: first, God's people should render to Him all that He deserves (including praise); second, out of a fear of wrath the wicked should refrain from their evil ways (vv. 10-12). Like Asaph, let us hope the unregenerate will recognize the awesome handiwork of the Lord and choose to fear and honor the God of Jacob.

Psalm: 77   Type: Lament – Personal   Author: Asaph

Remembering God's Marvelous Works

If you have ever been unable to sleep because of a troubled spirit, this psalm provides a solution: remember and rejoice! Asaph had such a disturbing night – He prayerfully cried out to the Lord all night long, but found no comfort (vv. 1-3). He remembered how on other occasions he would sing through the night praising God for his deliverance, but no such song was in his heart now (vv. 4-6). The nation was suffering a severe crisis and Asaph felt that God, perhaps in righteous anger, was not answering their prayers and had, in fact, abandoned His people (vv. 7-9). In the first ten verses Asaph is self-focused and miserable, referring to himself more often than the Lord.

However, a transforming change in the psalmist's disposition occurs in verse 10: renewed comfort and hope came to Asaph as he remembered and verbalized how God had miraculously delivered the newly liberated Israelites from Pharaoh's army (vv. 10-15). He mused on how God had opened up the Red Sea to allow Israel to pass through, had immobilized Pharaoh's pursuing chariots by a cloud burst, and then closed the sea in upon them after Israel had safely passed (vv. 15-20). Asaph joyfully concluded that there is no god as great as the God of Israel (v. 13). His circumstances had not changed, but his outlook had; Jehovah's past wonders proved He has a plan for His people and this encouraged Asaph that God would demonstrate His mighty wherewithal again on their behalf. Likewise, in times of distress may we remember God's past handiwork and joyfully declare to Him in faith: *"You are the God who does wonders; You have declared Your strength among the peoples"* (v. 14).

Psalm: 78   Type: Liturgical – Covenant   Author: Asaph

A Historical Lesson

J. G. Bellett concisely summarizes this poem, which "traces the history of God's ways in grace, and Israel's ways in perverseness, from the Exodus to David."[112] In this lengthy psalm, Asaph is obeying the divine directive to pass down the Law of the Lord and a roster of His mighty deeds to the next generation (vv. 1-7). The psalmist reviews both Jehovah's past mighty deeds on behalf of the Jewish nation, and how their forefathers failed to obey Him and were then consequently punished (v. 8). Ephraim's disobedience and discipline is provided as a specific example (vv. 9-11). In verses 12-39, Asaph recounts the Egyptian plagues, the Hebrews' subsequent exodus, the forty-year wilderness experience that followed, and also the complaining and rebellion of the people during that time despite all that God had done and provided for them. Their forefathers, while in rebellion to His will and doubting His goodness, demanded God do miraculous feats (vv. 17-10). God responded by proving His love for them through disciplinary judgments (vv. 21, 34, 40).

In verses 40-72, Asaph revisits God's tremendous demonstration of power in the Egyptian plagues (vv. 40-53), how He brought the Jews into a special land for an inheritance, and then provided them a godly king, David, to shepherd them (vv. 54-72). How did they respond to God's wondrous works and rich blessings? They continually rebelled against Him. For example, they set up high places and honored false gods, instead of worshipping only Jehovah in Jerusalem. The Hebrew word *nacah* occurs three times in this psalm, more than another chapter in the Bible, and is rendered "to test" (vv. 18, 41, 56). Asaph's point is that it is not good to test the Lord's love in this way (i.e., through rebellion). Jehovah is a great God who does marvelous works on behalf of His people, but He loves us too much to permit us to persistently wander outside of His will – this is a worthy message to be passed on to the next generation.

Psalm: 79   Type: Lament – Communal   Author: Asaph

A Plea for God to Judge Israel's Invaders

Asaph may have written this poem and Psalm 74 at the same time, as his lament over foreign invaders destroying Jerusalem, desecrating the temple, and slaughtering God's people is similar (vv. 1-2). The morbid scene described does not seem to fit any historical situation during David's reign. The description of unburied rotting corpses littering the countryside and being devoured by predators (v. 3) would be reminiscent of the Babylonian invasion in Jeremiah's day, but this occurred four centuries after Asaph's writings. Whatever the situation, Asaph acknowledges two facts: first, Israel was a reproach among the nations (v. 4); second, the desolation was God's punishment for the past sins of the nation (v. 8).

The psalmist therefore pleads with the Lord to turn from His jealous anger and redirect His wrath upon Israel's enemies (vv. 5-7), and to do so, if for no other reason, for His name's sake (v. 9). The invaders were taunting God to rescue His people, if He was indeed able to (v. 10). So the psalmist asks the Lord to preserve and deliver the Jewish captives and return to their oppressors sevenfold the devastation they had caused – in so doing, Jehovah would preserve His reputation among the nations (vv. 11-12). Asaph closes the song by promising that if the Lord answered his prayer, *"His people, the sheep of His pasture"* would be forever grateful and praise Him forever (v. 13). God's people choose their sin, but the Lord chooses the consequences of their sin. Asaph teaches us to lament our sin and accept divine chastening for it, but also to rise up from failure in grace and seek restoration.

Psalm: 80   Type: Lament – Communal   Author: Asaph

A Prayer of Restoration

This poem continues the previous psalm's tone of deliverance and restoration, but with a set of softer allegories (i.e., gruesome invasion details are not rehashed). Asaph speaks of Israel as a vine brought out of Egypt that once flourished because of God's care, but had now been trampled on by invaders. Isaiah, Jeremiah, and Hosea all use similar imagery in their prophecies (Isa. 5:2; Hos. 10:1). For example, Jeremiah wrote that the nation of Israel, as a political reality, was a noble grape vine (Jer. 8:13), which God planted in the world, but because of wicked leaders and corruption He would permit Babylon to trample it (Jer. 2:21).

The psalmist commences with an appeal to the Great Shepherd, who is enthroned in His holy temple above the cherubim and has authority over the sheep of His pasture in both the Northern and Southern Kingdoms, represented by Ephraim and Benjamin, respectively (vv. 1-2). Asaph prays for national restoration, that God's face (an expression of divine favor) would again shine upon His people (v. 3) and that His anger and their chastisement for sin would come to an end (vv. 8-13).

Besides the imagery of the trampled and uprooted vine, Asaph also speaks of Israel as a firstborn son who had been cut off from his family (vv. 14-16). Jehovah first explained the importance of this relationship to Moses at the burning bush (Ex. 4:21-22). God had adopted the nation of Israel (Rom. 9:4); He considered the nation as a firstborn son with a privileged status among the nations. Through Jehovah's covenant with Abraham, Israel had been singled out from among the nations as a special object of God's favor: *"For I am a Father to Israel, and Ephraim is My firstborn"* (Jer. 31:9). The firstborn son had a privileged position in the family, including the right of family leadership and the greatest share of inheritance. Israel was God's son and heir to the Promised Land (Ex. 4:22), but now the son had lost his inheritance and prestige. Asaph prays that God would revive and restore His son, *"the man at God's right hand"* (the literal meaning of Benjamin's name), to a place of favor (vv. 17-18). The refrain of verses 3 and 7, *"Restore us, O God,"* is again repeated in verse 19 to close the psalm.

It is noted that the nation's continued rejection of Messiah has delayed, but not cancelled, its entry into its inheritance, *"for the gifts and calling of God are irrevocable"* (Rom. 11:29). In fact, this very passage tells us that the hardening of Israel is temporary (*"until the fullness of the Gentiles has come in"*; Rom. 11:25), not permanent. Jehovah will not fail to bestow His firstborn with his inheritance. Additionally, we observe that while God's dealings with the Church are different than with His covenant people, the plea to purify, to revive, and to restore what is becoming corrupt is still a virtuous prayer anytime!

Psalm: 81   Type: Liturgical – Covenantal   Author: Asaph

Worship God and Obey His Word!

This festive psalm celebrates Israel's deliverance from Egypt and is traditionally connected with the Feast of Tabernacles, which was instituted by God to commemorate that event and the following wilderness experience (Lev. 23:33-43). The writer draws from this historical situation to show how God had liberated His people from bondage when they chose to obey Him (vv. 6-7), and that He had sustained them in the wilderness because they had not worshipped foreign gods (vv. 8-10). Obedience results in divine blessing! Hence, Asaph asserts God would remove their present affliction, if only they would wholeheartedly submit to God. One of the implications of this is that they should obey God's Law concerning the Feasts of Jehovah (vv. 3-5).

This, then, is the reason the psalmist commenced with a summons for the people to worship God with joy and sincerity and to sing praises to Him with musical accompaniment (vv. 1-2). As Asaph turns to the nation's current situation, he confirms it is because God's people did not submit to Him that He has allowed them to suffer the destructive consequences of going their own way (vv. 11-12). However, if they would repent and again obey His commands, God promised to subdue their enemies and bless them with agricultural prosperity (vv. 13-16). May we learn from Israel's failures and not doubt God's Word; rather, let us trust and obey, even when it does not seem sensible to do so.

> When we walk with the Lord in the light of His Word,
> What a glory He sheds on our way!
> While we do His good will, He abides with us still,
> And with all who will trust and obey.
> Trust and obey, for there's no other way
> To be happy in Jesus, but to trust and obey.
>
> — John Sammis

Psalm: 82   Type: Liturgical – Temple   **Author: Asaph**

God's Judges Warned

In Psalm 45, David employed the Hebrew *elohim*, a plural noun normally translated "God" in the Old Testament, to acknowledge the king was God's representative on the earth. Although not often rendered in this fashion, *elohim* is also used in this poem to identify those who are to be honored as representatives of God's authority (see also Ex. 21:6). Elohim occurs four times in this psalm, twice in reference to "God" (vv. 1, 8), and twice to designate "the gods" or "mighty ones," who were Israel's judges (and over whom God presided; vv. 1, 6). In this psalm Asaph implores God's judges to champion the weak and the oppressed, and to be just and impartial in their decisions, lest God's foundations of law and order be corrupted on the earth (vv. 2-5). Wherever God delegates authority, there is also accountability (Rom. 13:1); thus, the Jewish judges were severely warned to fulfill their offices with the utmost integrity (vv. 6-7). In Psalm 8 we witnessed another example of this reality: man was created to represent God's authority on the earth and was held directly accountable to God when he failed to properly do so (Gen. 3; Heb. 2:5-8). Psalm 82 concludes with the writer acknowledging the Creator's sovereignty over the earth and that everyone was ultimately accountable to Him (v. 8). It is good for us to remember we all must stand before the Lord and give a personal account (Rom. 14:10-12), and those who represent God's authority on the earth have even more reason to be concerned on that day (Heb. 13:17)!

It is noted the Lord Jesus quoted verse 6 to combat the Pharisees' charge that He had blasphemed because he claimed to be "the Son of God" (John 10:34). The Lord reasoned that, if God called those who were His representatives "the sons of God," how could they accuse Him of blasphemy? While it is true that the Lord Jesus was representing God's authority on the earth at that time, He is the only One to be worshipped as "the Son of God" in His essence and personage for all time (John 1:34, 9:35-38). Only the Lord Jesus could say, *"I and My Father are one"* (John 10:30) – the "Everlasting Father" must have an eternal Son (Isa. 9:6).

Psalm: 83   Type: Lament – Imprecatory   Author: Asaph

A Prayer to Judge Enemies

Asaph laments the threat of Israel's many enemies and calls on the Lord to vindicate His people, as He had done in the past by granting them victory (v. 1). To eliminate any confusion of the matter, the psalmist lists the specific enemies who were conspiring against Israel and God Himself at that time (vv. 2-8). The writer then recalls the type of historical victories he desired God to again grant them, such as when Deborah and Barak confronted Sisera (vv. 9-12; Judg. 4-5). Asaph also employs metaphors to describe the destruction he wanted God to inflict on their enemies: let them be like windblown chaff or a fire-consumed forest, and let them experience the upheaval of a violent tempest (vv. 13-16). The decisive answer to Asaph's prayer would be an ample recompense on these foes for afflicting those Jehovah loved (vv. 17-18). This would teach their oppressors that Jehovah was their Protector and the one true God.

Psalm: 84   Type: Liturgical – Song of Zion   Author: Korahites

Longing to Be With God

In Psalms 42 and 43, David expressed his yearning to be in God's presence at the tabernacle (the proper place of worship). The writer of this psalm is on a pilgrimage to the temple (vv. 6-7), and likewise conveys his deep longing to be in God's courts (vv. 1-2, 10). The name of the author is not known, but it was sung by or accredited to the sons of Korah. The psalmist seems to picture the temple scene in his mind and then expresses his envy of the priests who stand at the two altars in the temple (vv. 3-4). In fact, all who sought refuge there were welcome: *"Even the sparrow has found a home, and the swallow a nest for herself, where she may lay her young – even Your altars, O Lord of hosts, my King and my God"* (v. 3). It was not uncommon for sparrows and swallows to build their nests in the heights of the temple sanctuary and even among the altars. Because the birds had sought rest and safety in the temple, the priests did not disturb their nesting patterns, even if they took up residence on the altars.

The sparrow is a worthless bird; it doesn't sing, it is not beautiful to look at, and there is very little meat on it to eat; thus, in the Lord's day two sparrows were sold for a mere farthing (Matt. 10:29). The sparrow was a worthless bird that found significance in Jehovah's presence. The swallow is a restless bird, darting to and fro, yet the swallow too found tranquility in the house of God. What is the spiritual lesson for us? Like these common birds, all believers, in the spiritual sense, were once worthless and restless, but now have found spiritual significance and peace with God in the refuge of Christ.

It is noteworthy that both altars are mentioned in this psalm. The purpose of the Bronze Altar was the judgment of sin; this is where the animal sacrifices were placed. No such sacrifices were burned on the Golden Altar, but sacrificial blood from the animals offered on the Bronze Altar was placed on the horns of the Golden Altar to create a connection between the two. Through Christ's blood, the realities shadowed in both altars are established for the believer. The Golden Altar speaks of Christ's continuing work to perfect our worship and service and the total blessing of His intercessory ministry. This ensures whatever Christ accomplishes within His people will be appreciated by God as the sweet-smelling offering. The Bronze Altar typifies Christ's death; the Golden Altar, His life now. In the Bronze Altar, we see Christ judged, but in the Golden Altar we see Christ caring for His saints. In the Bronze Altar we gain peace with God, but through the Golden Altar the believer enjoys the peace of God. Wondrous is the typology within the altars, but it is even greater to experience what they represent: the peace, the significance, the security of being in God's presence, and having our sacrifices to God sanctified and presented by Christ Himself.

The psalmist was confident God would refresh pilgrims en route to Jerusalem. For example, the Valley of Baca was a waterless area, but when the rain did fall, the valley became full of springs and pools of water. This illustrated God's blessing to faithful pilgrims during their strenuous journey to the temple (vv. 5-7). The arriving pilgrims prayed God would strengthen and bless their king, so that he could continue to protect the nation (vv. 8-9). The poem concludes with the writer declaring his love for God's dwelling place – he would rather be with the Lord than anywhere else, especially the tents of the wicked (v. 10). He was confident that the Lord had heard his prayer and would continue to bless, to protect, and to bestow good to all those who trust in Him and walk uprightly (vv. 11-12). Indeed, this is an essential criterion for receiving God's favor in any age!

Psalm: 85   Type: Lament – Communal   Author: Korahites

Revive Us Again

The timing of this psalm cannot be determined, but the writer acknowledges a past chastisement for sin and that God had forgiven His people of their iniquities (vv. 2-3). It would appear this psalm was written after the return of the Jews from Babylon. Although many captives had made their way back to Israel, the psalmist prays that the God of their salvation would revive them again (perhaps speaking of full restoration); this would certainly result in their rejoicing in Him (vv. 1, 4-7). Perhaps Psalm 85 is the answer to Asaph's prayer in Psalm 79 to preserve and rescue the Jewish captives. The writer declares he will listen to what the Lord has to say because He promises salvation to His saints and does so to manifest His glory in the land (vv. 8-9). His people, therefore, should refrain from repeating their previous folly. In providing peace and prosperity to His people, God would demonstrate His attributes of love, justice, mercy, righteousness, and faithfulness (vv. 10-13). The writer confirms God cannot negate any aspect of His holy character to offer salvation to man; thankfully, mercy and truth, and righteousness and peace, converge on humanity's behalf in the finished work of the Lord Jesus Christ (v. 10; Rom. 3:21-2, 5:8-9). On this secure basis, we too can plead with the psalmist, *"Will You not Yourself revive us again?"* (v. 6; NASV).

Psalm: 86   Type: Lament – Personal   Author: David

Petitioning a Good and Great God

David says much about the nature of God and of his own character in this poetic supplication for preservation and mercy (vv. 2-3). He accredits God with being good, great, forgiving, merciful, compassionate, gracious, long-suffering, truthful; He is alone in majesty, unique in wondrous works – there is no god like Him (vv. 5, 8, 10, 15). Of himself, David states he is poor and needy, but living a consecrated life for God (vv. 1-3). God had heard his previous prayers and had delivered him from death (vv. 13); hence, he completely trusted the Lord to both hear and act on his desperate plea now (vv. 6-7). David was in need of mercy, strength, instruction in God's way, and more reverence for God's name (vv. 1-3, 11, 16). Besides these personal needs, David asked God to preserve him and to judge the proud, violent men who sought his life (vv. 14, 16).

The Lord was David's help, so he asked God for a sign of His continued support in order that David's enemies might be ashamed and that he himself would be comforted (v. 17). David fully anticipated that the Lord would hear his prayer, that he would rejoice in the Lord and be able to praise His name forever, and that all nations would appreciate and honor Him too (vv. 4, 9, 12). David shows us our prayers should peer beyond our own needs to understand the character of God – consider what would prompt God to answer our supplication. In doing so, we might find much of what we are asking Him is not in His will for us. When praying, let us be careful not just to ask, but also to thank, to praise, and to worship God: *"For You are great, and do wondrous things; You alone are God"* (v. 10).

Psalm: 87   Type: Liturgical – Song of Zion   Author: David

Zion – The Glorious City of God

David continues the thought introduced in the last psalm: *"All nations whom You have made shall come and worship before You, O Lord, and shall glorify Your name"* (Ps. 86:9). In this poem David acknowledges the glorious aspects of Zion and how God will assemble the nations there in a future joyous day. Zion is God's magnificent city; it is where He chose to dwell and to be worshipped (vv. 1-3). In bygone days, His covenant people honored Him there, but in a coming day all nations will happily gather there as if it were their birthplace; five specific nations are noted to be among the throng of people (vv. 4-5). God will welcome the Gentiles into His city; in fact, all their names will be on a permanent register acknowledging their citizenship (v. 6). Because the Lord dwells in Zion, the city will be a source of blessing and comfort to all that reside there (v. 7). More than three centuries later, Isaiah prophesied of this future scene in Jerusalem:

> *For the nation and kingdom which will not serve you [the Jewish nation] shall perish, and those nations shall be utterly ruined. ... Also the sons of those who afflicted you shall come bowing to you, and all those who despised you shall fall prostrate at the soles of your feet; and they shall call you The City of the Lord, Zion of the Holy One of Israel* (Isa. 60:12-14).

> *It shall be that I will gather all nations and tongues; and they shall come and see My glory ... to My holy mountain Jerusalem, says the Lord* (Isa. 66:18-20).

Then, over a millennium after David's time, John wrote the following panorama of God's dwelling place during the Eternal State:

> *I, John, saw the holy city, New Jerusalem, coming down out of heaven from God, prepared as a bride adorned for her husband. And I heard a loud voice from heaven saying, "Behold, the tabernacle of God is with men, and He will dwell with them, and they shall be His people. God Himself will be with them and be their God. And God will wipe away every tear from their eyes; there shall be no more death, nor sorrow, nor crying. There shall be no more pain, for the former things have passed away"* (Rev. 21:2-4).

> *But I saw no temple in it, for the Lord God Almighty and the Lamb are its temple. The city had no need of the sun or of the moon to shine in it, for the glory of God illuminated it. The Lamb is its light. And the nations of those who are saved shall walk in its light, and the kings of the earth bring their glory and honor into it. Its gates shall not be*

shut at all by day (there shall be no night there). And they shall bring the glory and the honor of the nations into it. But there shall by no means enter it anything that defiles, or causes an abomination or a lie, but only those who are written in the Lamb's Book of Life (Rev. 21:23-27).

The future is exceedingly bright for the restored nation of Israel and all Gentiles who will humbly submit to the God of Jacob and receive His salvation in His Lamb – Christ!

Psalm: 88   Type: Lament – Imprecatory   Author: Heman

Hope in Suffering

Written by the wise Ezrahite, Heman (1 Chron. 16:41-42; 1 Kgs. 4:31), this sad poem expresses the thoughts of one who is persistently crying out to the Lord amid continuous suffering (vv. 1-2). Heman plundered the dictionary of gloom to articulate his misery and affliction in this poem. He viewed himself as a buried corpse that is soon forgotten; indeed, his friends had forsaken him (vv. 3-6). A dead man does not receive God's care; in fact, Heman attributed his sufferings to relentless waves of God's wrath for his sin – he was overwhelmed with grief (vv. 7-9). In grappling with his emotions, Heman surmised he did not want to live as though dead, because the dead cannot praise God (vv. 9-12). Having been estranged from loved ones and apparently rejected by God, the despairing psalmist continues to pray for deliverance, knowing God is his only source of hope to escape this ongoing death and darkness (vv. 13-18).

Without God, suffering would be a most miserable experience, but with God suffering is worked for good and we can be thankful for it (Rom. 8:28; Eph. 5:20). Our affliction may be the consequence of sin (as in this psalm), or for personal refinement (Jas. 1:2-3), or to prepare us for further blessing (Job 42:12), but it is always for the glory of God (John 11:4). Thus, Paul could confidently write, *"For I consider that the sufferings of this present time are not worthy to be compared with the glory which shall be revealed in us"* (Rom. 8:18). In this sense suffering for righteousness better prepares us for heaven!

Psalm: 89   Type: Lament – Personal/Messianic   Author: Ethan

The Davidic Covenant

The psalm can be divided into two major sections: the establishment of the Davidic Covenant by God's faithfulness (vv. 1-37) and the future fulfillment of this covenant despite Israel's failures (vv. 38-52). The author, Ethan the Levite, is named with Heman in 1 Kings 4:31 as being a wise man in the days of Solomon. While the specific occasion for the writing of this royal liturgy is unknown, the general backdrop of crushing military defeats caused the psalmist to request that God would honor His covenant with David (2 Sam. 7). A paradox existed in Ethan's mind: how could a merciful and faithful God not honor His covenant with David (i.e., that one of David's descendants would sit on his throne forever) by permitting the present slaughter of His people (vv. 1-4)?

Ethan repeatedly affirms his trust in the attributes of God, who is alone in majesty, rules creation, and had done many marvelous works to bless and protect His people (vv. 5-18). Hoping to invoke God's intervention, Ethan reminds Him of his special relationship and covenant with David, who was a young man with a sincere heart when God chose him from among the people to be His anointed servant (vv. 19-20). A special father/son-like relationship ensued between the Lord and David, with God vowing to bless and protect him, and to make him victorious before his enemies (vv. 21-27). God unconditionally promised David an everlasting royal dynasty; though God would chasten His covenant people if they rebelled, He would not forget His promise to David (vv. 28-37; 2 Sam. 7:12-16).

Having substantiated the Davidic Covenant, the writer then describes the present situation to apparently prompt God to honor his vow to David and reverse the dire situation (vv. 38-39). A powerful enemy had overcome the present king in battle, broken his protecting walls and strongholds, and cast his throne down to the ground in shame (vv. 40-45). Ethan acknowledges his life was now in jeopardy and petitions God to remember and to honor His covenant with David by rescuing the psalmist from certain destruction – his hope was in the Lord alone (vv. 46-51).

If God intervened to deliver Israel and thus prevent the line of Davidic kings from being extinguished, then Ethan's quandary would be resolved. Of course, he did not understand that there were both conditional and unconditional aspects of God's covenant, and God always reserves the right to chasten and refine His people as necessary. In that matter, we can also praise the Lord. As in previous books, Book 3 concludes with a doxology in verse 52.

Book 4

The writers of fourteen of the seventeen psalms in Book 4 are unknown. Book 4 commences with the oldest psalm in our Bibles, Psalm 90, which was composed by Moses. David wrote Psalms 101 and 103.

Psalm: 90   Type: Lament – Communal   Author: Moses

Human Mortality and God's Eternality

The Hebrew superscript accredits Moses with the authorship of this psalm. Given the tone and content of the poem it was likely composed during the forty years' wilderness experience in which the older generation slowly perished for doubting God's goodness at Kadesh-barnea (Num. 14). No doubt continuously burying friends and family members as the nation aimlessly trekked through the desert marking time weighed heavy on Moses' mind. How did Moses find comfort while immersed in this scene of flickering human mortality? He contrasted the everlasting nature of God with the finiteness of humanity (vv. 1-6). The everlasting and immutable God was present before anything was created (v. 2). Accordingly, a thousand years to man is but as the passing of a day, or even a night watch of a few hours, to God (v. 4). Man's existence on the earth is brief before he returns to the dust of the earth, but in all generations the faithful have found God to be their eternal Refuge and safe dwelling place (vv. 1, 3).

In comparison to the eternal God, man's earthly sojourn is like grass that withers in the heat of the day or like sleep that passes in the morning (vv. 5-6). Man's suffering and short lifespan (around 70 to 80 years), occurs because of God's judgment of original sin and of ongoing sin (vv. 7-10). Realizing the reality of this pitiful and unchangeable situation, Moses requests two consolations from the Lord. The first is that the faithful would receive divine wisdom to behave properly during their limited days on the earth (vv. 11-12). The second is that God would show compassion and mercy to those loyal to Him and turn their sorrowful existence into a joyful and satisfying one (vv. 13-14). The latter request is further substantiated in that God's people had already suffered much in the will of God while slaves in Egypt (v. 15). Moses anticipated two desirable outcomes if God granted his requests: God's splendor would be displayed in His servants, and the next generation would witness the glory of the Lord (vv. 16-17).

This poem shows Moses understood the proper value of things in eternity, that is, in relationship to what we do in the will of God. He turned his back on the riches and fame Egypt offered in order to suffer the reproach of Christ (Heb. 11:24-26). After God called him forty years later, he proceeded towards Egypt with nothing but the rod of God – God was his full sufficiency. What motivated this dangerous pilgrimage to do God's will? Moses wanted to see the glory of God and wanted his children to know of God's majestic power also: *"Let Your work appear to Your servants, and Your glory to their children"* (v. 16). Similarly, if our children are to see the glory of God, we must surrender to the Lord what we have and number each day in wisdom for eternity.

Psalm: 91   Type: Thanksgiving – Song of Trust/Messianic
          Author: Unknown

The Secret Place of the Most High

Whereas Psalm 90 presents mortal man in contrast to the eternal God, Psalm 91 declares Christ as the perfect Man who is dependent on God in contrast to mortal man who is not. There are several words and expressions repeated throughout Psalms 90–91 that interconnect these songs and assert the believer's security: *"dwelling," "make us glad,"* and the frequent use of *Elyown* – "the Most High." The psalmist affirms the Lord is his Refuge and Fortress and therefore he will be victorious when solicited to evil or when attacked by the wicked (vv. 1-2). The writer will not fear because God's truth will shield him from the enemy's deceitful tactics and God's wing will protect him from heinous attempts at harm, such as the fowler's snare, deadly pestilence, flying arrows, and night terrors (vv. 3-8). In fact, the poet declares no calamity (apart from the will of God) can befall those who enjoy the Lord as their Refuge (vv. 9-10). God has even charged His holy angels with watching over and assisting His people and the innocent from evil plots (vv. 11-12; Matt. 18:10; Acts 5:19, 11:7).

While tempting the Lord to sin, the devil misquoted verses 11 and 12 of this psalm (see Matt. 4:6): Satan added *"at any time,"* and left out *"to keep you in all your ways."* Two important particulars are observed in their interchange. First, the devil is never more dangerous than when he quotes (misquotes) God's Word – he does so to deceive. Second, the Lord uses direct quotations from God's Word, the Shield of Truth (v. 4), to deflect the enemy's assault (Matt. 4:4, 7, 10). If we follow the Lord's example, we too will evade the lion's attack and trample the serpent under our feet (v. 13); both metaphors are used in the New Testament in the context of a believer's victory in Christ over Satan (Rom. 16:19-20; 2 Cor. 11:3-15; 1 Pet. 5:7-9). Because Psalm 91 is referred to during the temptation of Christ as recorded in Matthew 4 and Luke 4, the poem is considered Messianic in nature and is sometimes referred to as "The Psalm of Temptation." In verses 14-16, God promises His people seven blessings to overcome evil trials: His love, His name, His ear (i.e., the opportunity to pray to Him), His presence in trouble, His deliverance, His honor, and His satisfaction in life. Thus, every evil device against the believer is completely ineffective for those who rest in the salvation of the Lord, *"under the shadow of the Almighty"* (v. 1). Isaiah confirms we experience intimacy with God and His protection when we stay near to Him:

> *For thus says the High and Lofty One who inhabits eternity, whose name is Holy: "I dwell in the high and holy place, with him who has a contrite and humble spirit, to revive the spirit of the humble, and to revive the heart of the contrite ones"* (Isa. 57:15).

In the balances of eternity, there is much more at stake presently than our creature comforts, our personal rights, our family reputations, or our being proven innocent of wrongdoing. It is only through obedience, submission to authority, and brokenness that we experience reviving power and divine security. Hence, every satanic device employed against the believer affords him or her opportunity to draw near to God and experience the wonder of His fellowship and the power of His deliverance. These amazing benefits are lost to some degree when we withdraw from the intimate secret place of the Most High to defend ourselves, or worse, resort to the same debased behavior of our oppressors. Carnality opposed in the flesh can only have one outcome – more carnality: *"the wrath of man does not produce the righteousness of God"* (Jas. 1:20).

Psalm: 92   Type: Thanksgiving - Personal   Author: Unknown

The Blessed Should Praise God

The first verse summarizes the entire song: *"It is good to give thanks to the Lord, and to sing praises to Your name, O Most High"* (v. 1). It is appropriate for man to thank God for His loving-kindness, faithfulness, lovely thoughts, and good works and to sing praise to Him with the accompaniment of musical instruments (vv. 2-3). Specifically, the unknown psalmist praises the Lord for vindicating the righteous by destroying forever the wicked, speaking as if this triumph had already occurred (vv. 4-5). These evildoers abruptly sprout up like grass, but flourish only for a brief time because they are opposed by God, who is sovereign over all things and reigns forever (vv. 6-9). Because the wicked will be vanquished, the writer conveys his personal confidence in God, his Rock, to also lift him up in power and joyful vitality; thus, there is no reason to fear evildoers, but rather every reason to praise God (vv. 10-15)!

Psalm: 93   Type: Liturgical – Enthronement   Author: Unknown

The Eternal King on His Eternal Throne

This short poem celebrates the Lord's sovereign dominion over the earth, and also anticipates the future day when He, as the enthroned Jewish Messiah, will reign in righteousness and His glory will fill the earth (Ps. 45:6-7; 1 Cor. 15:23-27). Isaiah prophesied of that exciting event:

> *They shall not hurt nor destroy in all My holy mountain, for the earth shall be full of the knowledge of the Lord as the waters cover the sea. "And in that day there shall be a Root of Jesse, who shall stand as a banner to the people; for the Gentiles shall seek Him, and His resting place shall be glorious"* (Isa. 11:9-10).

The eternal God is robed in majesty and strength and is situated high above the world He created and rules (vv. 1-2). His might is far greater than a devastating flood or the raging waves of a tumultuous sea (vv. 3-4). Because His house is filled with holiness (i.e., no corruption abides there), God's commands over all creation are sure. This psalm affirms that God is actively ruling over the affairs of men with the utmost power and dignity; He should therefore be obeyed and honored by all.

Psalm: 94   Type: Lament – Communal   Author: Unknown

Vengeance Belongs to the Lord

Moses reminded the Israelites before they entered the Promised Land that vengeance and recompense for wrongdoing was the Lord's business (Deut. 32:35). God's wrath against wickedness and injustice is not a distasteful aspect of God's character, as some think, but rather an outward manifestation of His holy perfection. God's goodness and righteousness are demonstrated in both welcoming the repentant sinner into heaven and casting the proud rebel into hell. The psalmist recognizes this truth and calls on the Judge of the earth to invoke vengeance on the pompous wicked who persecuted His people (vv. 1-3). To further motivate the Lord to action, the writer laments what those who deserved His wrath were doing: boasting of their evil; oppressing God's inheritance (His people); slaying widows, strangers, and orphans; and gloating that the God of Jacob did not perceive or did not care about their evil deeds (vv. 4-7). In respect to the last offense, the writer implores the wicked to consider their ways: surely the One who created the ear hears, and the One who formed the eye sees; the implication is that their Creator was not ignorant of their malevolent escapades and would justly recompense them (vv. 8-11).

The psalmist proclaims there is both blessing and hope in the midst of suffering. To adequately teach His people the Law, they must experience the chastening consequences of breaking it. God's reproof is a proof of His love for His people; it is a rich blessing to them (vv. 12-13; Heb. 12:6). Having steadfast confidence that God will not forsake His people, but will surely punish all those who afflict them instills hope in the minds of the oppressed (vv. 14-15). This reality was the writer's hope and saved him from despair – he knew the Lord would "stand up" on his behalf and right the wrongs he had suffered (vv. 16-19). The Lord was his Fortress, Rock, and Refuge, and he realized the wicked and their corrupt rulers would be cut off, for they had no portion in the Lord (vv. 20-23).

In the New Testament, Paul quotes the previously mentioned command of Moses, but adds this instruction for believers in the Church Age:

Repay no one evil for evil. ... Beloved, do not avenge yourselves, but rather give place to wrath; for it is written, "Vengeance is Mine, I will repay," says the Lord. Therefore ... do not be overcome by evil, but overcome evil with good (Rom. 12:17-21).

During the dispensation of the Law, God demonstrated man's sin and need for a Savior because no one could keep the Law (Rom. 3:20; Gal. 3:24). However, in the Age of Grace, believers have the indwelling Holy Spirit and are commanded to fulfill the greater intention of the Law – to love selflessly, for example, by giving to others in lieu of merely not stealing from them (Rom. 13:8-10). Acknowledging God's righteous standard is the focus of keeping the

Law, but demonstrating His irresistible love in righteousness is paramount in fulfilling the Law – and this we must do to win the lost to Christ! Christians, therefore, should desire to pluck lost souls out of hellfire much more than they desire to get even for wrong done to them. God will deal with all injustice!

Psalm: 95   Type: Praise/Liturgical – Enthronement
Author: Unknown

Let Us Worship the Lord

Psalm 95 commences a series of five "enthronement" psalms similar to Psalm 93. William Kelly suggests that these psalms (Ps. 95-99) form a collective series that actually climaxes with Psalm 100, a hymn of praise:

> The first of the six psalms (Ps. 95) summons the people of God, in the Spirit of prophecy which animated the godly, to rejoice in Jehovah no longer to be hidden but revealed in Christ Who brings in salvation, glory, and rest; but no blessing is without hearing His voice. In the second the summons goes forth beyond Israel to the nations and peoples; as the third is the new song that is sought. The fourth demands a new song of Israel; and the fifth is the answer. This is completed by Psalm 100, which expresses Israel in the joy of grace, while owning their own portion, inviting all the earth to shout aloud to Jehovah.[113]

The writer of this psalm begins by exhorting God's people to joyfully sing and praise the Lord, and to worship Him as the awesome God and magnificent King above all other gods (vv. 1-3). It is appropriate for created beings to worship their Creator, the One who controls and maintains the existence of all things – Paul offers these same divine accolades to the Lord Jesus Christ (vv. 4-6; Col. 1:16-19). With the apex of praise reached in verse 6, the writer then warns his countrymen, *"the people of His pasture, and the sheep of His hand,"* against repeating their forefathers' error of disbelief at Kadesh-barnea (vv. 7-8).

The consequences of this particular instance of doubting God's goodness after enjoying His intimate presence and witnessing His wondrous works was crushing: an entire generation perished in the wilderness under His displeasure (vv. 9-11). The writer of Hebrews applies this historical incident to exhort fellow-believers not to have hardened hearts of disbelief towards the Lord, for to do so results in the loss of blessing and disciplinary chastening (Heb. 3:7-19). As shepherds usually lived among their sheep to ensure their proper care and protection, the analogy of the Great Shepherd with his sheep in verse 6 is a lovely expression of God's abiding presence with His people. Indeed, the writer of Hebrews reminds us of the Lord's words and their application:

For He Himself has said, "I will never leave you nor forsake you." So we may boldly say: "The Lord is my helper; I will not fear" (Heb. 13:5-6).

Surely, the One so powerful, so good, so intimate, and so faithful deserves our worship too!

Psalm: 96   Type: Liturgical – Enthronement   Author: Unknown

Worship the Lord in the Beauty of Holiness

Three times in the first two verses the poet urges those who had experienced God's salvation to *"sing unto the Lord"* not by singing songs of dead rote, but new songs which reflect the soul's joy and enthusiasm over receiving fresh mercies from the Lord day after day (vv. 1-2). Those who have experienced God's salvation have the privilege of declaring His glory and His marvelous doings to the nations, so that they might revere and praise Him also (v. 3). He is their Creator and the One who is above all false gods (vv. 4-5). The aura of God's presence saturated His temple with honor, majesty, strength, and beauty (v. 6).

Such a great God should certainly be sought out by His people in the beauty of holiness (i.e., with sins confessed and cleansed) and He should receive from them offerings of praise and gifts befitting of His glory (vv. 7-9). In fact, everyone should praise the One who reigns over the world and will judge in righteousness all peoples and nations (v. 10). Furthermore, all creation should honor the Lord and praise His holy name (vv. 11-12). The last verse previews the Second Advent of Christ to the earth when this reality will occur and the lament of the redeemed will abruptly cease, for the Lord shall rule in righteousness and peace over all nations, the curses on the earth shall be lifted (Gen. 3:17-19; Rom. 8:20-22), and the whole earth will be full of His glory (v. 13; Isa. 2:2, 62:1-7)!

Exodus 15 records the first occurrence of singing in the Bible as well as the lyrics of Scripture's first song. Euphoria swept through the Israelite ranks as they marched into the wilderness beyond the Red Sea as a redeemed people under the shadow of Jehovah's cloud. God's redemption of His people was complete; they had been purchased by blood in Egypt and had been powerfully delivered from Egypt through the sea. As then, it is a great privilege for the redeemed to sing praises to the Lord, day after day. To do so powerfully reflects the believer's salvation (i.e., it demonstrates the Lord resides within him or her) to a lost world that desperately needs to see Christ (v. 2). The redeemed must sing, come before the Lord with appropriate gifts (1 Cor. 16:2; Heb. 13:15-16), and worship Him in the beauty of holiness (1 Cor. 11:27-32)!

Psalm: 97   Type: Liturgical – Enthronement   Author: Unknown

God Judges the Evil We Should Hate

The psalmist visualizes the awesome appearance of the Lord when He comes to the earth to judge wickedness: He will be veiled in threatening clouds of darkness and accompanied by flashes of lightning, the mountains shall melt at His presence, and the whole earth shall quake (vv. 1-6). The author warns idolaters that they will then be judged and their false gods will be exposed for what they are – phony deities (v. 7). In light of this future event, the poet warns God's people to hate what is evil and to rejoice in the One who will judge it (vv. 8-10). The writer of Hebrew describes a similar scene at the Lord's

Second Advent to the earth, when He shall shake heaven and earth and remove all that is evil. The writer then exhorts believers:

Therefore, since we are receiving a kingdom which cannot be shaken, let us have grace, by which we may serve God acceptably with reverence and godly fear. For our God is a consuming fire (Heb. 12:28-29).

At that time, divine revelation will fill the earth and delight the hearts of all the righteous (v. 11). In the interim prior to this event, it is befitting for God's people to rejoice in Him, remember His holiness, and thank Him (v. 12)!

Psalm: 98   Type: Liturgical – Enthronement   Author: Unknown

Sing Praises to the Lord

This poem is similar to the previous in that the writer calls on everyone to sing praises to the Lord, who is coming to the earth to impartially judge its inhabitants in righteousness (vv. 1, 9). The psalmist had much to celebrate with spiritual songs and musical instruments; God had honored His covenant with Israel and sustained them through many threatening circumstances and hardships (vv. 3-6). His salvation for Israel was evident to the nations then, and centuries later at Calvary it would again be manifest. Before the Gentiles, God's own right arm was stripped bare and suffered righteously in order to offer salvation not only to the house of Israel, but to all people (vv. 1-3; John 3:16).

Although the Law revealed the righteousness of God, it could only condemn as no one could keep it (Rom. 3:19). God therefore displayed His righteousness in a new way apart from the Law, that is, by judging an innocent, sinless substitute in the place of sinful and condemned humanity (Rom. 3:21-22). There was only one possible substitute, God's own Son, whom Isaiah referred to as God's *"right arm"* (Isa. 59:1-2, 16). Seeing then the great salvation we have in Christ, we too can praise God with Israel, the nations, and indeed with all creation; the Lord, the eternal King of the saints, deserves our worship (vv. 7-8).

The Beginning of Wisdom

Accordingly, this psalm previews a future scene in heaven when the redeemed will be gathered out of the nations and will proclaim:

> *Great and marvelous are Your works, Lord God Almighty! Just and true are Your ways, O King of the saints! Who shall not fear You, O Lord, and glorify Your name? For You alone are holy. For all nations shall come and worship before You, for Your judgments have been manifested* (Rev. 15:3-4).

Psalm: 99   Type: Liturgical – Enthronement   Author: Unknown

Reverence for the Holy God

This is the last in a series of five enthronement psalms. While six other psalms speak of God's holiness, the word "holy" appears four times in this short poem, which is more than any other psalm. Specifically, God's name is declared holy (v. 3), His essence is holy (vv. 5, 9), and His inhabitation is holy (v. 9). Consequently, the psalmist describes the awesome and majestic position the One who sits between the cherubim held above not just His covenant people, but all the nations of the world (vv. 1-2). He longs for all people to reverently tremble before Jehovah, and to offer Him the appropriate worship and praise (vv. 3, 5). Beyond the motivation of God's awesome holiness, the psalmist also proclaims that God is worthy of worship for the mercy He has extended His people through the ages in response to their prayers (vv. 6-8). Verse 9 repeats the refrain in verse 5: it is most appropriate for the Lord's people to worship the Lord in His holy mountain, Zion. When this psalm was written, worship would have been offered at the temple in Jerusalem, but in the Church Age, it is through Christ that we may come directly into the holy throne room of heaven to worship and to pray (Heb. 4:15-16). This is a great privilege that is often neglected by believers today.

In response to His disciple's request for Him to teach them how to pray, the Lord Jesus commenced the instruction by addressing His Father in this way: *"Our Father which art in heaven, hallowed be Your name"* (Matt. 6:9). Charles Haddon Spurgeon commented on this verse:

The proper study of a Christian is the Godhead. The highest science, the loftiest speculation, the mightiest philosophy which can ever engage the attention of a child of God is the name, the person, the work, the doings, and the existence of the great God whom he calls his Father.[114]

God, His name, and His dwelling place transcend all that is common and earthly. God is holy; He is separate from all else! All that is associated with Him, including His name, should be revered.

Psalm: 100 Type: Praise   **Author: Unknown**

Joyfully Praising the Creator

This psalm is an exhortation to celebrate the Lord's rule and to joyfully praise Him. The goodness of the Creator's abiding love for His covenant people is declared in this lovely metaphor: *"Know that the Lord, He is God; it is He who has made us, and not we ourselves; we are His people and the sheep of His pasture"* (v. 3). It was not enough for the Jews to merely know they were God's sheep; their Creator wanted them to understand that He Himself knew they were His sheep. He loved them and longed to care for them and He wanted them to rest in His love. Centuries later, while warning his countrymen of the forthcoming judgment for their idolatry, Jeremiah acknowledged the Jews belonged to Jehovah and they were like an inheritance to Him (Jer. 10:16). This is a charming gesture; God confirmed His long-suffering love for His people even when they were in rebellion. In the Church Age, Paul declared the extent of God's sustaining love to all believers:

> *For I am persuaded that neither death nor life, nor angels nor principalities nor powers, nor things present nor things to come, nor height nor depth, nor any other created thing, shall be able to separate us from the love of God which is in Christ Jesus our Lord* (Rom. 8:38-39).

The Lord desires His people in every age to rest in His immutable truth, goodness, and everlasting mercy (v. 5), and to cherish the security of His inexhaustible grace. To do so will likewise enable us to serve Him with gladness (v. 2), and to joyfully sing praises in His presence (v. 1). Today, the Church can cherish many of the same divine sentiments expressed to Israel long ago: the Lord is our God, our Creator, our Owner, and our Shepherd (v. 3); thus, we add our affirmation to the psalmist's appeal:

> *Enter into His gates with thanksgiving, and into His courts with praise. Be thankful to Him, and bless His name. For the Lord is good; His mercy is everlasting, and His truth endures to all generations* (vv. 4-5).

Psalm: 101   Type: Liturgical – Royal   Author: David

A Personal Commitment to Holiness

In the wilderness of Sinai, God conveyed His profound yearning for His people: *"Consecrate yourselves therefore, and be holy, for I am the Lord your God. And you shall keep My statutes, and perform them: I am the Lord who sanctifies you"* (Lev. 20:7-8). In the same vein, David was not content to merely praise God's rule of mercy and truth (v. 1) without any personal action on his part; rather, he wanted his own life and kingdom to be marked by wisdom, purity, and willing subjection to God (v. 2). Knowing "the eye gate" and friends are two things that often cause the righteous to fall away, David personally committed not to look on any wicked thing or to keep company with any vile person (vv. 3-4). Rather, he pledged to surround himself with faithful, blameless companions and servants, and not to tolerate slander, arrogance, lying, or deceitful behavior among his companions (vv. 5-7). Looking beyond the boundaries of the palace, David further promised to purge wickedness from the nation of Israel (v. 8). A holy God deserves the service and worship of a holy people, who can have no expectation of His favor or communion if they are in sin. This is a timeless reality, one that John affirmed in the dawn of the Church Age:

> *God is light and in Him is no darkness at all. If we say that we have fellowship with Him, and walk in darkness, we lie and do not practice the truth. But if we walk in the light as He is in the light, we have*

fellowship with one another, and the blood of Jesus Christ His Son cleanses us from all sin (1 Jn. 1:5-7).

King David knew God's blessing and fellowship were contingent on his personal commitment to holy living and therefore pledged the Lord he would remain pure. May each believer do the same!

Psalm: 102   Type: Lament – Penitential/Messianic
Author: Unknown

The Afflicted Plead With God

The Hebrew superscription of this poem reads: *"A prayer of the afflicted, when he is overwhelmed and pours out his complaint before the Lord."* The oppressed psalmist pleads with the Lord to be attentive to his prayer and to quickly respond to it (vv. 1-2). Whatever the calamity was, it is obvious from the psalm's contents that it was adversely affecting the entire nation, especially the capital city of Jerusalem. As the days of unbearable misery dragged on, the writer laments that his heart was depressed, and he had lost his strength, appetite, and will to live (vv. 3-7). While the psalmist continued to mourn and weep with ashes on his head, his enemies mocked his pitiful condition (vv. 8-9). In despair and presumably approaching death, he wondered why God permitted his suffering – why had God levied His wrath on him (vv. 10-11)?

These verbalized quandaries pose a prophetic beacon leading us to our suffering Savior at Calvary. J. G. Bellett observes this Psalm commences in a very unusual way in that it opens with the lament of "the Man of sorrows" and then concludes with His praise:

> He sees Himself deserted by His followers, reproached by the foe, and sustaining the righteous anger of God – the indignation and wrath due to others falling on Him (vv. 1-11). We then listen to God's answer to this; and that answer pledges Him life and a kingdom, and display in His glory, rehearsing also the theme of praise with which Israel and the nations will then celebrate Him (vv. 12-22).[115]

The Beginning of Wisdom

The transition from agonizing in prayer to praising God in verse 12 is quite sudden: *"You, O Lord, shall endure forever, and the remembrance of Your name to all generations."* By recalling to mind God's sovereignty and past faithfulness to the nation of Israel, the brokenhearted poet transitioned from misery to joyful expectation: it was time for the Lord to act on behalf of His people (vv. 12-13). He was confident Jehovah would reestablish His people and rebuild Zion, and then the nations would join Israel in praising the Lord (vv. 14-22). In verse 23, the writer returns to lamenting his present situation – he prays the Lord will extend his life, not end it prematurely (vv. 23-24). The acknowledgement that all creation, including himself, would perish like a garment before an eternal, immutable God was a statement of confidence that God controlled all things and had the power to deliver him out of his distress (vv. 25-27). God would be faithful to His people throughout their generations (v. 28).

From a scientific point of view, the description of creation growing old and wearing out in verses 25-26 is consistent with our understanding of nature as described in the Second Law of Thermodynamics, which deals with system decay. Entropy (a measurement of system disorder) of all creation cannot decrease; it can only increase or remain the same. As the psalmist notes, entropy is increasing: *"Of old You laid the foundation of the Earth, and the heavens are the work of Your hands, they will perish, but You will endure; yes, they will all grow old like a garment"* (v. 26). The universe is winding down and will eventually "wear out." Genesis 2:1 declares God "finished" all that was to be created (v. 25); therefore, until God chooses to destroy creation, the natural order He put in place shall be maintained. Since creation, neither matter nor energy can be either created or destroyed, which is the First Law of Thermodynamics.

Verses 25-27 refer to the eternal Creator and Sustainer of all things and are thus rightly applied to the Lord Jesus Christ by the writer of Hebrews to affirm Christ's deity (Heb. 1:10-12). In the messianic sense of this psalm, verses 24b-28 contain God the Father's exuberant response to the prayer of His rejected and suffering Son in verses 1-11, 23-24a. In its practical application, the psalmist learned he was able to defeat his feelings of despair and discontent by recalling to mind that the Lord is sovereign over all things. Indeed, God is in control and everything is as He allows it. Nothing occurs in creation, including our trials, which does not first gain His approval. If we truly understand who Christ is, this means that we all should be able to say with Paul:

> *I know how to be abased, and I know how to abound. Everywhere and in all things I have learned both to be full and to be hungry, both to abound and to suffer need. I can do all things through Christ who strengthens me* (Phil. 4:12-13).

> *Now to the King eternal, immortal, invisible, to God who alone is wise, be honor and glory forever and ever. Amen* (1 Tim. 1:17).

Psalm: 103 Type: Praise   **Author: David**

A Bouquet of Praise

As David mused on all the ways he had experienced God's mercy and goodness, his soul boiled over with joy and his heart erupted in praise (vv. 1-2). He reminisced how God had demonstrated His lovingkindnesses and tender mercies towards him by: redeeming his life from destruction, forgiving his sins, strengthening him when he was weak, delivering him from oppression, providing satisfying things for him to eat, and healing his infirmities (vv. 3-6). In pondering the history of the Jewish nation, David also rejoiced in all the evidence of God's loyal love to His covenant people despite their failures and frailty (v. 7). God's mercy and grace are so inexhaustible towards those who fear Him that somehow an omniscient, omnipotent Creator chooses not to remember confessed sins or to punish sinners to the full measure they deserve (vv. 10-12).

God has not compromised His righteous character in extending to us these manifold blessings, but rather His just demands against sinners were reckoned in full at Calvary; Christ suffered and died in our stead (Rom. 5:9). Though man is not much more than dust and has a brief sojourn on the earth, God is compassionate to those who will revere and obey Him (vv. 14-16). Just as it is natural for a Father to have pity on His own children, God graciously extends infinite mercy to those who honor and trust Him (vv. 13, 17). After reviewing God's covenant faithfulness to Israel (v. 18), David is moved to call on the angels, God's mighty ministers and messengers, to praise the Lord with him

The Beginning of Wisdom

(vv. 19-21). Indeed, it is proper for all the works of creation to praise the Lord (vv. 22). David concludes the psalm as he started, by exhorting his soul to *"bless the Lord"* (v. 22).

In this poem as in everything, God's behavior is intimately connected with His holy character. As we learn from Scripture why God does what He does, we are able to understand more of His attributes and nature. This is a paramount reason to study Scripture, as God the Father desires that each believer be conformed to the moral image of His Son (Rom. 8:29). We are to know and, by the power of the Holy Spirit, pattern ourselves after God's character. For example, because God is slow to anger and quick to forgive (vv. 8-9) we should be as well (Ps. 30:4-5, 145:8; Eph. 4:32). God's children are to accurately represent their heavenly Father; let us live up to the family's holy image!

Psalm: 104 Type: Praise   **Author: Unknown**

Praise the Glorious Creator

Psalm 103 and Psalm 104 begin the same way, with the call *"bless the Lord, O my soul."* But where the previous poem focused mainly on God's past mercies to Israel, this psalm praises the Lord for His awesome power and immense goodness as demonstrated throughout creation (v. 1). The writer speaks of the splendor, majesty, and luminous essence of the One who formed and arranged all the elements of creation, including the creation of spiritual beings (vv. 1-4; Rev. 4:2-3). God created the foundations of the earth and then covered much of it with water (Gen. 1:2) before ordering the atmosphere, oceans, lakes, rivers, and springs, and establishing an evaporative water cycle to maintain life on the earth (vv. 5-9; Gen. 1:6-10; Eccl. 1:7). Besides providing drinking water for His creatures, the abundance of water ensured plenty of vegetation to furnish both man and beast with food (vv. 10-18). In verse 15, wine is used to speak of *joy* and olive oil of *comfort*, thus God's newly fashioned habitat for mankind provided not only for his necessities, but also for his contentment.

Additionally, God arranged the sun and the moon to mark time in man's new world; this design allowed man plenty of time to labor in daylight hours and yet to obtain needed rest and sleep at nighttime. From a scientific standpoint, the arrangement of our earth with its sun and moon has aspects unparalleled in the rest of known space. The size of the earth's moon is uniquely large, approximately one fourth the size of the earth itself. What does this accomplish? A large moon stabilizes the axial rotation of our planet at 23.5 degrees, which ensures temperate seasonal changes worldwide and allows the growth of vegetation over a vast portion of the planet in lieu of a narrow band centered at the equator. The size of the moon also causes significant tidal mixing of the oceans' cold and warm water masses, which provides control of the planet's temperature and prevents thermal stagnation of various bodies of water.[116] Science permits man to observe God's intricate design in nature with our limited understanding, and those wise enough to comprehend that design requires a Designer will agree with the psalmist: *"O Lord, how manifold are Your works! In wisdom You have made them all"* (v. 24)!

The writer proclaims God's sovereign rule over our planet and the resulting dependence of all living things upon the Lord, even the huge leviathan (vv. 25-30). Seeing such evidence of God's power and wisdom in creation, the poet erupts with praise: *"May the glory of the Lord endure forever; may the Lord rejoice in His works"* (v. 31). Indeed, the writer pledges to continue to praise God and to pray that He will remove sinners from the earth (vv. 32-35). In the style of the preceding psalm, this poem concludes as it began: *"Bless the Lord, O my soul! Praise the Lord!"* (v. 35). The only difference here is the addition of the phrase *"Praise the Lord!"* The English phrase is translated from two Hebrew words, which first appear here in Psalms: *halal Yahh* (a contracted form of *Yehovah* – God's personal name). However, this Hebrew phrase, translated "Hallelujah," is found once more in each of the next two psalms and then twenty times in Book 5; this brings the entire collection of poetry to a crescendo of praise in the final book!

Psalm: 105   Type: Thanksgiving – Historical   Author: Unknown

God Is Faithful to Israel

In this poem, the writer retraces several historical events from the call of Abraham to the wilderness experience of his descendants in order to thank God for His faithfulness to the Jewish nation (vv. 12-41). The psalmist begins with a series of exhortations to his fellow countrymen: give thanks to the Lord and call on His name, sing praises to Him and talk of His awe-inspiring works, glory in His name, seek the Lord, and do not forget His faithfulness (vv. 1-5). It was appropriate for Israel to remember and praise the Lord, because the Lord had remembered them. Because of His unconditional covenant with Abraham, which was also confirmed with Isaac and then Jacob, Jehovah brought their descendants from Egypt into the Promised Land (vv. 7-11).

The historical survey in verses 12-41 shows God's dependability to safeguard and provide for His covenant people. It covers: the preservation of Abraham, his descendants' journey to Egypt to escape famine, the exaltation of Joseph and the expansion of the nation in Egypt, their subsequent deliverance from slavery by Moses, and the following wilderness experience in which God supplied their every need (e.g., shade from the sun, water to drink, and bread from heaven and quail to eat). The poet writes the Lord had fulfilled His Word so that His redeemed people could abide with Him in a new land, that is, if they chose to obey His commandments (vv. 42-45). The last verse seems to be the main point of the psalm: if the Lord's people truly appreciate all He has done, they will rejoice in Him and demonstrate their love for Him through obedience. The Lord Jesus declared the same truth to His disciples the night before His crucifixion: *"If you love Me, keep My commandments"* (John 14:15). In any dispensation, practical obedience to revealed truth demonstrates love for God.

While speaking to the Jews, the Lord used the wilderness image of *"the bread from heaven"* (v. 40) to declare Himself as God's only provision for their salvation. Seven times in John 6 the Lord Jesus declared Himself to be the *"bread of life"* that came from heaven; He taught that if anyone ate of Him (i.e., appropriated His sacrificial work by believing on Him), that person would receive eternal life: *"And*

Jesus said to them, 'I am the bread of life. He who comes to Me shall never hunger, and he who believes in Me shall never thirst'" (John 6:35).

Thankfully, through a new and everlasting covenant, God could righteously forgive Israel's sin, for the first covenant (the Law) only brought condemnation to Israel. The new covenant was secured at Calvary and was sealed by the blood of the Lord Jesus Christ; it was made *"with the house of Israel and house of Judah"* (Heb. 8:8), as prophesied in Jeremiah 31:31-32. Thankfully, as Paul explains in Ephesians 2:11-3:7, Gentile believers are a second benefactor of this covenant and are permitted to share in all the blessings promised to the Jewish nation. Those of us who are Gentiles can also praise the Lord for His faithfulness to the nation of Israel!

Psalm: 106 Type: Thanksgiving – Historical   Author: Unknown

A Confession of Israel's Past Unfaithfulness

The previous poem praised God for centuries of dependability; in contrast, the final poem of Book 4 confesses Israel's long history of unfaithfulness to God and the just consequences of their rebellious deeds. The unknown psalmist then pleads with God to deliver His people from captivity and to restore them. Before overviewing Israel's long, rebellious history, the writer acknowledges two fundamental truths: first, *"give thanks to the Lord, for He is good! For His mercy endures forever"* (v. 1); second, *"blessed are those who keep justice, and he who does righteousness at all times* (v. 3)! This is a concise summary of the psalm.

This poem links God's blessing to man's continued obedience and the necessity of God's tempered anger and mercy when man is not. Although the nation was in sin at that time (v. 6), the psalmist wanted to be one of the obedient ones who received God's goodness so that he could praise the Lord (vv. 1-5). Verse 1 contains the first occurrence of the phrase *"mercy endures forever"* to be found in Psalms, but the expression occurs thirty-two more times in Book 5, where it highlights the importance of God's mercy to Israel, and all mankind. Certainly this psalm declares God's unfailing goodness and enduring mercy to

His covenant people, despite their failures. In this respect, Hamilton Smith notes the prophetic content of the psalm:

> The psalm prophetically looks on to the time when Israel's long captivity among the nations is reaching its close, and God is about to regather the nation under the reign of Christ. In that day the godly will recognize that all the blessing of the nation depends on the enduring mercy of the Lord. In the light of the goodness and mercy of the Lord the psalmist confesses the sin of God's people (v. 6), owning every stage of their failure (vv. 7-46), and finally appeals to God to save and regather the nation for His own praise (vv. 47-48).[117]

As a statement of national confession, the writer recounts the sins of the nation in the wilderness while journeying to the Promised Land (vv. 7-33). These included murmuring and complaining against God and His leadership, unbridled rebellion, and idolatry. Furthermore, these offenses occurred while God worked marvelous feats in their presence. After being led into the Promised Land, the Israelites failed to drive out the pagan inhabitants as God commanded; instead, Israel worshipped and sacrificed their own children to the false gods of Canaan (vv. 34-46). Accordingly, the era of the Judges was marked by repeated failure of the Jews to obey Jehovah. This was followed by divine chastening until brokenness and repentance was achieved, and then a divinely chosen judge was sent to deliver them from their oppressors (Judg. 2:16-23). Apparently, the Jews were scattered among the nations at the time this song was composed. Therefore, based on Jehovah's past dealings with Israel and because of His national covenant (v. 45), the writer pleads for an immediate rescue and the return of Jewish captives back to Israel (v. 47). The doxology in verse 48, which closes out Book 4, is similar to the one in Book 1, [*"Blessed be the Lord God of Israel from everlasting to everlasting! Amen and Amen"* (Ps. 41:13)], with the addition of the closing phrase, *"Praise the Lord!"*

Book 5

The final book in Psalms contains fifteen poems written by David, one by his son Solomon, and twenty-eight whose authorship is unknown.

Psalm: 107   Type: Thanksgiving – Communal   Author: Unknown

God Rescues His Redeemed

The unknown writer calls for the redeemed to thank the Lord for all His goodness, especially for rescuing the Jews and bringing them back into the land of Israel (vv. 1-3). There is no superscript for this psalm or other internal information which would identify the historical setting; perhaps it was written during or shortly after the return from Babylonian captivity. The author acknowledges four cases in which the Lord provided deliverance to those pleading for His help; He therefore deserves the praise of His people. The poem is thus repetitious in it construction, which involves: a description of the dire situation (vv. 4-5, 10-12, 17-18, 23-27), an urgent plea for help (vv. 6, 13, 19, 28 are virtually identical), divine rescue (vv. 7, 14, 20, 29-30), and exhortation to praise the Lord for His faithfulness and mighty deeds (vv. 8-9, 15-16, 21-22, 31-32).

The same call for men to praise the Lord is issued in verses 8, 15, 21, and 31. The first case speaks of those who lost their way in the wilderness and were hungry and thirsty, but Jehovah provided for them and led them to safety. The second instance describes the liberation of Jews previously in rebellion and bondage. The third occurrence relates how those who suffered from sickness and were near death were healed when they sought the Lord. Lastly, desperate sailors ready to perish in a powerful tempest were rescued when they cried out to the Lord for help.

The poet then describes God's absolute dominion over nature. He punishes the wicked by drying up their wetlands (vv. 33-34) and He transforms a desert into a well-watered habitation where the needy may prosper (vv. 33-38). The writer then informs his audience how Jehovah uses providence to humble the proud and reward the contrite and upright with good things (vv. 39-41). The wise will appreciate these evidences of God's loving-kindness to the redeemed and praise His name (v. 42).

Psalm: 108 Type: Thanksgiving – Personal   Author: David

Triumphant Praise

This is a poem of triumphant praise; David asserts his confidence in God's great mercy and past record of faithfulness (vv. 1-4). David therefore expected that Israel's enemies would be brought low with God's help (vv. 7-13), God's beloved people would be delivered (v. 6), and God would be exalted over all the earth (v. 5).

The expression of verse 1 seems somewhat strange: *"O God, my heart is steadfast; I will sing and give praise, even with my glory."* A similar statement occurs in Psalm 30:12, *"To the end that my glory may sing praise to You and not be silent."* Also in Psalm 57:8, *"Awake, my glory! Awake, lute and harp! I will awaken the dawn."* How are we to understand the expression *"my glory"* in reference to praising God? The explanation to this question is found in the New Testament, when Peter quotes Psalm 16:9: *"My heart is glad, and my glory rejoices"* this way to his Jewish audience: *"Therefore my heart rejoiced, and my tongue was glad."* Henry Morris explains the meaning of Peter's declaration:

> It becomes clear, then, that in such passages "my glory" simply means "my tongue." In fact, the word was translated "tongue" in these and other similar passages in the Greek Septuagint translation of the Old Testament. But why, then, did the inspired Hebrew text here use the words "my glory" instead of the usual Hebrew word for tongue? The answer probably is that, when our tongues are used to praise the Lord, they do, indeed, become our glory! Mankind alone has the ability to speak, for the simple reason that God desires to communicate with us so that we can respond in praise to Him. This is our glory![118]

May we use our tongue to proclaim the glory of God! We are not to glory in ourselves, but in Him whom we are to represent and honor in all that we do and say.

Verses 1-5 are nearly identical to Psalm 57:7-11 while verses 6-13 are the same as Psalm 60:5-12. It is likely that these two portions of Scripture were arranged as this psalm for a liturgical purpose.

Regardless, the final verse poses a true battle cry for every generation of saints: *"Through God we will do valiantly"* (v. 13a).

Psalm: 109 Type: Lament – Imprecatory   Author: David

A Prayer of Vindication

Full of holy zeal and purified contempt, the psalmist pleads with the Lord to execute vengeance on his enemies in various ways. Their perverse words, deceitful ways, false accusations, and unprovoked strife deserved God's immediate wrath; furthermore, they had returned evil and brutality for David's kind friendship and were, in his estimation, unfit for mercy (vv. 1-5). Specifically, David prayed that his wicked enemies would: be opposed (v. 6), be found guilty and condemned (v. 7), lose status and power (v. 8), die and that their children would become vagabonds (vv. 9-10), be plundered and made destitute (vv. 11), be pitiless (v. 12), and have all posterity cut off (v. 13). Continuing his petition of a thousand deaths, David prayed that God would render retribution to his enemies for their ancestral sins (vv. 14-15). Some further rationale for this imprecatory prayer is then provided. David's enemies had not only falsely accused and slandered him (v. 20), but also had taken advantage of the poor and brokenhearted (v. 16), and were prone to curse others (vv. 17-19). The scorn and oppression that David had suffered had seriously weakened him and soured his heart; he was in desperate need of the Lord's help and deliverance (vv. 20-25). What motivated David to pen this stalwart of imprecatory prayers? If his wicked persecutors were brought low, they would surmise that it was David's God who had vindicated him – this would accordingly prompt David's praise (vv. 26-31). For more information on Imprecatory Prayers and their place in the Church Age, please review the section on *Psalm Types* as well as the discussion on Psalm 35.

Psalm: 110　Type: Liturgical – Royal/Messianic　　Author: David

The Royal-Priest

This Messianic psalm is referred to about thirty times in the New Testament, including fourteen quotations which are directly applied to the Lord Jesus. This means this poem is referenced more in the New Testament than any other Old Testament passage. Though David was divinely inspired to pen the psalm, *Yahweh* (Jehovah) is the speaker throughout all seven verses. As recorded in the Gospels of Matthew, Mark, and Luke, the Lord Jesus quoted verse 1 to confront the Pharisees' ignorance. In doing so He both proved the psalm's authorship by David and acknowledged its divine inspiration:

> *And He said to them, "How can they say that the Christ is the Son of David? Now David himself said in the book of Psalms: 'The Lord said to my Lord, "Sit at My right hand, Till I make Your enemies Your footstool."' Therefore David calls Him 'Lord'; how is He then his Son?"* (Luke 20:41-44).

The point is it was prophesied that Jehovah would cause one of David's descendants to be enthroned with Him as David's "Lord" (*Adonai*). The Lord Jesus was showing the religious leaders of His day that the Messiah must be a man (i.e. a descendant of David), but also God incarnate for the great King David to revere Him as Lord. The Pharisees seemed to understand the implications of the only logical answer to the Lord's question, because they refused to reply (Matt. 22:46). The Lord Jesus is God incarnate – the Word of God became flesh (John 1:14).

Returning to the psalm, Jehovah promised to bestow David's Lord with an everlasting priesthood after the order of Melchizedek (v. 4; Gen. 14:18-20), and promised Him an everlasting earthly kingdom once Jehovah vanquished His enemies (v. 1). This will be accomplished when David's Lord returns to the earth with Jehovah's authority (the rod of strength) to execute judgment *"in the midst of His enemies"* (v. 2). This phrase refutes the doctrine of post-millennialism which teaches that Christ wars from heaven until the earth is made perfect to welcome His Second Advent.

At this time, glorified saints adorned in holiness will eagerly accompany the Lord into battle (v. 3; Rev. 19:14). David's Lord will then rule over the nations (vv. 5-6). He will do so with divine vigor, having drunk from the brook on the way; this possibly speaks of divine enablement from the Holy Spirit (v. 7; John 7:37-39). John confirmed all authority to judge mankind has now been given to the Lord Jesus by His Father (John 5:22). John also witnessed the fulfillment of this prophetic psalm in a vision: when the Lord Jesus Christ returns to the earth to defeat the Antichrist, his armies, and all who took the mark of the beast; Christ will then rule the remnant of the nations with a rod of iron (Rev. 12:5, 19:7-21). Today, we can thank the Lord that we are still in the Church Age, the great parenthesis between verses 1 and 2. Presently, the Lord Jesus is patiently calling sinners to repent and to trust in Him alone for salvation, but in a coming day the Lord Jesus will have His rightful throne on earth and be honored by all men. Maranatha!

Psalm: 111 Type: Praise   **Author: Unknown**

Praise for God's Wonderful Works

William Kelly observed that Psalms 111-113 "are plainly a trilogy in suited succession, following up that which set out the exaltation of Messiah on high and the coming day of His power out of Zion. The first two of the three are acrostics, but all are the praises of Yah (Hallelu-yah) for the deliverance of His people by Messiah."[119] In this alphabetical poem, the psalmist praises God's awesome and righteous works of redemption. The writer begins by vowing to praise the Lord in the congregation for His wonderful and beneficial "works" (mentioned five times in this song) to those who fear Him (vv. 1-3).

The psalmist acknowledges that the Lord's gracious feats were to be remembered, as these demonstrated His enduring love and covenantal commitment to His people (v. 4). He had provided them with food and a special land for an inheritance and, beyond all this, redemption (vv. 5-9). Because the Lord had displayed His holy character in all His gracious actions, He should be feared and His name revered – *"Holy and awesome is His name"* (v. 9). Indeed, the psalmist concludes by stating a foundational principle: *"The fear of the Lord is the beginning of wisdom"* (v. 10). This implies that those who have the proper disposition towards the Lord will have the wisdom to do His commandments and praise His name! Amen.

Psalm: 112 Type: Wisdom   **Author: Unknown**

Blessings for the God-Fearing

Psalm 111 is a song of praise to the Lord for righteously working on the behalf of those who fear Him (His redeemed); Psalm 112, also an acrostic, enumerates these blessings, which are received by those who demonstrate the fear of the Lord by obeying His commandments. In summary, it is wise to fear the Lord (Ps. 111:10), and those who do so are blessed (v. 1). A person who fears the Lord will be characterized by uprightness, faithfulness, and generosity. The following verses promise various blessings to such a person: a mighty posterity on the earth (v. 2), wealth and prosperity (v. 3), divine discernment (v. 4), God's goodness (v. 5), spiritual stability (v. 6), an anxiety-free existence (vv. 7-8), and strength and honor (v. 9). In contrast to all these blessings for the God-fearing, the wicked, who are estranged from God and His goodness, are ready to perish (v. 10). To summarize, the wicked are full of envy and anxiety, but have no power to inflict harm on the righteous or to improve their pitiful situation. In conclusion, it is worth repeating: *"Blessed is the man who fears the Lord"* (v. 1).

Psalm: 113 Type: Praise   **Author: Unknown**

Praise the Lord Always

Psalms 113 through 118 form the *Hallel*, a collection of songs traditionally sung during national festivals, especially the Feasts of Jehovah. Summarizing Psalm 113, William MacDonald suggested "the first five verses present God as the One who is *infinitely high*, the last four as the One who is *intimately nigh*."[120] Although the Lord is exalted in heaven above, the writer of this psalm calls on all His people below to praise Him, knowing that the Lord is intimately aware of every story behind every tear of the brokenhearted, and that they would be blessed in due time (vv. 1-3). The Lord is worthy of praise because He is alone in majesty, unique in essence, and transcends all created things (vv. 4-5). The Lord is to be admired because He powerfully and compassionately intervenes in human affairs (v. 6), such as assisting the homeless (vv. 7-8) and consoling and healing the barren woman (v. 9). Though this gracious and kind God transcends the universe, He still chooses to help those of the lowest estate; indeed, such a glorious God deserves the continual praise of His people.

In the ancient times, a Jewish woman considered herself blessed of God if she could marry, conceive, bear, and nurture many children; thus, a barren woman keenly felt unsatisfied in life (v. 9). Yet, God uses situations such as this and many more, to bring us to a point of desperation for Him. Why? Perhaps the best answer to this question is: it is how an all-wise God chooses to work for our good and for His glory. Isaiah expounds on this reality:

> For thus says the High and Lofty one Who inhabits eternity, whose name is Holy: "I dwell in the high and holy place, with him who has a contrite and humble spirit, to revive the spirit of the humble, and to revive the heart of the contrite ones (Isa. 57:15).

May each believer be able to look beyond the visible realm of suffering and unfulfilled expectations to draw near to a faithful God. It is through obedience, submission to authority, and brokenness that we experience His reviving power.

Psalm: 114 Type: Praise   **Author: Unknown**

Praise to the God of Jacob

This poem, traditionally sung just prior to the Passover meal, recounts God's mighty power exhibited in delivering His people from slavery in Egypt and bringing them into Canaan (v. 1). Jehovah opened the Rea Sea and peeled back the waters of the Jordan River to permit the Jews passage (v. 3). He unsettled the mountains by His awesome holy presence (v. 4) and caused refreshing water to flow from a desert rock to satisfy the thirst of His people (v. 7). Jehovah then pitched His tabernacle in their midst, thus making the Jewish nation His own sanctuary (v. 2). Employing personified creativity, the psalmist boldly interrogates the sea and mountains to ascertain why each responded as noted in the previous verses (vv. 5-6). The answer is obvious; all creation recognizes the Creator's power and authority and emphatically obeys His will.

In closing, the writer reminds the earth that the God of Jacob is powerful, even able to wring water from dry rocks; he then urges the earth to continue to tremble at the Creator's presence (vv. 7-8). Perhaps the psalmist is using satire to show that the material world is more willing to honor the Lord than many animate human beings are. For man, *"the fear of the Lord is the beginning of wisdom"* (111:10). The song honors the God of Jacob for His many mighty feats to establish the Jewish nation in the Promised Land.

Psalm: 115 Type: Liturgical – Temple   Author: Unknown

To God Alone Be the Glory

Given its thematic content, the prohibition of idols, it is possible that this is another psalm set after the end of the Babylonian captivity, as God had punished His people in Babylon for idolatry and had returned them to Israel as a purified nation. The psalmist declares Jehovah is sovereign over creation, and therefore anyone who worships pagan gods deserves His vengeance. Because mercy and truth mark Jehovah's character, the writer calls on Him to defend the honor and glory of His name against those who belittle His people with questions such as *"So where is their God?"* (vv. 1-2). Jehovah thinks and speaks, hears and sees all, and does what He pleases; in contrast, though they may have mouths, ears, and eyes, idols can do none of these things (vv. 3-7).

Consequently, those who create their own powerless and senseless gods to worship are no better off before the One true God than their idols – they all are spiritually impotent (v. 8). In our modern society, idolatry still exists in many forms, but at its core is the veneration of self. People may no longer bow down before manmade images, but we demonstrate by how we spend our time and resources what is most important to us, and in whom we really trust. Unfortunately, the Lord is often ignored and forgotten, today, just as He was when this psalm was written.

Hence, the writer admonishes his countrymen not to trust in idols, but rather in the One who truly has the power to be *"their Help and Shield"* (vv. 9-11). Indeed, the Creator of heaven and earth had blessed them greatly and would continue to do so for generations, if His people continued to fear and obey Him (vv. 12-15). God, not idols, owns and inhabits the heavens, and He created the earth as a place for humanity to dwell and honor Him (v. 16). Realizing this purpose and also that the dead cannot praise God from their graves, the psalmist vows to praise the Lord with other believers (vv. 17-18). Truly, all men should *"Praise the Lord"* (v. 18)!

Psalm: 116   Type: Thanksgiving – Personal   Author: Unknown

The Redeemed Love the Lord

The writer begins by expressing his love for the Lord and a renewed commitment to render life-long service to Him (vv. 1-2). He then explains why in verses 3-4: the Lord had heard his desperate plea for preservation and had delivered him from certain death. His prolonged life now provided him an opportunity to testify to others of God's goodness, and to beseech them to likewise trust in a gracious, righteous, merciful God who longs to assist the needy (vv. 5-6). He had learned to rest in his trustworthy God, even when death was lurking nearby; he urged others to do the same so that they too might experience His peace and tranquility in life (vv. 7-11).

It should be natural for all those who have experienced God's free gift of salvation to ask: *"What shall I render to the Lord for all His benefits toward me?"* (v. 12). The writer pledges to pay his vows (v. 14) and to contribute offerings (v. 13) in order to praise the Lord in the congregation of His people (vv. 17-19). Knowing that the death of His saints is precious to God, the writer gladly will praise Him, for God

The Beginning of Wisdom

chose to prolong his life on earth to do so (v. 15). We do not know the length of our earthly sojourn, but we can choose to *"praise the Lord"* each and every day God permits us to do so.

Psalm: 117 Type: Praise   Author: Unknown

Everyone Should Praise the Lord

Psalm 117 is only two verses in length and comprises just sixteen Hebrew words. It is not only the shortest psalm, but is also the smallest chapter in the Bible. Psalm 117 is also the 595th of 1,189 chapters in the Bible, which makes it the center chapter in the canon of Scripture. What is the paramount message of this epicenter? The psalmist calls on all people from all nations to praise the Lord in verse 1 and then provides the rationale in verse 2: *"For His merciful kindness is great toward us, and the truth of the Lord endures forever. Praise the Lord!"*

Clearly, the God of the Jews is also the God of the Gentiles, though the latter group was not directly included in God's covenant with Israel (Eph. 2:11-15). The New Covenant sealed with Christ's own blood permits the fulfillment of God's covenant promise to Abraham and His descendants and includes this provision: *"In you* [Abraham] *shall all families of the earth be blessed"* (Gen. 12:1-3). Paul explains that believing Gentiles in the Church Age have been grafted into the covenant promises of Abraham through Christ (Rom. 11:17), and indeed receive the promised blessings of that commitment (Eph. 3:1-9). If you are a Gentile saved by grace, then this psalm is for you; add your voice to the psalmist's and *"Praise the Lord!"*(v. 2).

Psalm: 118 Type: Thanksgiving – Personal/Messianic
Author: Unknown

The Lord's Loving-Kindness

Psalm 118 is the final song in the Jewish *Hallel*; it celebrates God's patient faithfulness to Israel, and previews a future day when Israel will be restored to God and honored by all nations. Fittingly, it is also the final Messianic poem in the book of Psalms. The psalmist begins by calling all Israel to acknowledge the goodness of the Lord and His forever-enduring mercy (vv. 1-4). The writer testifies to the congregation that he had put his trust in the Lord and had been rescued from a grave danger; it is for this reason they too should trust in the Lord instead of men (vv. 5-9). Surrounded by an overwhelming hostile force, the poet had cut down his enemy in the name of the Lord, who helped him (vv. 10-13). He had not only survived but was victorious because the Lord was his strength; for this reason, the writer promises to enter into God's courts with manifold praise (vv. 14-21). In his mind, Israel was like a rejected stone among the nations, which now had been exalted to its rightful place as a cornerstone and a testimony of God's greatness (vv. 22-25).

The psalmist concludes by requesting continued salvation and prosperity for the people at the hand of the one who *"comes in the name of the Lord"* (vv. 25-29). This psalm was sung at Passover, and its lyrics would have been on the minds of the people when Christ entered Jerusalem on what is commonly referred to as Palm Sunday. Thus, it was no accident that it was openly proclaimed by the people when the Lord descended down the Mount of Olives into Jerusalem a few days before Passover and His crucifixion: *"Blessed is He who comes in the name of the Lord"* (v. 26). Jesus Christ is the one who comes in the name of the Lord, offering life and blessing.

Verse 22 is quoted several times in the New Testament, where it is evident the reference to the rejected cornerstone relates to Israel's refusal of Jesus Christ as their Messiah. The psalmist says, *"this is the day which the Lord has made"* (v. 24). The Lord Jesus Himself acknowledged that this verse spoke of Him (Matt. 21:42; Luke 20:17), as did the apostles (Eph. 2:20; 1 Pet. 2:6-7). After being rejected by the Jewish nation, the Lord suffered and died at Calvary and was resurrected to the highest station in heaven, and in a future day He will return to the earth to establish His throne as Israel's King.

The Hebrew word *yowm*, normally translated as "day," appears frequently in the Old Testament; however, only about twenty times is it used in the Hebrew expression that correlates to the English phrase, "on that day" or "this is the day." This expression first appears in Leviticus 16:30 in reference to the Day of Atonement. We find it again in Psalm 118:24 to refer to a specific day that God had marked on His calendar since before the foundations of the world were laid – the day propitiation was offered by His own Son for all humanity's sins (Heb. 2:9; 1 Jn. 2:2). It was the day redeeming blood flowed from Immanuel's veins to ensure the redemption of all those who exercise faith in God's message of salvation. The psalmist wrote of this spectacular day:

> *The stone which the builders rejected has become the chief cornerstone. This was the Lord's doing; it is marvelous in our eyes. This is the day the Lord has made; we will rejoice and be glad in it* (vv. 22-24).

The Church often sings the latter portion of this Psalm as a praise chorus, without regarding its proper context. In other words, we are proclaiming it in a different way than the Spirit of God intended. While it is true that the Lord is sovereign over each of our days, the focus of our joy is not *our day*, but *the day* Christ was rejected of men and judged by God for our sins. The content of this psalm is a capstone on the revelation of all the fullness of Christ and His work mentioned in the other messianic psalms. May we treasure the full value God breathed into the text of Psalm 118 three thousand years ago and, like the psalmist, let us rejoice and be glad in what God has accomplished through Christ!

Psalm: 119 Type: Wisdom   **Author: Unknown**

Delighting in God's Word

Psalm 119 is not only the longest poem in the book of Psalms, but it is also the lengthiest chapter in the Bible; in fact, with its 176 verses, it is longer than fourteen Old Testament books. Psalm 119 is also the most familiar of the alphabetical-acrostic psalms. It is divided into twenty-two sections, one for each letter of the Hebrew alphabet. Each section contains eight verses with each verse in the section starting with the particular letter emphasized in that portion. The first eight verses begin with the first letter of the Hebrew alphabet, *aleph*, the next set of eight verses commence with the second letter, *beth*, and so forth. Each section reveals God's order, virtues, attributes, law, ways, and commandments for His people to consider and appreciate. William Kelly provides the following short overview for each of these twenty-two sections:

Aleph. All here is introductory and general: the return after wandering and sorrowful experience; Jehovah's law or doctrine written within under the new covenant.

Beth. Here is the washing of water by the word, God purifying the heart by faith, in moral death to natural energy just where it might be strongest.

Gimel. Jehovah's goodness is asked according to and in His word, the delight and guide of the Israel of God, whosoever might despise.

Daleth. The heart prefers abasement from and with God to ease without Him, but looks for enlargement to do His will with alacrity.

He. The need of Jehovah's teaching, in order to obey and be kept, is here spread before Him.

Vau. The taste of the grace of Jehovah, of His salvation as here expressed, is next craved for courage and fidelity.

Zain. "The word" is owned as hope and comfort in the midst of pride and ungodliness; the name gives motive to obey.

Cheth. Here the heart rises to Jehovah Himself; so that wicked men's hands were powerless to make the law forgotten, or His mercy unseen everywhere.

Teth. It is a soul profiting by affliction, and confiding all the more in Jehovah, to learn His statutes, better than thousands of gold and silver.

Yod. Jehovah is looked to as a faithful Creator, and those that fear Him counted on. As He afflicted for good, so would He show loving-kindness.

Caph. Here the prayer is instant, as the iniquity grows apace, and weakness is realized in the severest trial. It is not the hope of the Christian, who like Christ are to go on high; but deliverance, as Israel expect and shall have, by judgments executed manifestly on the enemy.

Lamed. The stability of Jehovah is seen on high. His purpose emanates thence infallibly, but establishes the earth too, the universe being His servant. Then its moral power is owned, and by it the conviction that the soul is His, attending in the midst of malice to His testimonies, and in the sense of total failure feeling the all-embracing value of what expresses His mind.

Mem. Here it is love of Jehovah's law, leading to meditation, and with blessed results in wisdom and moral ways.

Nun. In this stanza the light of the word for himself is acknowledged, and its judgments for wickedness.

Samech. Wavering and evil-doing are deprecated as heartily as Jehovah's law is loved. But the need of being sustained is expressed, as on the other hand Jehovah's summary dealings with the deceitful and wicked; for indeed He is to be feared.

Ain. Hence he looks for Jehovah to act, not only on His servant's behalf but in vindication of His law.

Pe. The intrinsic and real efficacy of Jehovah's revelation is here expressed, with the spiritual desire created by it.

Tzade. Here the righteousness of Jehovah's judgments and testimonies predominates, which he forgot not, if others did.

Koph. Dependence is the great resource in the evil day, and indeed always, with confidence in Jehovah, but according to His word.

Resh. If persecutors are more felt, so are Jehovah's judgments on behalf of faithfulness as well as life in power.

Schin. This stanza goes farther: awe at Jehovah's word, yet joy in what He says. Fruit of loving the expression of divine authority, praise rises fully, and peace without stumbling. Obedience is deepened by having all our ways out before Him.

Tau. It is the worthy end of a psalm most instructive in experience for the individual and the nation: a brief summary.[121]

Some believe this alphabetical format was used to enhance memorization, while others believe it assisted Hebrew children in learning their letters. Because of its literary sophistication and unique scholarship, it is possible that Ezra wrote Psalm 119 as a teaching tool for post-exilic Jews. On the other hand, the rabbis of the Talmud and Midrash contend that David wrote Psalm 119 because the phrase "your servant," which when found in the Psalms always refers to David, is found thirteen times in this poem.

The main theme of this song is "God's Word." In fact, God's Word is referred to by title or description in every verse of the poem, except four (vv. 84, 121, 122, 132). At this time, God's Word would refer to His revealed truth in written form. This would not only include the books of the Law (the Pentateuch), but also all Old Testament writings available at that time. Accordingly, in this poem God's word(s) is (are) mentioned forty-seven times, the Torah (the Law) twenty-five times, and God's commandments twenty-two times. Throughout the song the psalmist shows how God's Word directly reflects Jehovah's holy character. God's Word is what God is; He is true (vv. 43, 105, 160), merciful (v. 58), good (v. 68), eternal (vv. 89, 160), righteous (vv. 123, 160), upright (v. 137), pure (v. 140), and awesome (v. 161).

What attitude should believers have towards God's Word? Believers should long for it (v. 40), trust it (v. 42), delight in it (vv. 16, 24, 47, 77, 92), love it (vv. 48, 97, 127, 140, 163, 167), hope in it (vv. 49, 81, 116), draw comfort from it (v. 50), believe it (v. 66), and esteem it above all else (v. 128).

What should believers do with God's Word? They should seek it with their whole heart (v. 2), keep it (vv. 7, 17, 44, 55, 56, 57, 60, 69, 112, 134), be cleansed by it (v. 9), memorize it (v. 11), declare it (v. 13), rejoice in it (vv. 14, 111, 162), meditate on it (vv. 15, 23, 78), understand it (vv. 18, 144), learn from it (vv. 26, 33, 64, 135), be refined by it (vv. 29, 80), observe and obey it (vv. 32, 34, 166), be revived by it (vv. 37, 154, 156, 159), sing it (v. 54), and diligently seek it (v. 94). God's people should not wander from it (v. 10), nor forget it (vv. 16, 93, 109).

What benefits does God's Word have for His people? If obeyed, they are blessed (vv. 1-2); kept from sin (v. 3); kept from shame (v. 6); may offer acceptable praise (v. 7); receive life (v. 93); and obtain wisdom (v. 98), direction (v. 105), understanding (vv. 130, 169), and peace for their souls (v. 165). The psalmist also thanks the Lord for chastening him in love when he did not obey God's commandments (v. 75). It is also fascinating that he beseeches God to intercede with Himself on his (the psalmist's) own behalf. This is likely a reference to the ministry of intercession of the second Person of the Godhead in heaven. Several other Old Testament passages identify Him also: For example, Jacob referred to this Intercessor as his Redeeming Angel (Messenger; Gen. 48:16).

In this psalm, we see the writer was oppressed by those of higher rank and social status for his beliefs. Instead of compromising the truth or abandoning the faith, he strengthened himself by learning, meditating, and obeying God's Word. He loved God's Word; it was his rule for life and his divine source of direction, wisdom, comfort, and salvation. May we have the same conviction and obtain the same blessing by loving and obeying God's Word, and then may we seek to fellowship with those who do the same (v. 62). Most importantly, may each of us delight in the Lord as our portion (v. 57).

Psalm: 120 Type: Ascent   **Author: Unknown**

A Prayer of Deliverance

Psalms 120 through 134 compose the *Songs of Ascent*, but there is wide speculation as to what this title actually means. These psalms were likely sung by faithful pilgrims en route to Jerusalem to attend annual feasts (Deut. 16:16-17). Some believe this collection of poems was sung by the captives who returned to Israel from Babylon in the fifth and sixth centuries B.C. Alfred Barnes notes that some Jewish rabbis thought these songs will be raised by the people as they ascend the fifteen steps going up into the temple as foretold in Ezekiel's vision (Ezek. 40:22, 37).[122] In any case, the *Psalms of Ascent* symbolically portray God's people venturing out of the world and into His presence to praise and worship Him.

The psalmist prays to be rescued from liars and treacherous people who wanted to war against him, though he sought to be at peace (vv. 1-2). In verse three, the writer asks the same question in two different fashions; essentially, he inquires, "What sentence shall be handed down to a lying culprit?" The answer is in verse 4: God will rain down sharp arrows and coals of fire on him for the evil that he has done. Although the psalmist laments he had to dwell among the barbarous people of Meshech in the far north and the hostile Ishmaelites to the east in Kedar, the writer confirms that God would deliver him, a man of peace, from the hatred of these people groups. Interestingly, throughout Scripture the Ishmaelites picture the outworking of the flesh (Gen. 16; Gal. 4:22-23). The flesh nature that each of us possesses is in hostility with the Law of God that we understand in our minds (Rom. 7:18-23; Gal. 5:17). This battle is only won by not permitting the flesh nature to rule, which requires us to remain in God's presence and under the control of His Spirit (Rom. 8:13). We too must leave Kedar (v. 5) and come to God for help!

Psalm: 121 Type: Ascent/Thanksgiving – Song of Trust
Author: Unknown

Preservation of the Pilgrim

Jewish pilgrims had to trek a dangerous course to arrive at Jerusalem. Traveling through the Judean hill country, the writer contemplates the source of his help and security. So when the writer says he will lift up his eyes to the hills for help, he is proclaiming that His hope is in the God of Jerusalem (v. 1). His security is not in the hills themselves, for these often relate to challenges in life, but in the Creator of heaven and earth (v. 2). This is significant as Jeremiah noted that these same hills (the high places) were full of idols in his day and were under God's judgment (Jer. 3:23). The psalmist, then, is affirming his trust in Jehovah and repudiating paganism. As a result another person, perhaps a priest, affirms to the writer that God, who never sleeps, will indeed preserve him from evil through the journey and even from afflictions such as sun stroke (vv. 3-7). Because the psalmist had put his trust in the Creator and not in created things, the Lord will faithfully preserve Him throughout His life (v. 8).

Psalm: 122 Type: Ascent/Liturgical – Song of Zion   Author: David

Joyful Expectations of Jerusalem

David recounts his delight at being a pilgrim journeying to Jerusalem and the joy of arriving within its city walls (vv. 1-2). Jerusalem was a thriving city situated on a hill and surrounded by hills, with a significant population living, working, and worshipping closely together. It was God's dwelling place among His people and the seat of justice for the nation (vv. 3-5). For this reason David requested that his fellow countrymen pray God would keep Jerusalem, its inhabitants, and God's sanctuary within its walls safe and secure (vv. 6-9). David's joys and burdens concerning Jerusalem strongly align with those that believers should have for their local assembly in the Church Age; it should not be neglected (Heb. 10:25). May we also enjoy worshipping, serving, and praying with a close-knit group of people who love the Lord and want to see Him exalted in their midst!

Psalm: 123 Type: Ascent   Author: Unknown

Longing for God's Mercy

In lifting up his eyes to heaven, the writer affirms what he trusts in – the Lord's mercy (v. 1). This is the main theme of the psalm as the word "eyes" is found four times and the word "mercy" three times in the song. The writer therefore likens himself to a diligent slave patiently waiting for his master's orders; this is an expression of his fortitude to wait on the Lord to answer his prayers of deliverance (v. 2). Although he, along with God's people, were ridiculed and despised by the proud, the writer was confident that God would extend mercy to them; the poet was content to pray and wait for it (vv. 3-4).

The scoffing stemmed from those at ease, according to verse 4. If you are doing anything for the Lord, expect to be criticized. Criticism often originates from those unburdened in ministry who unfortunately have the extra time to burden you in yours. Evaluate criticism for potential constructive benefits, especially when it comes from those who love you unquestionably, and then cast the rest aside and forget about it. Do not be influenced to waste time by defending yourself against a pharisaical spirit. The devil often entices God's people to do this very thing, which pulls them from the work to invest in non-eternal matters – pray for mercy in such times and remember that in time God will judge the matter.

Psalm: 124 Type: Ascent   **Author: David**

Without God, We Lose

The pilgrim-writer acknowledges that "if" God had not been on Israel's side, they would have been decimated by their many enemies (vv. 1-2). Everything depended on that *if*. Without the Lord's protection and help, His people would have been washed away by the raging flood of hostility against them (vv. 3-5). For this reason the writer praises the One who created heaven and earth; He alone had enabled them to escape their enemy's evil devices (vv. 6-8). Paul proclaimed this same timeless truth to believers in the Church Age: *"If God is for us, who can be against us?"* (Rom. 8:31).

Psalm: 125 Type: Ascent/Thanksgiving – Song of Trust
           Author: Unknown

Surrounded by the Lord's Protection

One great benefit for the righteous is that the Lord surrounds them with His everlasting protection, which the psalmist likens to the natural safeguard of the ancient hills encircling Jerusalem (vv. 1-2). Though wicked nations might threaten the nation, the Lord would not permit His people to be tested beyond measure, lest the nation be overcome

The Beginning of Wisdom

with evil and turn away from the Lord (v. 3). Paul reminded Christians of a similar truth:

> *Therefore let him who thinks he stands take heed lest he fall. No temptation has overtaken you except such as is common to man; but God is faithful, who will not allow you to be tempted beyond what you are able, but with the temptation will also make the way of escape, that you may be able to bear it* (1 Cor. 10:12-13).

If we trust in ourselves, we will fall prey to temptation and become depressed, but by relying on God's revealed truth and assistance, we experience deliverance. He promises not to permit us to be overwhelmed by a trial if we rely on Him. Testing is needed to refine and build up our faith (Jas. 1:1-2), but God does not want us to fail in such times; rather, He desires we triumph in His power and be further strengthened for the next challenge. Faith that is not tested will not be trusted in times of adversity. With this understanding, the writer prays that God would bless those who continue in uprightness, notwithstanding hardship (v. 4). The psalmist concludes God's people should remain loyal to the Lord despite adversity, lest they turn aside and suffer God's judgment along with the wicked (v. 5). In the Church Age, true believers will not suffer God's wrath with the wicked (Rom. 5:9), but will be divinely chastened in the same way a disobedient child receives parental correction (1 Cor. 5:5-6; Heb. 12:6). Thankfully, *"If we are faithless, He remains faithful; He cannot deny Himself"* (2 Tim. 2:13). Therefore, we can agree with the psalmist: *"They who trust in the Lord ... cannot be removed"* (v. 1).

Psalm: 126 Type: Ascent   Author: Unknown

Sowing Tears – Reaping Joy

The psalmist recounts the immense joy and jubilant singing of the Jewish captives returning to Jerusalem, perhaps from Babylon – this euphoric experience was like a hopeful dream that had finally come true (vv. 1-2). The writer accredits the Lord with ending their captivity and then prays that He would also bless and fully restore them in the land (vv. 3-4). Allen P. Ross explains:

> He [the psalmist] compared the returning exiles to streams in the Negev (the desert south of Judah), which in the dry season have little or no water but which in the rainy season overflow their banks. Under God's "showers of blessings" the highways from the east would be full of returning captives.[123]

The writer expands the illustration to include the agricultural principle of sowing and reaping. Presently, the land of Israel was barren, but as more captives returned in obedience to the Lord and sowed the land in tears (i.e., agonizing labor in God's work), this would return the land to productivity; they would eventually reap joy (vv. 5-6). Paul also discussed sowing and reaping, deriving a similar application:

> *Do not be deceived, God is not mocked; for whatever a man sows, that he will also reap. For he who sows to his flesh will of the flesh reap corruption, but he who sows to the Spirit will of the Spirit reap everlasting life. And let us not grow weary while doing good, for in due season we shall reap if we do not lose heart. Therefore, as we have opportunity, let us do good to all, especially to those who are of the household of faith* (Gal. 6:7-10).

Because the enemy will oppose any true work of God, the Lord's servants should expect to sow in tears (engage in arduous and often heart-breaking labor) to accomplish God's will; later, they will reap the full measure of blessing in joy.

Psalm: 127 Type: Ascent/Wisdom   Author: Solomon

Children Are God's Heritage

The opening line reflects Solomon's style of wisdom as expressed in Ecclesiastes: without the Lord's blessing, all that we do under the sun is vanity – it counts for nothing. William MacDonald expounds this spiritual principle: "There is a saying, 'Little is much if God is in it,' but the reverse is also true: 'Much is nothing if God is not in it.' And that's what this Psalm says: unless our activity is ordered and directed by the Lord, it is a waste of time and energy."[124] Whether we attempt to build a house, guard a city, or raise food, without the Lord's enablement all of our efforts are futile (vv. 1-2).

This realization is similar to what the Lord taught in Matthew 7:24-27: if a man builds his life on the sand of humanism (i.e., what is not of God), he will certainly fall into chaos when the storms of life challenge him, but those who build their lives on God's bedrock of revealed truth will endure trials and have His praise. This fact is perhaps no more evident than in family life. Are we truly counting on God to direct, endorse, and bless all the affairs of our homes? A Christian family is not a household of Christians, but a Christian household. It is more than Christ dwelling within the hearts of family members; it is a family that is pursuing the heart of God. If the Bible is not at the center of family life and all home affairs, that home cannot be called a true Christian home. The vital focus and end objective of every Christian household is the glory of God!

While in general it is God's plan for children to be born from the marriage union of a husband and a wife, Malachi reminds us God is not merely seeking offspring, but rather a "godly seed" who will live for Him (Mal. 2:15). The principle is that God is more interested in the quality than the quantity of children. To have more children than what parents can spiritually, emotionally, educationally, and economically care for is not wise. As the prophet Ezekiel informed the parents of his day, children are born unto the Lord – they are for Him (Ezek. 16:20). The psalmist declares the same truth: *"Children are a heritage from the Lord"* (v. 3), and then explains:

> *Like arrows in the hand of a warrior, so are the children of one's youth. Happy is the man who has his quiver full of them; they shall not be ashamed, but shall speak with their enemies in the gate* (vv. 4-5).

The psalmist reminds us we are only stewards, not owners, of the children that God graciously entrusts to our care. If reared in the ways of the Lord, these skillfully sharpened and straight arrows become a rich blessing to all. In ancient days, older children ensured the defense of the family against the attacking enemy. Children must be trained up for the

Lord to be a blessing to others and to further the kingdom of God. Untrained children, not surprisingly, remain foolish (Prov. 22:15) and predictably absorb what outside influences fill their void of understanding. Children are natural sponges; they are compelled to learn and to develop an understanding of the world in which they live. God forbid that believing parents through careless neglect should rear up pagans to revile His name. May we count on the Lord and His Word alone to build up our homes!

Psalm: 128 Type: Ascent/Wisdom   **Author: Unknown**

The Blessed Home

The Lord richly blesses those who fear and obey Him (v. 1). As we learned in the last psalm, working apart from the Lord is vanity, but working under His authority and in accordance with His ways prompts His blessing (v. 2). To illustrate this concept, the writer shows how a man's home becomes a fruitful abode when those within it fear the Lord.

The poet likens a virtuous wife to a fruitful vine adorning the home with beauty: *"Your wife shall be like a fruitful vine in the very heart of your house"* (v. 3). In ancient times, fruit-bearing vines were commonly planted adjacent to the exterior walls of homes. Practically speaking, the custom optimized ground space, provided protection for the vine, and allowed easy access to the delicious fruit. From a cosmetic sense, cold barren walls were transformed into radiant color, for the fruitful vine was an ornament of beauty. Yet, neither the bountiful fruit nor the adorning aspects of the vine developed naturally – a labor of love was necessary to achieve both. To become fruitful, the fragile vine required a *place* to be nurtured, a *purpose* to guide development, and specific *provisions* to ensure fruit-bearing. With these three key aspects in mind, the foliage illustration highlights God's general plan for a married woman: she is to be the keeper of the home (1 Tim. 5:14; Tit. 2:5); there, she is to be a helper to her husband and to nurture her children (Gen. 2:18; Tit. 2:4), but to do so, she also requires stable direction and tender support; this type of love and care is to be received from her husband (Eph. 5:25-29).

The Beginning of Wisdom

Likewise, the upright man in this psalm is blessed with olive plants around his table, speaking of children (v. 3). Children, God's heritage to parents, also require special care to thrive in a world hostile to the things of God. Entire families normally traveled together to attend the Feasts of Jehovah, so this poem, when rehearsed during the pilgrimage, was a great encouragement to all. A virtuous wife and thriving olive plants are a tremendous blessing to a God-fearing man and to each other. After acknowledging one of God's chief blessings to the upright (i.e., family), the writer asked the Lord to further bless the God-fearing by securing Jerusalem with peace (v. 5). This benefit would permit parents longevity so that they would be able to enjoy their grandchildren (v. 6). Thus, the blessings of a godly family could be enjoyed by several generations: *"Blessed is everyone who fears the Lord, who walks in His ways"* (v. 1).

Applying this to the nation of Israel, Hamilton Smith suggests this psalm pictures God-fearing saints who are anticipating the millennial blessing: "In this psalm the thoughts of the godly remnant are carried beyond the time of building, watching and fighting, to millennial rest and prosperity."[125] Then all God's children will be at home with Him.

Psalm: 129 Type: Ascent   **Author: Unknown**

A Prayer for Suffering Israel

Speaking for the nation of Israel, the psalmist encourages the nation to testify how the Lord had delivered them from their oppressors in the past (vv. 1-2). So severe was their suffering that the cuts from their enemy's whip were likened to long furrows plowed on their backs. But God showed mercy by cutting their cords of bondage and releasing His people. The writer then prays that God would judge all those who persecute Israel and hate Zion; they do not deserve God's blessing, but rather His wrath (vv. 5-8).

Psalm: 130 Type: Ascent/Lament – Penitential   Author: Unknown

Waiting for the Morning

The writer pleads for God's mercy in the midst of a deep trial; this was apparently divine chastening for sin and was affecting the entire nation (vv. 1-2, 8). The psalmist rightly proclaims that if God dealt justly with sinners, no one would be able to stand before Him (v. 3). Thankfully, God is long-suffering and merciful, and will extend forgiveness to those who fear Him; at the time of this writing, forgiveness was possible through blood atonement for sins as prescribed in the Law (v. 4). This meant that the psalmist could hope in God's word and wait patiently for the Lord's pardon and deliverance (i.e. a new morning of blessing was imminent; vv. 5-6).

In the face of suffering, holding to revealed truth is a wise recourse for believers in any dispensation. Hence, the writer reminds Israel their hope for mercy and their redemption were in the Lord alone (vv. 7-8). Let us not forget that, just as sure as a new day always dawns, our complete salvation in Christ is at hand – this is the Church's blessed hope (Tit. 2:13; 1 Jn. 3:2-3)! The Lord Jesus said, *"I ... am the root and the offspring of David, and the bright and morning star"* (Rev. 22:16). Dark times will precede the curtain call of the Church Age, yet believers have the hope of their *Bright and Morning Star*. He shall come for His beloved bride at the dawning of the Day of the Lord, and then the *Sun of Righteousness* (Mal. 4:2) shall rise in His full strength and flood the earth with His glory!

Psalm: 131 Type: Ascent/Thanksgiving – Song of Trust
Author: David

A Child of Faith

David was on a lifelong pilgrimage to grow in grace and mature in his love for the Lord. He was pursuing God with childlike humility and dependence, not in arrogance and selfish ambitions, which he once yearned for in the same way a nursing baby desires to be nursed (vv. 1-2). Now weaned, so to speak, David desired that all Israel would follow his example in growing maturity and hope in the Lord, without religious pride, intellectual superiority, or a spirit of self-sufficiency (v. 3). James puts the matter this way: *"God resists the proud, but gives grace to the humble"* (Jas. 4:6); this is a timeless truth for all believers.

Psalm: 132   Type: Ascent/Liturgical – Covenantal
Author: Unknown

There Is Hope in David's God

The setting of this congregational prayer is uncertain. It may have been uttered by returning captives from Babylon, who after observing the destroyed temple and city wondered about God's promises to David concerning Zion being His perpetual dwelling place with a descendant of David ruling there. Another possibility is that the poem was written by Solomon when he brought the Ark of the Covenant into the newly-constructed temple and prayed for the Shekinah glory of God to dwell at that location.

The theme of the poem is stated in the opening plea of the congregation (or Solomon) for God to remember David, his afflictions, and his desire to build God a house (vv. 1-5). The prayer recounts how the Ark of the Covenant was joyfully found in Ephrathah, after being returned by the Philistines (vv. 6-8; 1 Sam. 6). It remained in Kirjath-jearim for twenty years before David conveyed it to Jerusalem – God's permanent earthly footstool, that is, the location He chose to be worshipped (1 Sam. 7:1-2; 2 Sam. 6). Having confidence that God would honor His covenant with David, which He freshly reiterated at this time, the congregation rejoiced (vv. 11-18). Zion would again be filled with the glory of the Lord, Israel's enemies would be put to shame, and a descendant of David would again reside on the throne in Jerusalem. This prayer has not been fully realized, as war and desolations are determined against the Jews until their previously "cut off" Messiah (Dan. 9:25-27) returns to crush the satanic rebellion that threatens their existence; then, the prophesied Heir of David will rule in Zion and over His people forever (Isa. 62:6-7; Zech. 14:16-17).

Psalm: 133 Type: Ascent/Wisdom   **Author: David**

The Blessedness of Unity

The timeless benefit of blessed unity among God's people is introduced in verse 1 and then portrayed in two word pictures in verses 2-3. Unity and love among the brethren are likened to the fragrant anointing oil that flowed down Aaron's beard and priestly attire at His consecration as high priest, and as the dew that falls upon the mountains and flows downward to renew and sustain life below (vv. 2-3). The special anointing mixture used to consecrate priests and holy things for the Lord's service contained olive oil (Ex. 30:22-32). Oil is a fluid that is both active and enabling, as shown in the operation of a lamp where oil is drawn from a reservoir through a wick to produce light when burned.

The Holy Spirit is generally depicted as an active fluid in Scripture, such as blowing wind (John 3), seven flames of fire (Rev. 4), or rushing water from a rock (John 7). In one of Zechariah's visions, he saw two olive trees supplying oil to a lampstand. God used the expression *"Not by might nor by power, but by My Spirit"* (Zech. 4:6) in reference to the influence of the oil as a picture of the Spirit of God. The Holy Spirit enables and accomplishes the will of God through others in a powerful and unseen fashion. Paul tells us that it is only through the work of the Holy Spirit that lovely unity will occur among God's people (Eph. 4:3); this is apparently what is symbolized by the oil and the dew in verses 2-3. Such an outworking of the Holy Spirit among God's people propagates the sweet aroma of Christ in the world and likewise refreshes our hearts (2 Cor. 2:14-16).

James ties strife and division with the work of the devil: *"For where envying and strife is, there is confusion and every evil work"* (Jas. 3:16; KJV). On the other hand, the unity of God's people is precious to Him: *"Behold, how good and how pleasant it is for brethren to dwell together in unity!"* (v. 1). As previously mentioned, the Holy Spirit works to maintain unity among believers, but believers must labor to keep it (Eph. 4:3). This is accomplished by humbling ourselves and putting the interests of others ahead of our own (Phil. 2:2-4). A busybody inserts his or her interests into the affairs of others, but a Christ-minded believer puts the welfare of others above his or her own interests – this type of attitude ends strife. Having the mind of Christ ensures His people are unified and doing *"all to the glory of God"* (1 Cor. 10:31). David desired the blessing of brotherly unity in his time, and we should likewise yearn for it in the Church today.

Psalm: 134 Type: Ascent/Liturgical – Temple   Author: Unknown

A Benediction of Praise

This poem is a benediction and a fitting conclusion for the *Psalms of Ascent* (Ps. 120-134). The writer asks the priest and Levites, who faithfully served in the temple day and night, to praise the Lord with uplifted hands, and to beseech God to bless those pilgrims who had come to Zion to worship Him (vv. 1-2). The psalmist was certain that the Creator of all things would bless those who had obeyed the Law and journeyed to Zion (v. 3).

Psalm: 135 Type: Thanksgiving – Historical   Author: Unknown

Worship Jehovah, Not Idols

Continuing the petition in the previous psalm, the writer calls on the priests and Levities serving the Lord in the temple to praise the Lord, for He is good and His name is pleasant (vv. 1-3). Unlike false gods, Jehovah deserved their worship, for He alone is sovereign over creation. This was demonstrated in His choice of Israel as His special people, and in nature's manifestation of His rule in rainfall, lightning, and wind (vv. 4-7). Furthermore, God's sovereignty was proven in the judgments of Egypt, which released His people from bondage and initiated the subsequent defeat of every enemy who opposed their entrance into Canaan (vv. 8-12). God will also show His rule and power by vindicating His covenant people in a future day, in fulfillment of His promises to Abraham and David (vv. 13-14). Clearly, Jehovah is superior to the pagan gods fashioned by men: idols which cannot speak, hear, breathe, etc. (vv. 15-18). Observing these evidences of Jehovah's sovereignty, the psalmist calls on the entire nation to praise the One who dwelt among them in Zion (vv. 19-21). He then closes the song in the same way he began, with celebratory praise – *"Praise the Lord."*

Verse 4 and Exodus 19:5 inform us that God considers Israel His special treasure. Three times in Scripture, Jehovah confirms His love for the Jewish nation by referring to them as *"the apple of His eye";* as such, He vows to cherish and defend them (Deut. 32:10; Lam. 2:18, KJV). The prophet Zechariah warned the nations to beware, *"for he who touches you* [Israel] *touches the apple of His eye"* (Zech. 2:8). The Lord will restore to Himself a refined Jewish nation at His Second Advent and judge all those who have harmed her (Zech. 12-14; Rom. 10-11); this is a divine ultimatum that no nation should forget!

Psalm: 136 Type: Thanksgiving – Historical   Author: Unknown

The Lord's Mercy Endures Forever

The construction of this liturgical psalm lends itself to antiphonic congregational worship. That is, the first part of the verse contains an accolade of praise to be uttered by part of the congregation or a Levitical official, and then the full congregation responds with the refrain, *"for His mercy endures forever"* to further endorse the initial statement. This format is consistent for each of the twenty-six verses. The theme of the poem is stated in verses 2-4: *"Give thanks to the God of gods ... the Lord of lords ... to Him Who alone does great wonders ... for His mercy endures forever."* Subsequent items of praise fall under one or more of those three headings. Some of the great wonders worthy of praise include God's: creative acts (vv. 5-9), care for and preservation of Israel from their Egyptian exodus to their arrival in Canaan (vv. 10-24), and provision of food for all creatures (v. 25).

The writer concludes by calling on the congregation to bestow thanks to the *"God of Heaven"* (v. 26). This is the only time this phrase appears in Psalms, and is a term predominantly used in post-exilic books such as Daniel, Ezra, and Nehemiah in acknowledgement that God was no longer dwelling among His rebellious people. Ezekiel describes the glory of the Lord leaving the temple and returning to heaven at the time of the Babylonian invasion, which God permitted to remove widespread idolatry from Judah (Ezek. 10). Then, according to the prophecy of Jeremiah (Jer. 25:11), the Lord brought His people home again but their idols remained in Babylon. More than any other people on the planet, the Jewish people experientially know that God's mercy is inexhaustible and endures forever!

Psalm: 137 Type: Lament – Imprecatory   Author: Unknown

A Captive's Plead for Vengeance

The sour tone of this psalm reflects the dismal disposition of a Jewish captive, and likely of the nation, while exiled in Babylon. Their homeland had been brutally conquered, many Jews had been slaughtered, many others were taken as slaves to Babylon, and Jerusalem and the temple had been destroyed. In that pagan land, Jewish captives understandably did not feel like rejoicing; in fact, they did not want to sing the songs of Zion when taunted to do so by their captors (vv. 1-4). When they thought of Zion, there was nothing to sing about; instead, the musicians hung their harps in the willow trees. This melancholy outlook is then contrasted with the Jews' intense love for Zion (vv. 5-6). The psalmist vows to remember Jerusalem, and if he forgets, he asks that the Lord would cause him to forget his playing skills as a musician, and that he would become a mute also (i.e., unable to sing). The words of verse 5, *"If I forget you, O Jerusalem,"* have been a rallying cry for displaced and discouraged Jews down through the centuries of oppression.

The remainder of the song focuses on the intense bitterness of the invasion and the ensuing captivity. The poet pleads with God to render back to the Edomites and Babylonians the same ruthless treatment they had inflicted on His people (vv. 7-9). This poem records one of the most intense imprecatory prayers found in Psalms. (See the discussion concerning imprecatory prayers in the *Psalm Types* section.) The enraged writer even petitions God to dash their enemies' children against the rocks to reimburse them for the slaughter of the Jewish children during the invasion (v. 9). As God promised Habakkuk, He would punish the Babylonians after He had finished using them as a rod of reproof against Israel, but what the psalmist failed to realize was the captivity was God's response to Judah's deep-seated idolatry (Hab.

Devotions in Psalms

1-2). The Jews could not be joyful in the Lord with such bitterness, even if God answered their prayer for vengeance. God had a different plan in mind, and that was for His people to recognize their sin, repent, accept their punishment as just, and then experience spiritual revival.

As Ezra and Nehemiah record in their books, national revival did break out after Jewish captives were permitted to return to Jerusalem by the Persians, who granted them permission to rebuild the temple, and later the city. After returning to Israel by faith, they experienced a spiritual awakening; then their singing could not be restrained (Neh. 12). In fact, spiritual revival prompts praise, worship, thanksgiving, and a desire to return to the Lord a portion of what He has graciously bestowed. May the Church too become desperate for God, reach up to heaven with clean open hands, and may God visit His people again with vitalizing power (Ezra 9 -10)!

Psalm: 138 Type: Thanksgiving - Personal   Author: David

Revived by Answered Prayer

This psalm is one of particular interest to a weary soul. Indeed, David's heart had been revived by the revelation of God's word in direct response to his prayer. J. G. Bellett remarks:

> In Psalm 56 the soul rejoiced in *the word* above all. All in God was matter of praise, but above all, His word, His promise, His covenant. 'In God will I praise His word' (Ps. 56:4, 10). In this Psalm *the word* is praised again – esteemed above all God's name or revelation of Himself.[126]

Because God had answered David's prayer, he vowed to praise the Lord in His temple; this would demonstrate David's contempt for false deities who might be looking on (vv. 1-3). In fact, David desired that all kings would hear God's word, see His glory, and would follow David's example of praising Jehovah alone (vv. 4-5). It was right to praise the Lord; though exalted in heaven, He continues to justly move on behalf of the brokenhearted and needy, while rejecting the proud (v. 6). For this reason, David expresses his confidence in the Lord to powerfully deliver him from his enemies and to revive him in the midst of trouble (v. 7). The poem then concludes with David acknowledging God's sovereign rule in his life and requesting the Lord to grant his petition for deliverance (v. 8).

Psalm: 139 Type: Lament – Personal   Author: David

The Omnipresent, Omniscient, Omnipotent God

"In the beginning, God created the heavens and the earth" (Gen. 1:1). Before there was anything, God eternally existed. God is not creation, as some teach, for creation came subsequent to the eternal God. If God was created, He would be the effect of a cause, subject to the laws of a superior being, and thus, changeable and not eternally existing – the premise is illogical. However, as David expresses in this song, God permeates His creation (vv. 7-12), is aware of all that goes on within it, including our thoughts (vv. 1-6), and powerfully manages it according to His will, including the formation of embryos in the womb (vv. 13-16). Because David realized every aspect of his life was searched out, planned, and meticulously controlled by the Lord, he could praise the Lord for His wondrous works and precious thoughts towards him (vv. 17-18). Accordingly, he knew he could trust the Lord to thwart his enemies, whom he detested because they despised the Lord's name (vv. 19-22), and also to further examine and refine his inner man (vv. 1, 23-24). Hamilton Smith reminds us that godly saints desire this type of spiritual scrutiny and enhancement:

> The godly man welcomes the searchings of God into the inmost recesses of his heart, desiring that he may be delivered from every evil way and led "in the way everlasting." In the experience of the psalmist the consciousness of the omniscience of God at first plunges his soul into the deepest distress as he thinks of his own broken responsibilities towards God. When, at length, he realizes that God's "works" and God's "thoughts" are toward him in grace, the omniscience of God becomes the source of his deepest comfort.[127]

Divine inspection of David's heart would both prove his loyal devotion to the Lord, and permit God to further test and enrich David's character. He knew he could not hide his thoughts and doings from the Lord, so he desired to transform all his contemplations and deeds to those that would please Him. This is the proper response to the omnipresent, omniscient, omnipotent God. Concerning one's devotion to the Lord, David shows us that there is no middle ground; what God opposes is what we must reject, and what God approves of is what we should desire also (Eph. 5:11).

Psalm: 140 Type: Lament – Imprecatory   Author: David

Praying for Protection and Justice

David pleads with the Lord to preserve him from his vile, wicked enemy, who continually planned evil and war against him (vv. 1-2). With cutting words and poisonous speech, these proud and violent men were threatening to overthrow David; they hoped to ensnare him in one of their traps in order to kill him (vv. 3-5). David then calls on his God, the strength of his salvation, to continue to protect his head in battle and not to allow his enemies to pompously gloat over his demise (vv. 6-8). Entering into the imprecatory stage of his prayer, David asks for God to return the evil purposed against him back on his slanderous enemies and to let them fall prey to their own evil devices (vv. 9-11). Because God championed the cause of the poor and afflicted, the psalmist knew that the righteous would have cause to praise the Lord and that the upright would dwell peacefully in His presence (vv. 12-13). David was perhaps thinking of Sodom and Gomorrah, destroyed by fire from heaven, when he asked for the Lord to heap burning coals on his enemies. In the Church Age, Paul poses a different approach to overcome one's enemies:

> *Beloved, do not avenge yourselves, but rather give place to wrath; for it is written, "Vengeance is Mine, I will repay," says the Lord. Therefore, "If your enemy is hungry, feed him; if he is thirsty, give him a drink; for in so doing you will heap coals of fire on his head." Do not be overcome by evil, but overcome evil with good* (Rom. 12:19-21).

Before the days of sulfur matches and when a burning fire in the hearth or oven was a necessity of life, carrying hot coals in a vessel to one's neighbor was a polite gesture of friendship. The believer whose heart is right with the Lord does not want his or her enemies destroyed, but rather yearns for them to experience salvation in Christ, so that as many as possible might rejoice together in Him.

Psalm: 141 Type: Lament – Personal   Author: David

A Prayer of Consecration and Liberation From Evil

At the evening sacrifice, with the smoke billowing upwards from the lamb offered on the Bronze Altar and the aroma of the sweet incense ascending up to God from the Golden Altar, David lifts up his hands and his voice to God (vv. 1-2). He prays for further sanctification and for deliverance from the wicked. Having suffered much from his enemies' slander and false accusations, David requested that God would grant him wise speech (v. 3) and that he would not be tempted to sin by worldly luxuries or sensual allurements (v. 4). He affirmed he would not reject the reproof of the righteous, for their counsel was like anointing oil that refreshes the soul. David also asked that the wicked would realize his words were true before they were destroyed (vv. 5-7). The wicked posed a serious threat to David; he therefore desired that the Lord would continue to be his life-preserving Refuge and also that the wicked would be ensnared by their own evil devices (vv. 8-10).

This psalm is in fact a prayer of David for deliverance from evil and evil men. While teaching His disciples how to pray, the Lord Jesus highlighted the fact that with God's help, believers would not be led into temptation, and thus delivered from evil (Matt. 6:13). This attitude of humble dependence was at the heart of David's prayer life and should be at ours as well. Although the human heart is *"deceitful above all things, and desperately wicked"* (Jer. 17:9), under God's control our hearts can beat for the Lord – David's did; he was a man after God's own heart (1 Sam. 13:14).

Psalm: 142 Type: Lament – Personal   **Author: David**

Recalling God's Deliverance

The Hebrew superscript accredits the authorship of this poem to David; it was penned while he was hiding from Saul in a wilderness cave. (See Psalm 57 for a discussion of David's various cave experiences.) In this psalm, David recalls a previous prayer (one that the Lord had evidently answered) for mercy during a life-threatening circumstance (vv. 1-2). Speaking to the Lord, David acknowledges the Lord was fully aware of his situation, his weakened emotional state, and that there was no one who could or was willing to help him (vv. 3-4). Accordingly, David's only option was to put his full trust in his heavenly Refuge; God was his portion – all that he had and needed (v. 5). Surrounded by his enemies and deserted by his friends, David likened his dire situation to that of incarceration in prison. He therefore prayed for deliverance so that he could again praise God's name in the company of the righteous (vv. 6-7). David's humble desperation for God and his subsequent divine rescue reminds us of his declaration in Psalm 51: *"The sacrifices of God are a broken spirit, a broken and a contrite heart – these, O God, You will not despise"* (Ps. 51:17). C. H. Mackintosh puts the matter this way:

> We must be really brought to the end of everything with which self has aught to do; for until then God cannot show Himself. But we can never get to the end of our plans until we have been brought to the end of ourselves.[128]

Like David here and Jacob in Genesis 32, it is when we come to the end of our personal agendas, plans, and strength that we experience a new beginning with God.

Psalm: 143 Type: Lament – Penitential   **Author: David**

An Urgent Plea for Deliverance

This poem displays a variety of moods as it transitions among several subjects: penitence, crisis, desperation, recollection, fervency, urgency, appeal, and prayer. This song is the last of seven *Penitential Psalms* in the book of Psalms; it also is an urgent request by David to be rescued from those who sought to murder him. He was fully aware that all men fall short of God's moral goodness and deserve condemnation, so he prays for God's salvation on the basis of grace alone (vv. 1-2). Overwhelmed, desolate, and exploited, the psalmist laments his situation before the Lord (vv. 3-4). Remembering God's past judicial responses against the wicked for their oppression of the innocent, David lifts up his empty hands to the Lord to show his complete dependency and urgently begs God for help (vv. 5-9). David asks God to revive his soul and spiritually guide him in the way of righteousness so that he would always walk according to God's will (vv. 10-11). David concludes his prayer by reminding the Lord that he was His servant and by again requesting the Lord to cut off his enemies and deliver him from trouble (v. 12).

Psalm: 144 Type: Liturgical – Royal   Author: David

A Declaration of Trust

David apparently compiled this poem by extracting portions from other psalms to declare his trust in the Lord in a unique but uniform manner. In this psalm, David is careful to extend praise to the Lord for his military victories that had subdued the region and established his rule over it (v. 1). The Lord had enabled him to fight, so in practice David viewed the Lord as his Rock, Fortress, Tower, Deliverer, Shield, and Refuge (v. 2). Before asking the Lord for victory in a forthcoming battle, David wonders why a God so magnificent and high would stoop to notice and intervene in the affairs of men, especially to help him (v. 3). In comparison to the Lord, the life of a man is like a mist that quickly evaporates in the morning sun or a fleeting shadow at day's end (v. 4).

Facing a deceitful enemy as strong as mighty waters, David petitions the Lord to supernaturally intervene to ensure his victory (e.g., to use lightning to scatter his enemies; vv. 5-8). He then expresses his confidence in the Lord to grant his request and hence vows to sing a new song of praise after the triumph, for which he again petitions God

(vv. 9-11). Victory for King David meant the subjects of his kingdom would prosper like thriving plants, economic benefits would be obtained (e.g., barns full of harvested crops), and an atmosphere of peace would be enjoyed by all (vv. 12-14). When God intervenes on behalf of His anointed, victory is assured and those under His authority are blessed (v. 15). Thus, this royal psalm climaxes with this wonderful conclusion: *"Happy are the people whose God is the Lord!"* (v. 15). Amen!

Psalm: 145 Type: Praise   **Author: David**

Great Is the Lord

This is another acrostic psalm, each verse beginning with a successive letter of the Hebrew alphabet. However, the Hebrew alphabet has twenty-two letters while it is observed there are but twenty-one verses in this poem. For unknown reasons, the letter *nun,* the fourteenth letter in the Hebrew alphabet, is missing in the Masoretic text. The ancient Greek, Syriac, and Latin versions include a *nun* verse between verses 13 and 14; this verse is identical to verse 17, except the first word matches the alphabetical listing. Some Hebrew texts found among the Dead Sea Scrolls in 1946-1956 AD also contain this verse. Alfred Barnes surmised that at some point the *nun* verse was probably omitted to ensure an identical cadence of three equal parts, each having seven verses.[129]

The Hebrew superscript titles this poem *"A Praise of David."* This is a unique title in Psalms and a fitting commencement of the book's final doxology, as formed by the last six psalms. It is noted that the word "praise" is found 222 times in Psalms, with 45 of those occurrences in Psalms 145-150; the final poem is a crescendo of praise, containing thirteen separate exhortations to praise the Lord.

Because the Lord is so great, far beyond human comprehension, David opened the psalm by declaring he will praise the Lord every day forever (vv. 1-3). God's many good and righteous feats are so awesome that believers from generation to generation should remember them, meditate on them, and rehearse them with an attitude of praise and appreciation (vv. 4-7). Transitioning from God's doings to His holy character, David declares that His God is good, righteous, gracious, slow to anger, full of compassion, and great in mercy (v. 8). Our God is good to all, including those who reject His kindness, which means everyone, and especially His saints have good reason to praise His name throughout their generations (vv. 9-13).

God's works inspire praise to His name; thus, David instructs the congregation to praise the One who is faithful to all His promises, who lifts up those who fall, who provides food for everyone, and who satisfies the needs of all living things (vv. 14-16). The Lord is righteous and holy in all His works, and near to all those who fear Him and call upon Him in truth (vv. 17-19). Hence, the Lord preserves those who love Him, but the wicked will be destroyed; thus, David is determined to praise His great God forever, and so should we (vv. 20-21).

Psalm: 146 Type: Praise   **Author: Unknown**

Praise for God's Help

This poem, as well as the remaining psalms, commence and conclude with *halal yahh* (*"Praise the Lord"*). After twice vowing to praise God his entire life (vv. 1-2), the psalmist exhorts the congregation to put their trust in the Lord and not mortal men because their agendas and strength die with them (vv. 3-4). In contrast, happy is the man who trusts and hopes in the God who created the heaven and earth (vv. 5-6). For example, the Lord delivers the oppressed, provides food for the starving, releases captives, heals the blind, bestows favor to the righteous, and protects the sojourner, the orphan, and the widow; yet, he confounds the wicked and spoils their devices (vv. 7-9). Thankfully, a sovereign, gracious, eternal God rules over the affairs of men – such a God is deserving of our praise: *"Praise the Lord"* (v. 10).

Psalm: 147 Type: Praise   **Author: Unknown**

Praise for the Great and Gracious God

It is fitting and pleasant for men to praise the only God who is praiseworthy (v. 1). As demonstrated by returning Jewish captives from

Babylon and reestablishing Jerusalem, God extends grace to those who repent and humble themselves before Him (vv. 2-3). The One who is infinite in knowledge, perfectly controls the universe, and rejects the wicked but heals the brokenhearted is worthy of praise (vv. 4-6). The psalmist instructs the congregation to praise God with music, for He is the Creator of all, the Sustainer of life, and yet He specially delights in each soul that trusts in Him (vv. 7-11).

The writer then calls on those living in Jerusalem to praise the Lord for blessing them with security, peace, and bountiful provisions (vv. 12-14). God is so great that He controls the earth and the forces of nature (e.g. wind, rain, snow, frost, and hail) with mere words (vv. 15-18). One of God's greatest acts of grace was to reveal Himself and His Law to initiate fellowship with a specific people-group, the nation of Israel (vv. 19-20). Such a great God who extends manifold grace to heal and who wondrously reveals Himself through creation and His Word is worthy of praise – *"Praise the Lord"* (v. 20).

Psalm: 148 Type: Praise **Author: Unknown**

Creation Praises the Creator

The psalmist summons all creation above the earth (e.g. sun, moon, and stars), and also the heavenly angels to praise the Lord. This is appropriate as God fashioned all that was created – creation demands a Creator and the Creator must be honored by His creation (vv. 5-6). The writer then calls on all that pertains to the earth: sea creatures, forces of nature, mountains, plant life, animal life, creeping things, fowls, and kings and those they rule (both young and old) to praise the Lord (vv. 7-12). The psalmist declares God is worthy of praise, not only because He raised up a king to serve His covenant people, but because His own name and intrinsic splendor is much greater than the sum total of all His creative acts. Consequently, every created thing is invited to join this gigantic choir to *"Praise the Lord"* (v. 14)!

Psalm: 149 Type: Praise **Author: Unknown**

Israel Joyfully Praises God

The psalmist calls on Israel to praise the Lord, their Maker and King, by singing a new song in unison, accompanied with musical instruments and dancing (vv. 1-3). It is noted that the Hebrew verb `asah, translated as *"their Maker"* in verse 2, is the same plural verb in Genesis 1:26, where it is rendered *"let us make"* – Israel was literally to praise their Makers, their triune God. It was appropriate for Israel to joyfully praise Jehovah who had created their nation by an unconditional covenant and then beautified them with many acts of grace (vv. 4-5).

A noticeable transition occurs in verse 6: singing believers become reigning saints with Christ. The writer instructs the Jewish nation to continue singing praises to God as they go forth into the world with sharp swords to execute His justice on the wicked (vv. 6-9). Those who opposed Jehovah were to be opposed by those who wanted to honor Him in Israel. Today, we do not lift a literal sword to avenge the Lord's name in the same way Israel did during the dispensation of the Law. Christians are to skillfully use His Word, a living and powerful Sword (Heb. 4:12), to penetrate the hearts of the unregenerate with love and truth, so that they might be converted and saved; then they, together with us, will *"Praise the Lord"* (v. 9).

Psalm: 150 Type: Praise **Author: Unknown**

An Overture of Climactic Praise

We come to the final psalm, the grand finale of climactic praise which commenced in Psalm 145. Because God is so majestic in essence and in His mighty works, the psalmist calls on His people to lift up praise to Him in His heavenly sanctuary (vv. 1-2). Praising God through joyful singing, dancing, and an assortment of musical instruments was appropriate (vv. 3-5). The last verse of Psalms provides a fitting summary: *"Let everything that has breath praise the Lord. Praise the Lord!"* (v. 6). The breath that every living thing has received from the Lord should be returned to the Lord in exhaled praise – *"Praise the Lord!"* (v. 6).

Proverbs

Proverbs

Introduction

Scholars have debated what *mashal*, the Hebrew word rendered "proverb" in the Old Testament, actually means. Observation tells us that a proverb is a pithy maxim, often of a metaphorical nature, to express a simile. This understanding would agree with what many believe is the literal meaning of the word proverb, "to be like"; this prompts the reader to consider an association of things. Proverbs, then, is a collection of succinct common-sense sayings, which by comparison or contrast convey a practical certainty that should be heeded. The book of Proverbs provides a lengthy contrast of wisdom and foolishness. Such practical wisdom will assist the younger generation from repeating the mistakes of their parents (1:5).

Biblical wisdom is not knowledge alone, nor philosophical speculations about our existence; it is learning and experiencing the principles of a God-honoring life. While six different Hebrew words are translated "wisdom" in Proverbs, the first to appear and the most common word in the book is *chokmah*, which means "to have skill." Just as sailors, singers, and craftsmen have expertise in their related professions, believers are to be competent in godly living. Knowledge can be memorized, but wisdom is dynamic; it must think through what is known to render the most profitable response. Wisdom skillfully applied will guide righteous, honest, pure, and orderly behavior.

Proverbs is a treasure-tome of godly wisdom addressing a vast number of timeless topics. Where the books of the Law decree righteous statutes to be obeyed, Proverbs goes further to direct proper attitudes and discretion in daily living. Moral conduct is explicitly declared to us in God's Word; however, discerning between wise and foolish, helpful and harmful, and profitable and worthless behavior is more difficult. This is especially true in questionable areas of conduct –

The Beginning of Wisdom

thankfully, Proverbs provides meaningful guidance and stern warnings for such facets of daily living.

Purpose

Proverbs is different from any other book in our Bibles in that it cannot be classified as historical, prophetic, Law, nor narrative in nature. While it certainly belongs with the other books of wisdom, it is clearly distinct from them in format and purpose. We do not need to read far into Proverbs to understand what the purpose of the book is; the writer tells us in the opening verses. Notice the author's fourfold intention for his book:

> *To know wisdom and instruction; to perceive the words of understanding; to receive the instruction of wisdom, justice, judgment, and equity; to give prudence to the simple, to the young man knowledge and discretion* (1:2-4).

Proverbs is God's textbook for teaching His people to have wise and disciplined behavior, to learn proper reasoning skills, to understand moral ethics, and to impart prudence. Prudence is the opposite of gullibility; it is "street-smart" discretion. While learning wise and discreet behavior is profitable for readers of any age, the focus of Proverbs is to instill these virtuous qualities into the younger generation (1:4). In fact, Solomon invokes the term *"my son"* some fifteen times in the first seven chapters to address his own children or possibly other young pupils. After chapter 7 the expressions *"wise son"* or *"foolish son"* are repeatedly used to convey the same tenor. To this end, Proverbs provides a character sketch of a spiritually mature person who has God's approval – both young and old should aspire to this.

Because individual proverbs contained easy to understand sayings and are couched in a concise poetic format, memorization was encouraged and retention enhanced. Frequent word-pictures throughout the book also assist us with understanding a particular proverb's meaning and application. This ensures that all of God's people will find Proverbs a valuable source of guidance in all life's affairs. It is noteworthy that the authors do not address the Jewish nation per se, but rather individuals who must make right choices daily; thus, Solomon's appeals to the wise, those who *"will hear and increase learning"* (1:5).

Proverbs

We cannot force others to change their ways or correct their bad bents, but with God's help each believer can become more Christ-like by yielding to God's Word.

The overall purpose of Proverbs, then, is to teach God's people godly character and wise conduct so that they can avoid the pitfalls of sin and of foolish behavior. If wisdom is learned, if prudence is gained, if godly character is shaped, and if divine counsel is heeded, believers will be able to live "skillfully" before the Lord.

As will be explained further, the "fool" in Proverbs is not a mentally-challenged person, but someone who rejects divine knowledge and wisdom: *"The fear of the Lord is the beginning of wisdom, and the knowledge of the Holy one is understanding"* (9:10). *"The fool has said in his heart, 'There is no God'"* (Ps. 14:1). A person who has no time or respect for God is a fool because he is morally and spiritually bankrupt and doesn't even know it. Accordingly, in Proverbs, foolishness is closely linked with death, which more normally speaks of the entire realm that is in conflict with life, than merely a single event that ends physical existence. May God's people learn wisdom and avoid the deadly foolishness Solomon warns us of in Proverbs.

Divisions/Outline

The content of Proverbs is difficult to classify because of the wide range of subjects addressed, often within the same chapter. C. I. Scofield suggests four main topical divisions for Proverbs:

1. Fatherly Exhortations Addressed Mainly to the Young, chps. 1-9
2. Wisdom and the Fear of God Contrasted with Folly and Sin, chps. 10-24
3. Proverbs of Solomon Selected by the Men of Hezekiah, chps. 25-29
4. Supplemental Proverbs by Agur and Lemuel, chps. 30-31[130]

Some have divided Proverbs according to authorship and themes, such as William MacDonald's outline:

1. Introduction, 1:1-7
2. Proverbs of Solomon on Wisdom and Folly, 1:8-9:18
3. Proverbs of Solomon on Practical Morality, 10:1-22:16
4. Proverbs of Wise Men, 22:17-24:34

5. Proverbs of Solomon Compiled by Hezekiah's Men, chps. 25-29
6. The Words of Agur, chp. 30
7. The Words King Lemuel's Mother Taught Him, 31:1-9
8. The Ideal Wife and Mother, 31:10-31[131]

Regardless of how it might be outlined, Proverbs addresses a host of beneficial topics: sound business practices, disciplined living, generosity, control of the tongue, gossip, rearing children, moral purity, handling peer pressure, managing anger, maintaining a good marriage, self-control, curbing greed, social relationships, picking good friends, substance abuse, grief, lying, laziness, ignorance, death, anxiety, and many more. If we want to be successful (from the eternal perspective) in life, we need to read, understand, and practice the wisdom imparted in Proverbs.

Authorship

According to the text and the Hebrew superscripts, Solomon, a man impressively gifted with divine wisdom (1 Kgs. 4:29-34), is the main author of Proverbs (1:10, 10:1, 25:1). According to 1 Kings 4:32, Solomon uttered some three thousand proverbs and wrote one thousand and five songs. Solomon was a prolific writer, but the Lord has determined to only preserve a small portion of Solomon's literary works for our benefit, perhaps because he did not walk with the Lord in his autumn years.

The writers of Proverbs 22:17-24:34 are identified as *"the wise"* (22:17, 24:23). Perhaps these men were known for their profound wisdom prior to Solomon's time and he therefore chose to include some of their writings with his own. Many of the sayings in this section are warnings (i.e., *"do not ..."*) and also require two to four lines to complete the thought. The proverbs contained in chapters 25-29 were written by Solomon, but compiled nearly three centuries later by Hezekiah's men (25:1). Agur and Lemuel contributed Proverbs 30 and 31 respectively; their identities are unknown. Given their names, they are not likely of Jewish descent; furthermore, Lemuel is referred to as a king (31:1) and there is no Jewish record of such a man ruling in Israel. Some have suggested that Agur and Lemuel may have been alternate names for Solomon, but this seems unlikely. The acrostic construction of Proverbs 31:10-31 is a distinct stylistic change from the previous nine verses, which were written by Lemuel. This abrupt transition suggests that an unknown author may have penned that portion of the text at a later date.

Date and Historical Setting

Since Solomon reigned as Israel's king from 971 to 932 B.C., his literary works would have been composed during that timeframe. The final compilation, assuming the men of Hezekiah completed the arrangement, would have been about 700 B.C. Sid Buzzell suggests that "Solomon wrote the Song of Songs in his early adult years, Proverbs in his middle years, and Ecclesiastes near the end of this life as he reflected on his experiences."[132] This seems reasonable, as several early chapters in Proverbs are addressed to a son of a marriageable age, and as Ecclesiastes is his reflection on a full life of experiences and disappointments. Regardless of the authorship or the timing of compilation, the Spirit of God has inspired and maintained a collection of priceless wisdom for humanity to benefit from – Proverbs is a book of heavenly guidance for earthly living.

Observation

Unlike Ecclesiastes, which focuses on the nature of man, Proverbs is occupied with the wider subject of wisdom, which is centered in the fear of the Lord. It is observed that when Solomon refers to God in Proverbs, he uses "Jehovah" as a general rule, rather than the less personal term of "God"; the latter is rarely found in the book, and then mostly as a modifier. However, in Ecclesiastes, Solomon uses the term "God" almost exclusively, until he speaks of the fear of Jehovah at the end. Jehovah supplies His covenant people with the very wisdom they require to maintain fellowship with Him; what revelation is needed is supplied. The secular axiom proclaims, "Ignorance is bliss," but Proverbs declares that it is foolish to live in willful ignorance. This highlights the wonderful double benefit of studying and heeding Proverbs: joyful communion with the Lord, and His blessing!

Devotions in Proverbs

Proverbs 1

Wisdom's Warning

Solomon introduces the purpose of the book in the opening six verses; verse 2 provides the summary: *"To know wisdom and instruction, to perceive the words of understanding."* Wisdom here refers to "skillfulness" in life and instruction means "to teach by discipline." Both are required to gain understanding, which is literally "learning from the unhappy experiences of others or of oneself."

The writer intends to teach his audience practical wisdom for daily living, rather than engaging in high-minded philosophical conjectures. Learning requires a two-way interaction. First, the student must be willing to *receive* instruction (v. 3); indeed, a wise man will listen and carefully process what has been heard and seek wise counsel as needed to ensure sound decisions (v. 5). Second, the teacher must be willing to *give* prudence and knowledge to the young and *"the simple,"* those who are naïve and untaught (v. 4). If teachers pass along to their pupils what they know to be true and honorable, and if their students rightly absorb it, wisdom is gained. In this process of learning, students then become able to mentally assess and reason out the deeper meaning of clever proverbs and thought-provoking riddles (v. 6). A wise man has ears to hear, a mind to learn, and a heart to heed instruction.

In verse seven Solomon states, *"The fear of the Lord is the beginning of knowledge."* *"The fear of the Lord,"* a phrase occurring eleven times in Proverbs, is to be the fountainhead of all human knowledge; J. N. Darby explains:

> All true knowledge, all moral knowledge begins by putting God in His own place. Nothing is right or true without that. For to leave Him out falsifies the position and relationship of all. I may know physical

> facts and what are called laws (that is, abstractions from uniform facts), but that is all, without it. Not that there are no instituted relationships, for there are, as parents, husband and wife, and others now man is fallen. But right and wrong refer to each in its place. And not only is the fear of God a motive, which maintains their authority in the heart, but, if I leave God out, what has instituted them and given them their authority is wanting. Each stone has its own place in the arch, but if the keystone be wanting, none can keep theirs.[133]

One cannot gain insight into spiritual things, such as discerning between good and evil, apart from recognizing God's true character and choosing to revere Him and what He says. The fools in verse 7 reason life apart from God's existence, thus obscuring its true meaning with a haze of humanism. The Hebrew word for this type of fool is *'eviyl*, and rightly describes the person who arrogantly despises the value of God's wisdom; in fact, he or she holds the things of God in contempt. *'Eviyl* is employed nineteen times to address one of three types of fools spoken of in Proverbs and is the most aggressive form of foolishness. The most common word for "fool" in the book (found forty-nine times), is *kesil* – a close-minded, stubborn, and silly person. *Nabal* is translated as "fool" three times in Proverbs and identifies a person who lacks any spiritual perception and is vile in nature. Because the "scoffer," *les*, makes an appearance seventeen times in Proverbs, he too earns a standing in the gallery of fools; he devalues God's word, is a deliberate troublemaker, and loathes correction. So while the term "the simple" is used in Proverbs to speak of the naïve, the words for "fool" and "scoffer" are reserved for those who willfully choose an outlook in life (a worldview, if you will) that ignores or rejects divine revelation. The term, then, does not speak of mental faculties so much as it does of rebel disposition.

Understandably, Solomon warned his son of this dangerous intellectual snare and then implored him to listen to his instruction and to faithfully obey God's commands in order to receive honor among men and divine blessing (vv. 8-9). Similarly, Paul was concerned that such high-sounding fools would adversely influence believers in Colosse: *"Beware lest anyone cheat you through philosophy and empty deceit, according to the tradition of men, according to the basic principles of the world, and not according to Christ"* (Col. 2:8). True friends will draw us closer to God, but *"bad company corrupts good morals"* (1 Cor. 15:33; NASV). Solomon advised his son to pick his friends carefully and not to associate with thrill-seekers, those motivated by greed and get-rich-quick schemes, or those who enjoyed doing evil, such as harming the innocent, stealing, and committing murder (vv. 10-19). Unfortunately, many young people have been inducted into questionable groups and violent gangs because there was little parental involvement or godly wisdom in their upbringing.

Thankfully, the voice of the wicked is not the only one yearning to be heard and heeded in this chapter. Wisdom, personified as a woman, publicly calls out to everyone, but scoffers, fools, and the simple-minded despise her instruction (vv. 20-23). Despite her earnest pleading, many reject her counsel – when calamity befalls them, she promises to mock them with condescending laughter (vv. 24-27). When the consequences of rejecting the Lord are fully realized, it will be too late to benefit from wisdom; thus, she will ignore the foolish in the day of their destruction (vv. 28-30). It will be too late then to obtain God's mercy: *"Therefore shall they eat of the fruit of their own way, and be filled with their own devices"* (v. 31; KJV). Why did the foolish perish? Because they ignored or rejected divine truth and wisdom's warning not to be indifferent in the things of God (v. 32). Paul also warned of judgment, saying, *"For the wrath of God is revealed from heaven against all ungodliness and unrighteousness of men, who suppress the truth in unrighteousness"* (Rom. 1:18). Anyone thumbing their nose at what God has revealed about Himself deserves His wrath. However, those who cherish wisdom have nothing to fear, for they shall dwell safely in the presence of the Lord (v. 33). The actions and consequences of the foolish in verse 32 are contrasted with those of the wise in verse 33; this sets the tone for the remainder of the book.

Proverbs 2

Wisdom's Path

In this chapter, each verse begins with a successive letter of the Hebrew alphabet. Using eight verbs in the first four verses, Solomon reminds his son that obtaining wisdom is not easy; it requires persistent effort. Wisdom can only be possessed by: receiving, treasuring, memorizing God's commands (v. 1); listening and learning with understanding (v. 2); asking questions to gain discernment (v. 3); and conscientiously searching out wisdom's deeper significance (v. 4). To ensure his point is understood, Solomon resorts to the simple language of *cause and effect*; the three "ifs" in verses 1, 3, and 4 "then" lead to the outcomes in verses 5-9. What is the result of diligently pursuing wisdom? To know and fear the Lord. Moses affirmed mankind is not responsible to know what God has not revealed, but we are to strive to understand and obey what He has disclosed to us: *"The secret things belong to the Lord our God, but those things which are revealed belong to us and to our children forever, that we may do all the words of this law"* (Deut. 29:29). The paramount reason to study Scripture is to learn what God reveals about Himself; He is the source of true wisdom. Man cannot gain true wisdom by his own efforts, but those who sincerely seek after God will generously receive His wisdom (v. 6).

To be aware of God's greatness prompts us to fall on our faces in wonder and awe before Him. Paul prayed that the believers at Colosse would be *"increasing in the knowledge of God"* because he knew such knowledge would lead them into spiritual wisdom, strength, and fruitfulness (Col. 1:9-11). Understanding who God is and what He has done and will do promotes our spiritual vitality. Most of our doubts and anxieties arise from a diminished view of God's true nature and of the power of His gospel message centered in the Lord Jesus Christ. For the wise, searching for truth always leads to walking in truth and closer communion with God.

Gaining and yielding to divine wisdom has a positive moral benefit for believers: they increase in righteous living and in blameless conduct (v. 9), and they enjoy inner peace because they are settled in the truth (v. 10). These wisdom-seekers have God as their shield of protection (v. 7); He will preserve their way in justice (v. 8). In this sense, wisdom is a valuable protection against being influenced by wicked people. Knowing and surrendering to wisdom prevents God's people from being corrupted by sinful people through deceit and perversion (vv. 11-15) or through seduction and immoral behavior (vv. 16-17).

Solomon's rebuke of the adulterous wife in verse 17 is noteworthy: *"Who forsakes the companion of her youth, and forgets the covenant of her God."* The Hebrew word for "companion," *alluwph*, means "to be familiar and intimate, as with a foremost friend." In committing adultery the Jew not only violated the seventh of the Ten Commandments, but the penalty for this crime was death; there was no grace under the Law for the sin of adultery. Solomon indicated this woman broke her marriage covenant with her husband *and* with Jehovah; the marriage covenant in not just a lifelong commitment between a man and a woman, but with God also. Such a commitment sets a husband and wife apart for a lifetime of mutual intimacy and companionship. By seeking intimacy with someone else, the unfaithful wife had severely damaged God's design for marital companionship. True intimacy and disclosure only has value in marriage when guarded by an unwavering commitment.

Wisdom, purity, and discretion walk together on the way of life, but immorality seductively lures her victims down the path of death (vv. 18-19). With this said, to merely escape the corrupting influences of wicked people is not the measure of a wise person; he or she must actively progress in wisdom, that is, in knowing God, practicing godliness, and maintaining upright companions (v. 20). It is wise to seek to be wise; otherwise, we are otherwise. As in the previous chapter, Solomon concludes this one by contrasting those who pursue true wisdom and those who do not. The Jews who lived in the fear of the Lord would have His blessing in the Promised Land and those who did not would be removed from it in judgment; they have no inheritance (vv. 21-22). The first two chapters completed, Solomon has finished the preface for Proverbs: If true wisdom from above is heeded, the believer can be kept from the various forms of evil that sin has ushered into the world (see also 1 Jn. 2:15-17).

Proverbs 3

Wisdom's Reward

Like all conscientious parents, Solomon wanted the best for his children and for them to experience the rewards of heeding godly wisdom. Hence, he here warns his son not to forget his law, but rather to keep his commandments (v. 1), and to let mercy and truth guide his earthly sojourn (v. 3). As confirmed by Moses at Mount Sinai (Ex. 20:12) and by Paul in the New Testament (Eph. 6:1-3), to obey one's parents is to invite God's blessing in life, namely, longevity and prosperity (v. 2). The notion of longevity here includes quality of life; otherwise, it would be but an affliction to endure. Practically speaking, an uncorrected child would be socially miserable and a nuisance to society. His or her sinful ways and rebellious manner would probably lead him or her to an early grave. Samson, Absalom, and Eli's sons are good examples of wayward children who were each recompensed with a life cut short. However, a well-trained, compliant child earns the favor of God and man (v. 4). It is not only wise to be law-abiding and respectful to God-ordained authority, but it is also personally profitable to do so.

The father-instructor then issues four specific charges to his son, each of which carries a reward if heeded (vv. 5-12): trust the Lord even when your reasoning and emotions tell you to do otherwise (vv. 5-6), remain humble and God-fearing (vv. 7-8), honor the Lord by rendering your best to Him (vv. 9-10), and appreciate the value of His correction when you have erred from the path of righteousness (vv. 11-12). The Lord becomes the cherished object of the heart that has departed from evil. Under the Law, the benefits of obeying Him include: fewer troubles, better health, enhanced prosperity, and experiencing God's favor. Commenting on the exhortation in verse 6 to trust in God's wisdom alone for daily living, William Kelly warns:

> The great danger for all, though for some of thought and experience more than others, is to seek counsel from within. Yet experience should have taught the reflecting a less flattering tale. All Scripture re-echoes what is here written, "Be not wise in thine own eyes." The bait of Satan was to become so, and man has ever coveted it. How blessed when we learn our folly and find an incomparably better wisdom open to us![134]

Since wealth cannot guarantee genuine happiness, Solomon affirms that wisdom, personified as a woman, is more valuable (vv. 13-15). She readily blesses and sustains those who embrace her (vv. 16-18). In creating the world, God showed the vital connection between knowledge, understanding, and wisdom; man must also rightly ascertain this association to navigate safely through life's experiences (vv. 19-23). This requires that we do more than just hold on to truth; truth must hold us to the right course. Those who do this will be able to steer clear of trouble, sleep soundly at night, have confidence for tomorrow, and better discern the entrapments of the wicked (vv. 24-26).

Solomon then issues five prohibitory precepts to wisely guide his son's relationships with others. Do not withhold proper wages from hired servants (v. 27). Do not hold back from assisting the poor when you are able to do so (v. 28). Do not plot evil against your neighbor or falsely accuse him (v. 29). Do not strive with others without a just cause (v. 30). Do not envy those who profit from violence (v. 31). An explanation is provided for the latter prohibition – God opposes, even mocks, these perverse people and there is no way they will escape divine judgment (vv. 32-35). In contrast, the humble, the wise, and the righteous (traits which are connected throughout Proverbs) receive divine blessing, grace, and glory. In summary, living wisely for God ensures the most favorable existence possible while living on a sin-cursed planet; that is, it imparts a daily confidence in the Lord that produces inner peace and outward good. Such a person has a settled mind and yearns for their glorious inheritance to come. Indeed, wisdom rewards all who embrace her.

Proverbs 4

Fatherly Wisdom

Child-rearing in Proverbs focuses mainly on the shaping and protecting of a child's heart (3:1, 4:21, 23, 23:15). Unlike the mind, where reason is invoked and choices are made, the heart is "formed" and behaves as it has been conditioned. For example, exercising faith in the Lord is a decision of the heart; it is not an intellectual response. This is why it is easier for children to trust the Lord than well-educated or sin-hardened adults (Luke 18:17). Over time, godly training stimulates the mind to make proper choices, and the heart is formed emotionally in purity and godly values, though it is inherently defiled by a propensity to sin. Solomon, the son of David and Bathsheba, was taught the commandments of God and the way of wisdom, which he had to actively keep seeking (vv. 3-4). By quoting his father David in verses 4-9, Solomon was passing down the instruction he had received from his father to his children (vv. 1-2).

In this chapter, Solomon is apparently pleading with a particular son to treasure in his heart the instruction that he had received, to pursue wisdom, and not to depart from the right path that had been set before him (vv. 10-12, 20-23). F. C. Cook summarizes the ever-recurring parable of the journey of life: "In the way of wisdom the path is clear and open, obstacles disappear; in the quickest activity there is no risk of falling."[135] Thus, Solomon implores his son, as David advised him, to go after wisdom and instruction, personified as a woman, and to never let her go (vv. 5, 7, 13). Coupled with these exhortations is the warning to not trod the treacherous wide path of wickedness, but rather remain on the straight and illuminated path of the just (vv. 14-16).

To consort with the wicked, that is, to speak their perverse words and to engage in their violence, is like running in the dark and unwittingly falling into destruction (vv. 17, 19, 24). What is in one's heart eventually passes over one's lips. In contrast, when one receives wise instruction and guards his or her heart from corruption, that person enjoys a full, healthy life (vv. 4, 22) and receives honor for their good conduct (vv. 8-9). One can avoid much trouble in life by looking straight ahead and focusing on the known path of righteousness (vv. 25-27). The glory of God is evident in the lives of all those who heed true wisdom, which is fostered in the fear of the Lord (v. 18). Clearly it would be wise for us to heed Solomon's counsel as well; our hearts must be pliable to God's Word (2:2) and protected from debasing influences – *"for out of it* [the heart] *are the issues of life"* (v. 23).

Proverbs 5

The Foolishness of Immorality

How are we to understand Solomon's warning to his own son regarding not lusting after the immoral (*"the strange,"* KJV) woman, when he himself had seven hundred wives and three hundred concubines, many of whom were foreign women (1 Kgs. 11:3)? Though Solomon did marry these women, clearly he did not exercise

Devotions in Proverbs

wisdom in this aspect of his life (Deut. 17:17). In time, his many wives turned his heart from the Lord (1 Kgs. 11:4-8). As in the Song of Solomon, here he apparently wants to set the matter straight; God's design for marriage is one man and one woman bound by a covenant for life (Matt. 19:5-6). The central message to his own son, then, is one that married men should heed today: do not lust for what is outside the will of God (i.e., the unchaste woman), but rather seek to be faithful and satisfied with your own wife!

Solomon begins by telling his son to "listen up" and gain vital wisdom and discretion on an important matter – avoiding immorality (vv. 1-2). The seductive words, attire, and body language of a strange woman are captivating, deceptive, and lead to one end: death (vv. 3-6)! While one's unchecked lusting may be temporarily gratified through adultery, it is a terrible offense against one's own body (6:32; 1 Cor. 6:18), one's spouse (Mal. 2:13-15), and the Lord, which is why it was punishable by death (Lev. 20:10). Adultery is an act of rebellion against God's regulations for marriage and family order. Therefore, Solomon warns his son to avoid the seductive woman altogether; adultery has too high of a price tag associated with it (vv. 7-8). Besides invoking God's anger, suffering personal guilt, and losing the respect of others, immorality has long-term consequences such as the loss of wealth, health, and longevity (vv. 9-14). On this point, H. A. Ironside writes:

> To learn by painful experience, if the Word of God is not followed, is a bitter and solemn thing. God is not mocked; what is sown must be reaped. The unsteady hand, the confused brain, the bleared eye, premature age, and weakened powers, regretful days and nights of folly that can never be forgotten: these are a few of the physical results of failing to heed the advice of wisdom. In the Spiritual realm parallel results may be: lack of discernment, weakened spiritual sensitivities, undependable behavior, wasted time, and loss at the judgment seat of Christ.[136]

Solomon then explains the benefits of maintaining moral purity in marriage. When a man genuinely cherishes and cares for his wife and is faithful to her, the sexual interaction they share is enhanced and mutually gratifying (vv. 15-19). In this way the marriage covenant protects and enhances what is shared privately between a husband and wife. The wife is likened to a refreshing cistern which is abundantly

The Beginning of Wisdom

satisfying. Solomon warns his son not to drink from another man's cistern, but rather to be satisfied with his own wife (vv. 15, 20). All sexual energy and desires should be reserved and channeled into one's own marriage. On this matter of marriage fidelity, Matthew Henry writes:

> Let him then scorn the offer of forbidden pleasures when he is *always ravished with the love* of a faithful virtuous wife; let him consider what an absurdity it will be for him to be *ravished with a strange woman* (Prov. 5:20), to be in love with a filthy harlot, and *embrace the bosom of a stranger,* which, if he had any sense of honor or virtue, he would loathe the thoughts of. "Why wilt thou be so [stupefied], such an enemy to thyself, as to prefer puddle-water, and that poisoned too and stolen, before pure living waters out of thy own well?"[137]

Whether she is spoken of metaphorically or in plain language, a man is to have his own wife and none other. Let him enjoy his own vine, his own cistern, his own well – his own wife! William Kelly explains that though we live in a sin-cursed world, a society can still be blessed by God by yielding to His design for marriage and home-life:

> In contrast with the fleshly lusts which war against the soul, and even here have no result but shame, Jehovah set up the holy relations of marriage in the sinless paradise of Eden. What a safeguard for man when an outcast through his own sin! What folly and ungodliness the dream of a Plato, which would dispense with the reality of one's own wife, one's own husband, one's own children in his ideal republic! Certainly there was no wisdom, nor understanding, in such a scheme. It is vagrancy of the most debasing kind. How gracious of Him to warn and guard weak passionate man from his own ruinous will![138]

After reviewing both the rewards for marital faithfulness and the repercussions of immorality, Solomon reminds his son of two more important reasons to avoid adultery. First, although others may be unaware of the sin, God sees it and will judge the offenders (v. 21). Second, sin is deceitfully enslaving and when a man departs from the path of wisdom, his unchecked lusting eventually destroys him (vv. 22-23). In summary, we should be mindful of the long-term consequences of immorality and ignore the flesh's desire for immediate pleasure in that which is outside of God's will. God created the sexual relationship as a means of emotionally strengthening the bond of marriage in such a way that permits a husband and wife to enjoy full disclosure and intimacy in a way sex outside marriage can never obtain.

Proverbs 6

The Foolishness of Laziness, Adultery, and Disunity

Solomon levies a barrage of parental warnings to his son in this proverb. These represent the common instruction of both parents and were to be cherished daily throughout the son's life (vv. 20-23). While the prohibitions and consequences of associating with the wicked (vv. 12-15) and the unchaste woman (vv. 24-35) are repeated, several new topics of wisdom are also conveyed:

- Do not carelessly enter into a financial agreement in which you are assuming liability for another person. Examples would be co-signing a loan agreement, putting up collateral to secure a loan for someone, or assuming the high-interest responsibility of another. Jews were not to charge each other interest on loans, but rather help each other during times of financial distress (Lev. 25:35-37). While financially helping friends and family is noble, one should avoid such obligations with strangers. If one discerns that he or she has erred or was deceived in entering into such an agreement, that person should humbly go to the other party and ask to be released from their act of indiscretion (vv. 1-3).

- Do not be lazy and irresponsible (e.g., tarry in bed); rather, follow the ant's example of diligence and labor now, so you will not be in need later (vv. 4-8). The sleep of a laboring man is sweet, but the idleness of a sluggard results in poverty (vv. 9-11; Eccl. 5:12). Sleeping when one should be working is inconsistent with God's command to Adam: *"In the sweat of your face you shall eat bread"* (Gen. 3:19).

- Do not keep company with scoundrels and worthless persons; such are known by their perverse speech, secret gestures (signals) to fellow conspirators, and their propensity for mischief and sowing discord among friends (vv. 12-14). There is no deliverance for a person set on doing evil; that person ensures his or her own sudden demise (v. 15).

- Do not associate with an immoral woman; avoid personal destruction by ignoring her beauty, seductive speech, and sensual gestures (vv. 24-29). It is foolish to commit adultery because it damages one's own soul, incites jealousy and rage in others, and prompts God's inevitable judgment (vv. 32-35). Illicit sex is like playing with fire – the guilty will eventually get burned (vv. 27-28).

- Do not despise a thief who has stolen because he is starving (v. 30). Such a person was not considered guiltless and was to make sevenfold restitution for his crime; yet, he was to be granted judicial mercy, for his crime was on the basis of necessity. In contrast, there was to be no mercy for those guilty of adultery (v. 31).

Solomon reminds his son of seven things God hates: a proud look, a lying tongue, murder, devising wicked schemes, a swift inclination to do mischief, a false witness, and those who sow discord among God's people (vv. 16-19). These abominations include one sin of attitude, one of thought, two of speech, two of action, and one of influence, showing that the full product of the first six sins results in the latter offense of discord and division. Beware, brethren, when you cause needless division among God's people – the Lord hates it!

In the practical sense, Christian fellowship is dependent on how much we determine we have in common with other believers. While it is true that we will not be able to have the same degree of fellowship with all believers, we should strive to walk as far as we can with all those who have been redeemed by the precious blood of Christ. So often believers cast others aside because of some difference in thinking, though they hold much more in common than what they disagree about – this wrong mindset hinders the fellowship Christ desires for the members of His body to enjoy. The fact of the matter is that those in the Church are not going to agree on everything on this side of glory (Eph. 4:13). Coming into unity with all brethren in Christ will be one of the purest blessings of heaven. Until then, we should conclude that only God knows His own mind perfectly and endeavor to maintain the unity that the Holy Spirit secures for us (Eph. 4:3).

Proverbs 7

The Foolishness of Fornication

Solomon solemnly warns his son of the consequences of being enticed by the immoral woman and then being led captive by one's own lusts, the end of which is immense sorrow and misery. He therefore again urges his son to obey his commandments and bind them to his heart (vv. 1-3). His son is further instructed to embrace wisdom as a sister, rather than to foolishly consort with a strange woman (vv. 4-5). In Solomon's illustration, he pictures a young man void of understanding strolling down a dark street in which an immoral woman resides (vv. 6-8). Seeing her prey, this skilled seductress appeals to all five senses of her next naïve victim:

- Flattering speech and fair words – hearing (vv. 5, 18).
- Spicy attire – sight (v. 10).
- A kiss – taste (v. 13).
- Seductive gestures – touch (v. 13).
- Perfumed bed – smell (v. 17).

While women are generally excited by emotional interaction with the opposite sex, men are aroused through sensual stimulation. Accordingly, the inexperienced young man of this story, after having all five of his senses bombarded by this seductress, does not resist her temptation. She further affirms to her quarry that they will not be caught, for it is dark (v. 9). She had a private location for them to enjoy each other all night (v. 16); everyone else was away, including her husband (vv. 19-20). She is not only a married woman, but also a religious woman: *"I have peace offerings with me; today I have paid my vows"* (v. 14). Her proclaimed spirituality was an attempt to make her immoral conduct seem more acceptable. Many ignorant fools through the ages have fallen for this same ploy. Stirred up in his lusting, he casts reason aside (v. 21) and yields to her urging: *"He goes after her straightway, as an ox goes to the slaughter"* (v. 22). He is not the first casualty, for she has brought many strong men down into destruction (vv. 26-27).

We learn in this chapter that the sexual sin of the woman is to lure (v. 21) and the sexual sin of the man is to follow (v. 22). It seems that after one thousand wives and concubines Solomon finally understood that unchecked gazing leads to more lusting and more lusting promotes immoral behavior. He said, *"The eye is not satisfied with seeing, nor the ear filled with hearing"* (Eccl. 1:8). Our flesh nature is never gratified – it always wants more than what is reasonable and what God permits. Practically speaking, a wife needs to work at appealing to her husband's senses to arouse him, while her husband should appeal to his wife's emotions to affirm security and his singular devotion. The goal is mutual satisfaction, so there will be no need or desire to look elsewhere for sexual gratification.

The home is a safe haven for a wife and mother (Ps. 128:3; 1 Tim. 2:5); it is her God-given domain of service and responsibility (1 Tim. 5:14; Tit. 2:4-5). But the unchaste woman is loud and boisterous; she does not want to abide where God would have her be; rather, she gladly wreaks havoc in other marriages and families as witnessed in this sorrowful narrative.

Proverbs 8

Cherish Wisdom

In the previous proverb, the immoral woman's seductive words entrapped the simpleminded, but in this poem, Solomon permits Wisdom (i.e., a personified attribute of God) to have her say. As in Proverbs 1, she is quite vocal in proclaiming her message (vv. 1-4). She cries out to all men, but especially to the simpleminded and the foolish, to receive her counsel and instruction so that they may obtain understanding (v. 5). These individuals should trust her, for she speaks in plain terms what is true and righteous; there is nothing perverse or inaccurate in her speech (vv. 6-9).

Accordingly, the understanding that she imparts should be diligently sought and is more valuable than silver, gold, or rubies (vv. 10-11); in fact, those who heed her counsel will enjoy prosperity, peace, and honor (vv. 18-21). Wisdom possesses understanding and strength; it is by these that the kings of the earth are able to effectively rule their various dominions (vv. 14-16). Those who are wise will search her out and cherish her early in life (v. 17). Prudence walks with Wisdom (v. 12), and she too proclaims an important message for all to hear: *"The fear of the Lord is to hate evil; pride and arrogance and the evil way and the perverse mouth I hate"* (v. 13). This is a warning that we would do well to heed today!

The tone of the poem changes in verse 22. As Wisdom reminisces of bygone days in eternity past, a broader reflection of divine emotion, character, and attributes are revealed than just what is associated with wisdom alone. As C. I. Scofield suggests, this can be none other than a fuller expression of what is associated with the second person of the Godhead:

That wisdom is more than the personification of an attribute of God, or of the will of God as best for man, but is a distinct foreshadowing of Christ, is certain. Proverbs 8:22-36, with John 1:1-3; 1 Cor. 1:24; and Col. 2:3 can refer to no one less than the eternal Son of God.[139]

So, while the divine attribute of wisdom has always existed, because God is self-existent and is eternal, the One spoken of in verses 22-36 is more than an attribute, but enjoys a tender familiarity with God the Father Himself. This is seen in verses 22-29, which speak of a time before time, the dawning days of creation, and the extraordinary process of laying the foundations of the world; these read synonymously with John 1:1-3:

In the beginning was the Word, and the Word was with God, and the Word was God. He was in the beginning with God. All things were made through Him, and without Him nothing was made that was made.

The Beginning of Wisdom

The Word, the Lord Jesus Christ, is not only the delight of His Father (v. 30), but also invigorates those sons of men who keep His way with joy and blessing (vv. 31-32; John 14:6). Indeed, those who heed God's message of wisdom (receive the Living Word) obtain wisdom, blessing, favor with God, and eternal life with Him (vv. 33-35). Those who reject it sin against the Lord and wrong their own soul and suffer eternal death (v. 36). Speaking of the Lord Jesus, the Living Word of God, John writes:

> *He who believes in Him is not condemned; but he who does not believe is condemned already, because he has not believed in the name of the only begotten Son of God* (John 3:18).

Initially, Wisdom, as an attribute of God, spoke her warning, but then the One who possesses all wisdom and much more is heard to express His devotion for His Father and His passion for the sons of men to receive life and not suffer death. Then as well as today, His message is clear: *"For whoever finds me finds life"* (v. 35)!

Proverbs 9

Wisdom Is Praised

Continuing his literary style of personification, Solomon presents Wisdom as a hospitable homemaker. She invites all who lack understanding to reject foolishness and make their abode with her; her enormous house is well furnished; her guests will lack nothing and receive all that is needed for godly living (vv. 1-6). The way in which people respond to Wisdom is then contrasted. A just man desires instruction and a wise man requests correction because of the benefits gained: more understanding and increased wisdom (v. 9). Because of his pride, the scoffer will not receive reproof; instead, he will resent the one offering rebuke, even if it is justified (vv. 7-8). In such cases it is best not to waste time admonishing the uncorrectable fool; the outcome of doing so is worse than the beginning (26:4). Harry A. Ironside contrasts the response of a scoffer and of a wise man to rebuke:

The more shallow and empty a man is, the less willing he is to listen to godly counsel; whereas, the truly wise are glad to learn from any who can correct and instruct. As a rule, the less a man knows, the more he thinks he knows. The more he really does know, the more he realizes his ignorance and his limitations. Hence the value of godly counsel from those who seek to be exercised by God's Word. Reproof will only be wasted on the scorner. He will delight in ridiculing all who endeavor to turn him from his folly, however pure their motives.[140]

The theme of Proverbs is succinctly stated in verse 10: *"The fear of the Lord is the beginning of wisdom, and the knowledge of the Holy one is understanding."* To know God is knowledge. In his early years, Solomon's son learned that *"The fear of the Lord is the beginning of knowledge, but fools despise wisdom and instruction"* (1:7). Now that Solomon's son is advancing in the school of life, Wisdom instructs him that it is foolish to live without God in the world. True wisdom is inseparable from the fear of the Lord; it is man's starting point in understanding the mind of God and enables him to resolve questions otherwise inscrutable.

Those who heed Wisdom's invitation will find life and blessing, but those who do not will be responsible for their own destruction (vv. 11-12). To further accentuate this point, Solomon compares Wisdom's house of blessing to the home of an immoral woman who brings death to all those who enter into it (vv. 13-18). William MacDonald explains the words of the seductress, *"Stolen water is sweet, and bread eaten in secret is pleasant"* (v. 17): "Basically she means that illicit intercourse is attractive because it is forbidden and because there is the intrigue of secrecy about it. When fallen human nature is forbidden to do a certain thing, that prohibition stirs up the desire to do it all the more (Rom. 7:7-8)."[141] Hence, the sensual invitation of the provocative woman is quite enticing to the inherent wanton instinct of the young man. Essentially, Solomon is posing a dramatic question: "Whose house will you abide in, my son? Will it be Wisdom's house of peace, blessing, and eternal life, or the abode of the foolish?" In the latter house one learns through experience that pursuing temporary pleasure leads to death and misery. May we too count the long-term cost of sin and choose to abide with the Lord in His wisdom.

Proverbs 10

Wisdom and Godly Fear Contrasted With Folly and Sin

This chapter begins the next major division within the book, chapters 10-24, which is strictly proverbial in nature. Solomon's passionate plea for his son to heed wisdom, reject foolishness, and avoid evil companions (including the immoral woman) transitions into a much broader contrast between wisdom founded in godly fear and the folly associated with a wasted life of sin. The poetry in Proverbs 10 through 24 contains 375 stand-alone pithy moral axioms to guide daily living. This section is not thematic in nature like the previous nine chapters. Many of the thirty sayings in Proverbs 22:17-24:22 and the additional six sayings of Proverbs 24:23-34 are posed as warnings, i.e., "do not ..." and usually require two to four lines to complete the thought. This format stands in contrast to the one verse expressions which characterize Proverbs 10:1-22:16. Sid Buzzell comments further regarding the literary style used by Solomon in this middle section of the book:

> Most of the verses in chapters 10-15 are contrasts (in antithetic parallelism); the second line in most of the verses begins with "but." Only a few of the verses in 16:1-22:16 are contrasts; most of the verses are either comparisons (in synonymous parallelism) or completions (in synthetic parallelism), with the conjunction "and" introducing the second line in many of the verses.[142]

In the absence of a central thematic development, the author has chosen to simply highlight points of wisdom and foolishness as compared and contrasted in the next fifteen chapters.

The Wise and Their Reward:
- Wise children are a delight to their parents (v. 1).
- Living a righteous life in the fear of the Lord avoids the pitfalls of sin and earns God's blessing, an honorable name to be remembered, and a long and joyful life; such shall be sustained by the Lord (vv. 2-3, 5-7, 27-30).
- Diligent hands will not lack God's blessing (v. 4).

- The wise gladly receive God's commandments and correction, walk in righteousness, rely on the Lord, speak edifying words of health and understanding, and are marked by a disposition of love and forgiveness (vv. 8-18).
- The wise refrain from much talking, choosing rather to speak choice words which encourage and edify others (vv. 19-21, 31-32).
- The righteous have God's blessing, peace, and eternal life (vv. 22-25).

The Foolish and their Punishment:
- Foolish children cause their parents grief (v. 1).
- Engaging in wickedness does not profit, earns shame, results in violence, and shortens one's life; such shall lose what they have obtained and perish by their own devices (vv. 2-3, 5-7, 27-30).
- *"Violence covers the mouth of the wicked"* (v. 6): F. C. Cook suggests that the violence the wicked has done is "like a bandage over his mouth, reducing him to a silence and shame, like that of the leper or the condemned criminal whose face is covered."[143]
- Laziness results in poverty and frustrates others (vv. 4, 26).
- The foolish are self-sufficient, they wink to betray their lying lips, and they will not receive reproof; they are proud, violent, slanderous, and harbor resentment in their hearts which stirs up strife in others (vv. 8-18).
- The wicked speak perverse things, and in the multitude of their words their foolishness and sin is apparent (vv. 19-21, 31-32).
- The wicked shall ultimately suffer sorrow, anxiety, and shall perish in just retribution (vv. 22-25).

During difficult times, the Lord's people may be tempted to compromise wisdom and righteousness to alleviate their distressing circumstances. However, the end of such reasoning will only make matters worse, for *"He who walks with integrity walks securely"* (v. 9) and *"the Lord will not allow the righteous soul to famish"* (v. 3). When things go wrong, we should not go wrong with them; the One who created the universe knows all about it and is in full control to work the challenging situation for good (Rom. 8:28).

Proverbs 11

Righteousness and Lawlessness Contrasted

The Righteous and the Wise:
- The righteous engage in honest business practices (v. 1), demonstrate wisdom in humility (v. 2), are guided by integrity (vv. 3, 5); their righteous living and godly fear preserve them from self-initiated calamities (vv. 4, 6-10, 23).
- The upright seek godly counsel in decisions and bless others. They are long-suffering, discrete, and slow to speak; they conceal offenses from others, do not repeat gossip, and avoid ungodly companions (vv. 11-14, 21-22).
- Honorable people are a delight to the Lord, who duly rewards them; they are marked by grace, mercy, frugality, the pursuance of righteousness, and the avoidance of debt (vv. 15-20, 24-26).
- The wise will flourish in the earth because they diligently seek to do good, thus leading others to the Lord as channels of blessing (vv. 27-31).

The Wicked and the Foolish:
- The wicked employ deceitful business practices (v. 1) and are proud, which prompts their shame (v. 2). They rely on perverse speech (vv. 3, 5) and trust in their riches; however, their iniquity will eventually lead them into destruction (v. 4, 6-10, 23).
- The wicked are void of wisdom, depend on their own judgment, despise those who have offended them, repeat gossip, cannot keep a secret, associate with evil companions, and cause others to suffer by their perverse speech (vv. 11-14).
- The wicked are an abomination to the Lord and are known by their deceitful ways, cruelty, and by spending money they do not have; these behaviors result in their own ruin (vv. 15-21, 24-26).
- A woman's outward beauty can be negated by indiscretion (v. 22).
- Those seeking mischief will find it, procuring trouble not only for themselves, but also their household; in the end they will achieve nothing, but the wise will be honored (vv. 27-30).

Harry A. Ironside suggests genuine humility is evidence that one possesses God-fearing wisdom:

> Nothing is more detestable in God's sight than pride on the part of creatures who have absolutely nothing to be proud of. This was the condemnation of the devil – self-exaltation. ... Humility is an indication of true wisdom. It characterizes the man who has learned to judge himself correctly in the presence of God.[144]

Although our determination and natural abilities may secure for us fame and wealth, such status will be short-lived if accompanied by pride and character that is not God-fearing: *"The righteousness of the blameless will direct his way aright, but the wicked will fall by his own wickedness"* (v. 5). Let us therefore not trust in the uncertainty of riches, but rather let us put our confidence in the Lord, who freely bestows to us all good things to enjoy (1 Tim. 6:17-19; Jas. 1:17).

Proverbs 12

Righteousness and Lawlessness Contrasted

The Righteous and the Wise:
- The righteous love instruction and obtain favor from the Lord; they shall not be moved (vv. 1-3).
- The just ponder righteous thoughts, speak uprightly, and their endeavors are established by God; they are commended for their wisdom, prudence, and long-suffering nature (vv. 5-8).
- The righteous man cares for his animals, diligently labors to provide for his family's needs, tells the truth, and learns from the wise lest he repeat their mistakes (vv. 9-16).
- The truth and words of wisdom and health that promote joy and peace are marks of a righteous person (vv. 17-20).
- Those who speak truthfully declare the integrity of their hearts and are a delight to the Lord; these will not be overtaken by evil (vv. 21-22).
- The prudent man is able to keep a secret, respects authority, is diligent with his hands, is not wasteful, and chooses his companions

carefully; such a man is blessed in life because he walks in the ways of righteousness (vv. 24-28).

These latter verses would suggest that it is foolish for someone to convey any bit of knowledge that they may possess on a particular topic in order to appear wiser than they really are. Such vanity will be exposed with each shallow attempt to seem deep.

The Wicked and the Foolish:
- The wicked hate reproof, are rejected by God for their evil devices, and will not be established (vv. 1-3).
- The counsel of the wicked is deceit and their words are murderous to others; God will overthrow all who have such evil in their hearts – they shall be despised (vv. 5-8).
- The wicked are cruel to animals and rely on other evil men and their schemes to obtain gain; they are prone to lie, to reject counsel, to laziness, and to wrath, but are noble in their own eyes (vv. 9-16).
- Lying, deceit, hurtful speech, and being led by evil imaginations of the heart are characteristics of a wicked person (vv. 17-20).
- Those who speak lies are an abomination to the Lord and shall suffer much mischief (vv. 21-22).
- The fool proclaims the folly in his heart, is slothful, is easily seduced by wicked men, and is careless with his possessions; such a man will suffer loss and be forced to work for others (vv. 24-28).

Pondering the first seven verses of this chapter, William Kelly offers this insightful synopsis:

> As original uprightness was lost in the fall, even if there be a new nature by grace, soul discipline is ever needed, and blessed in the genuine humility that values knowledge from on high. Pride and vanity are alike disdainful of reproof, and therefore go from bad to worse. Those unwilling to own their faults or to submit to God's faithful dealings sink below humanity.[145]

In verse 4, Solomon contrasts the immense blessing a virtuous wife can be to her husband with the detrimental influence that a self-seeking and tumultuous woman can have on him: *"An excellent wife is the crown of her husband, but she who causes shame is like rottenness in his bones."* When a wife ministers to her husband in such a way as to promote healthy stature and spiritual vitality, she becomes a crown to her husband's head. However, if a wife influences her husband to forsake reason, doubt God, and transgress His Word, she is akin to an aggressive bone cancer. Instead of a "helpmeet," she is a "tripmate," and consequently, her husband's spiritual prominence wanes before God and man. A wife bent on discouraging her husband with harsh words, or worse, hindering his spiritual growth Godward, is likened to a cancer that rots his bones. Without healthy bones, we would be reduced to a spasmodic blob of gushy tissue. Bones provide structure and stature to the body. How does one maintain healthy bones? Solomon answers this question: *"And a good report makes the bones healthy"* (Prov. 15:30). *"Pleasant words are like a honeycomb, sweetness to the soul and health to the bones"* (Prov. 16:24). Truth, grace, honesty, encouragement, respect, and devotion all convey a "good report" to one's husband and promote healthy bones. Praise the Lord for such faithful helpers!

Proverbs 13

Righteousness and Lawlessness Contrasted

The Righteous and the Wise:
- A wise son receives parental instruction (he gladly learns from the experience of others), and speaks with discretion (vv. 1-3).
- The righteous man hates lying and is diligent with his hands; such a man is established in life because of his just behavior (vv. 4-6).
- The righteous man is more than what he possesses, he delights in understanding the truth, seeks godly counsel, labors diligently to obtain necessities and uses them discerningly; he honors the law and authority in general, and savors knowledge and understanding (vv. 7-16).
- The prudent man is a faithful representative of what is good, receives reproof and thereby honor, is faithful to complete a task properly, has wise companions, leaves an inheritance for his grandchildren (vv. 17-22).

- The wise man follows the divine pattern of discipline to train his own children because he loves them; he understands that both grace and restraint are a necessary part of child rearing (v. 24).
- The wise man is satisfied with what he obtains by diligent labor (vv. 23, 25).

As Derek Kidner surmises, the overall point of this terse chapter seems to be "that size of your resources matters less than the judgment with which you handle them."[146] Accordingly, the wise discerningly use what they diligently obtain, whereas the slothful fool often squanders the little he does have.

The Wicked and the Foolish:
- The depraved son scoffs at rebuke, and is prone to violence and destructive speech (vv. 1-3).
- The wicked man is lazy and a liar; such a man is loathsome to others and will be overthrown in shame (vv. 4-6).
- The wicked man measures himself by his possessions, is proud and prone to stir up contention, uses unethical means to obtain wealth, despises law and order, and transgresses according to his own folly (vv. 7-16).
- The wicked man is prone to mischief and foolishness, and suffers poverty and shame because he does not receive instruction, but rather associates with fools; such a man will lose his possessions and be in want until the day of his destruction (vv. 17-25).

Solomon reminds us of two important realities concerning division among God's people. First, God intensely loathes those who sow discord among His people (6:19). Second, pride is a primary fountainhead from which strife springs (v. 10; 1 Tim. 6:4-6). Commenting on verse 10, *"By pride comes nothing but strife, but with the well-advised is wisdom,"* Harry A. Ironside writes:

> It is an old saying that "it takes two to make a quarrel." Contention begins when the effort to maintain a foolish dignity prevails, or the heart covets what belongs to another. The strife soon ceases when the offended one meets his offender in lowliness and grace. Wisdom

enables the well-advised to give the soft answer that turns away wrath.[147]

All the disunity and contention within the Church today is the result of our pride in one form or another. Nothing good can come from pride! This is why Paul admonished the believers at Philippi to follows Christ's example of selfless humility: *"Let nothing be done through strife or vainglory; but in lowliness of mind let each esteem others better than themselves"* (Phil. 2:3; KJV). As R. C. Chapman attests, this is the best defense against the pride that naturally consumes us:

> In 1 Corinthians 15:28 we read: *"Then shall the Son also Himself be subject,"* and in Revelation, *"The throne of God and of the Lamb."* Christ is forever the Shepherd and forever the Lamb, and it is the lowly or little Lamb, the diminutive being used. There is an infiniteness in the lowliness of the blessed Lamb, and He is now at the utmost of His lowliness. Satan took upon himself the form of a master, being created a servant; instead of serving in obedience he would be lord, and "the condemnation of the devil" is in his self-will; he chose to take to himself what belonged only to God. What a rebuke to the devil the exaltation of the Son of God will be to all eternity – a mirror in which to see his own folly! Acquaintance with the Cross of Christ brings me to nothing! Let any thought of self-exaltation be to me as a serpent; I have nothing to do but to kill it![148]

Strife is the devil's way to get one's way, but lowliness permits God to judge legitimate wrongs His way, which is always the best way. How do we know this is true? Vengeance (justified wrath for sin) is the Lord's alone (Rom. 12:19); only He can rightly dispense wrath to humble the proud heart (Job 40:11-12); the wrath of man does not work the righteousness of God (Jas. 1:20).

Proverbs 14

Righteousness and Lawlessness Contrasted

The Righteous and the Wise:

The Beginning of Wisdom

- A wise woman is industrious and through wise preparation seeks to build up her home (literally she is a *"home-maker"*) (v. 1).
- The upright fear the Lord; they understand knowledge, exercise wisdom, and are preserved by their discreet speech, sound administration, and a faithful testimony (vv. 2-8).
- The righteous make amends for wrongdoing, carefully consider the integrity of others' speech, fear the Lord and depart from evil; they shall flourish and be happy in life (vv. 9-17).
- The prudent seek knowledge and are honored (v. 18).
- The righteous exercise mercy and truth and are happy and respected for selflessly helping others (vv. 19-22).
- The wise will prosper in their labors, limit their words, and speak truthfully; their confidence is in the Lord (vv. 23-28).
- Because the righteous have knowledge, wisdom, and a sound heart, they are slow to wrath, quick to show mercy to the poor, and have the hope of being exalted and living with God after death (vv. 29-35).

The Wicked and the Foolish:
- A foolish woman is slothful and permits her home to fall into disarray and chaos (v. 1).
- The perverse despise the Lord. Their foolishness is founded in pride; they are prone to lie and scoff at wisdom and knowledge and therefore should be avoided (vv. 2-8). As an example, they can justify killing their oxen, needed for farming, so that they do not have to clean stalls (v. 4).
- The fool offers no restitution for his sin, but rather goes his own way. He haphazardly accepts the words of others, is self-confident, and is quick to anger and prone to rage; this person shall be overthrown and suffer death (vv. 9-17).
- Those void of understanding (i.e., the gullible and the simple-minded) engage in foolishness (v. 18).
- The wicked despise their neighbors, devise evil, and do not care for the needs of others (vv. 19-22).
- The fool labors with his lips instead of his hands; he or she speaks rashly, deceitfully, and without reverence for the Lord (vv. 23-28).

- Because the wicked are void of knowledge, they are hasty in judgments, prone to envy, and do evil; consequently, their foolishness is apparent to all and they will suffer shame, wrath, and death (vv. 29-35).

From a theoretical standpoint, a society that adheres to absolute morality rather than moral relativity would be characterized by less violence. If naturalism were true, more aggression would be expected in a society in which each individual pressed for his or her own personal security and survival over the wellbeing of others. If naturalism were not true, this realization may still be observed, for as a people ignore their moral programming, their consciences, that society will primarily be occupied with pursuing personal gain and selfish indulgences, rather than the good of others. In either case, moral behavior where self is preeminent and the welfare of others is ignored will lead to the demise of a society, not to its beneficial development. Solomon warns, *"As righteousness leads to life, so he who pursues evil pursues it to his own death"* (11:19). *"Righteousness exalts a nation, but sin is a reproach to any people"* (v. 34). Moral relativity devolves human society into chaos, while the pursuit of divine righteousness leads to prosperity – God's blessing. Ultimately, a society's conduct is a direct reflection of their attitude towards God, and where God is not revered, man will not prosper.

Proverbs 15

Righteousness and Lawlessness Contrasted

The Righteous and the Wise:
- The skillful speech of the wise is founded in knowledge; it defuses anger, soothes, refreshes, and heals (vv. 1-4). Harry A. Ironside further explains the wise person is one who possesses restraint when his or her feelings are moving otherwise:

It takes far more true character to meet an angry man in quietness of spirit, and to return cool, calm words for heated, hasty ones. The man who controls his tongue shows that he has his personal feelings in subjection. The man who returns malice for malice reveals that he does not yet know how to rule his spirit. Grievous words only add fuel to the flame; a gracious demeanor will go far towards cooling the angry passions of another.[149]

- The Lord loves those who receive instruction, disperse wisdom, walk uprightly; their prayers delight the heart of God and they shall have a joyful existence (vv. 5-14).
- Happiness is not achieved in things, but rather by a disposition of the heart that both fears the Lord and rejoices in Him; this results in a willingness to sacrificially love others (vv. 15-17).
- The wise man honors authority, seeks godly counsel, is industrious, speaks seasoned words at the appropriate time, and is slow to anger; such a man will be joyful and have God's favor (vv. 18-25).
- The Lord is pleased with those who consider a matter before speaking what is pure and beneficial; the just do not profit through dishonest means and, thankfully, the Lord promises to honor their prayers (vv. 26-29).
- The wise are humble and will be honored because they fear the Lord and are willing to listen to and heed reproof in order to gain understanding (vv. 30-33).

The Wicked and the Foolish:
- The words of the fool are perverse, grievous, stir up anger, and produce anxiety in others (vv. 1-4).
- The Lord hates those who snub authority, loath wisdom, and reject reproof and correction; these shall suffer sorrow, devastation, and ultimately death (vv. 5-14).
- Depression results when the meaning of life is determined by temporal things and human relationships; a self-focused existence in lieu of a God-focused one is detrimental to one's spiritual vitality and results in misery, trouble, and hatred (vv. 15-17).
- The foolish man despises authority and godly counsel, is slothful, is wrathful, and stirs up strife with his words; such a man is proud and will be destroyed by the Lord (vv. 18-25).
- The Lord hates even the thoughts of the wicked because they are greedy, speak evil, and pursue dishonest gain; the Lord does not

assist them, but permits them to suffer the peril of their own making (vv. 26-29).
- The foolish bring about the demise of their own soul because they do not fear the Lord, nor do they desire to hear reproof and gain understanding (vv. 30-33).

How can an omnipresent God be far from the wicked (v. 29)? While God is omnipresent, He visibly reveals Himself to man within the realities of time and space in order that man might be aware of His abiding presence. God cannot have communion or fellowship with the wicked, so in this respect He is far from them, that is, He remains unknown by them though He is actually quite near to them (Rom. 10:6-7). The great privilege of the righteous is to know the Lord and to personally abide with Him while they fulfill their divine calling (John 14:16; 1 Cor. 7:24).

Proverbs 16

Righteousness and Lawlessness Contrasted

The Righteous and the Wise:
- The righteous commit themselves and all their endeavors to the Lord; as a result, their pure thoughts and ways will be established, and God will bless them with wise speech (vv. 1-3, 9, 33).
- In the fear of the Lord, the righteous depart from evil and pursue mercy, truth, and wisdom; God blesses them with peace and a joyful disposition (vv. 6-7, 16-17, 20-23).
- It is better to live simply with a modest income in righteousness, than to have much in wickedness (vv. 8, 19).
- Human government was established by God; therefore, those in authority must represent God's righteousness in their decisions – such a leader avoids wrath and is appreciated by the people (vv. 10, 12-15).
- Being slow to anger, exercising discretion, and only speaking words which encourage and edify others are characteristics of the wise (vv. 24, 32). Ambitious men have conquered nations, but were defeated because they could not control themselves; thus, self-

The Beginning of Wisdom

mastery, as evidenced by a well-controlled tongue, is one of life's greatest victories.
- Gray hair in one's autumn years is a crown of beauty because it symbolizes God's reward for righteous living, a long life (v. 31).

The Wicked and the Foolish:
- Though the ways of man may be well-prepared and seem right, these ultimately lead to death; God knows and will judge all unclean thoughts and motives in such things (vv. 1-2, 25).
- The Lord works all things for His glory, even the evil and proud doings of the wicked, who in no way will escape His fierce judgment (vv. 4-5, 18).
- The wicked use unjust weights to cheat others (v. 11).
- A wrathful leader destroys his people and a wicked ruler is an offense to God (vv. 12, 14).
- The perverse man creates evil in his mind, conveys it with critical gestures and facial expressions, and then gossips his evil imaginations to others; this stirs up violence and causes division among God's people (vv. 27-30).

We read in verse 1: *"The preparations of the heart belong to man, but the answer of the tongue is from the Lord"* (v. 1). There are many instances of this truth in Scripture, but perhaps one of the best is contained in the book of Ezra. In a spirit of humility, Ezra prepared his heart to seek the law of the Lord, to do it, and to teach it (Ezra 7:10). God responded by stirring King Artaxerxes's heart to grant all that Ezra desired to do and even more than what he requested (Ezra 7:27). Ezra understood what it meant to prepare his heart, and to wait on the Lord, but do we? Is there any adversary, any political figure, or any earthly authority that can move against the will of God? Why then do we fret and worry about what only God can control? Ezra, recognizing God was with him, stepped forward in faith (Ezra 7:28). As a result, God blessed him with wise speech and he was used to bring revival to Israel. A contrasting example is found in King Rehoboam, who cherished the counsel of men rather than a word from the Lord; as a result, he did evil in the sight of God. Why? Because he had not prepared his heart to seek the Lord (2 Chron. 12:14). Solomon stated such behavior results in death (v. 25). Whatever is right and true among men originates with

God. Accordingly, we prepare ourselves for service as we read, memorize, meditate on, and yield to God's Word (v. 3). The Holy Spirit will guide a prepared heart to seek and serve the Lord (Matt. 10:19; Luke 21:12-15)!

Proverbs 17

Righteousness and Lawlessness Contrasted

The Righteous and the Wise:
- It is wise to be content with little, rather than to have much and be in turmoil (v. 1).
- God tests the hearts of His people to better refine them (v. 3).
- Grandchildren demonstrate parenting success or failure; children glory in fathers who wisely reared them up for the Lord (vv. 2, 6).
- Those in leadership must represent God's authority by telling the truth and not accepting bribes (vv. 7-8).
- It is wise to express love by releasing and forgiving the offenses of others, instead of causing division through gossip or contentious words (vv. 9, 14, 17).
- A joyful spirit is therapeutic to everyone (v. 22).
- It is wise to spare one's words (vv. 27-28).

Solomon informs us that a true friend loves at all times, especially during seasons of adversity (v. 17). On this point, D. L. Moody colorfully remarked: "a true friend is like ivy – the greater the ruin, the closer he clings."[150]

The Wicked and the Foolish:
- The wicked respect the deceitful ways of a liar, mock the poor, and rejoice in the calamites of others; they will not go unpunished (vv. 4-5).
- The fool refuses correction and his folly is perilous to the righteous; an evil man is rebellious in all his ways (vv. 10-12).

The Beginning of Wisdom

- Those who return evil for good, justify the wicked, condemn or punish the just, exalt themselves, or take bribes to pervert justice will be judged by God (vv. 13, 15, 19, 23, 26).
- A foolish child prompts parental sorrow and grief (vv. 21, 25).
- A fool does not value wisdom, sells himself into poverty, and babbles without discretion (vv. 16, 18, 24).

Solomon wrote, *"He who covers a transgression seeks love, but he who repeats a matter separates friends"* (v. 17). Gossip is like a dangerous virus that sweeps through whole communities through personal interactions. It secretly infects each person it comes in contact with, unless that person has acquired immunity against it. The consequences of this dangerous infection are realized much later, and may be long-lasting, and may even result in death. Gossip, or slanderous whispering, does not propagate the truth in love, but has the objective of degrading another's character, thus damaging his or her reputation and ministry. Those who repeat gossip needlessly infect others with this dangerous virus. Praise God for those who are immune to this sin as shown by neither listening to nor repeating what would unnecessarily infect others with evil and inevitably cause them harm. U. S. Naval Admiral Hyman Rickover summarized gossip this way: "Great minds discuss ideas. Average minds discuss events. Small minds discuss people."[151] The spiritual mind muses upon Christ and eternal truth. What kind of mind do you have? The tongue is the tail of the heart that wags out of the mouth, for *"those things which proceed out of the mouth come from the heart, and they defile a man"* (Matt. 15:18). Whatever is in your heart will eventually come out your mouth.

Proverbs 18

Righteousness and Lawlessness Contrasted

The Righteous and the Wise:
- The righteous value the Lord's name and do not want to blaspheme it through inappropriate behavior (v. 10).
- The righteous understand that humility precedes honor (v. 12).

- The wise seek knowledge and wisdom, not flattery; they fully consider a situation before answering it, as the first appearance of things is usually not the reality of the matter (vv. 13-17). A wise person does not grip a one-sided story!
- The wise understand that the tongue can encourage, edify, and promote friendships, or it can cause great devastation, even separating friends unnecessarily (vv. 19-21, 24).
- The wise man understands that a godly wife is a great blessing from the Lord and she should be treated as such; God created and is pleased with marriage (v. 22).

The thought of verse 24 is better conveyed in the NASV: *"A man of too many friends comes to ruin, but there is a friend who sticks closer than a brother."* It is not in the multitude of so-called friends that help is found, but in a true and loving friend. Every believer is the Lord's friend and He will never fail us, His friends, even when everyone else may (John 15:13-15).

The Wicked and the Foolish:
- It is foolish to isolate one's self from human accountability and wise counsel to pursue personal desires (vv. 1-2).
- With wickedness comes contempt, dishonor, and scorn; it is foolish to respect such a person, especially at the expense of the righteous (vv. 3-5).
- The words of a fool stir up contention and cause destruction and those who gossip inflict deep wounds (vv. 6-8).
- Laziness and carelessness results in great waste (v. 9); yet, it is foolish to seek honor and security through obtaining wealth (vv. 9, 11).
- In the multitude of words a fool is gratified, and identified (v. 20).

Verse 10 reads, *"The name of the Lord is a strong tower; the righteous run to it and are safe."* Why could David charge a giant named Goliath in battle? The honor of God's name was at stake! The people were unconcerned that the name of their God was brought into disrepute, but David felt the matter keenly: *"Then David said to the Philistine, 'You come to me with a sword, with a spear, and with a javelin. But I come to you in the name of the Lord of Hosts, the God of*

The Beginning of Wisdom

the armies of Israel, whom you have defied'" (1 Sam. 17:45). David courageously defended the Lord's name because he understood that *"the name of the Lord is a strong tower; the righteous run to it and are safe"* (v. 10). Likewise, our conduct must consider Christ and His name first in all things, for we are His saints. Believers compose the household of God, His living temple on earth to shine forth His virtue; God forbid that we disdain His name before the nations through corrupt or cowardly conduct.

Proverbs 19

Righteousness and Lawlessness Contrasted

The Righteous and the Wise:
- The wise walk in the fear of the Lord and value integrity more than wealth or the shallow friendships it can buy (vv. 1, 4, 6-7, 16, 22, 23). Zeal alone will not preserve one's walk with the Lord; we must also be men and women of integrity.
- The righteous seek wisdom and understanding to walk in purity; they are also slow to anger and able to absorb the offenses of others without reviling back at them (vv. 8, 11, 20).
- The wise man understands that a prudent wife is far better than a great inheritance, but a contentious wife is a constant irritation (vv. 13-14). A wise man today should realize the same truth, but with the added understanding that he should only marry "in the Lord" (that is, in His will; 1 Cor. 7:39), not just "in Christ" (that is, a fellow believer).
- Those who give to the poor are blessed by the Lord (v. 17).

The Wicked and the Foolish:
- A fool is known by his or her perverse lips, ignorance of spiritual things, swiftness to do evil, and a heart that rages against the Lord; such a person shall perish (vv. 1-3).
- The false witness scoffs at justice and thus shall be punished (vv. 5, 9, 28-29).
- Slothfulness and idle hands mark a hungry fool (vv. 15, 24).

- A foolish son should be corrected, instructed, and chastened early on in his life; else, he will destroy the family name later (vv. 13, 18, 26-27).

The goal of child training is to instruct and encourage godly conduct and correct ungodly behavior such that repentance and restoration are achieved. Inevitably, there will be times that parents grow weary of training their children, but we are under the divine mandate to be diligent in discipline, an important part of child training: *"Chasten thy son while there is hope, and let not thy soul spare for his crying"* (v. 18; KJV). Whether it is church discipline or parental discipline, the focus of all correction is to bring about proper behavior, which begins with repentance and has the triumphant finale of restoration. The rod is never alone; it always has reproof as its partner. Yet, there are many occasions when reproof or exhortation are unaccompanied by the rod (13:1). Children should receive much encouragement, instruction, and exhortation for sins of ignorance; the rod is reserved for those specific offenses that involve blatant disregard of what is known to be forbidden. Parents must be faithful to lovingly train their children with a godly sense of impartial justice in which appropriate punishment for offenses is neither excused nor abused.

Proverbs 20

Righteousness and Lawlessness Contrasted

The Righteous and the Wise:
- It is honorable to cease from strife, to allow the Lord to vindicate offenses, and to rely on wise counsel to assist others to achieve peace and contentment (vv. 3, 5, 22).
- Even a child is known by his actions; therefore, a wise man need not boast, for his revealed integrity is a testimony to others, including his children, of his goodness (vv. 6-7, 11).
- Godly authority rightly discerns evil and judges it accordingly (vv. 8, 26, 28).
- Words formed in wisdom and knowledge have great value (v. 15).

- The righteous seek wise counsel before rendering important decisions; they also count the cost of a project before initiating it (v. 18).
- It is wise to avoid an overzealous flatterer (who will just as easily slander you behind your back) and also a gossiper (who will eventually betray your confidence) (v. 19).
- A wise child will honor the position of parental authority despite its imperfections; such a child will seek to conceal his or her parents' faults rather than to belittle them publicly (v. 20).
- Wisdom is to be valued over strength, and is generally shown by the gray hair of the elderly (v. 29).

The Wicked and the Foolish:
- The fool is controlled by alcoholic beverages (v. 1).
- It is foolish to needlessly provoke those in authority to anger (vv. 2-3).
- The sluggard will suffer hunger (vv. 4, 13).
- A fool boasts in his own accomplishments; he both justifies and excuses his own sins (vv. 6, 8, 14).
- A foolish child reviles his parents, despises their authority, and shames them before others; such a child will experience life without God's favor (v. 20; 19:26).
- The wicked pursue "get-rich-quick" schemes and handle money frivolously; in the long run, they will possess less than what they originally did (v. 21).
- The human conscience reveals God's standard of righteousness; only the Lord knows the hearts of men, and He will not only judge wickedness, but wrong motives as well (vv. 24, 27).
- Besides suffering a guilty conscience, frauds and cheats will reap God's wrath (vv. 10, 17, 23, 25).

There is a moral connection pertaining to purity in each of the proverbs in verses 6 through 12. Verses 5 and 30 are also connected: *"Counsel in the heart of man is like deep water, but a man of understanding will draw it out"* (v. 5). *"Blows that hurt cleanse away evil, as do stripes the inner depths of the heart"* (v. 30). Biblical counseling uses the illumination of God's Word to explore the dark recesses of man's depraved heart, then draws out into the light what is not of God and what must, consequently, be eradicated. After the sword of truth wields evil thinking a mortal blow, the counselor then implants what is living and true into the heart-void just created. Accountability is then applied to ensure that what is Christ-like holds fast and that evil does not creep back in and, if so, it is punished. According to verse 30, experiencing the repercussions for sin is a necessary part of our sanctification process; Harry A. Ironside wrote:

> A skillful surgeon is not always concerned to immediately heal a wound because added suffering may be required to purge the system of poisonous matter. There is often a probing and consequent inflammation that is very painful but good in its final result. So it is with God's dealings when sin has been tolerated by His children. Stripes and sorrows may be laid on them, but only that the inner parts of the being may be purged of all hidden evil by self-judgment and full confession in His presence.[152]

It is biblical counseling and not humanistic philosophies that God's people will find most beneficial in correcting bad bents and in resolving difficulties with others.

Proverbs 21

Righteousness and Lawlessness Contrasted

The Righteous and the Wise:
- God blesses His people through upright authority (v. 1).
- The righteous understand God values their godly behavior more than their gifts; they therefore delight in living justly and will be rewarded for doing so (vv. 3, 8, 15, 21).
- Because the wise plan for the future, are diligent, and act appropriately, they will not suffer lack (vv. 5, 20, 29).
- The wise do not require punishment to learn; they eagerly receive instruction to gain further understanding (v. 11).
- The righteous should avoid the wicked because they continually crave and devise evil and will be overcome by it (vv. 10, 12).

- The righteous attend to those in need, and the Lord blesses them for doing so (v. 13).
- Those who control their tongue keep themselves from trouble (v. 23).
- The righteous know that all true wisdom, understanding, infallible counsel, and safety are in the Lord (vv. 30-31).

The Wicked and the Foolish:
- Man judges by appearance, but God knows our thoughts and intentions; hence, He will humble the proud. Those who rebel against Him can do nothing acceptable in His sight (vv. 2, 4; Tit. 1:15-16).
- Hasty fools and lovers of pleasure shall suffer lack, but the fraud, the robber, the false witness, and the one who ignores wisdom shall perish (vv. 5-7, 16-17, 28).
- The fool squanders his resources (v. 20).
- Like a drone in a beehive, the sluggard is self-focused and selfish; he yearns for the fruit of labor, but detests the work required to produce it (vv. 25-26).
- The sacrifices and thoughts of the wicked are putrid to God (v. 27).

Likely drawing from his own marital experiences, Solomon surmises: *"Better to dwell in a corner of a housetop, than in a house shared with a contentious woman"* (v. 9). *"Better to dwell in the wilderness, than with a contentious and angry woman"* (v. 19). Solomon addresses the quarrelsome wife on five separate occasions in Proverbs. Everyone is under authority, and Paul informs us when we oppose that authority we are opposing the counsels of God (Rom. 13:1-2). Therefore, attempting to control, defame, or taint the authority which God has placed over us (in this case, the husband's position) is an insult to Him and His order.

Husbands who are constantly ridiculed, diminished, and consequently controlled by their wives do not achieve honor in the eyes of their children and, in the end, usually become spiritual washouts in the home and in the church. A husband locked into this nagging and belittling existence soon will have no motivation to think for himself. Matrimony of this sort is nothing less than torture. The husband seemingly has only two escapes: he can either docilely settle into lowly servitude or abject isolation. Neither avenue of evasion will benefit the family. In the former, the husband lives with his wife but not for her; in the latter, he does neither. Wives, encourage your husbands in spiritual leadership, but don't nag! Rather, compliment your husband when he does what is right. If you cannot say anything kind to your husband, then be silent; "waters that babble in their course proclaim their shallowness, while, in their strength, deep streams flow silently."[153] Provoke him unto love and good works through your godly, quiet conduct. Husbands, your biblical mandate is to sacrificially love your wife and be a good spiritual leader. If these two ministries are pursued, your wife will most likely not resort to nagging or manipulation to get you to do what you really know you ought to do anyway.

Proverbs 22   Author: Solomon (vv. 1-16)/Wise Men (vv. 17-29)

Righteousness and Lawlessness Contrasted

The Righteous and the Wise:
- A respectable reputation, loving friends, and wealth accompany the righteous, who are marked by humility, prudence, and the fear of the Lord (vv. 1, 3-4, 11).
- God is no respecter of persons; rich or poor, the diligent and the righteous will be exalted (vv. 2, 29).
- It is wise to assist the poor; it is also wise to avoid putting up security and going into debt (vv. 7, 9, 16, 26).
- Those who listen and yield to divine wisdom, and trust in the Lord, will have a joyful spirit and be equipped to speak fitting words for Him (vv. 17-21).

A series of proverbs, as such as we have in this chapter, requires the reader to progress from a basic understanding of a string of platitudes to understanding context, deriving application, and guiding wise behavior. Derek Kidner suggests verses 17-21 describe how a reader must engage with Scripture to derive wisdom and benefit from it. He poses this in the form of helpful questions:

Does he read with alert concentration (v. 17)? How much is retained and ready for passing on (v. 18)? Does he receive it in the spirit in which it is given – to deepen his trust (v. 19), guide his decisions (v. 20), and strengthen his grasp of truth (v. 21)? Does he see himself as the virtual envoy of those whose knowledge of the truth depends on him?[154]

The wicked and the fool do not approach God's Word with this level of interest or intensity; rather, they ignore or reject it.

The Wicked and the Foolish:
- The fool is oblivious to the entrapments of evil and suffers for his ignorance, but the perverse intentionally pursue sin and thus reap God's wrath (vv. 3, 5, 8).
- Scoffers and bitter people are to be avoided; they stir up strife among God's people and instill into others their own sour behavior (vv. 10, 24-25).
- The slothful offer ludicrous excuses not to work (v. 13).
- By embracing the immoral woman and committing fornication, a man suffers great harm to himself and ensures God's wrath (v. 14).
- Those who oppress the poor will suffer their same plight (vv. 16, 22-23, 27).
- The wicked move boundary markers in an attempt to steal land from their neighbors (v. 28; also 23:10).

Thankfully, in the present dispensation of grace, the believer's inheritance is centered in infallible truth and the eternal benefits of Calvary. Yet, there are those today who attempt to remove these distinguishing landmarks of grace and replace them with the doctrines of men. Believers must be careful not to allow sacred truth to be pushed into human oblivion. One of the most obvious areas this is occurring in Western society is in the realm of child rearing; on this important matter, we would do well to learn from a page in Jewish history.

After Joshua died, the Jews ceased to teach their children about the Lord (Judg. 2:8-12), and as a result, the next generation did not know Him. The aftermath of Joshua's death illustrates the fallacy of depending upon any spiritual influence outside the family to maintain your family's spiritual welfare. The new generation forsook the Lord and embraced other gods, so God seized the role of the parent to teach them by the rod of military invasion who He was and what He expected of them (Judg. 3:1-2). All this occurred because the parents did not reverence God before their children. Untrained children, not surprisingly, remain foolish (v. 15). They predictably absorb from outside influences what seems appropriate to fill their void of understanding; thus, to leave a child to himself is to ensure his ruin. Children are natural sponges – they are compelled to learn and to develop an understanding of the world in which they live. May we learn from Jewish history and use Scripture to teach our children about the Lord, so that they might intimately know Him and also know the way they should go in life (v. 6). They may later choose to rebel against the Lord, but this godly heritage will always be with them to show the way back to the path of righteousness.

Proverbs 23

Righteousness and Lawlessness Contrasted

The Righteous and the Wise:
- It is wise to labor for and be satisfied with life's necessities, rather than being a workaholic to gain unneeded wealth, or longing for what the wealthy may offer with insincerity. It is good to remember that riches have a tendency to abruptly vanish without warning (vv. 1-8).
- It is wise to apply one's heart to instruction and learn knowledge, and then to be faithful to pass it down to the next generation. Also, we see the rod of reproof is a necessary part of child training (vv. 12-14, 19, 22, 25).
- Wise parents rejoice when their children fear the Lord, speak wisely, choose good companions, and do not envy sinners (vv. 15-18, 20-21, 24-25).

The Wicked and the Foolish:
- The fool rejects wisdom, so it is foolish to correct him (v. 9).

The Beginning of Wisdom

- Immoral women (or persons) and intoxication are two pitfalls to be avoided; both make their victims senseless and ultimately destroy them (vv. 27-35).

Solomon warns his son not to lust after the provocative woman who uses her feminine features to lure men into immorality. The ultimate goal of pornography is to promote fornication; the former stirs up unlawful lusting, the latter satisfies those lusts through immoral sexual acts. If we are to abstain from fornication, we must put up a mental defense that will maintain a pure thought-life. We cannot lust in our members and expect to be holy in conduct. Indeed, the Lord Jesus taught that if a man looks on a woman with lust, he has already committed sexual immorality with her in his heart (Matt. 5:28). Physically we are what we eat, but spiritually we are what we think: *"For as he thinks in his heart, so is he"* (v. 7). By properly controlling our thought-life, we control our behavior! When we choose not to stimulate our flesh through suggestive media, we will find it easier to maintain a Christ-honoring thought-life. Unchecked lusting leads to sin and broken fellowship with God (Jas. 1:14); He cannot commune with us while we are in sin (1 Jn. 1:5-7). A believer cannot change the reality of the wicked society in which he or she is a part, but, on a personal level, he or she can determine to remain pure and to pursue precautionary measures to maintain practical holiness.

Proverbs 24

Righteousness and Lawlessness Contrasted

The Righteous and the Wise:
- A life and home established in godly knowledge will be strong and blessed by God (vv. 3-5, 14).
- The wise seek the mind of God in the unity of godly counsel (vv. 6-7).
- The spiritual nature of the righteous is known by how much opposition it takes to discourage them (v. 8).
- The wise understand that God knows their abilities, works, and thoughts; therefore, there are no excuses which can fool Him from

accurately judging our motives and behavior, especially if we are willfully silent amid injustice (vv. 11-12). Believers are instructed to *"have no fellowship with the unfruitful works of darkness, but rather expose them"* (Eph. 5:11). Silence condones sin!

On the matter of being a silent spectator of unrighteousness, William MacDonald writes:

When innocent people are being led off to gas chambers, ovens, and other modes of execution – when unborn babies are destroyed in abortion clinics – it is inexcusable to stand by and not seek to rescue them. It is also useless to plead ignorance. As Dante said, "The hottest places in hell are reserved for those who in a time of great moral crisis maintain their neutrality."[155]

- The righteous learn from their falls (their mistakes), and then get back up and press on in grace; they do not rejoice when the Lord's wrath falls on their enemies (vv. 16-18).
- The wise do not compromise righteousness by extending preferential treatment or honor to those who do not deserve it; rather, their honesty refreshes everyone (vv. 23, 26).
- The righteous are not vengeful when wronged, but permit the Lord to judge the offense (v. 29).

The Wicked and the Foolish:
- Evil men should not be envied; in fact, they ought to be avoided. They are vicious people who are fit for destruction (vv. 1-2, 19-20).
- Those who hold the things of God in contempt cannot understand or appreciate wisdom (v. 7).
- Those who scheme to do evil sin against God, for *"the devising of foolishness is sin"* (v. 9); those who commit evil are an abomination to God and men (vv. 8-9, 15).
- God and His designated civil rulers have the authority to punish the rebellious, who show by their evil behavior that they do not fear the Lord (vv. 21-22).
- An unrighteous judge is despised by the people and those who rebuke him shall be rewarded (vv. 24-25).
- The wicked lie and stir up strife without cause (v. 28).

- The slothful fool does not plan his neglect or his inevitable ruin, for unattended fields and vineyards return to their natural state (vv. 30-34).

Verse 3 reads, *"Through wisdom a house is built."* From the earliest pages of Scripture, we see God's plan for the family. The husband is to be the head of and the provider for his family, while the wife is to bear children, nurture them, and keep and maintain the home. In Ruth 4:11, both Leah and Rachel are acknowledged as the ones who *"built* [Hebrew verb *banah*] *the house of Israel."* Later, Solomon would write: *"The wise woman builds* [*banah*] *her house, but the foolish pulls it down with her hand"* (14:1). *"Through wisdom a house is built* [*banah*], *and by understanding it is established"* (v. 3). The wise mother rests in God's wisdom and strength to build and to keep her home, for *"except the Lord build the house, they labor in vain that build it"* (Ps. 127:1). In general, what mankind builds rots, corrodes, degrades, and otherwise loses value over time. Building a home, however, has eternal value. This observation does not diminish the father's responsibility as the spiritual leader of his family, but it does highlight the significance of a virtuous woman laboring to build up her home; her investment of time and energy literally impacts eternity! If you have experienced failures in parenting, admit your errors and faults. Children don't need to see perfect parents, just honorable ones! Practically speaking, falling is not what makes one a failure, but wallowing in self-pity and choosing to stay down does: *"For a righteous man may fall seven times and rise again, but the wicked shall fall by calamity"* (v. 16).

Proverbs 25   Author: Solomon, as arranged by Hezekiah's men

Various Warnings and Exhortations

Proverbs 25-29 is a collection of more than a hundred proverbs written by Solomon, but compiled nearly three centuries later by Hezekiah's men (v. 1). This section includes a variety of unrelated proverbs, which I will endeavor to summarize by chapter. Proverbs 25 commences with wise instructions for leaders.

Just as God does not reveal everything about Himself to man, it is appropriate for kings or other rulers to conceal certain information from their subjects; however, it behooves him to fully investigate the truth before rendering a decision (vv. 2-3). Removing the influence of wicked counselors and assistants will enable leaders to rule more effectively and righteously (vv. 4-5). If you exalt yourself in the presence of authority, expect to be humbled, but when you are promoted by those in authority, you will receive honor (vv. 6-7). Those who strive with others without a just cause will be humbled and those who do have a legitimate complaint should handle the matter privately, with patience, and with well-chosen words; this is especially important when communicating with rulers (vv. 8-12, 15).

The chapter continues with a motley assortment of pithy sayings. A trustworthy servant refreshes those in authority, but he that is unfaithful causes immense anguish, especially in times already desperate (vv. 13, 19). He who boasts of himself does so in vain (vv. 14, 27). Disciplined living promotes peace; therefore, we should eat what is required to maintain healthy bodies; gluttony is harmful to the body. In general, what is in excess of God's enough is nauseating, not ecstasy (vv. 16, 27). Do not become a nuisance in your neighbor's home; your relationship will be adversely affected if you take advantage of their hospitality too often; rather, your infrequent visits should refresh your neighbor (v. 17). Be discerning; glad tidings and jubilant songs have their place, but not among the heavyhearted – encourage the suffering, but do not annoy or provoke them to malice (v. 20).

On the subject of anger, Solomon reminds us: *"The north wind brings forth rain, and a backbiting tongue an angry countenance"* (v. 23). Bearing false witness against one's neighbor also stirs up wrath (v. 18). As we have previously learned, *"A soft answer turns away wrath, but a harsh word stirs up anger"* (Prov. 15:1, also see v. 15). Regardless of the world's injustices and our sufferings, what we do when we feel angry is our choice. We are completely responsible to God for the way we respond when angry and to others who are angry. Neither past hurts, nor enduring wrongs, nor physical adversity is holy ground for inflicting others with unrighteous behavior. Despite the circumstances, a Christian should seek to secure a right response to the wrong behavior of others. The goal is to serve others by provoking them to proper behavior, not to further incite them to greater sin by our self-focused behavior. Thus, Solomon suggests that the evil deeds of one's enemy can be overcome by rendering good in exchange (vv. 21-22), but if that is not possible, it is best to withdraw from conflict and allow the Lord to judge the wrongdoing (v. 24).

Proverbs 26   Author: Solomon, as arranged by Hezekiah's men

Various Warnings and Exhortations

How should we handle a fool? He should not be honored, nor should his words be valued (vv. 1-2). The only correction he seems to understand is what causes him physical pain (v. 3). Do not respond to a fool according to his folly, that is, do not stoop to his level of egotistical foolishness: if he boasts, do not boast; if he rails, do not rail; be silent if silence will condemn him (v. 4). However, there are times in which wisdom is required to refute the blatant ignorance of a fool with his own words; this is so he will not become more conceited and cause harm to others (v. 5). Ignore the counsel of fools, for they are undeserving of responsibility or respect (vv. 6-9). A fool rarely learns from the consequences of his folly, but is prone to repeat his foolishness; God will judge his stupidity and transgressions (vv. 10-11). It is foolish to think of yourself as wise (v. 12). A sluggard will always be able to justify his laziness (vv. 13-16).

If you are not part of the problem or the solution, do not get involved in a dispute that does not pertain to you, otherwise you will escalate it further (v. 17). Do not resort to malicious flattery, but speak the truth in love when a response is necessary; do not use sarcasm and personal jabs and then claim you were just joking; this behavior stirs up strife (vv. 18-19, 25). This type of communication is deceitful and indicates bitterness resides in one's heart; such internalized resentment eventually ruins that person (vv. 24, 26-28).

Solomon likens the sin of propagating gossip to throwing more wood on a fire: *"Where there is no wood, the fire goes out; and where there is no talebearer, strife ceases. As charcoal is to burning coals, and wood to fire, so is a contentious man to kindle strife"* (vv. 20-21). The laws of physics have determined that there are basically two ways to stop a chemical reaction which produces a flame: remove either the fuel or the oxygen from the combustion process. Solomon uses this similitude to teach us how to stop gossip. First, do not allow the gossiper to whisper in your ear; this stops the gossip from spreading as you did not become aware of the information. This response removes the wood from the fire, so to speak. If the gossip is not heard and repeated, the rumor soon dies out. Second, pouring water on a fire robs the combustion reaction of needed air, which abruptly extinguishes the flame. This resembles the proactive behavior of bringing the gossip and gossiper to the attention of the one being hurt by it. When this happens, the truth of the matter quickly comes out and the gossip is dealt a deadly blow and the gossiper is rebuked by his or her own folly. Much damage has been done within the Body of Christ through the spread of rumors and hearsay – may we pull the wood and throw the water on the fire of gossip!

Proverbs 27   Author: Solomon, as arranged by Hezekiah's men

Various Warnings and Exhortations

Much of the counsel in this chapter pertains to interpersonal relationships. In the first six verses, Solomon warns against accepting the world's ideologies, which are centered in self-confidence and self-dependence; the believer must be diligent in life, yet always depending on the Lord. It is prudent to plan and labor for the future, to attempt to avoid life's pitfalls, and to protect what we have, but ultimately our lives unfold according to God's will (vv. 1, 12-13; Jas. 4:13-15).

We are then given several warnings and instructions regarding our interactions with others. First, let others praise you; self-exaltation is unbecoming for a believer (vv. 2, 21). Take care; because the fool is illogical and uncorrectable, his wrath does much damage, but someone with an envious and vindictive heart is even more destructive because he or she is self-seeking (vv. 3-4, 22).

What characterizes true friendship? William Kelly offers this practical insight:

> It is the property of real love, to prove its activity; if it abide hidden when called to speak or work according to the heart, it betrays self

rather than true affection. Even if there is a faultiness, love is bound to give "open rebuke." Indifference passes for much in this world, but it is the reverse of love, and cares for self, when it hides to spare danger and yet pretends affection. A friend's wounds, on the contrary, are faithful, for God's will is thus done, even though misunderstood and resented for a while.[156]

A true friend is loyal to both encourage and correct, face to face, even when it is uncomfortable to do so; he or she desires that you reach your full potential to serve God (vv. 5-6, 9-10, 17, 19).

Concerning the matter of possession, those who do not have much, appreciate the essentials of life more than those spoiled with luxuries; those who value and diligently care for what God has provided will be sustained (vv. 7, 23-27). There are family consequences when a man neglects his responsibilities in the home, especially godly leadership (v. 8). "A man who wanders from his home," suggests William MacDonald, "is one who is discontented and restless; he is like a bird that strays from its nest, shirking responsibilities and failing to build anything solid and substantial."[157] Flagrant unsolicited praise is to be dreaded; it is usually insincere and shows a lack of sensitivity because of the repugnancy it inflicts to a humble recipient (v. 14). A contentious wife is not easily restrained or consoled; she does not realize her offensive behavior degrades her marital relationship (vv. 15-16).

Solomon surmised, *"the eyes of man are never satisfied"* (v. 20); he also stated, *"The eye is not satisfied with seeing, nor the ear filled with hearing"* (Eccl. 1:8). Many socially-acceptable activities are not beneficial for our spiritual growth (1 Cor. 10:23). Human nature has a drive for distraction and a thirst for amusement. The word "muse" means "to think," the prefix "a-" means "no" or "not," and the suffix "-ment" means "an activity." The next time you crave amusement, understand why it is enjoyable – it is a "non-thinking activity." Usually, Satan does his best programming of the believer's mind during those times; when we refuse to muse, the filth just oozes in. Seasons of rest and relaxation rejuvenate our mental and physical wherewithal and enable us to better service for the Lord. Family fun and entertainment is emotionally therapeutic, but we must not let down our guard! Once smut is allowed to protrude through the frontlets of our minds, it affixes itself to our neurons and becomes difficult to remove. God forbid that what Christ has redeemed (the spirit, soul, and body of the believer) should become defiled by mental garbage (1 Cor. 6:19-20; 1 Thess. 5:23).

Proverbs 28 Author: Solomon, as arranged by Hezekiah's men

Various Warnings and Exhortations

Proverbs 28 and 29 are composed of thirty antithetical contrasts in which the second line begins with the conjunction "but." This entire section illustrates the vast disparity between the ways and destiny of the wicked and those of the righteous. The wicked are hard-hearted, conceited cowards who disregard justice, ignore the poor, profit by unfair means, and lust after riches. They ignore or forsake the Law of God, excuse their sins, praise evildoers, stir up strife, and cause the righteous to stray. Such evildoers are destined to experience calamity and will ultimately perish before the Lord, who in the meantime ignores their prayers. The righteous fear the Lord and in that knowledge they humble themselves, walk wisely, confess and forsake their sins, and trust the Lord during challenging times. They stand boldly for the truth, keep God's Law, uphold justice, and assist the poor; they will be saved from upheaval and shall prosper because they are blessed by the Lord.

Another key subject addressed in this chapter is right and wrong attitudes towards the poor (vv. 3, 6, 8, 11, 15, 22, 27). The Jews were to be a hospitable people, especially to their destitute brethren. Moses exhorted the nation: *"You shall not oppress one another, but you shall fear your God; for I am the Lord your God"* (Lev. 25:17). Besides our care for fellow believers in need, Solomon reminds us to also attend to the necessities of the poor in general: *"He who has pity on the poor lends to the Lord, and He will pay back what he has given"* (Prov. 19:17). *"He who gives to the poor will not lack, but he who hides his eyes will have many curses"* (v. 27). The Lord rewards those who attend to the needy.

In the Church Age, through the power of the Holy Spirit, believers are able to fulfill God's fuller intention of the Law – to demonstrate divine love for each other (Rom. 13:10). A Jew who refused to steal kept the Law, but to fulfill the Law an individual has to selflessly give to another. Hence, Paul exhorts believers not only to care for each other and the poor, but also to extend compassion to those who oppose us. If they are hungry and thirsty, we are to provide them food and drink (Rom. 12:20). He explains that such kindhearted acts *"overcome evil by doing good"* (Rom. 12:21). Such conduct is a tangible and lasting testimony of Christ in our communities.

Proverbs 29   Author: Solomon, as arranged by Hezekiah's men

Various Warnings and Exhortations

While this chapter contains twelve different contrasts, these may be categorized under three main headings. The first is the wise man and his ways juxtaposed with the foolish man and his folly. Because the fool cannot rationally contemplate wisdom, it is a waste of time to reason with him (v. 9). The fool rejects the benefit of correction; he is also prone to babble what is on his mind and to interject himself before he thinks through a matter (vv. 1, 11, 20). A wise man longs for the company of the righteous, defuses the wrath of others, and properly trains his children so that he may delight in them; he is slow to speak and limits his speech to what is needful and helpful (vv. 3, 8, 10-11, 15, 17, 21).

The second contrast in this poem is the benefits of just civil leaders as opposed to the pitfalls of their evil counterparts. God instituted human government to teach us submission to His authority; hence, rulers are ministers of God to do good to their subjects and are accountable to God if they do not (v. 26; Rom. 13:1-4). When those in authority affirm God's revealed Word, show compassion to the poor, and execute godly justice, the people in their care are happy and flourish. However, when the wicked rule, strife, wrath, deception, injustice, the acceptance of bribes, the heeding of lies, and the neglect of the poor are commonplace; the people mourn, suffer, and seek seclusion (vv. 2, 4-8, 12, 14, 18).

King Solomon warns that the Lord will not tolerate pride, especially in those who rule His people: *"The fear of the Lord is to hate evil, pride and arrogance, and the evil way"* (8:13). *"By pride comes nothing but strife"* (13:10). *"Pride goes before destruction and a haughty spirit before a fall"* (16:18). *"A man's pride will bring him low, but the humble in spirit will retain honor"* (v. 23). God hates pride (Prov. 6:16-17). This is seen in the life of King Uzziah; when he served the Lord obediently, he was blessed. When he went his own way, God judged his pride and he suffered with leprosy of the head for the remainder of his life. We do well to remember this valuable lesson and bestow the Lord with the honor He deserves instead of trying to retain it for ourselves.

The third contrast of the chapter is a familiar one: the behavior and character of the righteous assessed together with those of the wicked. (The theme here is broader than relations with governmental authorities.) The righteous care for the poor and deplore behavior contrary to God's Law; they trust and rejoice in the Lord and are honored because of their humility (vv. 6-7, 10, 23, 25, 27). The wicked resort to flattery, scorn, and theft to get what they want and cause others to suffer because of their rage and escalating sin; they neglect the poor and fear men more than God (vv. 5-8, 12, 16, 24-25, 27).

Proverbs 30

The Wisdom of Agur

Proverbs 30 is written by Agur, the son of Jakeh, to Ithiel and Ucal who, like Agur, are not mentioned elsewhere in Scripture (v. 1). In comparison to God's creative power, knowledge, and wisdom, Agur humbly confesses he is dumbfounded and stupid (vv. 1-4). It is possible that when he says he is the most ignorant man, he is using a bit of irony in confronting those who proclaim to be wise. He then uses a series of five questions to reveal the greatness of God as revealed in nature and to show that those who profess to be "wise" are otherwise. Only God can be the right answer to each of these questions. Because God is holy, high above all that He creates, His words are pure and should be trusted and obeyed, but never added to; to do so ensures His rebuke (vv. 5-6). Without divine revelation and illumination, man could not know God at all (1 Cor. 2:9-14).

In the first of six numerical sayings, Agur requested *"two things"* from the Lord: that he not fall prey to the vanity and lies of others, and that he would have adequate provisions in his autumn years of life, but not the abundance of wealth (vv. 7-8). He then explains the latter request, saying, *"Lest I be full and deny You, and say, 'Who is the Lord?' Or lest I be poor and steal, and profane the name of my God"* (v. 9). Both of Agur's requests, first for godly character and second to alleviate those circumstances that might compromise it, have the same goal. Agur, knowing his own fragility, humbly asked God for godly integrity despite life's circumstances; this was to ensure that he never dishonored the Lord's name.

Therefore, Agur desired that he neither be rich, fearing he might forget the Lord, nor poor, fearing he might be forced to steal and, in so doing, disdain God's name. It is for this reason, the honor of God, that Paul exhorts believers to pursue Christ-honoring behavior: *"Let him who stole steal no longer, but rather let him labor, working with his hands what is good, that he may have something to give him who has need"* (Eph. 4:28). This Proverb illustrates that individuals can communicate blasphemy for the Lord's name without using actual words. We often say to our children, "actions speak louder than words," but we probably do not reckon the same principle in our breaking of God's laws. The believer sins because he or she chooses to, and our rebellious behavior insults God, affronts His holy character, and blasphemes His name. It is absurd to claim to be a Christian, a Christ-one, while we are diminishing His name through un-Christ-like conduct. Often, we think more about the personal consequences of our sin than we do about the hurt inflicted on the heart of God. Stealing offends God and degrades His name in the eyes of the unsaved.

Agur then continues by acknowledging that there was a generation of people in his day that showed contempt for God's name by their proud actions: false accusations and slander, cursing one's parents, self-justification and the excuse of sin, and oppression of the poor (vv. 10-14). Agur then refers to *five* earthly things to illustrate a lack of contentment within man's natural existence: the leech, the grave, a barren womb, parched land, and fire (vv. 15-16). The point seems to be that insatiable greed destroys. It is likely that verse 17 was inserted directly following this pungent conclusion to express that an arrogant child who scorns parental authority is just as appalling as someone mastered by greed, and will also experience an untimely end. Next, Agur identifies *four* things beyond his understanding: how the eagle maintains flight, how the serpent slithers across a rock, how a ship navigates in the sea, and how a man woos a maiden (vv. 18-19). These four things leave no lasting trace of their previous way; such is the lie of adultery when the guilty say, *"I have done no wickedness"* (v. 20). He then identifies *four* things that are unbearable to social order and hence cause turmoil and make people shudder: a servant who rules, a gorged fool, an unloved wife, and a maid who supplants her mistress (vv. 21-23).

In contrast to having people elevated to social positions they are not fit for, Agur identifies *four* creatures which are disproportionately wise for their small size: the diligent ant who prepares for the future, the nearly defenseless rock badger who safely dwells in rocky crags, the locust who demonstrates unity of purpose without a leader, and the easily-caught lizard (perhaps a spider; NKJV) who is still able to venture into any part of the king's palace virtually unnoticed (vv. 24-28). Though these are humble and lowly creatures, they are wise in their doings and God provides for them – we should learn from their example.

Agur concludes his proverb with his last numerical saying; he acknowledges the noble bearing of *four* creatures: the strong lion, the strutting rooster (NASV), and the bold he-goat, and a smug king who is surrounded by his invincible army (vv. 29-31). In God's order, all creatures, small and unpretentious or powerful and prominent, are cared for by Him. Likewise, despite God's predetermined calling for our lives (lowly or noble), this proverb exhorts everyone to be humble before the Lord. True humility will cause us to reverence the Lord (vv. 1-9), to be in submission to His will (vv. 10-17), and to be in awe of who He is (vv. 18-31). If we are marked by this mindset, we will want to pursue peaceable behavior that properly deals with unlovely and sinful thoughts, and refrain from speech that stirs up strife and works to exalt oneself (vv. 32-33).

Proverbs 31

Drunkenness Is a Curse; the Virtuous Woman Is a Blessing

As previously noted, the acrostic poetical construction of verses 10-31 is different from the style of the initial nine verses, which were written by Lemuel. Some have suggested that this abrupt stylistic change in the middle of the chapter indicates that an unknown author may have penned that portion of the text at a later date. King Lemuel determined to share the wise counsel his mother gave him, namely, to avoid intoxication and the sexual temptation of wayward women (vv. 1-2). Those who represent God's authority should not become inebriated (1 Tim. 3:8). A drunken governor will pervert justice, forget what is noble, and disregard problems that need resolution; rather, he must rule in righteousness and care for the poor and needy (vv. 4-9).

The subject matter turns from the right endeavors of a godly, sober king to the character and blessings of a virtuous woman, detailed in verses 10-31. The word translated as "virtuous" in verse 10 is derived from the Hebrew word *chayil*. Derek Kidner suggests that the modern sense of "virtuous" does not reflect the root idea of this Hebrew word, which implies "she has a lot in her."[158] In this original application, the narrative paints the portrait of a wholesome, industrious, efficient, and profoundly able wife. She is an incredible example of biblical femininity.

The wife in this chapter has won her husband's full confidence. In verse 11, we read *"the heart of her husband safely trusts her."* Verse 12 continues with *"She does him good and not evil all the days of her life."* She is the ultimate selfless companion who longs to serve her husband instead of placing expectations on him. Verses 12-19 describe a woman who rises early in the morning to greet the day with hard work. Matthew Henry clarifies the virtuous wife's mindset: "She doesn't love her bed too much in the morning."[159] The virtuous woman puts forth her best efforts in keeping the home and pleasing her husband. She is industrious and frugal. Neglect and ease are not words in her vocabulary. The woman in Proverbs 31 is industrious in the home and loyal to her husband; she is also compassionate. Verse 20 proclaims, *"She extends her hand to the poor, yes, she reaches out her hands to the needy."* One of the finest legacies a mother can impart to her children is an unselfish example. Children will pattern themselves after a recurring exhibition of selflessness.

Verse 23 reads: *"Her husband is known in the gates, when he sits among the elders of the land."* The gate of a city was commonly the location for business and the seat of government. The gate was the strategic location for any politician as he could shake hands with everyone who entered the city. How could the husband be devoted to his business at the city gate? Because he had a wife who was totally devoted to her business at home. He was not concerned about the daily activities of the home. This sphere of responsibility was delegated to his wife in whom he had the utmost confidence.

The practical and wise instruction of this woman to her children is captured in verse 26: *"She opens her mouth with wisdom, and on her tongue is the law of kindness."* She is not prone to speaking evil of others or spreading gossip about them. Her tongue is a skillfully-controlled instrument of instruction, edification, and healing. Solomon recognized the awesome power of speech, remarking, *"death and life are in the power of the tongue"* (18:21), and the virtuous woman is profoundly "pro-life" in her speech. Furthermore, if the mother speaks foolishly, the children will follow in her folly (13:20). The mother is the one who establishes the tone of response in her children. If she is prone to be quick to anger and unforgiving, her children will likewise tend to be easily enraged and bear a yoke of bitterness (22:24). However, if her speech is kind, discrete, and cheerful, her children will observe the power of life and peace as she interacts with others.

The mother's heart is the child's schoolroom.

— Henry Ward Beecher

Ecclesiastes

Ecclesiastes

Introduction

The title "Ecclesiastes" is found in the Septuagint (the Greek translation of the Old Testament) and is derived from the Hebrew word *Koheleth*, which is found seven times in Ecclesiastes. *Koheleth* means "caller" and is translated *"the preacher"* (e.g., 1:2, 12:8). In this largely autobiographical poem, the royal Preacher, Solomon, shares with us excerpts of his weary search for the significance of human existence. He will examine science, wisdom, philosophy, pleasure, materialism, as well as living for the moment as possible avenues of satisfaction. Is it possible for man to actually enjoy his earthly sojourn, that is, his life *"under the sun"*? It seemed to Solomon that all man's toil was utterly meaningless (1:2).

Purpose

Ecclesiastes highlights the sorrowful consequences of choosing to venture down wrong paths in life. Solomon entered into many political marriages with the daughters of pagan kings, who then brought strange gods into his palace, all of which degraded his relationship with Jehovah. He forsook God's Word, which he had known from his youth, in order to pursue selfish interests and sensual pleasures. Now writing in his autumn years, Solomon is disappointed, even disillusioned, all because of his own carnality.

It is not necessary for us to follow the royal writer in his regretful exploits to learn their end. In Ecclesiastes, Solomon examines his own life, especially his mistakes, and reflects on a lifetime of observations in an attempt to make sense of it all: "Why is man upon the earth?" and "How can man find satisfaction in life?" Ultimately, he will conclude that the answer to both questions is the same: *"Fear God, and keep His commandments, for this is the whole duty of man"* (12:13; KJV). Solomon's ontological quest led him back to the Lord, and to understand that man exists to please Him. This is perhaps why Solomon uses the less familiar term *"God"* exclusively throughout the book, until he acknowledges the importance of personally fearing *"Jehovah"* at the end. Recognizing and yielding to divine authority results in personal fellowship with the Lord and His blessing.

Whereas Proverbs provides hundreds of wise course corrections to help navigate through life, Ecclesiastes explores a panoramic view of life itself – what does it all mean and what is truly satisfying in it? It is important to realize Ecclesiastes is penned from a foolish humanistic perspective. This is one of the great paradoxes recorded in Scripture: how does the wisest man (of that day) play the world's greatest fool? As we will learn in Ecclesiastes, foolish humanistic reasoning results when divine wisdom is ignored.

Date and Historical Setting

Since Solomon reigned as Israel's king from 971 to 932 B.C., his literary works would have been composed during that timeframe. H. A. Ironside suggests the following order of his writings:

> Presumably he wrote the Song of Solomon when he was young and in love, Proverbs when he was middle-aged and his intellectual powers were at their zenith, and Ecclesiastes when he was old, disappointed, and disillusioned with the carnality of much of his life.[160]

If written at the end of Solomon's life, a date of 930 B.C. seems appropriate.

Authorship

The writer of Ecclesiastes does not mention his name, and provides limited information about himself. Jewish tradition has long ascribed the authorship of the book to Solomon, though today that determination is widely debated.[161] Solomon's authorship was broadly accepted throughout the Church Age until Martin Luther rejected the idea in the sixteenth century. Presently, many conservative Bible scholars do not believe Solomon produced this literary work, claiming much of the Hebrew grammatical construction used within it did not exist until after the Babylonian captivity. However, recent studies have called into question the validity of this linguistic evidence and reopened the possibility of Solomon's authorship on a grammatical basis.[162]

We do know that the author was a descendent of David and was also a king of Israel ruling in Jerusalem (1:1, 12). Although the word *"son"* in these verses can mean a grandson or later descendant, the primary sense best fits the text, as there was only one descendant of David who ruled over *all* Israel in Jerusalem – David's son Solomon. William MacDonald makes a case for Solomon's authorship by correlating information found in Ecclesiastes with what we know about Solomon elsewhere in Scripture:

> Solomon was a king in Jerusalem: of great wisdom (1:16); of great wealth (2:8); one who denied himself no pleasure (2:3); one who had many servants (2:7); and one who was noted for a great building and beautification program (2:4-6).[163]

Given the known inspired writers of Scripture, what we understand about them, and their writing styles and thematic works, it seems likely that Solomon is the author of Ecclesiastes. On this point, William Kelly poses the following conjecture:

> Even if the book had no such marks as Ecclesiastes 1:1, and 12, who does, who could, speak of wisdom as in the latter half of Ecclesiastes 1 but Solomon? Who could sit in judgment of all that is done under the heavens, and pronounce on its nothingness as in Ecclesiastes 2, but one with the weight of that great king? Was anyone that ever lived after him in Jerusalem entitled so truly as he to speak of great works that he made, of building and planting with every accessory; of servants within and without; of such possession of herds and flocks and on such a scale of grandeur; of wisdom remaining, notwithstanding vast accumulations of silver and gold and the peculiar treasure of kings? There is no real ground to imagine an anonymous writer personating Solomon: an idea quite alien to scripture, though reasonable in the eyes of worldly men used to fiction. Here all is intense and solemn reality, as he had proved too well who could speak beyond any.[164]

Accordingly, this author will proceed on the assumption that the book is Solomon's sorrowful reflection on life in general and his many poor choices (now his regrets) in particular.

Recurring Phrases and Ideas

Because Solomon confines his quest to understand the meaning of life to the material world, much of his efforts frustrate, even torment, him. The answer to this important question cannot be found through reasonings or experiments "under the sun"; one must get "above" the sun by contemplating divine revelation. This is why many of the recurring words and phrases throughout Ecclesiastes convey a general tenor of sadness: "labor" occurs 20 times; "evil," 18 times; "vexation of spirit" (KJV) or "grasping for the wind" (NKJV), 9 times; moreover, words such as "oppression," "sorrow," "grief," and "mourning" are plentiful.

The following is a list of key repetitive phrases and a brief explanation of their meaning:

"Vanity of Vanities" – Vanity describes the emptiness of life apart from God and His purposes. That which is futile has no lasting value and will only cause frustration.

"Under the Sun" – In short, this phrase refers to life on earth from man's perspective: man is born, he labors, he suffers, he experiences brief moments of fleeting joy, then he dies and leaves behind all that he gained in his brief existence.

"Eat, drink, and be merry" – Throughout Scripture this idea conveys natural man's propensity to satisfy himself through stimulation of the senses, which produces no lasting enjoyment or worth. This is temporal man behaving temporally: he disregards what is eternal, ignores accountability to his Creator, and instead indulges himself and lives for the moment.

"I perceive" – This is natural man trying to make sense of the material world without the aid of divine revelation, which means he cannot accurately reckon what is spiritually tangible and eternal.

In order to interpret the meaning of this book properly, it is important to understand that many of Solomon's conclusions are not correct or are only partly true. This reveals the futility of the *"under the sun"* perspective, that is, the fallacy of human reasoning apart from divine revelation. His dismal outlook is that life is *"vanity and grasping for the wind"* (1:14); it is not worth living. The material world will never be able to explain the spiritual significance of life. One must get above the sun (above the earthly viewpoint) and seek and accept what God reveals about our existence to enjoy it. This is Solomon's point: nothing on this earth will ever satisfy the deep longing of the human heart to be in communion with one's Creator – without Him, life is meaningless!

Overview

Synoptic comments will be provided according to the following outline of the book:

1:1-11: Introduction
1:12-2:26: Searching for the True Meaning of Life
3:1-5:20: Discerning the True Meaning of Life
6:1-8:15: Clarifying the True Meaning of Life
8:16-12:8: Applying the True Meaning of Life
12:9-14: Conclusion

Devotions in Ecclesiastes

Introduction
(1:1-11)

The Preacher, King Solomon, wastes no time in conveying to us the conclusion of his ontological investigation: man's presence on the earth is transitory and meaningless – all is vanity (vv. 1-2). Man observes the repetitive and predictable nature of his environment (e.g., the motion of the sun, the water-vapor cycle, seasonal changes, and the direction of the wind), and concludes that the earth will continue as it has forever (vv. 4-7). In the material world, the goals of human existence are reduced to survival and reproduction. Humanity is sequestered into a ceaseless, wearisome, cyclic routine – there is nothing remarkable about human existence. From this earthly perspective, man's life is brief and unsatisfying, full of labor and sorrow; one simply tolerates the boring drudgery of passing days until one passes out of them (vv. 3, 8). Yet, even the cyclical nature of the world that Solomon is speaking of is a mercy of God: enough variety to preclude boredom, plus consistency to uphold security.

Solomon further observes that our fallen nature has a natural drive for gratification and a thirst for amusement: *"The eye is not satisfied with seeing, nor the ear filled with hearing"* (1:8); *"the eyes of man are never satisfied"* (Prov. 27:20). Paul reminds us the flesh wants to do what it knows it should not do: *"For when we were in the flesh, the sinful passions which were aroused by the law were at work in our members to bear fruit to death"* (Rom. 7:5-6). He further acknowledges that his flesh was in constant opposition to what he understood God demanded of him (Rom. 7:23). He referred to this nature as the law of sin and he knew it was an abiding evil presence within himself (Rom. 7:25). The flesh, governed by the fallen nature, is never satisfied; it wants more than what is reasonable or lawful. For example, instead of eating what is necessary to maintain a fit body, the flesh engages in gluttony (Prov. 23:21, 28:7). However, after conversion Christians should be governed, not by the law of sin within them, but rather by the Spirit of God (Rom. 8:13). Moderation and self-control are a testimony to others that God is the One controlling a believer's actions (Phil. 4:5). Such behavior is evidence that yearning for fleshly gratification is no longer the goal in life, but rather that one is satisfied with knowing and pleasing God.

Before informing us of the details of his investigation, Solomon shares his conclusion: human life appears futile; man labors to eat, he eats to strengthen himself to labor, when he can no longer labor he dies and is forgotten (vv. 9-10). There is nothing new under the sun; what seems unique only appears to be so because previous occurrences of the same event were forgotten (v. 11). No matter how important a man tries to make himself, he soon passes off the stage of life into oblivion. If one only examines one's existence from this naturalistic viewpoint, this is a logical conclusion.

Searching for the True Meaning of Life
(1:12-2:26)

With his initial conclusion about human existence somewhat vaguely stated in the introduction, Solomon then retraces his intellectual pilgrimage in a much more personal way; he is in search of what constitutes a satisfying and meaningful life (1:12-15). Because Solomon, as a young king, petitioned the Lord for knowledge and wisdom to rightly lead His people instead of riches, power, and fame, God blessed him with these and as well as the wisdom he requested (1:16; 2 Chron. 1:10-12). Yet, his superb education, his many experiences, his observations of human behavior, and all his understanding could not resolve his unanswered meaning-of-life questions; this caused Solomon grief and sorrow (1:17-18). The more he learned, the more disgruntled and frustrated he became: *"Knowledge puffs up"* and makes one arrogant (1 Cor. 1:8); perhaps Solomon was suffering the consequences of philosophical conceit.

Having failed to achieve satisfactory answers through intellectual achievement, Solomon considered pleasure as a possible source of true happiness (2:1-2). Whatever he lusted after he pursued without restraint: wine, elaborate housing, beautiful gardens, servants to cater to his every whim, livestock, precious metals, music, and let us not forget the sensual pleasure he sought in his many wives (2:3-10). Yet, Solomon learned that no matter how much he pursued pleasure, he still longed for more. He concluded that there was no true lasting gratification in indulging one's lusts and that laboring for that which does not afford satisfaction is a futile enterprise (2:11).

Turning from pleasure, Solomon would next examine materialism as a source of satisfaction in life. His previous depressing conclusion caused Solomon to wonder if the wise man really had much of an advantage over the fool, since both were destined for the same fate (death), and no amount of wisdom could alter that appointment (2:14). His bewilderment was further fueled by the fact that both the wise man and the fool are both quickly forgotten after their funerals (2:16-17). Solomon believed that if he, the wise monarch, could not reason out this conundrum, no one after him was likely to do so; therefore, he diligently considered the matter (2:12). Solomon discerned wisdom was generally better than folly, for a person who walks in the light (true wisdom) is not as likely to stumble and fall into the traps of life, as compared to a fool who walks in the darkness of ignorance and stupidity (2:13). But aside from this, he concluded that there was no great distinction between these two contrasting courses in life and, thus, that expending much time to pursue wisdom was not justified (2:15).

After all, Solomon reasoned, could wisdom help him enjoy all the wealth that he had accumulated? No, it was destined to be passed on to his heir, who in foolishness might squander it away (2:18-19). Solomon had no control over events after his death; neither his wisdom nor all his endeavors could avert the possibility of a foolish, wasteful successor; this realization depressed him (2:20). The idea of one's death was made all the more distasteful by the fact that one's hard-earned possessions could be thoughtlessly dissipated (2:21). From an *"under the sun"* point of view, there is no enduring value to anything people do in life, because at death they do not have any more control of it; therefore, people may as well live for the moment and enjoy pleasure while God enables them to do so (2:22-24). Paul agrees with Solomon in that, without an afterlife, there is no reason to live but for the now;

The Beginning of Wisdom

however, the resurrection of Christ ensures all true believers a glorious life with Him forever – this is worth living for (1 Cor. 15:32)!

Solomon, the richest man in the world, then admitted that pleasure (like intellectualism and materialism) did not enhance his happiness. He then concluded that to live righteously before God is the only way to have true enjoyment while living under the sun; to live any other way provokes His displeasure which results in further shame and suffering (2:25-26). Solomon will expand this assessment in chapter 12; it suffices here to merely say that living for God and not for self results in His blessing, both now and through eternity!

Discerning the True Meaning of Life
(3:1-5:20)

In chapter 3, Solomon continues his research into human behavior and existence by observing a consistent and predetermined order to life which continues with relentless regularity. Leaving the experiment of materialism, Solomon assumes a fatalistic posture in his investigation: perhaps we should just take life as it comes and not try to find its meaning. Such is the undergirding of Buddhism and other world religions. Solomon provides fourteen pairs of contrasting activities to represent the entire gambit of human existence for example, he says birth is followed by death, planting precedes harvesting, clearing away debris permits building (3:1-8). His point is illustrated by summing the efforts of each pair, which is zero. That is, the tally of received benefits as compared to the effort or resources expended for each of the activities cancel out; therefore, man advances nothing despite all his toil (3:9-10). This assessment of life under the sun begs the question: is there really anything to be gained through human existence?

However, in verse 11, Solomon suggests an additional reason for human life which tips the scales in favor of it: that man (speaking of humanity) might know his Creator: *"He has made everything beautiful* [or appropriate] *in its time. Also He has put eternity in their hearts, except that no one can find out the work that God does from beginning to end."* By God's design there is an appropriate and designated time for each activity within His creation. Furthermore, God puts the sense of eternity in the human mind. Though living in a world governed by time, man instinctively ponders a forever existence beyond his present domain, though he cannot naturally surmise what that might be.

These unexplainable inklings of eternity and our lack of understanding of God's immutable accomplishments throughout time should cause man to humble himself before his Creator. Solomon thought this to be the proper response of humanity, remarks William Kelly:

> Of Himself we can only receive what God reveals; but this is not the question here discussed. The Preacher accordingly speaks his conviction that there is nothing better for them – nothing good in them – but to rejoice and to do good; as God had shown in His work (whatever man or Satan had done to the contrary) only what is excellent and appropriate.[165]

We learn from verse 11 that God has granted man a certain level of opportunity to recognize a distinct order in nature and to reason out the intricacies of that order. Although man cannot comprehend God's eternal purposes from nature, he can perceive God Himself. Enough information is available for him to conclude the intricate design in nature requires a Designer with immutable power and wisdom. While man can never fully understand God or creation through mere observation, there is enough revelation of truth to stimulate the human heart to think beyond the material world of time and space, and to ponder eternity (3:11-15). Fatalism, as previously explored by Solomon, suggests God neither hears, sees, nor cares about us, which means there is no opportunity for us to experience His grace and mercy; however, we know God has put eternal longings in the human heart to draw man to Himself.

Besides the testimony of creation to God's involvement, Solomon refers to the testimony of his own conscience: the sense of decency and righteousness within him demanded a time when the injustices of life would be judged (3:16-17). Paul confirms man was created with a moral fabric to guide his conduct in life; we refer to this as our conscience (Rom. 2:15). Sudden feelings of guilt and of impending judgment prove to us that we do not continue in well-doing, but have instead violated that moral law placed within us. Hence, the human conscience is an evidence of God's on-going and future involvement in our lives.

Solomon then considers the certainty of death, and wonders what advantage man has over the animals who suffer the same ultimate demise. His rationale is his own; his conclusions do not reflect God's assessment of the matter. Hence, apart from divine revelation, Solomon sees no advantage of man over the animals, as after death there is no more opportunity to know or to control earthly affairs – to experience life (3:18-21). He concludes the brevity of life is sheer vanity, so enjoy the fruit of your labors while you can (3:22). However, this egotistical philosophy of living for self cannot prompt lasting happiness.

In chapter 4, Solomon expresses his grief over the inequalities of life, especially the seemingly endless cruelty that man inflicts on his fellow man, and also his sorrow over humanity's general lack of concern and courage to assist those wrongfully treated or in need. A cynical Solomon suggests the oppressed are better off dead than continuing to suffer; given their lot in life, it would have been better if they had not been born at all (4:1-3). This defeatist attitude is a logical conclusion if one does not realize that God sees all, controls all, and will judge all injustices. In fact, God commonly uses such hardships to refine and mature His people. Suffering would be a most miserable experience if there was no hope that God was using our difficulties to better and to bless us (Jas. 1:2-3).

The Preacher then considers the efforts of various types of individuals to point out their inevitably profitless end: the frazzled workaholic who is driven by envy and covetousness and yet has no time to enjoy life; the lazy fool who does nothing to protect himself and barely survives, never experiencing life's fullness; and the secluded miser who has acquired more than he could ever consume, but keeps laboring anyway, though he has no heir for his fortune (4:4-8). In the latter case, Solomon observes the lonely miser chooses to endure his miserable existence without the benefit of human fellowship. Four examples, all selfish reasons, are then provided to suggest that it is wise and profitable to maintain good relationships with others. First, working together is more profitable; this is especially true if urgent assistance is needed after an accident (4:9-10). Second, one is able to keep warm at night because of another's body heat; human fellowship offers comfort and security (4:11). Third, close allies will assist in fending off an attacker. Fourth, a rope is much stronger when individual strands are tightly braided together than if not (4:12); one accomplishes more and is less likely to break under strain when part of a good group.

While Solomon understood the profitability of human relationships, he also recognized that they were transient in nature, often because man craves for what is new and different. He then improvises a story concerning a king who diligently worked his way up to the throne, but then became arrogant and unyielding. In turn, his subjects, who once lauded him as their man, wanted to replace him – it is in our nature to both change and to demand change (4:13-16). Even if one were to obtain the world's best benefits and highest honors, such things are temporary, unsatisfying, and therefore futile. Accordingly, all of life's inequalities lead to vanity: egotism fails to resolve Solomon's unanswered questions.

In chapter 5, Solomon continues his quest for the meaning of life by pondering the vanity of two things: humanized religion (which cannot fulfill man's deepest spiritual needs), and flawed governmental authorities (who cannot safeguard against injustice). Because man is a spiritual creature, he is prone to ponder the supernatural and to engage in religious activities. Apart from yielding to divine revelation, such activities are mere charades which cannot please God (John 4:24). However, Solomon's point is that even if one knows the truth, he or she may still embrace it in hypocrisy by offering rash vows, uttering meaningless jargon, or engaging in foolish traditions (5:1-6). This type of religious behavior does not please the Lord, but rather demonstrates a lack of reverence for Him and His word; thus, superficial spirituality is pure vanity (5:7). Solomon also counsels us not to despair when the helpless are exploited or when political injustice occurs. Such inequities will transpire because human rulers are imperfect; yet, every governing official is ultimately accountable to God and will be judged by Him in a future day (5:8-9).

The chapter concludes with Solomon considering the vanity of passing riches. All the money in the world cannot buy one's contentment; true happiness is unachievable through material possessions (5:10). Those who have much naturally want more. Being wealthy is not condemned in Scripture, but God's people are to use what they have to honor the Lord; they are neither to love money, nor to trust in their riches (1 Tim. 6:9-10, 17-19).

The Beginning of Wisdom

Besides the propensity for discontentment, another problem with accumulating wealth is that it attracts parasites – the more money you have, the more others will want to help you spend it (5:11). Furthermore, those who hoard their wealth instead of using it to benefit others must worry about losing it through some calamity they cannot prevent (5:13-14). If such a catastrophe would occur, what a pity to have had so much which could have been used for good, but to instead suffer regret and want at the end of one's life (5:15-17). In contrast, those who pursue a simple lifestyle, engage in an honest day's work, and choose to live within their means, enjoy a restful night's sleep; they benefit from a clear conscience and have little over which to be anxious (5:12). Because life is brief, Solomon surmised that the best scenario in life would be to appreciate and enjoy all good things received from the Lord and not to be encumbered with the abundance of things (5:18-20).

> I enjoy the luxury of few things to care for.
>
> — Hudson Taylor

Solomon covered a lot of ground in this section. Some summary points are: Human laboring, which is often motivated by greed, envy, and prestige, cannot alter God's immutable and mysterious order of things. Human laboring may result in benefits that can be enjoyed as God enables, but often are lost through rash behavior, religious tradition, moral corruption, covetousness, and calamity. God has placed a longing for eternity in man's mind which provides awareness of God's presence and should cause him to ponder his own feeble existence and live to honor his Creator.

Clarifying the True Meaning of Life
(6:1-8:15)

Solomon continues in chapter 6 to ponder wealth as a means of satisfaction. He now explains the harsh irony that burdened his soul: it was quite possible for a man like himself with vast wealth, power, and fame to be unable to fully enjoy what he possessed (6:1-2). He blamed God for this torturous dichotomy. The specific cause of this situation is not explained: perhaps the rich man's own selfish attitude prevented him from enjoying what he had (i.e., because he chose to hoard his wealth). The irony here is only enhanced if a man's wealth were to be enjoyed by a stranger, perhaps through theft or calamity. Even if a man did have a long life and was blessed with many children, what consolation are these things, if he could not appreciate his existence or receive a decent burial after his death (6:3)? Would not a stillborn baby – departing in anonymity and never knowing life's injustices, oppression, and maddening perplexities – be better off than the man who cannot enjoy the outcome of his labors and whose name is soon forgotten after his funeral (6:3-5)? Solomon thought so, remarking that even if a man could live two lifetimes, he would ultimately share the same fate as the stillborn infant, but at least the latter was not forced to endure an unsatisfying life of toil and trouble (6:6-7).

From this perspective, the wise have no advantage over the foolish, nor the rich over the poor. In fact, because the poor have learned to survive with little, they are more likely to be content with basic necessities, as compared to the rich who having much still lust for more (6:8-9). It is God who determines each person's lot in life, and no one can dispute the Creator's claim on them: things are as He wills (6:10-11). For this reason, no one else could inform Solomon how to best endure his vain life, or what would happen on earth after he left it. He concludes again that life is futile (6:12).

The point of chapter 6 is that man cannot determine what is best for himself during his earthly existence, because life's circumstances are foreordained by God. From this statement, Solomon further conjectures in chapters 7 and 8 that man cannot even fathom God's plans. The Hebrew word, *matsa*, which means "to discover" or "find out" occurs twelve times in chapter 7 and three times in chapter 8; it is only found once previously in Ecclesiastes. In this section, Solomon repeatedly applies this word in a negative tone to imply that man is incapable of discovering and understanding God's purposes in what goes on under the sun (7:13, 25, 8:17). With this said, it is noted that the sour tone of the narrative in chapter 6 is somewhat brightened in chapter 7. In the latter, Solomon utilizes paradox to share his ideas as to what types of behaviors are more profitable than others in mankind's pointless, incomprehensible existence. Solomon will now examine the experiment of morality as a means of obtaining satisfaction and enjoyment in life.

It is observed that the words "good" and "better" occur more frequently in these practical maxims of chapter 7 than in any other chapter in our Bible. We read, for example, that a good name, the evidence of an upright character, is to be valued more than costly perfume. Accordingly, those who live righteously before the Lord can have a joyful expectation concerning death; Solomon surmises that death can actually be more exciting than birth (7:1). Centuries later, Paul explained why: believers are ushered into the presence of the Lord (2 Cor. 5:8). Whether or not this was Solomon's intended import is unknown; generally speaking, he did believe the end of a thing is better than its beginning, presumably because one can better discover its meaning (7:8). Because death and suffering cause us to focus with painful clarity on the fundamental aspects of life, Solomon suggests the sadness experienced at a funeral, the rebuke of a wise person, and suffering in general are more profitable than fleeting delight and merriness, laughter, festive fanfare, etc. (7:2-7). He reasons we are not as mindful of the important issues of life, when we are engaged in mindless amusements.

Solomon then warns against being quick-tempered (7:9). Such behavior demonstrates a character weakness that is injurious to a good name and also brings out the worst in others; it is a destructive behavior. This is good counsel, but with a selfish motive: walk softly, do not be an extremist, be a compromiser to get along favorably with others so that you can better profit from your association with them. Another foolish activity is living in the past rather than facing the reality of one's present situation; it is better to courageously and cleverly tackle the affairs of life, rather than ignoring them by fantasizing about "the good old days" (7:10-12). A wise man understands that a sovereign and omniscient God is in control of all that happens during our earthly sojourn and that we really do not know what the future holds. This means we must explicitly trust Him, as He unfolds His immutable will in bestowing to us both times of prosperity and adversity. Solomon notes that from a human vantage point this mindset appears to be a mysterious contradiction (7:13-16).

Because foolhardiness and overzealous righteousness often led to premature death, and because there was no guarantee of divine blessing for living righteously, Solomon surmised that a middle-of-the-road policy was the best way to navigate through life's complexities (7:17-18). Of course, this is "under the sun" reasoning apart from divine wisdom, and must be regarded as such, that is, as a secular philosophy. Might does not make right; rather, wisdom is better than strength in resolving problems, though this approach does not guarantee favorable outcomes (7:19). The previous statements seem to be leading up to a logical conclusion: all men are imperfect creatures who sin and therefore need divine strength and wisdom to prevail in this life that they cannot understand (7:20). This realization should cause us to live before our Creator with more humility and be better accepting of what befalls us while sojourning on this sin-cursed planet (7:21-22).

Although Solomon had applied the full extent of his wisdom to unraveling life's great mysteries, he realized he had failed to do so, for such answers rest with God alone (7:23-24). Despite this daunting challenge, Solomon opted to continue his quest for understanding and a solution to the human saga; he especially wanted to understand why people abandon themselves to wickedness and shame (7:25). He considers the immoral woman who with cunning fervor seduces and ensnares her victims. What is her motivation? Would not a God-fearing man avoid her deadly entrapment (7:26)? As Solomon reflected back on his life, he realized that he had often had high expectations of people after first meeting them, but as he got to know them, his initial fond thoughts quickly diminished. In retrospect, he had found very few men, and no women (this reflects a carnal search and earthbound outlook) who were truly good and trustworthy (7:27-28). Humanity, in its present state of pursuing its own devices, was overall a huge disappointment to Solomon, though he reminds us that there was a day when man was not as he is now (7:29).

Originally, Adam was created "upright" or "innocent." Until Adam sinned, he reflected the character of God, for he bore God's image and likeness (Gen. 1:26). Adam was God's representative of Himself in creation before the fall of man (Heb. 2:6-8). After Adam sinned, he no longer bore the likeness of God, but his own likeness (Gen. 5:3). The Last Adam, Christ, is not just *innocent humanity,* as Adam was; He is *holy humanity* (Luke 1:35): indeed, *"For in Him dwells all the fullness of the Godhead bodily"* (Col. 2:9). Nowhere in Scripture do we read of Adam being "holy." God was not in Adam, but

"God was in Christ reconciling the world to Himself" (2 Cor. 5:19). Christ was fully human but had a different spiritual nature than Adam. As *holy humanity*, Christ could not sin, for there was nothing in His members that would respond to sin; His very essence repulsed sin and loathed its working.

When Adam sinned, he made a transition from *innocent humanity* to *condemned humanity* and was judged by God. Everyone coming from Adam is condemned as well (Rom. 5:12-14). Through the obedience of Christ came the offer of grace, forgiveness, and restoration (Rom. 5:15-21). Those who respond to the gospel of Christ become *redeemed humanity* and wait to become *glorified humanity* at Christ's return to the air for His Church (1 Thess. 4:13-18). In glorified Christ-like bodies the redeemed will then be ever with the Lord (Phil. 3:21; 1 Jn. 3:2). All that was lost by Adam's sin in the Garden of Eden is fully restored through the Last Adam, the Lord Jesus.

Despite the failure of human wisdom to resolve life's difficulties, a wise man was to be admired above a fool, for even his optimistic countenance reflected a more settled outlook on life (8:1). King Solomon then affirms that wisdom teaches one to be subject to and to respect those in authority; not to do so would result in unpleasant consequences (8:2-4). Those who obey the king need not fear punishment, though they would need wisdom to know how to best accomplish his commands (8:5-6). In this sense, wisdom would benefit the servant to understand what he did not know or could not control (8:7-8). These were aspects of life under the sun that the royal Preacher observed in a world in which rulers often exercised authority selfishly to the harm of their subjects (8:9).

He also observed that much of life was shallow and that man was gullible in discerning the reality of things; he cites the wicked man who covers up his corruption under a religious disguise and was then praised by others for his piety after his death (8:10). Solomon then suggested that delaying the just punishment of a criminal only serves to promote lawlessness and contempt for authority, all at the expense of the victims (8:11). While Solomon recognized that prompt, impartial justice was necessary for a society to function properly, he also believed that those who lived in fear of the Lord would generally prosper more than those who did not, yet he acknowledges there are troubling exceptions to this observation (8:12-14). Donald R. Glenn summarizes Solomon's main conclusion of this chapter:

> Having shown that there are enigmatic contradictions in the doctrine of retribution – righteousness is not always rewarded and wickedness is not always punished, and sometimes the wicked prosper and the righteous meet with disaster – Solomon again recommended the enjoyment of life. ... Man cannot control or predict adversity or prosperity; however, each day's joys should be received as gifts from God's hand and be savored as God permits (3:13; 5:19).[166]

In short, Solomon suggests that the best policy for enjoying life under the sun is to delight in your labor, or rather, the good God grants you through your labor, while you can (8:15). We must remember that Solomon is speaking of life apart from God; it is the way earthly man views life. It is no surprise then, suggests James Vernon McGee, that many atheists quote from the book of Ecclesiastes to further their agenda:

> This book of the Bible is like a black sheep in a flock of sheep. One can take many passages out of this book which seem to contradict the other portions of Scripture. They express ideas that are contrary to some of the great teachings of Scripture, which explains why this book has been a favorite among atheists. Volney and Voltaire quoted from it frequently. It fosters a pessimistic philosophy of life like Schopenhauer had. Some of the modern cults predicate the main thesis of their systems on this book. ...We must always remember that Solomon is speaking of life apart from God. ... So then it is no surprise that unbelievers would quote from this book.[167]

For the Christian, our life is hidden in Christ in heavenly places; therefore, we have the benefit of a heavenly vantage point, which is far above the sun. This revelation enables the believer to make sense of life, to enjoy it, and to live it to the fullest extent possible in grace.

Applying the True Meaning of Life
(8:16-12:8)

Despite his best efforts to understand the meaning of human existence, Solomon finally realized that no human philosophy, that is, no perspective "under the sun," could adequately explain what God had purposefully arranged in obscurity (8:16-17). However, it was still possible for him to experience a meaningful life, without comprehending the finer points of being. He would later conclude that we must obtain true wisdom from above the sun, which is centered in the fear of the Lord, to understand the eternal perspective for our existence.

In chapter 9, Solomon returns to the topic of death, which despite wisdom is unavoidable (hence his repeated admonitions to enjoy life to the fullest while you can). God is sovereign in dealing with the wise and the foolish. This means that certain sorrowful events in life may not be explainable and may not be the result of God's displeasure – for what man can know the mind of God (9:1)? All men eventually suffer the same fate: death. None can escape this end no matter how they live. But Solomon surmised since death was unavoidable that there must be divine retribution after death for those who choose to live wickedly, or this would be a gross injustice (9:2-3). His belief in a future day of reckoning lent meaning to life under the sun.

This meant that as long as man lived on the earth there was something to look forward to, but humanly speaking, there was nothing after death to hope in, for the dead are not cognizant of earthly affairs (9:4-5). This statement does not validate "soul sleep" after death as some teach; it should rather be understood to mean that the interactive physical and emotional life that one previously possessed on the earth is over at death (9:6). Simply put, life is preferable to death, but when it comes to the purpose of their temporary existence, the materialist sees no difference between man and animal. Hence, Solomon again reiterates his humanistic conclusion: live life to the fullest – enjoy yourself while you can and as God enables, because His foreknowledge has already preset your future (9:7-8); just make the best of life that you can!

The well-known maxim of verse 10, *"Whatsoever your hand finds to do, do it with your might,"* is still quoted today, often to spur others on in their service to the Lord. However, in its proper context, Solomon is urging us to exploit life's enjoyments, including the sensual aspects of one's marital relationship, to the fullest before death ends our opportunity to do so. In his view, these fleeting pleasures were connected with diligent labor, and therefore represented the best outcome of all one's toil under the sun (9:9-10). Although we are assured the Lord certainly knows (and directs) the future, Solomon observed that time and chance are seemingly immense factors in one's life – our best efforts, even when forged in wisdom, are often wiped out by unforeseen calamities (9:11); like a fish caught in a net, bad luck just happens and is unavoidable (9:12).

Besides this dismal reality, Solomon suggests another one that is equally heartbreaking: wisdom is not always appreciated, even when its beneficial outcome is obvious. He is in a quandary as to why man rejects the benefits of wisdom. This query is illustrated by the story of a poor man whose wise counsel saved his village from a mighty aggressor, but later, after the crisis was past, his wisdom was disregarded (9:13-16). Despite this reality, the Preacher concludes that words of wisdom spoken with humility are more powerful than the foolish utterances of kings. He remarks, *"Wisdom is better than weapons of war"* (9:17-18) – wisdom is superior to power.

Solomon continues on in chapter 10 to consider the undertakings of both the wise and the foolish in somewhat of a proverbial fashion, which makes his reasoning more difficult to discern. He introduces the notion that it is best to pursue a lifestyle of moderation with a word picture. Flies trapped in a perfumer's ointment die and soon cause a foul odor; likewise, though a man may wisely labor his entire life to gain a good reputation, it requires only a few moments of foolish indiscretion to void all that he has accomplished (10:1). While the wise know the right way and walk accordingly, the fool, even when he attempts to trek down the path of wisdom, invariably betrays common sense and proves himself to be senseless (10:2-3). The consequences of such behavior are even more troublesome if the fool is in authority. As a side note, Solomon suggests that if you are the recipient of a ruler's foolish rage, you are more likely to pacify him by a submissive, humble response (10:4).

The Preacher also observed another disquieting paradox: wise men, suited to leadership, often expend their lives performing mundane tasks

The Beginning of Wisdom

while fools are permitted to rule the people (10:5-7). Solomon therefore concluded that because positions of authority are not always determined on the basis of merit, but rather by chance or fancy, the observed value of wisdom is often nullified. Yet, foolish leaders or those who scheme to harm others eventually suffer from their own devices (10:8). Furthermore, a society that repeatedly ascribes dignity to folly will suffer eventual collapse (10:6). This type of behavior is apparent in various ways, but a prominent example today would be our modern society's appreciation of filth under the label of "art" or "free expression." Yet, such manifestations are merely the sinful foolishness of the corrupt human heart.

Solomon acknowledges that no activity in life is without risk, but just as a person sharpens an axe before splitting wood to expedite the work, yielding to wisdom and proper order lessens the likelihood of harm and enhances productivity while reducing effort (10:9-11). Understanding the obvious advantage of wisdom in life, a wise person will carefully select and speak gracious words. In contrast, a fool, no matter how hard he tries to speak prudently, is ultimately known by his idiotic and unconstrained babbling (10:12-14): *"In the multitude of words sin is not lacking, but he who restrains his lips is wise"* (Prov. 10:19). The fool's inefficient, random, and senseless ways are unprofitable and his ignorance of even simple affairs ensures he has no plan for the future (10:15). A people governed by such a gullible and immature person should be pitied, but those ruled by a man of character and wise fortitude are privileged (10:16-17).

Solomon continues providing proverbial insights as to the benefits of wisdom in life and the ills of foolish behavior: Laziness and neglect have a guaranteed outcome. Hence, it is better to maintain one's roof in good condition, rather than to suffer a greater expense of household damage due to a leaky one (10:18). Under the sun, money can buy any pleasure, but not happiness (10:19). Be careful not to speak ill of those in authority, even when you think no one is listening; the walls have ears, so to speak, and your careless murmurings might find their way to the king himself (10:20).

In chapter 11, Solomon ponders how the moral man might best enjoy the good life through the practice of moderation. To illustrate this point, the chapter commences with a word picture: sowing bread (or grain) in wet fields will produce a bountiful harvest later. The significance of this proverb is that the distribution of what is good is profitable (11:1). Accordingly, Solomon suggests that we be generous while we are able, as the opportunity to benefit others may be lost; we do not know when future catastrophes will strike (11:2-3). Furthermore, since the possibility of disaster is always lurking about, he advises prudent investments in a variety of endeavors, even *"to seven, yes to eight"* (11:2). In other words, "don't put your eggs all in one basket" – by one fall you may lose everything. Practically speaking, all ventures under the sun have some level of risk; therefore, do not be so cautious that you accomplish nothing in life; if one chooses to wait for certainty to act, you will waste your life away (11:4). Sensible risk and diligence are a normal part of a fruitful life; it is understood that some ventures will fail, while others will be successful, but nothing prospers from inaction (11:6-8). Solomon is not saying trust in your various investments; rather, as William Kelly suggests, his import is to seek wisdom from God and put your trust in Him:

> Earlier in the book is shown the folly of setting the heart on any object under the sun; and if any understood more deeply what is in man and in the world, as the writer in fact did, it is only the more profound sorrow. Receiving what God gives and using it all in His fear is wisdom. Now the Preacher exhorts to liberal action in assured faith, as he may well do who knows that the righteous and the wise and their works are in the hand of God.[168]

What is Solomon's advice in chapter 11? Life is brief, therefore take calculated risks while trusting in the Lord and go for the gusto, especially in one's youthful vitality, but behave with righteous prudence, for God punishes sin and often the consequences of juvenile sin occur later in life (11:9). In application, we should not let what we do not know hinder us from acting on what we do know; furthermore, prudence, moderation, and godliness should govern all that we do. For example, a farmer knows he must risk time and resources to sow seed in his fields in order to harvest a crop, but to do so in a lingering drought would not be prudent. Yet, if he waited to sow his fields until there was no threat of calamity, he would cease to be a farmer. Investments which minimize loss and provide for our necessities while trusting in God for the increase is Solomon's suggested way of life.

The Beginning of Wisdom

Continuing this train of thought into chapter 12, Solomon adds this exhortation concerning our dependency: *"Remember now your Creator in the days of your youth, before the difficult days come"* (12:1). Throughout one's life, a person should revere God, obey His commandments, and render faithful service to the Creator. The coming difficult days in this verse refer to the body's degradation that accompanies old age. To ensure his younger audience would be able to relate to his warning, Solomon colorfully describes the condition of those trudging on through their autumn years:

In the day when the keepers of the house shall tremble, and the strong men shall bow themselves, and the grinders cease because they are few, and those that look out of the windows be darkened and when the doors are shut in the streets, and the sound of grinding is low; when one rises up at the sound of a bird, and all the daughters of music are brought low (12:3-4).

It is natural for older women to fall, for men to slump over with age, and for the elderly to lose their teeth and eyesight (12:3). Additionally, they may lose their hearing and often suffer from insomnia, weakened vocal cords, fearfulness, and diminished natural desires (e.g. taste for food, sexual vigor, etc.; 12:4-5). As Paul puts it, the *"outward man is perishing"* (2 Cor. 4:16). Solomon remarks this unavoidable degenerative process is nature's way of preparing us for our long-lasting abode: death, man's eventual end under the sun (12:5). It would be wise, then, for us to honor God in our brief existence, for a dead and decaying body has no opportunity to do so (12:6).

Apparently, Solomon believed that the human spirit returned to God after death, but New Testament revelation informs us that only the spirits of the redeemed will be with the Lord after death (Phil. 1:23; 2 Cor. 5:8). The soul of the unbeliever descends into Hades where it waits to be reunited with a resurrected body, which will afterwards be condemned to the Lake of Fire at the Great White Throne Judgment (Luke 16:19-31; Rev. 20:11-15). After contemplating the distasteful inevitability of death and judgment, Solomon concludes this section at the very place he began his quest in chapter 1: life under the sun is vain, meaningless, and futile. This pathetic conclusion is unavoidable if one estimates the meaning of life from an earthly perspective.

Solomon has experimented with wisdom, natural science, religion, materialism, egoism, fatalism, moralism, and the pursuit of pleasure, none of which could satisfactorily resolve the difficulties in his mind concerning the purpose of man's existence. We must obtain wisdom from above the sun to understand the eternal vantage point and the reason for our living. True wisdom is inseparable from the fear of the Lord and enables us to begin to understand the mind of God and to resolve questions otherwise inscrutable (Prov. 9:10). This realization becomes the basis for Solomon's final conclusion.

Conclusion
(12:9-14)

The Preacher draws his ontological journey and literary work to a close; he sought to be a good shepherd of the people by sharing his wisdom and knowledge in the form of well-tested proverbs (12:9-11). He readily admits that he has not exhausted the subject matter, but in his estimation, further examination of the meaning of life from an "under the sun" outlook would only yield the same conclusion, regardless of how much effort he expended (12:12). Even if a person could read every book available, they would all reveal the same thing – the vanity of life. Solomon realized no human reckoning could adequately explain what God had purposefully arranged in obscurity (8:16-17). However, he did deduce that through wisdom and diligence it is possible to experience a meaningful life, without fully comprehending the meaning of one's vain existence.

While it is true that many aspects of our existence are beyond the realm of our senses and hence outside our acumen and understanding, some mysterious facets of our existence can be observed by their influences. In others words, we can validate the existence of something without fully understanding it. By applying what we do understand of earthly order, we are able to statistically verify improbable occurrences which defy natural law. This suggests something else at work beyond nature – a supernatural cause and presence among us.

In summary, the Creator has intentionally allowed us to perceive only a portion of absolute reality in order to prompt us to ponder the vast void beyond. God has constructed a cosmic stage, has put something bigger in motion than we can comprehend, and at the same time administers an unavoidable test for every conscious individual. As Solomon concludes, all such human quandaries about our existence may be duly satisfied by approaching a divine Creator in obedience to revealed truth. Former atheist C. S. Lewis came to this realization also: "I believe in God as I believe that the Sun has risen, not only because I see it, but because by it I see everything else."[169] For this reason, a philosophy that precludes the possibility of supernatural cause in nature will be a *doubting science*. The words of German philosopher Nietzsche illustrate this point well: "If you could prove God to me, I would believe Him all the less."[170] Those who willfully close their eyes to revealed truth will not see God!

King Solomon wisely instructed his readers to *"Consider the work of God"* (7:13). Man is to ponder God's nature, character, word, and works, but not without including Him in the exercise, or else his humanly-derived conclusions will of necessity be lacking. We must reason together with God. Why? Because without God's help man cannot understand or reason out what God has purposefully concealed: *"The secret things belong to the Lord our God, but those things which are revealed belong to us and to our children"* (Deut. 29:29). Because God alone holds absolute truth, He will always transcend human reasoning. Solomon surmised:

> *I saw all the work of God, that a man cannot find out the work that is done under the sun. For though a man labors to discover it, yet he will not find it; moreover, though a wise man attempts to know it, he will not be able to find it* (8:17).

The words of Louis Cassels to the intellectual sound true: "You can save yourself a lot of time and mental agony by recognizing at the outset that you cannot reason your way to a belief in God."[171] God spiritually calls and pleads with people to trust Him, but He does not force them heavenward against their will. Because reason and free choice are required to approach God, man is required to weigh out the evidence, wrangle over the possibilities, consider God's Word, and come to a logical conclusion which will cause him to act in good faith. God assists a true seeker every step of the way into a greater realization of Himself.

If we open our minds to God's calling and study Scripture to know His will, we find Christ the most wonderful answer to all our problems, the chief of which is sin. By this I do not mean that our lives will be filled with wealth and prosperity, and void of trials and difficulties, but rather that we will know a joy and peace beyond these things. Solomon concisely summed up man's purpose on the Earth: *"Fear God and keep His commandments, for this is the whole duty of man"* (12:13). This is the message of Proverbs, and finally of Ecclesiastes also. Whether or not this grand conclusion was prompted by direct revelation or was a logical assessment given man's accountability to his Creator cannot be asserted (12:14). What is obvious is Solomon knew that God had revealed His will to man and that there was an inescapable judgment for those who held that knowledge in unrighteousness.

Centuries later, Paul would affirm this immutable reality: *"For the wrath of God is revealed from heaven against all ungodliness and unrighteousness of men, who suppress the truth in unrighteousness"* (Rom. 1:18). He also acknowledged that God had written His moral law instinctively into the human heart; therefore, man could not claim ignorance as to what God expected in his behavior (Rom. 2:15). Whether Solomon was referring to only God's written Law or also to His moral law in the human heart, does not really matter, as both reflect the same standard of holiness. Solomon's point is that man has no excuse; God has revealed Himself, what He expects of man, and will hold man accountable.

In the Church Age, the whole duty of man is to obey (i.e., exercise faith in) the gospel message of Jesus Christ (1 Cor. 15:3-4). Those who experience His salvation are then called to live out this gospel message – they are to die to self and live for Christ (Gal. 2:20). By God's mercy, the believer escapes hell, and by His grace, he or she inherits heaven and all that Christ has (Rev. 21:7). The Lord Jesus Christ is both the beginning and the end of man's quest to uncover the meaning of life; through Him, believers obtain eternal life, one that is abundantly fulfilling even now (John 10:10). We conclude life under the sun, apart from knowing Christ, is vain and temporary, but what we have in Him above the sun is meaningful and eternal.

Song of Solomon

Song of Solomon

Introduction

Originally, this song was titled after the first verse, "The Song of Songs," but later it became identified with its author as the "Song of Solomon." The repetition of the word "song" in the first verse indicates that Solomon considered this expression his most important literary work. This grammatical construction is used to denote a superlative in Hebrew; Moses used this form to identify the supremacy of Jehovah; He is the *"God of gods"* and *"Lord of lords"* (Deut. 10:17). What is the topic of the greatest song that Solomon penned? The security and exhilaration of marital love.

At this present time, the divine institution of marriage is under immense attack! Not only are some in our postmodern culture trying to redefine what marriage is, but many have also concluded that it is an archaic tradition which is no longer relevant. Consequently, a smaller percentage of people are entering into that sacred covenant and, of those who do, fewer are staying married.

God's original design for marriage was affirmed by the Lord Jesus: one man and one woman committed to each other until death separates them (Matt. 19:3-8). Unfortunately, Old Testament history shows that divorce had become commonplace among God's covenant people long before Christ's earthly sojourn (Mal. 2:14-16). As evidenced in Solomon's own life, another departure from God's marital order was polygamy. In the ancient Jewish culture, it was not uncommon for a man to take a second wife, especially if his first wife could not bear him children (1 Sam. 1). Reigning kings usually took several wives in hopes of ensuring a lasting posterity and a long dynasty. Polygamy is never extolled in the Old Testament, but the ill consequences of it are recorded for our edification. The New Testament flatly rejects polygamy; no polygamist could be recognized as a church elder or deacon in the local church (1 Tim. 3:2, 12).

In this song, Solomon is not only acknowledging the importance of the marital commitment, but also the intimate lifetime companionship that God desires a married couple to share. These vibrant realities needed to be rediscovered in Solomon's day, and we need them reaffirmed today as well. The "Song of Songs" upholds God's design for what the marital union is to be. Although the exact meaning of its poetic narrative is difficult to assert, its theme is not, and for that reason this book has encouraged the Lord's people for over two millennia.

Purpose

While the main theme of this opus centers in the love shared between *"the beloved"* and the Shulamite maiden, the specific purpose of the book depends on the perspective from which it is evaluated. From a *literary* standpoint, the entire poem extols marital love. If we analyze it from a *dispensational* view, the special union between Jehovah and His covenant people, the nation of Israel, is paramount. If interpreted by the fuller work of *redemption*, as revealed in the New Testament, then we can see the marvelous union between Christ and the Church. Lastly, if reading the book from a *spiritual* standpoint, we understand that communion between the redeemed and the blessed Savior is to be maintained in purity and faithfulness. The latter vantage point encourages believers to live moral lives, lest they hinder the very fellowship that Christ yearns to enjoy with them. It also prompts believers to deepen their appreciation for their Beloved through meditating on Him in Scripture and communicating with Him in prayer.

Divisions/Outline

Throughout the song, *"the beloved"* refers to Solomon or perhaps, as some think, the shepherd-lover, while the Shulamite maiden is called his *"love."* Regardless of which dramatic interpretation one accepts as correct, the following generic outline by Hamilton Smith[172] seems to accommodate the various views of this book:

1:2-2:7: The Assurance of Love
2:8-3:5: The Awakening of Love
3:6-5:1: The Communion of Love

    5:2-6:12: The Restoration of Love
    6:13-8:4: The Witness of Love
    8:5-14: The Triumph of Love

If Solomon is identified as the Shulamite's beloved, then the progression in their relationship can be outlined in this manner: a courtship (1:2-3:5), followed by a wedding (3:6-5:1), and the maturing of the marital relationship (5:2-8:4). Some associate the beloved with an unnamed shepherd-lover; in this case, the storyline would be: the Shulamite reminisces about her old lover while in Solomon's court, expresses her desire to be with him, tells others about him, and/or secretly communicates with him (1:2-8; 2:8-3:5; 4:7-6:3); during this time Solomon's attempts to woo her to himself fail (1:9-2:6; 3:6-4:6; 6:4-7:10); and, finally, she is reunited and married to her shepherd-lover (7:11-8:14).

Authorship

The book's title and the first verse confirm King Solomon authored this splendid book. He is also mentioned by name throughout the song (1:5, 3:7, 9, 11, 8:11). Additionally, the writer is referred to as a *"king"* (1:4, 12, 3:9, 11, 7:5). At the time this book was written, Solomon was the King of Israel and had a harem of sixty wives and eighty concubines (6:8). Towards the end of his life this number grew to seven hundred wives and three hundred concubines (1 Kgs. 11:3).

Given Solomon's marital extravaganza, we may question why he composed this poem that features the relationship between one man and one woman, and how in Proverbs he could repeatedly warn his own son not to be overcome with sensual lusting. Clearly, Solomon did not exercise wisdom in this aspect of his life; he plainly ignored Moses' warning against a king marrying many women (Deut. 17:17). Regrettably, towards the end of his life, his many wives turned his heart from the Lord (1 Kgs. 11:4-8). In the Song of Songs, Solomon apparently wants to set the matter straight; God's design for marriage is one man and one woman bound by a covenant for life. Given the above understanding, some believe this literary piece is regarded as the "song of songs" because it was one of Solomon's earliest works, in which he describes his first love who he then marries. Regardless of the truth of this conjecture, the central theme of the poem is not to lust for what is outside the will of God; rather, seek to be faithful and satisfied with the wife of one's youth (Prov. 5:18-19)!

Date and Historical Setting

Since Solomon reigned as Israel's king from 971 to 932 B.C., his literary works would have been composed during that timeframe. Given that the Shulamite is a young maiden, it is suggested that Solomon wrote the Song of Songs in his early adult years. He likely wrote Proverbs as a middle-aged man, and Ecclesiastes near the end of his life as he reflected on all his experiences. The text itself gives us clues as to its timeframe. The first reference to spring in this song occurs in 2:11-13, and the second is mentioned in 7:12, which means the entire book spans an interval of more than one but less than two years.

Analysis of the Book

The explicit language describing the passion shared between the Shulamite bride and her beloved has caused some to question whether the book is divinely inspired and if it should have been canonized at all. Speaking to the book's divine inspiration, H. A. Ironside highlights how the Song of Solomon affirms God's design for marriage to the nation of Israel:

> Many of the Jewish teachers thought of it [the Song of Solomon] simply as designed of God to give a right apprehension of conjugal love. They thought of it as the glorification of the bliss of wedded life, and if we conceived of it from no higher standpoint than this, it would mean that it had a right to a place in the canon. Wedded life in Israel represented the very highest and fullest and deepest affection at a time when, in the nations surrounding Israel, woman was looked upon as a mere chattel, as a slave, or as the object of man's pleasure to be discarded when and as he pleased. But it was otherwise in Israel. The Jewish home was a place where love and tenderness reigned, and no doubt this little book had a great deal to do with lifting it to that glorious height.[173]

The Song of Solomon has always been a part of the Hebrew Bible, though a tradition developed among orthodox Jews did not permit a man under thirty years of age to read it because of its descriptive sensual content (e.g., 1:12-16). Regardless of its interpretation, this entire poem is a song of enduring devotion and expressed passion between a man and a woman who are unconditionally committed to each other – this upholds God's original design for marriage as declared in Genesis 2:24-25. For this reason, the bulk of this author's contemplations will be focused on deriving application pertaining to the institution of marriage, rather than expounding on potential typological and prophetic meanings of the poem.

Dramatic Observations

Some regard the Song of Solomon as merely a collection of detached romantic poetry, which lacks a central storyline; while portions of the book might be fitting for a wedding ceremony, they see no literal meaning or application to be derived from the composition. The fact that the same characters, figures of speech, and expressions are present throughout the entire book overturns this conclusion. On the contrary, conservative scholars observe a central narrative involving two or possibly three main participants, depending on how the narrative is understood.

There are two main dramatic understandings. First, Solomon, likely disguised as a lowly shepherd, interacts with a young beautiful Shulamite maiden and develops a relationship with her. He later reveals his true identity in a surprise visit and whisks her away to the palace to be his bride, thus fulfilling his promise to her. F. C. Cook, Jack Deere, H. A. Ironside, James V. McGee, C. I. Scofield, and Hamilton Smith are some Bible expositors that hold this view. Second, the Shulamite maiden has already committed herself to a shepherd-lover, but Solomon sequesters her in his palace against her will. Solomon's repeated attempts to woo her fail and she is eventually reunited with her beloved, who she then marries. In this view, the Shulamite bride is the heroin of the poem, and Solomon, the author, is the villain. William MacDonald prefers this understanding, a view popularized two centuries ago by Ewald, the great German critic, who has been called the father of higher criticism.[174] This author prefers the former and less awkward viewpoint, to which H. A. Ironside offers this dramatic overview:

King Solomon had a vineyard in the hill country of Ephraim, about 50 miles north of Jerusalem (8:11). He let it out to keepers (8:11), consisting of a mother, two sons (1:6), and two daughters – the Shulamite, (6:13), and a little sister (8:8). The Shulamite was "the Cinderella" of the family (1:5), naturally beautiful but unnoticed. Her brothers were likely half-brothers (1:6). They made her work very hard tending the vineyards, so that she had little opportunity to care for her personal appearance (1:6). She pruned the vines and set traps for the little foxes (2:15). She also kept the flocks (1:8). Being out in the open so much, she became sunburned (1:5).

One day a handsome stranger came to the vineyard. It was Solomon disguised. He showed an interest in her, and she became embarrassed concerning her personal appearance (1:6). She took him for a shepherd and asked about his flocks (1:7). He answered evasively (1:8), but also spoke loving words to her (1:8-10), and promised rich gifts for the future (1:11). He won her heart and left with the promise that someday he would return. She dreamed of him at night and sometimes thought he was near (3:1). Finally he did return in all his kingly splendor to make her his bride (3:6-7:3).[175]

Whether the Shulamite's beloved is actually Solomon or a shepherd-lover cannot be proven. However, the latter interpretation suggests Solomon was a kidnapper; such a perspective taints the book's theme of marital love. Furthermore, all of the Shulamite's romantic expectations seem fulfilled by Solomon's surprise appearance at her home and then their departure in the royal chariot to his Jerusalem palace (3:1-10, 6:12). Why would Solomon say to her, *"Rise up, my love, my fair one, and come away,"* if they did not share a mutual affection (2:13)? With this opinion stated, the author readily agrees with Jack Deere's assessment: "Probably no other book of the Bible has such a variegated tapestry of interpretation."[176] It is doubtful that Bible students will agree on the interpretation of the Song of Solomon on this side of heaven, but what we can concur on is that marriage, as God designed it, is a lifetime covenant of companionship between a man and a woman which is characterized by intimacy and unwavering commitment.

Thematic Interpretation

There are three main thematic interpretations of the Song of Solomon: allegorical, literal, and prophetic. Because of the vivid sensual language, many ancient scholars viewed the entire book as an allegory tracing the history of the Jewish nation from its conception to the coming of the Messiah, their Beloved. This type of allegorical meaning is represented in other portions of Scripture, such as Ezekiel 16.

As already discussed, the literal interpretation suggests that the book is an actual love story which confirms God's design for marriage. Commentator Roy Zuck holds this position:

> Some Bible teachers view the Song of Songs as an extended allegory to depict God's relationship to Israel or Christ's relationship to the church. However, since there is no indication in the book that this is the case, it is preferable to view the book as extolling human love and marriage.[177]

Yet, it is not absurd to see a prophetic meaning in the Song of Solomon. Nearly all of the prophetic books in the Old Testament foretell a future day when the Messiah will come and restore the nation of Israel to Himself. From this viewpoint, Jehovah is the faithful Husband waiting for the restoration of His unfaithful wife, Israel (Jer. 3:8; Hos. 3). Beyond this fact, this book does seem to contain a prophetic application for the Church, which Paul states was a mysterious truth not clearly revealed in Solomon's day (Eph. 3:1-11). From this vantage point, the *"daughters of Jerusalem"* in the song (1:5, 2:2, 2:7, 3:5...) represent the Jewish nation which is presently spiritually estranged from Jehovah, while the Church is the spotless bride patiently waiting to be united with her Beloved, the Lord Jesus Christ (Eph. 1:6). Like the Shulamite, the Church is also waiting for a surprise visit of her Groom to snatch her away to His superb palace! This interpretation would agree with the teachings of the Lord Jesus concerning future events involving the Church after its rapture to heaven: The Church returns to the earth with Christ at the end of the Tribulation Period as the bride (Rev. 19); there, the refined Jewish nation who receive the Holy Spirit are patiently waiting to receive Him as well. (They are like the virgins with oil; Matt. 25:1-14.) The marriage feast is then enjoyed by all believers.

The Song of Solomon is a marital opus of devotion and commitment between a husband and his bride. As already mentioned, several interpretations of the main characters and various thematic viewpoints are possible; however, it seems most fitting to assume a literal explanation of King Solomon and a young Shulamite woman being mutually consenting lovers who maintained moral purity in their relationship before and after they were married.

Characters

Who are the main characters in the Song of Solomon and who or what might they represent? As already mentioned, there is some question as to whether Solomon is the shepherd-lover or not. The following list of characters is supplied with the understanding that the shepherd and king are one and the same. Throughout the poem, then, the term *"beloved"* refers to Solomon (e.g., 1:14), and his *"love"* is the Shulamite bride (e.g., 1:15). If a prophetic meaning does exist in the song, it seems pertinent to interpret it in relation to the nation of Israel primarily, though a secondary application may pertain to the mysterious union of Christ and the Church.

Characters	Primary Significance	Secondary Significance
Solomon the Shepherd-King	Jehovah God	The Lord Jesus Christ
The Young Maiden	Believing Israel	The Church
The Daughters of Jerusalem	The Nations	Unbelieving Israel
Solomon's Companions	Angels	Angels
The Watchmen	The Prophets	Faithful Gospel Preachers

Song of Solomon

Overview

The first verse introduces the author and his estimation of this story as his highest work. The commentary for the remainder of the book will follow Hamilton Smith's outline:

1:2-2:7: The Assurance of Love
2:8-3:5: The Awakening of Love
3:6-5:1: The Communion of Love
5:2-6:12: The Restoration of Love
6:13-8:4: The Witness of Love
8:5-14: The Triumph of Love

Devotions in Song of Solomon

The Assurance of Love
(1:2-2:7)

The Shulamite maiden was swept off her feet during her first encounter with a young shepherd, whom I believe to be King Solomon incognito (1:2-4). Perhaps he had disguised himself and ventured from the palace secretly to enjoy a few moments of solitude in the countryside. The Shulamite's brothers had forced their sister to work long, grueling hours tying up vines and setting traps for little foxes in their leased vineyard (1:5-6). The fact that she refers to them as *"my mother's sons"* and that they *"were angry with her"* may imply they were half-brothers and she was suffering the injustice of a divided family (1:6).

In this ongoing situation, she was not able to attend to her *"own vineyard"* (1:6), that is, to properly care for her own body and its appearance. For this reason, the Shulamite insisted her new admirer not gaze upon her sunbaked skin, blistered hands, and filthy attire. Yet, her diligent subjection to her family despite the personal hardship made her all the more attractive to him (1:7). He responded to her plea by affirming kind words, telling her she was *"fairest among women"* (1:8-10). A friendship commenced that soon blossomed into mutual admiration and romantic expressions. The Shulamite maiden willingly received Solomon's kindness and genuine concern for her by saying his love was *"better than wine"* (1:2). He pledged to return someday and make her his wife. The Hebrew language conveys her acceptance of his love in verse 4: *"Take me away with you."* There seems to be a parenthetical jump forward in time in these early verses to clue us in to the fact that she is later brought to the palace and becomes the king's wife. But for now she can only anticipate marital intimacy with him, acknowledging if this did not occur, she would be like a veiled woman mourning the dead (1:7).

The remainder of this first section records the mutual desire, praise, and assurance of these two lovers as their courtship progresses into maturity. Genuine love must be nurtured to grow; it cannot be forced (2:7). Several principles for edifying conduct in our own marriages can be derived from the spectacular interaction of these two lovers. While the Song of Solomon contains many lessons in how both husbands and wives may satisfy one another's needs for companionship, four specific applications are noted in this first section.

First, they had doves' eyes for each other. The bridegroom proclaims to his bride, *"You have doves' eyes"* (1:15, 4:1). In turn, the bride speaks of her beloved as having *"eyes like the eyes of doves"* (5:12). As C. E. Hocking comments in his book, *Rise Up My Love*:

> The dove spoken of here is the 'rock pigeon,' which hides away from danger among the stony crevices of a rock face. Normally, like eyes, these doves are always seen in pairs. Both lovers describe the other's eyes as doves' eyes. Indeed, her eyes are a true mirror image of his and his eyes of hers....Beauty and constancy are suggested, for the dove has its mate alone before its eyes, and mourns when its mate is absent.[178]

Husband and wife are literally to have eyes only for each other. Men, your wives notice those quick glances at forbidden fruit, and each one of them bruises your fruitful vine (Ps. 128:3), and limits the ascent to true biblical companionship. Do you want your wife's affection or anxiety? Doves cannot rotate their eyes to see; they must turn their necks to look in different directions. Their fixed eyes convey single-hearted devotion to one another. Having doves' eyes for one another necessitates being with one another. A husband and wife must spend time together to nurture their relationship.

Second, the beloved accommodates the moods of his love. There are many factors, such as the need for security, emotional cares, and hormonal fluctuations that can affect a woman's disposition and mood. From a practical standpoint, husbands should be sensitive to their wives' mood changes and assist them as much as possible during times of irritability, anxiety, and depression. Hocking highlights the way the beloved accommodated his bride's needs:

The whole poem appears to oscillate between the country and the city, the vineyards and the banqueting house, the sovereign and the shepherd. She needs to be conducted from one scene to the other so as to assure her heart, for she is overly self-conscious. This her beloved does with great sensitivity, responding to her initial request to him, 'Draw me,' and so accommodating himself to her every mood until she is faint with love and finally requests 'stay (support) ye me.' The experienced attractions, responses, and triumphs over all obstacles led to the attained rest of betrothal.

We may note that she:
is drawn by him
is brought into the king's chambers
desires his kisses

is sustained by him
is brought to the banqueting house
enjoys his embrace

There is development elsewhere in the poem:
she suffers from sun scorching then
she is slaving away in the vineyards
we will run after thee

she is under his shadow
she is sitting down in his presence
love is not to be disturbed[179]

    Just as Christ satisfies every need of the Church, husbands should endeavor to satisfy every legitimate need of their wives. A properly satisfied wife will respond to her husband in the same way the Shulamite woman responded to Solomon – with total commitment and returned affection. God created woman to respond in this way upon the receipt of genuine sacrificial love.

    Third, husbands should compliment their wives. Mark the Shulamite's preoccupation with herself in this chapter; she uses the pronoun "I" eight times as compared to Solomon's single use. She is especially sensitive about her appearance. In contrast, Solomon focuses the majority of his speech (three of the five verses) on reassuring the Shulamite of his love and on his approval of her beauty. In general, women are more concerned about their outward presentation than men. Men may venture from the home into public without inspecting their image, but this would be unsettling for most women.

    Both Paul and Peter address the feminine practice of alluring with the outward appearance (1 Tim. 2:9; 1 Pet. 3:3). The woman's longer hair is referred to as her glory (1 Cor. 11:15); however, evidently at this time there were Christian women who were displaying their hair in elaborate hairstyles, flaunting themselves in costly apparel and decorative ornaments of gold and fine jewels, being flirtatious, and misusing their feminine assets to attract the attention of their male counterparts. Nothing is new under the sun, but time has shown that this enticing practice continues to degrade women and stumble men. With each passing generation, women are uncovering more of themselves and sexual perversion abounds. A woman has no scriptural grounds to be a seductress, except to her husband. A wife should endeavor to look her best for her husband in the home, but avoid being an embellished sex object in public. Clement of Alexandria summarizes this point bluntly, "Love of display is not for a lady, but a prostitute."[180]

Returning to the narrative, the exhortation is twofold. First, men need to understand the natural need for a woman to be noticed and appreciated (1:8-10) – to feel significant. Second, each husband should continually reassure his wife that she is the *"apple of your eye"* – to know the security of his love. She needs to know you have doves' eyes for her alone (1:15). The Shepherd-King in the Song of Solomon ministered to his love in this way, saying such things as: *"You are fairest among women"* (1:18). *"As the lily among thorns, so is my love among the daughters"* (2:2). *"You are all fair, my love; there is no spot in thee"* (4:7). Truly, a husband with such tender qualities casts a *"banner of love"* over his wife; in other words, his gentle affection towards his wife is easily observed by others (2:4).

Fourth, wives ought to use their words to build up their husbands. The Shulamite is swelling with kind speech about her beloved when she speaks to the daughters of Jerusalem (1:12-13, 2:3-7). The Shulamite never says anything negative about her beloved to others. There is no excuse to talk disrespectfully or disgracefully about one's husband to anyone else; *"let the wife see that she respects her husband"* (Eph. 5:33). A husband should show the same regard for his wife; matters of marital exhortation or correction should be done privately and with prudence. One of the deepest needs of men is to feel respected by their wives. Your husband may not have earned your respect, but you still must respect his position of authority, for it was issued by God. To disrespect his authority, unless its use is contrary to the Word of God, is to actively oppose God (Rom. 13:1-2; Acts 5:29; 1 Pet. 3:1).

Solomon provides wonderful insights within this intimate poem as to the appropriate and needful interaction between a husband and his wife to enhance their assurance of love. Let us pursue what is holy, meaningful, and edifying for our spouses, and may every husband be satisfied by the clusters of his own vine (7:7-8) and the refreshing drink from his own well (Prov. 5:15)!

From a devotional perspective, we have already noticed that the Shulamite is swelling with kind speech about her beloved. While this is an honorable behavior, we also observe that she spends more time *talking about him* to others (the daughters of Jerusalem) than *speaking to him* personally (e.g., 1:12-14, 2:3-7). This is a spiritual pitfall to avoid in interacting with our Beloved. Spiritual intimacy with the Lord is enhanced as we genuinely cooperate with Him and rely on Him. This requires us to mediate on His Word and obey what the Holy Spirit teaches us from it (John 14:15). The Lord speaks to us in this way, but we also must approach the throne of grace where He resides to speak to Him, that is, through prayer (Heb. 4:15-16).

While it is honorable to speak to others about the goodness of the Lord, let us not be guilty of neglecting our communication with Him. Nehemiah reminds us that our joy and strength rest in Him (Neh. 8:10) and the Lord Himself warned that we could do nothing without Him (John 15:5). The church at Ephesus was sound in doctrine and was doing good works, but yet received the rebuke of the Lord because they did not love Him as they once did (Rev. 2:4-5). Let us remember that doing good works in the Lord's name and gaining knowledge about Him does not necessarily equate to loving Him (Matt. 7:21-23). Husbands and wives naturally drift apart if they do not spend time interacting with each other and the same thing can happen if we ignore our Beloved, though He is not the one who withdraws (2 Tim. 2:13; Heb. 13:5).

The Awakening of Love
(2:8-3:5)

While there are references to the palace in the first section, the setting for this portion of the song is rural – the Shulamite's home. She recalls the day that her beloved made a surprise visit to her home (2:8-9). Apparently, Solomon requested that his *"darling"* accompany him on a walk through countryside. During this stroll he requested that she

The Beginning of Wisdom

come away with him (2:10-15) and she also expressed her devotion to him (2:16-17). The Shulamite then discloses the details of a troubling dream in which she could not find her beloved (3:1-4). She confidently asserts, *"I will seek him whom my soul loves,"* and later, *"I found him whom my soul loves"* (3:2, 4). The Shulamite and Solomon are engaged in a private and mutually exciting romantic adventure. Both actively communicate in colorful poetry their passion for each other. Their free speech throughout the entire book demonstrates the security and integrity of their love for each other; this serves as a good example for husbands and wives to follow, in spirit if not in form. The Hebrew poetry is both lovely and pure!

The following are passionate expressions of the bride towards her beloved:
> *Let him kiss me with the kisses of his mouth* (1:2).
> *A bundle of myrrh is my well-beloved to me, he shall lie all night between my breasts* (1:13).
> *Our bed is green* (1:16).
> *I am sick with love* (2:5).
> *Your lips, O my spouse, drop like the honeycomb; honey and milk are under your tongue* (4:11).
> *I am my beloved's and my beloved is mine* (6:3).
> *I am my beloved's, and his desire is toward me* (7:10).
> *Let us get up early to the vineyards ... there will I give you my love* (7:12).
> *Many waters cannot quench love, neither can the floods drown it* (8:7).

Solomon's passion is equally emphatic:
> *Rise up, my love, my fair one, and come away* (2:10).
> *Your hair is as a flock of goats that appear from Mount Gilead* (4:1).
> *Your lips are like a thread of scarlet* (4:3).
> *Your two breasts are like two young roes that are twins, which feed among the lilies. Until the day break, and the shadows flee away, I will go up to the mountain of myrrh and to the hill of frankincense* (4:5-6).
> *You are beautiful, O my love* (6:4).
> *How fair and how pleasant are you, O love, for delights* (7:6)!
> *This stature of yours is like a palm tree, and your breasts like its clusters. I said, "I will go up to the palm tree, I will take hold of*

its branches." Let now your breasts be like clusters of the vine, the fragrance of your breath like apples, and the roof of your mouth like the best wine (7:7-9).

If you are not familiar with the Song of Solomon, you may have been surprised or even stunned by the fervent poetic dialogue between these two lovers. Some may have even felt a bit embarrassed with the graphic references of disclosed affection. If so, we must remember we are reading the inspired Word of God! The unfettered passionate interlude of a husband and wife is one facet of companionship that God designed for us to enjoy. There is nothing shameful in a husband and wife intimately divulging their hearts to one other.

When the bride speaks of her beloved resting all night between her breasts (or upon her bosom), she is poetically speaking of her longing for sweet, uninterrupted communion with her husband, even to the daybreak. The sexual aspects of these lovers are completely veiled in secrecy and rightly so. Their mutual love for each other and enjoyed communion, however, is highlighted in Scripture. Details about the physical exchange between a husband and wife should remain concealed from others, unless as a mutual decision counseling is sought in this area. However, the outshining glow of two people in close, enthusiastic communion with one another cannot be concealed even if the couple tries. How did Abimelech know Isaac and Rebekah were married? He noticed Isaac caressing Rebekah (Gen. 26:8). Even this pagan king understood the marital language of a man to his wife, and as a result, their deception was discovered.

Although obligational love (commitment) holds the marriage together, disclosure builds intimacy, and shared passion imparts joy to the union. The romantic side of a marriage is just one way to share passion and build intimacy. However, we are creatures of habit and rote. If a couple is not attentive to one another, they may sail their marriage into the doldrums of stagnated romance. It is important to keep exploring new avenues of passion, as you did in your newlywed days.

The disclosure between husband and wife must remain pure, private, and undefiled by frivolous exposure to others. God warns against forsaking physical intimacy in a marriage (1 Cor. 7:2-5). The writer of Hebrews reminds us that, *"Marriage is honorable among all, and the bed undefiled; but fornicators and adulterers God will judge"* (Heb. 13:4). The marriage act is a gift in itself to be shared between a husband and his wife. However, the emotional entanglement and meshing of souls that occurs when two people pour themselves into one another during physical bonding is much more consequential than the fading moments of physical arousal. The sense of pleasing one's spouse surmounts the goal of mutual satisfaction. Those who engage in intimate activities outside of marriage will never experience the full emotional intimacy the marriage act was designed to promote because no commitment is present between the parties to allow for full disclosure!

Solomon then warns his lover of what would hinder their disclosure and companionship: *"Catch us the foxes, the little foxes that spoil the vines, for our vines have tender grapes"* (2:15). If foxes ran through the vineyards at a time when the grape vines were budding, their long tails tended to knock off the tender blossoms, which then diminished the fruitfulness of the vines. This was especially true if the vines were not supported. The reference to little foxes has a metaphoric meaning that denotes a problem with a relationship that requires resolution. Although these two lovers are not yet married, the reality is nonetheless the same; diligence and honesty are required to maintain intimate relationships. Sins of omission, pride, envy, evil-speaking, or impurity are the little foxes that not only grieve the Lord, but harm our relationship with others, especially with our spouse. The warning is that one must live purely with God to enjoy the most fruitful relationship with one's spouse. So let us keep short accounts with the Lord and also with those we love – a joyful marriage requires both godly wisdom and diligent work!

The Communion of Love
(3:6-5:1)

This particular poem of the book recounts the wedding of our lovers and the circumstances preceding it. Solomon led a regal wedding procession, including sixty sword-clad warriors, to the bride's home and brought her back to Jerusalem in his chariot (3:5-10). It is unlikely that the poor country folk of that area had ever seen such a sight as this, and no doubt the young Shulamite was stunned to learn her long-awaited beloved was the king himself. The couple then married (3:11), and although the festive wedding feast normally lasted a full week, the couple consummated their marriage that same night (4:16-5:1). After their wedding, but before they come together physically, Solomon again expresses his devotion to his new bride (4:1-7), asks for her full attention (4:8), and then praises her love and purity (4:9-15). The physical intimacy they shared in the night is immersed in poetic expressions of devotion and assurance. This indicates the sexual relationship of spouses is much more than just an act of physical gratification, but rather the mysterious and pleasurable meshing of two souls into exclusive oneness.

In Solomon's message of love, he provides a description of his charming bride beginning with her head and moving downward (4:1-6). Though her skin had been darkened by the sun, Solomon's assessment of her is one of complete acceptance (4:7): *"You are all fair, my love, and there is no spot in you."* Fair skin was desirable in Solomon's day; it was a sign of prominence and wealth, while the skin of those laboring outdoors in fields, groves, vineyards, etc. was darkened by the sun's exposure.

While Jehovah will certainly rejoice over Israel in the future day of her cleansing and restoration, the redemption typology of a Jewish King securing a peasant bride also points us to the mysterious relationship of Christ with His mainly Gentile Church, the object of His delight. On this point, H. A. Ironside writes:

> In this fourth chapter of the Song of Solomon, we hear the bridegroom expressing to his loved one the feelings of his heart toward her, and as we read these words, as we listen to these heart-breathings, we should remember that the speaker is really our Lord Jesus Christ, and that the bride may be looked at in various ways, as we have already seen. Prophetically, we may think of the bride as Israel, and the Lord God rejoicing over her in that coming day; individually, we may think of the bride as representing any saved soul, and the Lord expressing His delight in the one He has redeemed to Himself by His precious blood; or as that Church which Christ loved and for which He gave Himself.[181]

Initially, we were ungodly and enemies of God (Rom. 5:6, 10), but through our union with Christ, we have been reconciled with God and accredited a position of righteousness (Rom. 4:5). Even now, Christ continues to sanctify and cleanse His bride, and in a future day, He will present her to Himself without spot or wrinkle (Eph. 5:26-27). At that time she will experience the full communion of His presence, poetically displayed in this poem – this is the blessed hope of the Church.

The Lord Jesus said to His disciples the night before He was crucified, *"In My Father's house are many mansions: if it were not so, I would have told you. I go to prepare a place for you. And if I go and prepare a place for you, I will come again, and receive you unto Myself; that where I am, there ye may be also"* (John 14:2-3; KJV). The Church now is waiting for the glorious appearing of her Beloved, who will rapture her from the earth to ever be with Himself (1 Thess. 4:13-18; Tit. 2:13). Notice that the daughters of Jerusalem, the Jewish nation, are present throughout the story and observe this unique union with interest. It is also noted that the bride was summoned from her home after winter, but before summer; the fig tree was just putting out green figs (2:13).

The Jewish nation is allegorically likened to a trilogy of foliage: the vine, the olive tree, and the fig tree. Each one represents a distinct aspect of the nation's existence. The nation of Israel, as a political reality, is likened to a noble vine (a grape vine; Jer. 8:13), which God planted in the world (Jer. 2:21, 12:10); Israel was God's vineyard. The prophet Jeremiah told his fellow countrymen God had planted a beautiful vineyard (Israel), but Israel's shepherds had made it desolate (Jer. 12:10).

When Israel is spoken of as a fig tree in Scripture, the metaphor relates to the religious element of Israel, which was often fruitless for God (Jer. 8:13; Matt. 21:19-21). This reality was identified during one of the events in the life of the Lord Jesus (Luke 13:6-9). After preaching three years to the lost nation of Israel, Christ cursed the fruitless fig tree just before His death at Calvary. Less than forty years later, Jerusalem and the temple were destroyed and the Jews have not sacrificed since then.

At the end of the Tribulation Period, the refined Jewish nation will receive the Holy Spirit and obtain spiritual life in Christ – this is depicted by the olive tree and will be discussed momentarily. Once the

Jewish nation has experienced spiritual renewal, the vineyard of the Lord (i.e., the house of Israel; Isa. 5:7) will be again planted in Israel as a testimony to the nations of God's glory (Isa. 4; 60:1-5).

One of the signs that the Tribulation Period and the Second Advent of Christ are nearing is that the fig tree (i.e., religious Israel) will again shoot forth leaves after a long winter season of deadness (Luke 21:29-31). Leaves must precede fruit, but the fig tree will bear no fruit until the rebirth of the nation occurs in the latter days of the Tribulation Period. What might the new leaves speak of? This is likely a reference to the Jews reviving the old sacrificial system during, and perhaps just prior to, the Tribulation Period. It is of prophetic interest then that the bride (picturing the Church) is united with the Jewish king in marriage prior the spiritual revival of the Jewish nation. The marriage supper of the Lamb will be enjoyed by the Church in heaven prior to the Tribulation Period (1 Thess. 4:13-18; Rev. 19:7-9). Christ's own anticipation and excitement of being with His redeemed is pictured in Solomon's desire for his bride, whom he likens to a beautiful and fruitful private garden:

A garden enclosed is my sister, my spouse, a spring shut up, a fountain sealed. Your plants are an orchard of pomegranates with pleasant fruits, fragrant henna with spikenard, spikenard and saffron, calamus and cinnamon, with all trees of frankincense, myrrh and aloes, with all the chief spices – a fountain of gardens, a well of living waters, and streams from Lebanon (4:12-15).

Certainly, it is from Christ alone that the believer draws an abundant supply of mercy and grace; but, dear believer, have you ever considered your own heart as a garden in which He is to find His joy (4:9-10)? H. A. Ironside reminds the believer, "Your very life is as a garden which is to be for His pleasure. That is the figure you have here. It is the bridegroom looking upon his bride with his heart filled with delight as he says to her, '*You are to be for me, you are like a lovely garden yielding its fruit and flowers for me, set apart for myself*.'"[182] Indeed, the Lord Jesus longs to have His unspotted bride in His presence, but even now He is able to enjoy spiritual communion – holy pleasure with those who are sealed and enclosed gardens of grace. In the spiritual sense, the redeemed may also plead, *"Let my Beloved come into His garden, and eat His pleasant fruits"* (1:16). Yet, this is

The Beginning of Wisdom

impossible without steadfast devotion and consecrated effort on our part, for the Lord cannot enjoy communion in a barren and sin-diseased garden. It is also much better for us to revel in His satisfying love, a *"love better than wine"* (1:2), rather than to suffer the unpleasant consequences of His jealous love (1 Cor. 10:20-22).

Charles Spurgeon understood the Song of Solomon primarily as a poetic description of the love relationship between Jesus Christ and His redeemed people. In his 1872 sermon entitled *Better than Wine* (drawn from SOS. 1:2), he explained why Christ's love is better than wine:

Christ's love is better than wine because of what it is not:
- It is totally safe, and may be taken without question - you can't take too much.
- It doesn't cost anything.
- Taking more of it does not diminish the taste of it.
- It is totally without impurities and will never turn sour.
- It produces no ill effects.

Christ's love is better than wine because of what it is:
- Like wine, the love of Christ has healing properties.
- Like wine, the love of Christ is associated with giving strength.
- Like wine, the love of Christ is a symbol of joy.
- Like wine, the love of Christ exhilarates the soul.

Indeed, the refreshing and exhilarating communion of the Lord Jesus is better than wine. As the object of His love, may we maintain our purity and reserve our affections for Him. The Shulamite bride had an imminent expectation of her beloved's return to whisk her away to the marriage supper. May the Church live in purity with that same expectation (1 Jn. 3:2-3). Indeed, *"Blessed are those who are called to the marriage supper of the Lamb!"* (Rev. 19:9). Come quickly, Lord Jesus!

The Restoration of Love
(5:2-6:12)

In this poem the Shulamite tells of another distressing dream which describes a period of broken intimacy between our lovers and then their blissful restoration. Perhaps royal affairs or a journey had kept Solomon away from his wife for an extended period of time. In her dream, he comes to her bedroom at night, but she does not immediately respond to his tender call (5:2-3). This resulted in an anxious breech of marital communion. Those of us who are married know this disquieting feeling and also the joy that follows when humility pushes what is harmful out of the way. Jack Deere suggests this dream relates to an area of needed growth within the couple's relationship:

> The intimacy, joy, and physical desire of their wedding night did not fade as is often common in many marriages. They nourished their life together so that the joy of their married life increased rather than decreased. This does not suggest, however, that they did not encounter problems potentially harmful to their relationship. This section opens with the problem of indifference and offers a paradigm for the successful resolution of a serious marital problem.[183]

In her dream, the young wife had already put off her coat, washed her feet, and retired for the night. She was comfortably settled in her bed and nearly asleep when she heard a gentle knock at her door and the soft whisper of her husband calling to her. Although she knew it was her beloved, her preoccupation with personal ease caused her not to respond to his initiation. She did not want to be bothered and feigned sleep.

While the Shulamite lingered in her warm and pleasant alcove, she heard her beloved's hand reach through the small hole in the door to the inside latch, but he does not open it. A wave of guilt swells and breaks over her conscience. She rushes from her bed to open the door, but her beloved has already departed. Indeed, it was her husband who had visited her moments earlier; his calling card, myrrh, was still dripping from the door latch. In her dream the Shulamite frantically searches for him, initially in the palace, and then in the streets, but she cannot find him. During her search, she is roughly treated by the city's watchmen who do not recognize her, though they snatch away her veil. Next, she inquires of the daughters of Jerusalem, if they have seen her beloved (5:8). Dumbfounded by the intensity of her commitment, they respond by asking her what is so special about him (5:9). In response to their question, the Shulamite provides them with a glorious, full-length description of her lover (5:10-16). By musing on the positive features of her husband, she unknowingly has prepared her heart to be restored to him. This is seen in her statement: *"I am my beloved's, and my beloved is mine"* (6:3), which is the inverse of her previous declaration in 2:16: *"My beloved is mine, and I am his."* This selfless focus is the proper priority of genuine love, and is what Paul teaches should govern interactions with one's spouse:

> *Because of sexual immorality, let each man have his own wife, and let each woman have her own husband. Let the husband render to his wife the affection due her, and likewise also the wife to her husband. The wife does not have authority over her own body, but the husband does. And likewise the husband does not have authority over his own body, but the wife does. Do not deprive one another except with consent for a time, that you may give yourselves to fasting and prayer; and come together again so that Satan does not tempt you because of your lack of self-control* (1 Cor. 7:2-6).

Thankfully, the Shulamite's selfish focus was rebuked by her own contemplations of her husband's goodness as she told others about him. The daughters of Jerusalem readily acknowledge such a man is indeed worthy of her love and they commit themselves to help her search for him (6:1). However, after inquiring where he might be found, the Shulamite admits she already knows where he is, saying, *"My beloved has gone down into his garden to feed his flocks"* (6:2-3). Now, all that is needed to complete the restoration of this marital couple is for them to come together and for the beloved to affirm his loyal love to his young wife. This he promptly does: *"You are beautiful, O my love,... my dove, my perfect one"* (6:4-9). It seems the absence of her husband is what caused the Shulamite's indifference towards him; this is why Peter instructs husbands to *"dwell with your wives"* (1 Pet. 3:7). Husbands must spend time with their wives to know them and to know how to properly attend to their needs. This section concludes with others agreeing with Solomon's assessment of his wife, and with the happy reunion of the two lovers (6:10-13).

This narrative reminds us of a similar scene in Revelation 3:20: the Lord Jesus is knocking on the door of believers' hearts who are a part of the lukewarm, materialistic church at Laodicea. He is a perfect gentleman and will not force Himself upon those who would rather live without Him, that is, who would rather live for themselves. Yet, His love is patient and He continues knocking and asking for access so that He might enjoy full communion with those He loves. Those who open the door of their hearts to Him eagerly receive His rule, and will enjoy His peace and blessing also. Unfortunately, there is much lethargy in the Church today, and few permit the Savior in to dine with them. As the Shulamite painfully learned, her beloved was not to be found in the world, but rather among his sheep. Likewise, the Lord will be found in the midst of His people (Matt. 18:20), and attending to their needs – this is what the Great Shepherd does (Heb. 13:20-21). Those who willingly gather unto Him instead of venturing into the world to find answers and gratification will never suffer the frantic anxiety of not knowing where there Beloved is.

Hence, the typological application of this unsettling dream poses a rebuke against today's pampered Church. Much of the modern Church is stranded in the spiritual doldrums of complacency and comfort. Like the Shulamite bride, the Church needs to be aroused from willful slumber. Those who have been redeemed and cleansed by the blood must venture out into the world and tell others of their wonderful Beloved. When the Shulamite opened and closed her bedroom door, the sweet-smelling myrrh on the latch was transferred to her hand (5:5), and the fragrance faithfully pursued her wherever she went. Paul reminds the believers at Corinth that they too were to be a daily fragrance of Christ in the world:

> *Now thanks be to God who always leads us in triumph in Christ, and through us diffuses the fragrance of His knowledge in every place. For we are to God the fragrance of Christ among those who are being saved and among those who are perishing. To the one we are the aroma of death leading to death, and to the other the aroma of life leading to life* (2 Cor. 2:14-16).

To be witnesses for Christ, to spread His gospel message, and to demonstrate His goodness and holy character through selfless deeds is how others will become familiar with our Beloved. Everything about the Lord Jesus is wonderful; *"He is altogether lovely"* (5:16). This means that if we are not complacent, others, like the daughters of Jerusalem, will find Him lovely and want to seek after Him as well. If we become self-focused and spiritually despondent, we may remain comfortable in this life, but as the dream indicates, there is a

The Beginning of Wisdom

tremendous cost to spiritual lethargy – communion with the Beloved is lost. On the flip side, those who are faithful to the Lord should expect to be roughed up by those who guard the philosophies and rudimentary affairs of this world. May every believer reckon himself or herself dead to self and alive in Christ (Gal. 2:20). Then we too will have the right realization of our relationship: *"I am my beloved's, and my beloved is mine"* (6:3). We are Christ's before all else. And, He is ours; there is no possibility of disappointment on our part.

The Witness of Love
6:13-8:4

This poem begins with the daughters of Jerusalem announcing their agreement with the beloved's assessment of the bride's beauty (6:13-7:5). Solomon then describes his bride's attractiveness and his complete sensual satisfaction in her (7:6-9). The bride interrupts his declaration of love to inform him that she longs to fulfill his pleasure and to be enjoyed by him (6:9-10). This poetic movement concludes with the young bride acknowledging she is also homesick and would like to visit her family, but only with her beloved by her side (7:11-8:3). She knows that, despite the huge social gap between their families, she is secure in her beloved's affection.

The Shulamite bride counted it a privilege to be completely reserved for her husband's pleasure (7:10). Here, as in the previous section of poetry (6:11), the Shulamite bride is likened to a flourishing grape vine loaded with fruit that only Solomon could taste and enjoy:

> *Come, my beloved, let us go forth to the field; let us lodge in the villages. Let us get up early to the vineyards; let us see if the vine has budded, whether the grape blossoms are open, and the pomegranates are in bloom. There I will give you my love* (7:11-12).

The metaphoric language of this passage is quite powerful. To alleviate confusion, we will call upon C. E. Hocking to simplify and clarify the similes and symbols:

> For her beloved, too, her breasts are as clusters of fruit. By means of this simile he is not describing their youthful and graceful beauty, but *rather their maturity and abundant fruitfulness.* Like dates, her fruit was sweet and nutritious *to his soul.* Every impression she makes upon him creates deep desires within him, so that he determines to make her his own. Note his repeated "I will.".... It remains for him to appeal to her: she must become all that he desires her to be. ... It is not the vine in budding and flowering stages that He seeks, but He would handle and taste its abundant fruitfulness. Hence his desire that her "breasts be as the clusters of the vine."[184]

The Shulamite was offering Solomon her best – fine clusters of "grapes" (mature, selfless, and abundant love) from her one "vineyard" (her own body, 8:12), and her best "wine" (prepared love to please his senses). Wine in the good sense symbolizes joy in Scripture: *"wine makes glad the heart of man"* (Ps. 104:15). Christ joyfully anticipated drinking wine with His disciples in the coming kingdom (Luke 22:18). Foresight and preparation are required for a wife to be able to joyfully give her best to satisfy her husband's need for affection. It took hard work to produce wine, and it cost the grapes everything (we speak of mature love that longs to satisfy). Some work is necessary for the wife to have something left to present to her husband in those few minutes of the day remaining after the children are occupied with sleep. Wives are encouraged to leave some vigor to share with one's husband. The clusters of grapes were visibly fresh, tantalizing to taste, and thoroughly satisfying.

The psalmist also refers to a virtuous wife as a fruitful vine that clings to the sides of her home: "Your wife shall be like a fruitful vine in the very heart of your house" (Ps. 128:3). In ancient times, fruit-bearing vines were commonly planted adjacent to the exterior walls of homes. Practically speaking, the custom optimized ground space provided protection for the vine, and allowed easy access to the delicious fruit. From a cosmetic sense, cold, barren walls were transformed into radiant color, for the fruitful vine was an ornament of beauty. For these blessings to be enjoyed, the vine's husbandman (caretaker) must provide it with adequate support and direction to ensure thriving foliage and proper direction of growth. The same is true for a married couple: *"So husbands ought to love their own wives as their own bodies; he who loves his wife loves himself. For no one ever hated his own flesh, but nourishes and cherishes it, just as the Lord does the church"* (Eph. 5:28-29). The fruitful vine will thrive in the home, if properly loved and cared for by her husbandman.

Generally, a wife will be most fruitful within the home; on this subject, Paul supplied instruction to both Timothy and Titus. To Titus he wrote that wives should be *"discreet, chaste, keepers at home, good, obedient to their own husbands, that the word of God be not blasphemed"* (Tit. 2:5; KJV). The Greek word translated *"keepers at home"* in this verse is *oikouros*. *Oikos* means "home" and *ouros* refers to "a guard"; thus, the keeper at home is literally the "guardian of the home." This is why Paul warned Timothy *"that the younger women [were to]... guide the house [their sphere of delegated responsibility], give no occasion to the adversary to speak reproachfully"* (1 Tim. 5:14; KJV). Satan eyes the disordered home as an opportunity to gain an "occasion" and promote further chaos within the family. Disorder leads to frustration and often an atmosphere of resentment, and then ill-temper invades family life. God designed the woman for unique fruit-bearing, and generally speaking, she will be the most productive within the sphere of the home. Scripturally speaking, the home is a base of operation for a wife and mother, but not the measure and boundary of her existence. For example, the industrious woman of Proverbs 31 both observed and assisted the needy. This is God's best plan for a married woman and where she will have the most ability to care for her children and refresh her husband. He created marriage and ordered the home with this purpose in mind.

Let us apply the vine and grape imagery for a final application for husbands. Drunkenness is consistently forbidden throughout Scripture. Paul exhorts believers, *"be not drunk with wine, wherein is excess; but be filled with the Spirit"* (Eph. 5:18). In moderation, the fruit of the vine may stir up joy, but if abused, it certainly will control our flesh. The vine expends much energy to bear clusters of grapes. The fruit requires time to develop and ripen; it is simply not available at all times. Likewise, the husband should be careful not to be too demanding of his wife; sexual moderation will ensure satisfying refreshment, but excess will certainly affect the quality of the "fruit" and the general health of the "vine" (wife). When a husband tenderly cares for his wife in an undemanding way, she will voluntarily yield an abundance of refreshment – this is a testimony of true, mutually satisfying love.

The Triumph of Love
8:5-14

In the previous section, the young bride mentioned that she was homesick, which resulted in the newlyweds visiting her family. This final section begins with the bride's brothers recalling their amazement at seeing their little sister leaning on the king's arm (8:5). Solomon recounts his pledge of love (8:5-6) and the bride speaks of the vastness and pricelessness of the love that they share (8:7). The bride then recalls how her brothers forced her to work long hours in isolation in a vineyard (8:8-9). Ironically, this vineyard was apparently owned by Solomon and leased to the Shulamite's brothers – it was the very location of the couple's first meeting (8:10-11). Now everyone, including the Shulamite's brothers, appreciates the marriage of these two lovers; as marital companions, they bask in each other's devotion and mutual satisfaction (8:12-14).

This marital bliss pictures the wonderful union between Christ and His bride, through which we delight the heart of our Savior and we enjoy full satisfaction in Him and with Him. From a relational standpoint, the Lord Jesus yearns to be with His bride and indeed is not complete without her: *"And He put all things under His feet, and gave Him to be head over all things to the church, which is His body, the fullness of Him who fills all in all"* (Eph. 1:22-23). Likewise, believers should long to be with their Beloved and love His appearing (2 Tim. 4:8; 1 Jn. 3:2-3). David expressed his deep longing of someday being in the Lord's glorious presence: *"As for me, I will see Your face in righteousness; I shall be satisfied when I awake in Your likeness"* (Ps. 17:15). Writing to persecuted believers, Peter also acknowledged the future joy that they would all have in the presence of their Savior after enduring much hardship on His behalf:

In this you greatly rejoice, though now for a little while, if need be, you have been grieved by various trials, that the genuineness of your faith, being much more precious than gold that perishes, though it is tested by fire, may be found to praise, honor, and glory at the revelation of Jesus Christ, whom having not seen you love. Though now you do not see Him, yet believing, you rejoice with joy inexpressible and full of glory, receiving the end of your faith – the salvation of your souls (1 Pet. 1:6-9).

Indeed, the marital love shared between Solomon and the Shulamite has been wonderful to observe, but their level of satisfaction and bliss is far less than what believers experience in the eternal bonds of God's love through their spiritual union with the Beloved, the Lord Jesus Christ. The hymn writer Henry Bennett eloquently expresses the delightful ecstasy of experiencing marital love in Him now and the anticipation of being with Him soon:

Satisfied with Thee, Lord Jesus, I am blest;
Peace which passes understanding, on Thy breast;
No more doubting, no more trembling, Oh, what rest!

Taken up with Thee, Lord Jesus, I would be;
Finding joy and satisfaction all in Thee;
Thou the nearest and the dearest unto me.

Listening for Thy shout, Lord Jesus, in the air!
When Thy saints shall rise with joy to meet Thee there;
Oh what gladness! No more sadness, sin nor care.

Returning to the narrative, verses 6 and 7 can be taken as a climactic summary of all we have learned concerning the wonders of marital love. Solomon is speaking in verse 6 and his new bride in verse 7:

Set me as a seal upon your heart, as a seal upon your arm; for love is as strong as death, jealousy as cruel as the grave; its flames are flames of fire, a most vehement flame. Many waters cannot quench love, nor can the floods drown it. If a man would give for love all the wealth of his house, it would be utterly despised.

The success of marital love requires a seal on the heart (affection) and on the arm (strength and tenacity). As stated previously, the two main ingredients of biblical companionship are intimacy and commitment – a marriage cannot thrive as God intends it to without both qualities. Love of this nature is both exclusive and lifelong; hence, it is as strong as death. True love is enduring; it cannot be quenched by adversity, for genuine *"love never fails"* (1 Cor. 13:7-8). Furthermore, we understand from these two verses that the Shulamite considers the communion she shares with her beloved as priceless.

We have traced the beginnings of this love from the moment Solomon first gazed on the young Shulamite and his heart was moved towards hers until they were united in marriage, and then as they grew together in their relationship as a couple. H. A. Ironside suggests that this is a beautiful picture of the secure love of Christ, which reaches us in our deepest need, and also of that glorious union with Him which will be consummated at the marriage supper of the Lamb (i.e., complete spiritual intimacy in His presence is a reality):

> Now you hear the bride exclaiming, "Set me as a seal upon thine heart, as a seal upon thine arm." The seal speaks of something that is settled. One draws up a legal document and seals it and that settles it. And so Christ and His loved ones have entered into an eternal relationship, and He has given us the seal, the Holy Spirit. "After that you believed, you were sealed with that Holy Spirit of promise." This is "the earnest of our inheritance until the redemption of the purchased possession."[185]

Believers are immensely blessed by Christ's unwavering love. There are four facets of secure love mentioned in verses 6 and 7 that certainly apply to His love for His own bride: the strength of love, the jealousy of love, the endurance of love, and the value of love – it is priceless! While the love shared between Solomon and the Shulamite might aspire to these grand merits, Christ's eternal unwavering love for His bride epitomizes them. She is set as a seal upon His heart and rests peacefully on His everlasting arm.

The Shulamite bride did not have much to offer Solomon other than her own vineyard (metaphorically speaking, her own body; 8:12). At first, the time she spent attending to the grape vineyards distressed her, for it was difficult to properly care for her own body while working strenuous hours in the hot sun: *"Do not look upon me, because I am dark, because the sun has tanned me. My mother's sons were angry with me; they made me the keeper of the vineyards, but my own vineyard I have not kept"* (1:6). But once in the palace, she was able to properly care for herself and to better prepare herself for her husband's

The Beginning of Wisdom

presence; at this point she states, *"my very own vineyard is at my disposal"* (SOS 8:12; NASV). This was a choice she had, to take good care of herself, then to wholly give herself to her husband. There are many aspects of being a good wife and homemaker, but here the Shulamite acknowledges the importance of attending to her own vineyard, then seeking to satisfy her husband with the sensuous fruits of a flourishing vine.

As people grow older, they change in various ways. Solomon colorfully describes the condition of those in their autumn years (Eccle. 12:1-7). It is natural for older women to fall, for men to slump over with age, and for the elderly to lose their teeth and eyesight – the outward body perishes. Likewise, the avenues of exchanging marital passion with each other will also change with age. Enjoy the changes, and seek to develop new expressions of mutual pleasure within the natural realm that God has given. This is the triumph of marital love!

Concerning the believer's spiritual union with Christ, Paul explains that though our physical bodies diminish in ability with time, our inner man (i.e., our spirit) is strengthened through the power of the Holy Spirit. This reality increases our resolve and ability to serve the Lord, our understanding and love for Him, and our desire to be with Him:

> *Even though our outward man is perishing, yet the inward man is being renewed day by day. For our light affliction, which is but for a moment, is working for us a far more exceeding and eternal weight of glory, while we do not look at the things which are seen, but at the things which are not seen. For the things which are seen are temporary, but the things which are not seen are eternal* (2 Cor. 4:16-18).

So while we may have decreasing ability to demonstrate love in our earthly relationships, our union with Christ ensures an increasing capacity to appreciate and demonstrate our devotion to Him. A billion years from now believers in heaven will still be learning of the Lord's inexhaustible grace (Eph. 2:7)!

In conclusion, the Song of Solomon not only acknowledges the importance of the marital commitment, but also the intimate lifetime companionship that God desires a married couple to share. Husbands are to tenderly and diligently care for their wives. They must spend time communicating with their wives in order to provide them beneficial emotional support. Husbands are to supply their wives' physical needs, protect them from harm, and be good spiritual leaders. Wives are to respect their husbands' authority as unto the Lord, help and support their husbands, be keepers of the home, and attend to themselves to better enhance romantic interaction with their husbands. The "Song of Songs" upholds God's design for what the marital union is to be, a pattern that must be affirmed today if we are to enjoy God's blessing in marriage.

Endnotes

1. C. I. Scofield, *The New Scofield Study Bible*, KJV (Oxford University Press, NY; 1967), p. 572
2. A. R. Fausset, Robert Jamieson, David Brown, *A Commentary, Critical and Explanatory, on the Old and New Testaments* (Logos Research Systems, Inc., Oak Harbor, WA; 1997), Job 1:1
3. William Kelly, *Eleven Lectures on the Book of Job*, STEM Publishing; Lecture 5: http://stempublishing.com/authors/kelly/1Oldtest/job11lec.html#a5
4. Roy Zuck, *The Bible Knowledge Commentary*, edited by J. F. Walvoord and Roy Zuck (Victor Books, Wheaton, IL; 1986), p. 719
5. C. H. Mackintosh, *Job and His Friends*, STEM Publishing: http://stempublishing.com/authors/mackintosh/Bk1/JOB.html
6. Mike Mason, *The Gospel According to Job* (Crossway Books, Wheaton, IL; 1994), p.40
7. Samuel Ridout, *Job*, STEM Publishing; Introduction: http://stempublishing.com/authors/S_Ridout/SR_Job1.html
8. William Kelly, *Eleven Lectures on the Book of Job*, STEM Publishing; Lecture 1: http://stempublishing.com/authors/kelly/1Oldtest/job11lec.html#a1
9. Samuel Ridout, op. cit.
10. C. H. Mackintosh, op. cit.
11. Mike Mason, op. cit., p. 60
12. Roy Hession, *The Calvary Road* (CLC Publications, Fort Washington, PA; 2014), pp. 102-103
13. Elisabeth Elliot, *On Asking God Why* (Revell of Baker Publishing Group, Grand Rapids, MI; 1989)
14. F. B. Hole, *Job*, STEM Publishing: http://stempublishing.com/authors/hole/Art/Job.html
15. Samuel Ridout, *The First Addresses of His Friends*, STEM Publishing http://www.stempublishing.com/authors/S_Ridout/SR_Job2.html
16. F. B. Hole, op. cit.
17. William Kelly, op. cit.; Lecture 2 http://stempublishing.com/authors/kelly/1Oldtest/job11lec.html#a2
18. Matthew Henry, MHCC derived from *Matthew Henry Commentary Vol. 3* (MacDonald Pub. Co., Mclean, VA), Job 5:1-5
19. H. L. Rossier, *Job's Three Questions and Three Answers*, STEM Publishing: http://stempublishing.com/authors/rossier/JOBS3QST.html
20. William Kelly, op. cit.; Lecture 2
21. F. B. Hole, op. cit.

22. J. N. Darby, *Synopsis of the Books of the Bible: Ezra – Malachi, Vol. 2* (Stow Hill Bible and Tract Depot, Kingston, England; 1948), p. 26
23. C. H. Mackintosh, op. cit.
24. William Kelly, op. cit., Lecture 3
http://stempublishing.com/authors/kelly/1Oldtest/job11lec.html#a3
25. Matthew Henry, op. cit., Job 9:14-21
26. J. N. Darby, op. cit., p. 29
27. Mike Mason, op. cit., p. 116
28. F. B. Hole, op. cit.
29. Roy Zuck, op. cit., p. 732
30. Mike Mason, op. cit., p. 127
31. C. I. Scofield, op. cit., p. 579
32. Samuel Ridout, op. cit., subdivision 2
33. A. R. Fausset, op. cit., 12:2
34. William Kelly, op. cit., Lecture 4
http://stempublishing.com/authors/kelly/1Oldtest/job11lec.html#a4
35. Roy Zuck, op. cit., p. 735
36. A. R. Fausset, op. cit., 14:12
37. William Kelly, op. cit., Lecture 4
38. W. H. Westcott, Extracted from Scripture Truth magazine Volume 9, 1917, page 82; STEM Publishing:
http://stempublishing.com/authors/westcott/Endurance_of_Job.html
39. Samuel Ridout, *The Second Addresses of His Friends*, STEM Publishing
http://www.stempublishing.com/authors/S_Ridout/SR_Job3.html
40. F. B. Hole, op. cit.
41. William Kelly, op. cit., Lecture 4
42. Roy Zuck, op. cit., p. 740
43. Mike Mason, op. cit., p. 205
44. Charles Spurgeon, *Morning and Evening* (Electronic Edition STEP Files, Parsons Technology, Inc; 1999), Evening November 19th devotion
45. F. B. Hole, op. cit.
46. C. H. Mackintosh, op. cit
47. Roy Zuck, op. cit., p. 743
48. William Kelly, op. cit., Lecture 6
http://stempublishing.com/authors/kelly/1Oldtest/job11lec.html#a6
49. Roy Zuck, op. cit., p. 745
50. William Kelly, op. cit., Lecture 6
51. Samuel Ridout, op. cit.
52. Mike Mason, op. cit., p. 245
53. William MacDonald, *Believer's Bible Commentary* (Thomas Nelson Publishers, Nashville, TN: 1989), p. 528
54. Warren Wiersbe, *The Bible Exposition Commentary* (Victor Books, Wheaton, IL: 1996, c1989), Jas 5:11
55. F. B. Hole, op. cit.
56. Roy Zuck, op. cit., p. 748

Endnotes

57 F. B. Hole, op. cit.
58 http://www.answers.com/topic/evangelista-torricelli?cat=technology
59 F. B. Hole, op. cit.
60 Roy Zuck, op. cit., p. 752
61 William Kelly, op. cit., Lecture 8
http://stempublishing.com/authors/kelly/1Oldtest/job11lec.html#a8
62 Samuel Ridout, *Job's Closing Monologue*, STEM Publishing
http://stempublishing.com/authors/S_Ridout/SR_Job5.html
63 Samuel Ridout, *The Testimony of Elihu*, STEM Publishing
http://stempublishing.com/authors/S_Ridout/SR_Job6.html
64 Stuart Briscoe, Edythe Draper, *Draper's Quotations from the Christian World – Soul* (Tyndale House Publishers Inc., Wheaton, Il. – electronic copy), Anger
65 Roy Zuck, op. cit., p. 758
66 Arthur W. Pink, *Gleanings in Exodus* (Moody Press, Chicago, IL; no date), p. 110
67 Albert Barnes, *Barnes' Notes Bible Commentary – Job* (Baker Book House, Grand Rapids, MI; 1981), p. 142
68 Asit K. Biswas, *Notes and Records of the Royal Society of London*, (Vol. 25, No. 1; Jun. 1970), p. 47
69 Roy Zuck, op. cit., p. 766
70 D. L. Moody, *Anecdotes and Illustrations* (Rhodes & McClure, Chicago, IL; 1877), p. 19
71 William MacDonald, op. cit., 535
72 James Catron, *Old Testament Poetry and Prophecy* (Emmaus Bible College, Dubuque, IA;1993), p. 8
73 http://www.pleaseconvinceme.com/index/The_Bible_Foreshadows_ Scientific_Discoveries
74 James Catron, op. cit., p. 8
75 William MacDonald, op. cit., 538
76 J. N. Darby, op. cit., p. 31
77 C. I. Scofield, op. cit., p. 600
78 William MacDonald, *Believer's Bible Commentary* (Thomas Nelson Publishers, Nashville, TN: 1989), p. 722
79 T. Ernest Wilson, *The Messianic Psalms* (Gospel Folio Press, Port Colborne, ON; 1997), Introduction
80 James L. R. Catron, *Old Testament Survey: Poetry and Prophecy* (Emmaus Bible College, Dubuque, IA; 1993), p. 13
81 William Kelly, *Notes on Psalms*, STEM Publishing:
http://stempublishing.com/authors/kelly/1Oldtest /Ps_nts.html
82 J. G. Bellett, *Short Meditations on the Psalms*, STEM Publishing:
http://www.stempublishing.com/authors/bellett/Psalms.html
83 Hamilton Smith, *The Psalms*, STEM Publishing:
http://stempublishing.com/authors/smith/PSALMS.html
84 William Kelly, *Notes on Psalms*, STEM Publishing:
http://stempublishing.com/authors/kelly/1Oldtest /Ps_nts.html

[85] William MacDonald, *Believer's Bible Commentary* (Thomas Nelson Publishers, Nashville, TN: 1989), p. 552
[86] William MacDonald, *Believer's Bible Commentary* (Thomas Nelson Publishers, Nashville, TN: 1989), p. 557
[87] Allen Ross, *The Bible Knowledge Commentary*, edited by J. F. Walvoord and Roy Zuck (Victor Books, Wheaton, IL; 1986), p. 798
[88] William Kelly, *Notes on Psalms*, STEM Publishing: http://stempublishing.com/authors/kelly/1Oldtest/Ps_nts.html
[89] Hamilton Smith, *The Psalms*, STEM Publishing http://stempublishing.com/authors/smith/PSALMS.html
[90] Allen Ross, *The Bible Knowledge Commentary*, edited by J. F. Walvoord and Roy Zuck (Victor Books, Wheaton, IL; 1986), p. 804
[91] William MacDonald, *Believer's Bible Commentary* (Thomas Nelson Publishers, Nashville, TN: 1989), p. 569
[92] Chuck Missler, *The Creator Beyond Time and Space* (http://www.direct.ca/trinity/cosmos.html)
[93] J. G. Bellett, *Short Meditations on the Psalms*, STEM Publishing: http://www.stempublishing.com/authors/bellett/Psalms.html
[94] T. Ernest Wilson, *The Messianic Psalms* (Gospel Folio Press, Port Colborne, ON; 1997), p. 58
[95] William Kelly, *Notes on Psalms*, STEM Publishing: http://stempublishing.com/authors/kelly/1Oldtest/Ps_nts.html
[96] Allen Ross, *The Bible Knowledge Commentary*, edited by J. F. Walvoord and Roy Zuck (Victor Books, Wheaton, IL; 1986), p. 815
[97] Hamilton Smith, *The Psalms*, STEM Publishing: http://stempublishing.com/authors/smith/PSALMS.html
[98] William Kelly, *Notes on Psalms*, STEM Publishing: http://stempublishing.com/authors/kelly/1Oldtest/Ps_nts.html
[99] William MacDonald, *Believer's Bible Commentary* (Thomas Nelson Publishers, Nashville, TN: 1989), p. 617
[100] Hamilton Smith, *The Psalms*, STEM Publishing: http://stempublishing.com/authors/smith/PSALMS.html
[101] Sam Wellman, *David Livingstone – Explorer & Missionary*: "Heroes of the Faith" series (Barbour Publishing, Uhrichsville, OH; 1995), chp. 16
[102] William MacDonald, *Believer's Bible Commentary* (Thomas Nelson Publishers, Nashville, TN: 1989), p. 624
[103] William Kelly, *Notes on Psalms*, STEM Publishing: http://stempublishing.com/authors/kelly/1Oldtest/Ps_nts.html
[104] Hamilton Smith, *The Psalms*, STEM Publishing: http://stempublishing.com/authors/smith/PSALMS.html
[105] C. H. Spurgeon, *Morning and Evening: Daily Readings* (Logos Research Systems, Inc., Oak Harbor, WA; 1995), September 9 AM
[106] William MacDonald, *Believer's Bible Commentary* (Thomas Nelson Publishers, Nashville, TN: 1989), p. 645

Endnotes

[107] Allen Ross, *The Bible Knowledge Commentary*, edited by J. F. Walvoord and Roy Zuck (Victor Books, Wheaton, IL; 1986), p. 842

[108] Hamilton Smith, *The Psalms*, STEM Publishing: http://stempublishing.com/authors/smith/PSALMS.html

[109] William Kelly, *Notes on Psalms*, STEM Publishing: http://stempublishing.com/authors/kelly/1Oldtest /Ps_nts.html

[110] T. Ernest Wilson, *The Messianic Psalms* (Gospel Folio Press, Port Colborne, ON; 1997), p. 151

[111] Matthew Henry, *Matthew Henry's Commentary on the Whole Bible* (Hendrickson, Peabody, MA; 1991 – electronic version); Ps. 74

[112] J. G. Bellett, *Short Meditations on the Psalms*, STEM Publishing: http://www.stempublishing.com/authors/bellett/Psalms.html

[113] William Kelly, *Notes on Psalms*, STEM Publishing: http://stempublishing.com/authors/kelly/1Oldtest /Ps_nts.html

[114] Edythe Draper, *Draper's Quotations from the Christian World* (Tyndale House Publishers Inc., Wheaton, IL – electronic copy)

[115] J. G. Bellett, *Short Meditations on the Psalms*, STEM Publishing: http://www.stempublishing.com/authors/bellett/Psalms.html

[116] Guillermo Gonzalez and Jay Richards, *The Privileged Planet* (Regnery Publishing, Washington, DC; 2004), p. 107

[117] Hamilton Smith, *The Psalms*, STEM Publishing: http://stempublishing.com/authors/smith/PSALMS.html

[118] Henry Morris, http://www.icr.org/article/8583

[119] William Kelly, Notes on Psalms, STEM Publishing: http://stempublishing.com/authors/kelly/1Oldtest /Ps_nts.html

[120] William MacDonald, *Believer's Bible Commentary* (Thomas Nelson Publishers, Nashville, TN: 1989), p. 728

[121] William Kelly, *Notes on Psalms*, STEM Publishing: http://stempublishing.com/authors/kelly/1Oldtest /Ps_nts.html

[122] Albert Barnes, *Notes on the Old Testament – Psalms, Vol. 3* (Baker Book House, Grand Rapids, MI; reprinted 1879), p. 227

[123] Allen Ross, *The Bible Knowledge Commentary*, edited by J. F. Walvoord and Roy Zuck (Victor Books, Wheaton, IL; 1986), p. 884-885

[124] William MacDonald, *Believer's Bible Commentary* (Thomas Nelson Publishers, Nashville, TN: 1989), p. 755

[125] Hamilton Smith, *The Psalms*, STEM Publishing: http://stempublishing.com/authors/smith/PSALMS.html

[126] J. G. Bellett, *Short Meditations on the Psalms*, STEM Publishing: http://www.stempublishing.com/authors/bellett/Psalms.html

[127] Hamilton Smith, *The Psalms*, STEM Publishing: http://stempublishing.com/authors/smith/PSALMS.html

[128] C. H. Mackintosh, *Genesis to Deuteronomy* (Loizeaux Brothers, Inc., Neptune, NJ; 1972), p. 122

[129] Albert Barnes, *Notes on the Old Testament – Psalms, Vol. 3* (Baker Book House, Grand Rapids, MI; reprinted 1879), p. 319

[130] C. I. Scofield, *The New Scofield Study Bible*, KJV (Oxford University Press, NY; 1967), p. 672
[131] William MacDonald, *Believer's Bible Commentary* (Thomas Nelson Publishers, Nashville, TN: 1989), p. 791
[132] Sid Buzzell, *The Bible Knowledge Commentary*, edited by J. F. Walvoord and Roy Zuck (Victor Books, Wheaton, IL; 1986), p. 902
[133] J. N. Darby, *Practical Reflections of the Proverbs*, STEM Publishing: http://stempublishing.com/authors/darby/PRACTICE/17006E.html
[134] William Kelly, *Proverbs*, STEM Publishing: http://stempublishing.com/authors/kelly/1Oldtest/proverbs.html
[135] F. C. Cook, *Barnes Notes: The Bible Commentary – Proverbs to Ezekiel* (Baker Book House, Grand Rapids, MI; reprinted from 1879 edition), p. 23
[136] H. A. Ironside, *Proverbs* (Loizeaux Brothers, Neptune, NJ; 1995), p. 39
[137] Matthew Henry, *Matthew Henry's Commentary* (MacDonald Publishing Co., McLean, VA: original 1706), Vol. III, p. 819
[138] William Kelly, *Proverbs*, STEM Publishing: http://stempublishing.com/authors/kelly/1Oldtest/proverbs.html
[139] C. I. Scofield, *The New Scofield Study Bible*, KJV (Oxford University Press, NY; 1967), p. 677
[140] H. A. Ironside, *Proverbs* (Loizeaux Brothers, Neptune, NJ; 1995), p. 54
[141] William MacDonald, *Believer's Bible Commentary* (Thomas Nelson Publishers, Nashville, TN; 1989), p. 813
[142] Sid Buzzell, *The Bible Knowledge Commentary*, edited by J. F. Walvoord and Roy Zuck (Victor Books, Wheaton, IL; 1986), p. 925
[143] F. C. Cook, *Barnes Notes: The Bible Commentary – Proverbs to Ezekiel* (Baker Book House, Grand Rapids, MI; reprinted from 1879 edition), p. 34
[144] H. A. Ironside, *Proverbs* (Loizeaux Brothers, Neptune, NJ; 1995), p. 67
[145] William Kelly, *Proverbs*, STEM Publishing: http://stempublishing.com/authors/kelly/1Oldtest/proverbs.html
[146] Derek Kidner, *The Proverbs: An Introduction and Commentary* (Inter-Varsity Press, Downers Grove, IL; 1964), p. 105
[147] H. A. Ironside, *Proverbs* (Loizeaux Brothers, Neptune, NJ; 1995), p. 87
[148] R. C. Chapman, *Robert Cleaver Chapman of Barnstaple*, by W. H. Bennet (Pickering & Inglis, Glasgow, Scotland; no date – 1st ed.), pp. 125-126
[149] H. A. Ironside, *Proverbs* (Loizeaux Brothers, Neptune, NJ; 1995), p. 104
[150] D. L. Moody, *Notes from My Bible* (Hard Press Pub., U.S.; 2012), Prov. 17
[151] William MacDonald, *The Disciple's Manual* (Gospel Folio Press, Port Colborne, ON; 2004), p. 290
[152] H. A. Ironside, *Proverbs* (Loizeaux Brothers, Neptune, NJ; 1995), p. 163
[153] William Henry Bennet, Robert Cleaver Chapman of Barnstaple (Pickering & Inglis, Glasgow, Scotland; 1902), p. 13
[154] Derek Kidner, *The Proverbs: An Introduction and Commentary* (Inter-Varsity Press, Downers Grove, IL; 1964), p. 149
[155] William MacDonald, *Believer's Bible Commentary* (Thomas Nelson Publishers, Nashville, TN; 1989), p. 852

Endnotes

[156] William Kelly, *Proverbs*, STEM Publishing: http://stempublishing.com/authors/kelly/1Oldtest/proverbs.html
[157] William MacDonald, *Believer's Bible Commentary* (Thomas Nelson Publishers, Nashville, TN; 1989), p. 859
[158] Derek Kidner, *The Proverbs: An Introduction and Commentary* (Inter-Varsity Press, Downers Grove, IL; 1964), p. 95
[159] Matthew Henry, *Matthew Henry's Commentary* (MacDonald Publishing Co., McLean, VA: original 1706, Vol. III), p. 975
[160] H. A. Ironside, *Proverbs* (Loizeaux Brothers, Neptune, NJ; 1995), p. 7
[161] *Megillah* 7a; *Sabbath* 30
[162] Donald R. Glenn, *The Bible Knowledge Commentary*, edited by J. F. Walvoord and Roy Zuck (Victor Books, Wheaton, IL; 1986), p. 976
[163] William MacDonald, *Believer's Bible Commentary* (Thomas Nelson Publishers, Nashville, TN; 1989), p. 877
[164] William Kelly, *Ecclesiastes*, STEM Publishing: http://stempublishing.com/authors/kelly/1Oldtest/ecclests.html, Introduction
[165] William Kelly, *Ecclesiastes*, STEMPublishing: http://stempublishing.com/authors/kelly/1Oldtest/ecclests.html, chp. 3
[166] Donald R. Glenn, *The Bible Knowledge Commentary*, edited by J. F. Walvoord and Roy Zuck (Victor Books, Wheaton, IL; 1986), p. 997
[167] James Vernon McGee, *Thru the Bible* Vol. III (Thomas Nelson Publishers, Nashville, TN; 1981), p. 128
[168] William Kelly, *Ecclesiastes*, STEM Publishing, http://stempublishing.com/authors/kelly/1Oldtest/ecclests.html, chp. 8
[169] Tentmakers: http://www.tentmaker.org/Quotes/atheismqu-otes.html
[170] Duane Litfin, *The Bible Knowledge Commentary* (Victor Books, Wheaton, IL; 1983), p. 733
[171] W. J. Federer, *Great Quotations: A Collection of Passages, Phrases, and Quotations Influencing Early and Modern World History Referenced according to their Sources in Literature, Memoirs, Letters, Governmental Documents, Speeches, Charters, Court Decisions and Constitutions.* (AmeriSearch, St. Louis, MO; 2001), "Blaise Pascal"
[172] Hamilton Smith, *The Song of Songs*, STEM Publishing: http://stempublishing.com/authors/smith/canticls.html
[173] H. A. Ironside, *Addresses on the Song of Solomon* (Loizeaux Brothers, New York, NY; 1950), chp. 1
[174] Ibid.
[175] H. A. Ironside, *Addresses on the Song of Solomon*, pp. 17-21, as summarized by Merrill Unger (Unger's Bible Handbook), pp. 299-300
[176] Jack Deere, *The Bible Knowledge Commentary*, edited by J. F. Walvoord and Roy Zuck (Victor Books, Wheaton, IL; 1986), p. 1009
[177] Roy B. Zuck, *Basic Bible Interpretation* (Cook Communications, Colorado Springs, CO; 1991)
[178] C. E. Hocking, *Rise Up My Love* (Precious Seed Publication, West Glamorgan, UK: 1988), p. 54

[179] C. E. Hocking, *Rise Up My Love* (Precious Seed Publication, West Glamorgan, UK; 1988), p. 187
[180] David Bercot, *A Dictionary of Early Christian Beliefs* – Veil (Hendrickson Publishers, Peabody, MA; 1998), p. 690
[181] H. A. Ironside, *Addresses on the Song of Solomon* (Loizeaux Brothers, New York, NY; 1950), chp. 4
[182] H. A. Ironside, *Addresses on the Song of Solomon* (Loizeaux Brothers, New York, NY; 1950), chp. 5
[183] Jack Deere, *The Bible Knowledge Commentary*, edited by J. F. Walvoord and Roy Zuck (Victor Books, Wheaton, IL; 1986), p. 1020
[184] C. E. Hocking, *Rise Up My Love* (Precious Seed Publication, West Glamorgan, UK; 1988), pp. 280-281
[185] H. A. Ironside, *Addresses on the Song of Solomon* (Loizeaux Brothers, New York, NY; 1950), chp. 7

CPSIA information can be obtained
at www.ICGtesting.com
Printed in the USA
FSOW04n0401020316
17335FS